Your Symphony of Selves

"This wonderful book urges us to look at ourselves and our lives in an entirely new way. We are not a single self, the authors teach us, but rather we contain multiple selves, each valuable in its own way. This lovely book will help you understand and embrace who you are and who you could be."

AYELET WALDMAN, AUTHOR OF *A REALLY GOOD DAY*

"This masterful, comprehensive exploration of the diversity within us is both fascinating and useful. With grace and erudition, the authors explore the nooks and crannies of our minds—and in the variety of 'selves' they find there is, paradoxically, a profound and healing sense of wholeness and freedom."

RICK HANSON, PH.D., AUTHOR OF *NEURODHARMA*

"This book exquisitely explores the age-old and yet seemingly new theme that we are made up of different 'moving parts.' Talking to yourself is not just reserved for eccentric people on subways but an inner psychodrama that can lead us toward a more integrated, 'together,' symphonic self. Now I can, and will, tell clients: 'Read this book, and then come back and talk to me!'"

STEPHEN LARSEN, PH.D., PROFESSOR EMERITUS
OF PSYCHOLOGY AT SUNY ULSTER

"This insightful book creates a landscape of perspective with profound implications for understanding the psychology of human beings. A must-read for every person interested in self-discovery."

BILL LINTON, EXECUTIVE DIRECTOR AND
CO-FOUNDER OF USONA INSTITUTE

"A profound, brilliant, and convincing account of the many entities that make up each of us. I hope it will have the success and influence it deserves."

"Based on what I've read in this book, I now more clearly recognize some of my own selves: my scientist self, my personal growth self, my spiritual self, my 'Am I kind of crazy sometimes?' self . . . and all of them are getting valuable ideas and practices to become more harmonious. My thanks to Fadiman and Gruber for this remarkable book!"

"A tour de force on the multiple manifestations—scientifically, artistically, religiously, and culturally—of the multiple persons and personalities each one of us inhabits. No matter how skeptical your point of view before you read this book, it will make you think, and you will take it seriously."

"Astoundingly, my various persona all seem to agree that Fadiman and Gruber have unpacked this complex topic in ways that are factual, insightful, and extremely useful—a must-read for most, if not all, of your selves."

"From the microbiome in our gut to the voices in our heads, each of us is a community, as the authors explain in this fascinating, delightful book. The illusion of a single unitary self interferes with clear thinking about everything from immunology to psychiatry to the nature of community. We are each a symphony of selves, and my selves highly recommend this book to your selves."

"In clear, practical prose, and drawing from a wealth of religious, philosophical, and psychological materials, the authors make a strong, clear case that is brilliantly couched as a seductive invitation: just stop believing you are a single self, and start to orchestrate and befriend the varied and fractious clan that you are."

ERIK DAVIS, AUTHOR OF *HIGH WEIRDNESS*

"James Fadiman has consistently been walking, exploring, and illuminating the cutting edge of culture for the past half century. This book is no exception, and with it, Fadiman and his scholar-writer partner, Jordan Gruber, intellectually investigate and prosaically dance in a way that recognizes and honors the many voices within us all."

DANA ULLMAN, MPH, CCH,
AUTHOR OF *THE HOMEOPATHIC REVOLUTION*

"This is a very special book! This idea of a 'symphony of selves' reflects what has always been understood among indigenous peoples—and so the book digs deeply into essential universal truths. A treasure to enjoy and learn with and from."

RICHARD KATZ, PH.D.,
AUTHOR OF *INDIGENOUS HEALING PSYCHOLOGY*

"The idea that our sense of self is illusory and that we all contain different selves may seem strange at first. But the great accomplishment of *Your Symphony of Selves* is that it doesn't just make this idea perfectly sensible, the authors show how it can help us better understand ourselves and how cultivating and integrating those multiple selves makes us healthier and happier."

ALEX SOOJUNG-KIM PANG, PH.D., AUTHOR OF
SHORTER: WORK BETTER, SMARTER, AND LESS—HERE'S HOW

"A tour de force that pulls together insights from psychiatry, philosophy, religion, neurology, the humanities, and the social and behavioral sciences. Profound, yet entertaining, it plumbs deeply into rarely explored depths of the human psyche. It even contains activities and exercises that its readers can employ, soon realizing that they may never be the same again."

Stanley Krippner, Ph.D.,
co-author of *Personal Mythology*

"My cousin James Fadiman has an uncanny ability to take a problem, turn it calmly in his hands, look at it from many angles, and solve it, always with a glint of amusement in his eye. Until I read this book he wrote with Gruber, it had never occurred to me that what enables those multiple angles is his sense that he isn't confined to a single self. He is a team! The ideas in this book seem simple, but that's the point: why make things hard when they could be easy?"

Anne Fadiman, author of
The Spirit Catches You and You Fall Down

"Nowhere are Fadiman and Gruber's words 'being in the right mind at the right time' more applicable than for the military fighter pilot. The world moving, quite literally, at Mach 1 creates an unforgiving cauldron where incoherent or incongruent thought yields catastrophic results. The difference between life and death depends on fighter pilots finding their mental best selves."

Buster Glosson, three-star general, USAF (Ret.),
author of *War with Iraq*

"In this fascinating book, the authors offer insights that enable us to kindly accept and value ourselves and others. They reveal an incredible opportunity for healthier living through embracing our different selves, leading to psychological cohesion and wholeness."

Darren Cockburn, author of *Being Present*

Your Symphony of Selves

DISCOVER AND UNDERSTAND MORE OF WHO WE ARE

James Fadiman, Ph.D., and
Jordan Gruber, J.D.

Park Street Press
Rochester, Vermont

Park Street Press
One Park Street
Rochester, Vermont 05767
www.ParkStPress.com

Park Street Press is a division of Inner Traditions International

Cataloging-in-Publication Data for this title is available from the Library of Congress

ISBN 978-1-64411-026-3 (print)
ISBN 978-1-64411-027-0 (ebook)

Printed and bound in the United States by P. A. Hutchison Company

10 9 8 7 6 5 4 3 2

Text design by Priscilla H. Baker and layout by Virginia Scott Bowman
This book was typeset in Garamond Premier Pro, Legacy Sans, and Futura with
Century and Gotham used as display typefaces

To send correspondence to the authors of this book, mail a first-class letter to the
authors c/o Inner Traditions • Bear & Company, One Park Street, Rochester, VT
05767, and we will forward the communication, or contact the authors directly at
info@yoursymphonyofselves.com.

Contents

Acknowledgments

One of the great joys of finishing a major project is being able to thank those who helped bring it about.

Jim: First and foremost, thanks go to my wife, Dorothy, and my daughters Renee and Maria. They've been urging me for years to write this book. Maria gets special credit for never letting up with "Dad, you HAVE to write that book." Even as I write these words, I can hear her voice.

While it may not be usual to thank your co-author, this book would never have happened if Jordan hadn't offered to help me—and then took charge of the endless files and notes from presentations I'd accumulated for decades. You enormously increased the quality and amount of material we had to work with and became the finest collaborator anyone could ask for.

Special thanks to Foster Gamble, who gave me one of my first opportunities to present my thoughts on this topic at the Mind Center (to an audience that, as it happened, included Jordan). That audience's response gave me the courage to keep digging into what seemed to me, from the onset, to be simultaneously obvious and spectacularly well hidden.

Jordan: Let me thank my wife, Gail, and our life partners, Linda and Mitch—as well as all of my close friends—for their support and remarkable good humor throughout my deep dive into this immersive project. In particular, I want to thank our daughter, Diana, not just for putting up with my many selves, but for showing me how powerful the healthy selves model was when faced with something like making a final choice between which of two colleges to attend.

As for Jim, we met again at a conference a year or so after the Mind Center event, and as we lived close by, we soon got to know each other. You have been in my life for many years now, always as a friend, but also as a mentor, and later (now) as a partner and co-author. The privilege of deeply collaborating with a mind and heart of your magnitude and merit cannot be overstated. Dorothy, thank you for letting me have so much of him and for your unconditional support the whole way through.

Thanks to Max Taylor, for your enthusiasm, research skills, and, most of all, sage advice. And to Joy Daniels as well, your steadfast presence and early review of many first drafts was invaluable. Great thanks to my niece, Ilana Gruber, who did a fantastic job on a super-short timeframe. And finally, let me express my endless appreciation for my mother, Lola Gruber, who at age eighty-nine has been patiently waiting for five long years to hold a physical copy of this book in her hands.

We would both like to thank the wonderful support team at Inner Traditions • Bear & Company. Jon Graham, when you not only accepted our manuscript but also shared with us your personal excitement, we knew we were home. Next came the unbelievably important and timely help of Patricia Rydle, who shepherded us through the early phases and helped us get through some extremely difficult publishing-process rapids.

Unlimited gratitude goes to our project editor, Kayla Toher, who not only helped us wrangle and keep track of an amazing assortment of materials, but whose word-by-word, sometimes letter-by-letter, editorial review smoothed away so many rough edges and ultimately cajoled us into making this a much better book.

We also are greatly appreciative of our copyeditor, Elizabeth Wilson; our publicity liaison, Manzanita Carpenter; and Kelly Bowen, who saw us through the acquisitions process. Special thanks to cover designer Aaron Davis and to the production team for piecing together the book's many elements. And Jeanie Levitan, we felt your eye on the process the whole way through, and we want to acknowledge you for assembling the kind of top-notch team where every interaction during the publishing process left us feeling we were in strong, capable hands.

Additionally, we would both like to thank all of the following for contributing in some way to the creation of this book: Ari Annona, Giselle Bisson, Dave Blazek, Ellen Bob, Rob Breszny, Dennis Briskin, Dennis Browe, Jeri Burns, Ari Cartun, Conrad Chaffee, Luba Schwartzman Chaffee, David Chilcott, Tammy R. Coffee, Brooklyn Cook, Joy Daniels, Erik Davis, Lisa Delan, Gabriel DeWitt, David Eagleman, Bill Eichman, Liz Elms, Liam Galleran, Cindy Lou Golin, Lion Goodman, Ray Grasse, Helen Green, Helene Gruber, Cathy Guisewite, Jeramy Hale, Molly Hale, Wynn Hausser, Rocío Herbert, Jean Houston, Anodea Judith, Yuri Koshkin, Luther Kitahata, Daniel Kottke, Chaim Koritzinsky, Stanley Krippner, Krisztina Lazar, Anne-Marie Lemonde, Andy Leventhal, Donna Lewis, Marty Lupowitz, Tom McCook, Karen Mckenzie, Annika Mongan, John Nadler, Carter Phipps, Jamie Prieto, Celia Ramos, John Rhead, Lori Schwanbeck, Marna Schwartz, Amber Seitz, Richard Smoley, Judith Springer, Darin Stevenson, Jackson Stock, Kinta Striker, Charles Tart, Tom Upton, Boris Vainer, Selene Vega, Sam Webster, Don Weiss, and Laura Wigod. And thanks to everyone on Ramona Street at Bistro Maxine, Coupa Café, and Joe & the Juice for providing caffeine, nourishment, and friendly smiles and conversation every step of the way.

Finally, special thanks to Jordan's cats and Jim's dogs, who regularly remind us that the shifting of selves is not limited to the human species.

Not So Radical After All

For many years I worked on understanding why healthy selves seemed to be such a radical idea when on so many levels it felt completely obvious. Only after we began our scholarship on the history of psychology did we come to recognize something very important: in early psychology, the only real issue was between two groups, one composed of scientists and philosophers who felt that every human being had selves, and another set of important clinicians—working to develop the first theories of mental illness—who felt that different selves appeared only in their patient populations.

Then there was a fundamental sea change in the early 1900s after which it was not okay to discuss selves at all. This sea change was so thorough and unchallengeable that for all practical purposes there has been no more discussion of healthy selves in psychology or psychiatry since then, though from time to time less healthy selves were theorized about and entered into common conversation.

Instead of seeing ourselves as proponents of a radical new view of human nature, what we realized is that we were simply continuing to explore and illuminate the way that people had been thinking prior to the general suppression of the idea. (We describe the reasons for that suppression and its remarkable success.)

When we discovered we weren't trailblazers, the project became a little less exciting, but it was also an enormous relief to realize that we were simply rediscovering a fully developed tradition and presenting it in contemporary terms. Selves have always been here—even in psychology—so we might as well learn to work with them.

—JAMES FADIMAN

From Lewis Carroll, *Alice's Adventures in Wonderland*

The Caterpillar and Alice looked at each other for some time in silence:
at last the Caterpillar took the hookah out of its mouth,
and addressed her in a languid, sleepy voice.
"Who are **you**?" said the Caterpillar.
This was not an encouraging opening for a conversation. Alice replied, rather
shyly, "I—I hardly know, sir, just at present—at least I know who I WAS when I got
up this morning, but I think I must have been changed several times since then."
"What do you mean by that?" said the Caterpillar sternly. "Explain yourself!"
"I can't explain *myself*, I'm afraid, sir" said Alice, "because I'm not myself, you see."

SECTION I

· · · · · · · · ·

Welcome from All of Us
to All of You

ONE

What This Is About and What We Hope to Accomplish

All human beings, including those who are healthiest and most success-ful, are composed of more than one self. When things are going well, each plays its rightful role as part of a harmonious symphony. We really *are* different people—or have different minds, parts, or personalities—in different moments and in different contexts.

This is not a new observation; it goes back thousands of years. And it is not difficult to understand, at least not in its basic form. Instead, it is extremely useful and beneficial. By appreciating what is actually so about ourselves and others, many things in our lives begin to make more sense.

Please consider the following questions:

- Have you ever argued with yourself? With whom were you arguing? Who was the other voice, or other voices? If you have ever argued with yourself and changed sides, who did that? When looking at that last cookie or piece of cake or candy, who says "yes" and who says "no"? Have you ever been by yourself or with your old friends and done something truly wild and crazy—something you would never do around your parents, children, co-workers, or boss? Who was it that acted that way? Was that same part of you embarrassed later on?

- Have you ever gotten so inebriated that you said or did things

that you would normally never do, or caused physical or psychological damage to yourself or someone else? Who did that? Who
got the hangover? And who eventually felt the shame or regret?

- Have you ever been so stressed that you did something you told
  yourself you would never do? Once you did it—or perhaps even
  while you were doing it—did another part of you already know
  you were making a big mistake? Would that part of you show up
  again if you experienced the same sort of stress?

Acknowledging these different parts of ourselves is what this book
is all about. To say, for example, that people merely have different
moods at different times misses our main thrust: the selves that compose us are actual, real, independent, and innately valuable parts of who
we are.

In addition to addressing questions like these, we will offer many
examples from ordinary day-to-day life, some of which will likely
remind you of similar experiences in your own life. We will also make
frequent reference to popular culture: books, movies, music, and cartoons. Finally, we will discuss the thoughts of a wide range of thinkers, writers, scientists, and artists who have grappled with this issue
throughout history.

The collected and synthesized information we are providing here
might at first puzzle you or disturb your equilibrium, or even upend
your theory of yourself and others. But it will likely change (for the
better) how you view and understand yourself (your selves) and others
(their selves).

As you read, we are hopeful you will do at least two things:

- begin to let go of the ways you tend to characterize who you are
  as a single, unitary, monolithic self; and
- begin to accept and appreciate your own selves and the selves of
  others.

These things—relatively easy to do—often provide immediate benefits
(as will be described).

Most of our ideas are easy to understand and may feel very familiar to you. They seem to make sense to most people once, based on their own life experiences, they bring them to awareness. For many, the prospect of living a better life—consciously noticing and working with what we are describing—proves an enticing possibility.

HOW THE SINGLE SELF ASSUMPTION LIMITS OPTIMAL HUMAN FUNCTIONING

The difficult part—the problem we all face—is that this way of looking at things is so rarely discussed that most people simply are not aware of it. A veil seems to exist that prevents us from directly experiencing or considering the idea that we are—or can be—a collection of harmonious healthy selves. (Going forward, we will refer to the "healthy selves" or "healthy normal selves" idea, worldview, or perspective.) This barrier or veil follows directly from the unexamined pervasiveness of what we call the "Single Self Assumption," which, in its simplest form, is the idea that:

Each of us is a single unified self.

As a result of the pervasiveness of the Single Self Assumption, the reality of experiencing ourselves as a healthy multiplicity is seldom considered. If it is brought up, it may be laughed away or simply dismissed. But, when we become aware of, question, and step beyond the Single Self Assumption, our worldview shifts. This alternative posits that greater health, functioning, and satisfaction come to people who understand and make practical good use of the recognition that selves are real.

The new assumption is that it is normal to have more than one self. Perhaps more importantly, optimal functioning and well-being *necessitates* acknowledging and working with all of our selves. Those who do this demonstrate increasing congruence among their words, behavior, and plans. They are seen by others as being coherent in their interactions and communications. They are also kinder and more compassionate.

Acknowledging and working with selves thus enables us to be more congruent, coherent, and, overall, what we describe as being more cohesive. Simply, our selves "hang together" in a well-integrated way. The more cohesive our selves are, the better our real-world functioning (what we do and how we do it) and our interactions and relationships (how we are felt, seen, and experienced).

To begin our discussion, here is an example of someone famous—literally a major rock star—who made effective use of his selves.

R.I.P. DAVID BOWIE, MASTER OF SELVES CHANGES

Following Bowie's death in early 2016, Helen Green's animated GIF of his many looks[1]—his many faces, perhaps his many selves—went viral. The image below is made from six of the many Bowie images that flash by in the animated GIF. Did Bowie consciously make use of—deploy or even invent—different selves when necessary?

Fig. 1.1. The evolving identity of David Bowie.
Used with permission of Helen Green.

Bowie himself said, "Even though I was very shy, I found I could get onstage if I had a new identity."[2] After reviewing his troubled early years, British psychologist Oliver James wrote, "What seems to have been the trigger for his shift from distressed and tortured to emotionally healthy, was his adoption of personas in his musical career."[3]

Referring to Bowie's album *The Rise and Fall of Ziggy Stardust and the Spiders from Mars,* James continues, "I believe the album's lyrics were an attempt by Bowie to create a dialogue between different parts of himself. . . . Bowie's legacy is the idea that we have many different selves and if we can only dare to confront them, we can choose who is to host our life at any one moment."[4]

WHAT'S DIFFERENT ABOUT THIS BOOK

Many books have been written about the idea of selves generally, and a few have been written specifically about healthy, normal selves (although not by that name). Our book differs from these other books in a number of ways:

- Our ongoing focus is on health and wholeness—not on pathology and dysfunction.
- We believe that since selves exist, denying their reality or trying to force them to go away is almost always a mistake.
- Many books in this general area also cover subjects such as trance, possession, and supernatural selves (such as angels, demons, and the like). We will lightly touch on some of this material, but only when historically relevant or otherwise appropriate.

Importantly, we do not have—nor are we striving to create—anything like a comprehensive theory. A major problem with having a full-on theory is that its proponents seem to inevitably spend a great deal of time and effort defending it, often focusing on the errors of competing theories. Instead, we have three working assumptions:

1. Healthy, normal* people have—and may be aware that they have—more than one self or personality.
2. Different selves are truly different—when a particular self is up front and in control, fundamental qualities and attributes of a person can change by a little . . . or a lot.
3. Ultimately, it is easy to see beyond the Single Self Assumption and have your life work better.

FIRST PREMISE:
WE ALL HAVE SELVES

The first premise—that healthy, normal people have more than one self or personality—is based on:

- our own experience of ourselves,
- what others have told us about themselves, and
- the observations, research, and intellectual and artistic reflections of a great many wise and aware people.

Fig. 1.2. "We Annoy Them, But No One Can Say We Bore Them."
From the comic strip *Cathy*. Used with permission of Cathy Guisewite.

---

*We distinguish *healthy* multiplicity—the experience of selves that most people have, especially healthy high-functioning people—from *pathological* multiplicity, originally known as "multiple personality disorder" (MPD) and later renamed "dissociative identity disorder" (DID). The older term, MPD, is generally used throughout because it is clearer and more descriptive.

Later, we will look at how selves usually manifest and how to work with them, but first we need to address two important points.

First, the core notion that we are composed of multiple selves *has very little to do with mental illness, deviance, or criminality.* As we see it, awakening to the reality that we have several selves is a key step toward health and creativity and away from illness and dysfunction. Having an understanding and appreciation of the existence of healthy multiplicity in yourself and others makes your life better. As we will discuss, many high-achieving and high-performing individuals inherently embrace and work with their own multiplicity, taking full advantage of the talents and vitality of their different selves.

While there are genuinely pathological cases—like those portrayed in movies like *Sybil* and *The Three Faces of Eve* and the TV show *The United States of Tara*—they are relatively rare. These cases can help inform us and are often quite fascinating, but they are not a good basis for modeling healthy, normal multiplicity and optimal functioning. Pathology is not what this book is about. We can learn a great deal from it, but it is not the basis of our discussion.*

The second point concerns the terminology used throughout this book to refer to our different selves, minds, or personalities.† While thinkers and artists throughout history have grappled with the idea of many selves, the concept for the most part remains elusive, surfacing for a while and then disappearing from both scientific and popular discussion. As a result, new and different terms for the same essential idea have come and gone.

For example, when interest in the pathological versions of multi-

---

*Given Jim Fadiman's transpersonal perspective—he was the co-founder of the Institute of Transpersonal Psychology—it is not surprising that this book focuses on health rather than pathology. As Jevon Dängeli puts it: "The conventional psychological perspective on health is that it is something obtained when pathology has been ameliorated. That is, health is the absence of pathology and suffering . . . transpersonal psychology is motivated to investigate and facilitate the emergence of optimal psychological health. It proposes that the study of positive states and qualities of functioning should be incorporated into our efforts at constructing a more complete and holistic understanding of the individual."[5]

†Chapter 8 presents a more complete roster of alternative terms for *selves.*

plicity skyrocketed in the 1970s and 1980s, thanks to popular books and movies, the term *alter* came into widespread use. More recently, the idea of doing therapeutic parts work has become popular. And the concept of hearing or talking to different voices within has a very long history.

We ask you to suspend any concerns you might have about the exact terms we are using to describe these different parts of who we are. We will usually refer to *selves, personalities, minds, parts,* or *self-states,** but when it makes sense or is helpful, we will use other terms as well.

We want to be clear, however, that we are not big fans of terms that soft-pedal or negate the main concepts being presented here. Your selves are not merely moods, urges, or whims, and to integrate a self against its will is not a benign act.

The bottom line is that a single, consistent, unitary self is almost never the way things are. We do not experience ourselves or other people in this single-minded way, nor do other people experience us that way either.

A Wide Range of Backup and Support

Importantly, the two authors of this book are most certainly *not* the only ones who have ever mused over the mechanisms of managing multiplicity as a means to more healthful and successful living. In fact, many thinkers, authors, and artists have made inquires into their own multiple minds, or have reflected on the different selves they've seen in others. In coming chapters you will come across supporting ideas and themes from the following wide variety of sources:

- philosophers, including Plato, David Hume, Bishop Butler, Friedrich Nietzsche, and Alfred North Whitehead
- psychologists, including Jean-Martin Charcot and Pierre Janet, two pioneering nineteenth-century French thinkers; William James

---

Self-states is a relatively recent term that appeals to progressive psychologists and neuro-scientists. We like it as well.

(the father of American psychology); Sigmund Freud; Alfred Binet (creator of the well-known IQ test); Carl Jung; and many others

- religious thinkers, including writers on Judaism, Christianity, ancient Egyptian religion, Hinduism, Pagan religions, and the Hmong
- novelists, essayists, poets, and other writers, including Lewis Carroll, Ralph Waldo Emerson, Kahlil Gibran, Hermann Hesse, Anaïs Nin, Marcel Proust, Salman Rushdie, Robert Louis Stevenson, and Virginia Woolf
- scientists—cognitive psychologists and others—many of whom come to conclusions similar to ours but through very different means, including Douglas Hofstadter, Marvin Minsky, Robert Ornstein, Dan Siegel, David Eagleman, and others
- twentieth- and twenty-first-century spiritual and self-development teachers, including Sri Aurobindo, G. I. Gurdjieff, Roberto Assagioli, and Jean Houston
- contemporary accounts addressing healthy normal multiplicity— an awareness of healthy selves seems to be picking up lately, with at least one excellent overview book published in 2015 (*On Multiple Selves* by David Lester) and one in 2016 (*Parts Psychology* by Jay Noricks)

SECOND PREMISE:
DIFFERENT SELVES ARE TRULY DIFFERENT
AND INHERENTLY VALUABLE

When someone is embodying a particular self or personality, there can be a wide variation in that person's fundamental qualities and attributes.

As we will show you throughout the book—and as we believe will be in accord with your own experience—different selves have the ability to bring to the fore different qualities, characteristics, and talents. This applies to a wide range of inner emotional and mental experiences, to external real-world abilities and capacities, and in some cases even to physiological differences (like changes in eyeglass prescriptions and blood pressure). Moreover, it looks like the creativity and abilities of high achievers in many fields are enhanced by their capacity to effectively and seamlessly shift into and out of their different selves.

Once you begin to acknowledge, experience, and appreciate your different selves, you will find that, for the most part, each one knows itself to be real—an independent, invaluable, and essential part of who you are. Treating your selves as truly different and of unique inherent value is of paramount concern.

Just How Different One's Selves Can Be: Timmy Loves Orange Juice

When Timmy drinks orange juice he has no problem. But Timmy is just one of close to a dozen personalities who alternate control over [him]. And if those other personalities drink orange juice, the result is a case of hives. The hives will occur even if Timmy drinks orange juice and another personality appears while the juice is still being digested. What's more, if Timmy comes back while the allergic reaction is present, the itching of the hives will cease immediately, and the water-filled blisters will begin to subside.[6]

This is an account of a mental hospital patient diagnosed with having more than one personality. For the staff, there was no doubting that he was different people at different times. So different, in fact, that even a concrete physiological reaction—one easily seen and measured—would come and go depending on which particular version of the man was present. When it was eleven-year-old Timmy, well, he loved orange juice and was just fine with it. However, when any of his other selves were front and center, hives appeared.

Anything that asks us to go far beyond our normal scientific and medical models can make us uncomfortable. In some ways, this story strikes many people as being so bizarre that they prefer to think that the whole thing had been made up. This particular story, however, was brought to us by the respected psychologist Daniel Goleman in "the newspaper of record," *The New York Times*.

Some hard-core skeptics think that this and other multiplicity-related accounts of measured and reported physiological changes must be made up. Keep in mind that these folks are generally committed to a view of the world that—a priori or ahead of time—says these things cannot possibly be true. But the data (which we will revisit in chapter 8)—the real experiences of scientists, therapists, and the many people who have experienced similar sorts of physiological changes—takes us in a very different direction.

THIRD PREMISE: ULTIMATELY, IT IS EASY TO SEE BEYOND THE SINGLE SELF ASSUMPTION

In a slightly expanded form, the Single Self Assumption can be stated as:

Each of us is—or ought to be—a single, unified self.

As a unified being with only one unchanging self or personality at our core, it naturally follows that we—and the people we know—should be fully consistent and therefore predictable in most situations. That is, we *ought* to be able to rely on people to be the way they *always* are. However, almost no one we know acts this way or experiences other people acting this way either.

The Single Self Assumption is pervasive, despite there being so little evidence for it and a great deal of everyday evidence for healthy multiplicity. The Single Self Assumption, embedded in the back of our minds, is rarely questioned in ordinary cultural discourse. The resultant lack of awareness of the idea—even the possibility—of healthy, normal multiplicity is so widespread that what we are describing in this book is nearly completely missing from the conversational map. Since the idea of healthy multiplicity is rarely considered, it is no surprise that most of us—despite our personal experiences to the contrary—hold an incomplete and suboptimal view of human reality. That is, since the prevailing consensus view of reality prevents us from talking about, thinking about, or considering healthy selves, it obscures and distorts reality.

Put more simply, the single-self view of human psychological reality—assumed by both conventional science and monotheistic religion—can limit us in many ways and prevent us from being fully happy and achieving our utmost potential. It is hard for your symphony of selves to play your own life music as sweetly, healthfully, and harmoniously as possible if you do not appreciate—let alone acknowledge—that you have a set of inner players capable of playing many parts.

Psychologically, psychiatrically, philosophically, scientifically, and theologically, the healthy selves worldview is conceptually off limits, a *meme non grata* rarely invited to the conversational table. But once it *is* brought into the conversation, most people seem to quickly understand it, and those who apply it in their own lives often experience immediate benefits.

While writing this book, we have discovered that it often only takes two or three minutes of ordinary conversation for most people to open to the notion of healthy multiplicity. Even those who first respond with dislike or disdain usually admit to us—once we have described how all this works in our own lives, and how it likely works in theirs—that they know what we are talking about. They tend to say something like, "Sure, of course, I really am different people at different times and in the different parts of my lives." Or sometimes they say, "Well, I've known this about myself for a long time, but I never talk about it." (We have been surprised by the number of people who report having a "twin self" who is responsible for some of their less honorable and most regrettable actions.)

Given the strength of the Single Self Assumption, many people have never considered their own experience of healthy multiplicity. But once the healthy selves worldview is brought up, those able to look beyond the Single Self Assumption begin to see the confusion and difficulty that flows from it begin to drop away from their lives. An obviously easier and better way to live is not just around the corner but already resides within you. As your selves come to look past the Single Self Assumption and experience what we are discussing here, most or all of you may naturally and readily choose to take increasing advantage of the totality of who you are.

Each of your selves, whether or not you ever name them or identify any of them with precision, is a very real being, entity, or self-state, an autonomous complex (as Jung called it) that has its own agenda, its own needs, and its own ways of working with your other selves and other people (and their selves). It is not just that you have different moods, aspects, or feelings; it is that there really are different alive autonomous parts of you—different selves, different personalities, different parts.

It's really quite striking: we have a culture-wide adherence to an assumed unity that rarely if ever exists, and a corresponding denial of what many of us already know to be so about the way that things actually are. Almost all of us have experienced what it means to be in a different self. For starters, please reconsider the kinds of questions asked at the beginning of this chapter: When you are arguing with yourself, who is arguing with whom? When you do something completely out of character, who is doing that? When you party too hard, who comes back thrashed to spend time with your mate, family, or co-workers?

Throughout this book, we will provide you with a wide variety of everyday examples, commonplace experiences, and cultural reflections of the healthy selves idea. For the most part, as previously stated, we will be short on theory and long on stories and examples.

We are betting that as soon as you start placing more attention on them, many of the ideas and concepts we present will feel familiar to you. Then, as soon as you start trying on and gently experimenting with your own healthy normal selves—as soon as you learn to acknowledge and appreciate the parts of you that already work well together—you will likely begin to validate these ideas.

A PREVIEW OF WHAT
YOU'LL FIND IN THIS BOOK

One of the most harmful illusions that can beguile us is probably the belief that we are an indivisible, immutable, totally consistent being. Each of us is a crowd with its own mythology and we are more or less comfortably crowded into a single person.

PIERO FERRUCCI, *WHAT MAY BE*

Our goal in this book is to give you a heads-up about your own and others' selves: their existence, their needs, the potential value and benefits that might come to you from considering them. What we hope for is that you will spend some time thoughtfully observing your own selves, and those of other people, before reaching any conclusions.

Think of it this way: the Single Self Assumption, to the extent it prevents us from even beginning to talk or think about the way things actually are, ends up surrounding us with a wall of disinformation. This wall prevents us from seeing what is true or validating experiences to the contrary. What we are doing is putting some windows into that wall so you can look through and see what's what.

We will make some recommendations and suggestions and provide you with a set of beginning resources. We will describe many of the systems and techniques that others have used to explore these inner territories and suggest possibilities for you to explore on your own. Just as good, though—and we will say this many times—it is important for you to go into your own life to understand these ideas, concepts, and possibilities. The best way to find out what works is to undertake an exploration of your own selves.

Section I—Welcome from All of Us to All of You

This beginning section introduces the book's most important concepts:

- Chapter 1 lays out the book's basic ideas and premises.
- Chapter 2 considers the pragmatic value of the healthy selves model, that is, the many advantages and benefits of opening yourself up to and working with a model of human reality that better reflects the ways things actually are.
- Chapter 3 presents a simple but powerful catchphrase—"mental health is being in the right mind at the right time"—showcasing stories and examples that illustrate the hows and whys of learning to more effectively move from one self-state to another.

Section II—Multiplicity All Around Us:
Cultural and Intellectual Reflections
This section provides a cultural tour of multiplicity from religious, philosophical, psychological, and scientific perspectives:

- Chapter 4 reviews, highlights, and reinforces our collective cultural knowledge. We move through a good number of examples from everyday language, consider the voices in our heads, and then move on to some popular cultural treatments in books, essays, movies, television, music, and other sources.
- Chapter 5 looks at the history of multiplicity in religions worldwide and throughout the course of Western philosophy. While the Single Self Assumption is deeply rooted, there have been significant exceptions in both religion and philosophy.
- Chapter 6 looks at multiplicity from the perspective of psychology and psychologists, from the days before psychology was a formal science to the present day. With some notable exceptions, the existence of selves—and certainly the idea of healthy normal selves—was off limits for most of the twentieth century. We will closely track who was and who was not open to multiplicity and how this changed over time.
- Chapter 7 explores material relevant to neuroscientists, Buddhists, and postmodern thinkers, all of whom tend to come to conclusions similar to ours but by different paths.

Section III—Understanding, Acknowledging,
and Working with Our Selves
This section, which is as close to a workbook as we will offer, contains many approaches and techniques that you might want to try or be aware of:

- Chapter 8 asks some basic questions, including "who's in there?" (how many selves exist), "what's what?" (what kinds of selves exist), and "where from?" (exploring the origins of selves). We look at what selves are, how real they are, and even why we have them.

- Chapter 9 considers how groups of selves organize and learn to cooperate. We consider a wide range of terminology, models, and metaphors. The desire to create a single "super self" is also considered.

- Chapter 10 looks at tools, techniques, and strategies for selves work. First steps, three main approaches, and then more than a dozen additional techniques and strategies are described. The chapter closes with a look at how helpful and useful these tools can be.

Section IV—Healthy Normal Selves in the Twenty-First Century

This section reviews current and future approaches to selves and provides a recap and some final advice:

- Chapter 11 considers organized responses, reactions, and approaches to working with selves. From spiritual and self-help teachers to organized therapeutic approaches, we will cover the highlights of several systems of thought and practice. We will also look at the response of larger cultural and social systems to the idea of selves.

- Chapter 12 presents the evolution of thought from the traditional continuum of dissociation, to the full spectrum of selves, to the expanded full spectrum of selves, and closes with a consideration of the healthy new normal.

- Chapter 13 concludes the book. It briefly recaps everything we have covered, addresses a few important pragmatic and theoretical loose ends, provides some personal reflections from the authors, and offers some final words on experiencing and working with your own selves.

- Finally, an appendix exploring dissociation—the term's origins and usage, as well as conceptual problems and suggestions—is also included.

AWARENESS HEALS

We conclude this opening chapter with some good news. Since what we are talking about is the way things actually are, it does not take much to let some light in—light that begins of its own accord to pierce the veil of the Single Self Assumption. This book, then, can fairly easily provide you with an enhanced appreciation of who you are.

For example, the very first time you avoid overreacting to something that someone close to you has said or done because you are aware that they are in a different self—perhaps a self that you can see only inadvertently made you mad or unhappy—you will feel tremendous relief. You will find you can more easily forgive them and move on, letting go of the offending incident rather than shifting (or being triggered) into a different self of your own that is confrontational and hurtful. Having more awareness of another person's selves enables you to stay more grounded and in a better self of your own.

Fortunately, awareness heals! Having been subjected to a constricted view of self and personality, and having lived under the consensus delusion of assumed unity for so long, many of us may need to let go of a good deal of old anger and resentment. A little bit of awareness goes a long way in initiating and sustaining this healing process.

If this book can help you realize what you have likely already directly experienced many times, we believe you will pick up the tent flap, peek underneath, and see for yourself that your selves are indeed quite real and inherently valuable. Fully seeing and embracing the world of vibrant healthy selves—both inside and outside of your own being—is a cohesive path to experiencing our selves and others as the complex beings we actually are. A more harmonious and richly resonant symphony of selves awaits you.

TWO

The Benefits of
the Healthy Selves Model

"Which you am I talking to now?"

Fig. 2.1. "Which you am I talking to now?" by James Thurber.
From *The New Yorker*, February 21, 1942.
Used with permission of www.CartoonCollections.com.

This chapter considers the many potential real-world benefits and advantages available to those who open to the healthy selves perspective. These include:

- living in a world that makes more sense;
- greater self-acceptance (selves acceptance) and appreciation;

- more compassion for your own selves and the selves of others;
- ability to make sense of inner dialogues, discussions, and arguments;
- increased physical and emotional energy;
- increased ability to access skills, talents, and creativity;
- greater acceptance and appreciation of others;
- less frustration and impatience with others; and
- increased ability to harmonize well with oneself (and one's selves) and with others (and their selves).

We will also discuss potential *disadvantages* of opening to the healthy selves worldview. (You may find some of these a little surprising.) After that we consider how the benefits and advantages of the healthy selves perspective can be valuable in the postmodern milieu, in which we face unprecedented numbers of options and choices in many areas of life.

We then use a set of diagrams or flowcharts for summary and review purposes. These make it easier to see what an awareness of healthy selves offers and are especially useful for people who have selves that appreciate orderly visual representations. The chapter closes with one final diagram that frames a discussion of the timing of benefits received.

A PRAGMATIC AND PERSONALIZED APPROACH TO POTENTIAL BENEFITS

Why focus on the pragmatic value of potential benefits and advantages? Our goal has always been to write a practical book, one that presents a more accurate and useful worldview that reframes confusing parts of reality and day-to-day experience. We focus on the model's pragmatic value because if something is not of real use to you in your day-to-day life—if you cannot "validate, corroborate, and verify" it[1]—then what we are saying in these pages would be of no value to you.

Our experience tells us that each person who opens to, embraces, and works with the healthy selves worldview will do so in their own way. Why? Since each of us embodies a unique system or constellation of selves, the various benefits and advantages will also be uniquely and idiosyncratically experienced. This is true both in terms of how much and how positively each benefit adds to our lives as well as the timing of those benefits.

We are *not* saying that everyone who opens to the healthy selves perspective will experience any *particular* benefit or *all* of the benefits and advantages described in this chapter. And, we are also not specifying an exact timetable for receiving and experiencing benefits. Instead, we are saying that many people are likely to experience a set of diverse and robust benefits. By knowing what these benefits and advantages are, and how you might experience them over time, you are more likely to notice available opportunities and make use of them.

HERSCHEL WALKER: A SELVES-CONSCIOUS SUPERSTAR

As a segue to the potential benefits, we wanted to bring to your attention someone who has been successful in many areas of life, someone who in many ways can be said to be an example of multiple personality *order*.

Valedictorian of his Georgia high school—itself a substantial achievement for someone who was written off early in grade school as an unintelligent stutterer—Herschel Walker is often ranked among the greatest multi-sport athletes of all time. His athletic achievements are many:

- He was a two-time All American college track star who briefly held the world record in the sixty-yard dash.
- As a college football running back, he was a three-time All American, set various NCAA yardage records, and won the 1982 Heisman Trophy as college football's most outstanding player.
- A professional football player for more than a decade, he was widely regarded as one of the NFL's premier running backs.
- He received an Olympic bronze medal in 1992 for the two-man bobsled.

- In a limited career as a professional MMA (mixed martial arts) fighter, he had no losses.

Herschel also once danced with the Fort Worth Ballet, was a contestant in Donald Trump's *Celebrity Apprentice* show, and was the winning contestant in season three of the television show *Rachael vs. Guy: Celebrity Cook-Off.* A born-again Christian, he has been referred to as a "Renaissance Man"[2] and a "Renaissance Jock."[3] He also founded and ran one of the largest minority-owned meat-processing plants in the United States. Herschel still rigorously trains his body by doing up to thousands of push-ups and sit-ups a day,[4] something he started doing after receiving some kindly coaching as a twelve-year-old boy who no longer wanted to be fat but who had no access to gym equipment. As a teenager, Herschel would watch hours of television daily and do push-ups and sit-ups during every commercial. As an adult, in 2015 it was reported that he had cut his push-ups down to 1,500 a day along with 2,000 sit-ups.[5]

Diagnosis and Autobiography

What makes Herschel Walker particularly interesting for our purposes is his very public admission and discussion of how he has learned to cope with his diagnosis of dissociative identity disorder, or DID. In fact, Herschel's 2008 memoir, *Breaking Free: My Life with Dissociative Identity Disorder,* has this as its main theme. He tells us he wrote the book, despite the stigma that it might bring, so that others would be more able to recognize similar symptoms in themselves and get professional help.* He also explains that "what made me different, and what characterized my distinct [condition], was that for the majority of my life, *the alternative personalities that I developed did far more good than harm.*"[6] (Emphasis added.)

After he retired from professional football, Herschel did indeed have some serious problems. He had anger issues that contributed to

---

*The authors have not met Herschel Walker in person. What we surmise here is based on reading his memoir and watching him in video interviews.

Fig. 2.2. Herschel Walker's *Breaking Free*

the loss of his marriage. And, somewhat infamously, on more than one occasion he apparently played Russian roulette . . . with a real gun and a real bullet. These problems eventually led him to seek help. In particular, during one episode Herschel was driving to the house of a friend who was "messing up his schedule" over the delivery of a new car. A murderous rage had come over Herschel, who found himself experiencing the following internal dialogue:

> Every few seconds, I'd hear a voice telling me, "No, Herschel, that's wrong. You can't shoot a man down in cold blood over this." Over that voice I'd hear another urging me on: "You've got to take care of business. This guy has done you wrong. You can't let him get away with that. Kill him." Over and over these two voices were shouting at me, each one pleading with me . . .
> "Do it."
> "Stop it."
> "Do it."
> "You can't."
> "Do it."
> Like the pulsing rhythm of a chorus, the two voices kept up a relentless beat.[7]

Fortunately, Herschel's faith—aided by his seeing a Jesus bumper sticker—intervened. The incident soon led him to working with Jerry Mungadze, a psychologist who diagnosed him with DID. Herschel recalls that "I knew that I needed to take a new direction in my life. The Herschel Walker who had driven to that house with murder in his heart and mind was not the Herschel Walker I had been for most of my life. Something was clearly wrong with me, and I had to figure out what it was. And quickly."[8]

Herschel's memoir reveals a number of distinct perspectives on what it means to have selves—both healthy and less so. At times, the book makes the familiar error that to have selves at all equates to having a mental illness. At other times, the book presents a progressive perspective on the mechanics of creating "alters" (alternative selves) as being the response of a healthy and creative survival mechanism. Finally, the idea of healthy, normal selves is also occasionally touched on.

With the help of Mungadze, Herschel—always an avid learner—came to understand that "there was inside of me a kind of chorus or a cast of actors each taking their turn to step into the spotlight to take charge."[9] Throughout the book, Herschel makes it clear that while the experience and usefulness of selves can exist in a normal range, when triggered by abuse or stress, things can get stuck and out of control. At that point, professional help is needed.

On the other hand, Herschel is equally clear that he is essentially a normal person and that in many ways it was his ability to make use of his selves that enabled him to achieve so much. Consider again the quote "For the majority of my life, the alternate personalities that I developed did far more good than harm."

Herschel understands that it was precisely his ability to fully immerse himself in his different selves—developed early on when he was a stuttering, overweight, and bullied schoolboy—that enabled him to accomplish so much. As we see from his achievements and his own testimony, for the most part Herschel's ability to utilize different parts of himself did not harm him or cause problems, other than in the difficult period soon after retirement from professional football. Instead, over the course of his lifetime, it was exactly *his ability to access and utilize his different selves that enabled him to excel* in a wide variety of sports, business, and personal endeavors and to, in effect, become a living legend.

Herschel has also demonstrated awareness of the importance of consciously working with his different selves. For example, consider what he said in a 2008 article in the *Star Tribune:* "People have to shift themselves and their personalities in so many different areas to be successful. . . . You don't want Herschel Walker the football player, babysitting your kids. Those are two different people."[10] Moreover, Herschel appreciated that being able to access the right self at the right time was directly connected to his ongoing multiple successes, including being a champion football player. He has talked about how he consciously developed parts of himself called "the Warrior" and "the General."[11] When he was in these personalities, he was hyper-focused: "I'd just get the ball and run. Whatever it took to get the job done."[12]

Ultimately, Herschel understands both that there is nothing inherently abnormal about multiplicity and that if you have a self that "struggles, that has faults" then "you got to get help." He says:

> Multiple personality disorder . . . people have demonized it because of *Sybil* and *Three Faces of Eve* and I'm just wanting for people to know that you are not a demon, you are not crazy, and you are not a freak. What it is, is, that you are coping with something . . . but you are normal. And that's what I want to show, that I'm normal. There was a time when I did some things that I did not like, but I'm normal. I'm like any other man that struggles, that has faults. But you can correct those faults, but you got to get help.[13]

His Diagnosis Respectfully Reconsidered

With all due respect to Herschel Walker's medical advisers, we would like to consider whether what we know about him really indicates the presence of a multiplicity *disorder*. First, Herschel has in many ways led an exemplary life. "People think it is negative but look at me. I don't do drugs. I don't drink. I have never done anything wrong. I have never been to jail."[14] As the *Star Tribune* article put it:

Walker was able to cope. . . . His outward appearance rarely changed. And his business acumen was not stunted. Instead, Walker said he was able to use different facets of his personality to run a successful food service business. . . . "The same person who was on the football field is not the same person you would see running a business," he said.[15]

What we have here, then, is a religious man who has never actually "done anything wrong," who has succeeded in many life arenas, and who is widely regarded as one of the greatest college and multi-sport athletes of all time. Lacking substantial cohesion, people with pathological multiplicity may hurt themselves and others and often lose track of memories, agreements, and time generally. Along these lines, it was ultimately the anger experienced by one of his selves that drove Herschel to seek help. But who among us has never experienced or acted on anger or frustration? And who among us has never experienced rage or had violent thoughts?

So while Herschel Walker—a super-successful religious world-class athlete—may have had one or more selves capable of disproportionate rage, violent thoughts, and even playing Russian roulette, *the issue was more about that particular self than it was about having more than one self in the first place.* Fortunately, when he experienced the intense dialogue and disagreement between the two parts of himself, Herschel quickly recognized the part that was close to being completely out of control—and sought help.

To this day Herschel Walker remains an advocate of making positive use of one's selves. He notes that his condition "can sometimes be a positive tool for good rather than something always negative and destructive."[16] Similarly, he states that "I want to do what I can to help remove the stigma of mental illness, to demonstrate how once it is understood . . . [it] can be channeled into something positive."[17] Ultimately, Herschel provides a clear example of how recognizing, developing, and using one's different selves bestows advantages and benefits and facilitates overall success.

BENEFIT: A WORLD
THAT MAKES MORE SENSE

Herschel Walker is just one real-world case study of how significant benefits in sports, business, and leadership can come from consciously working with selves. In this section, we turn to a different benefit, more amorphous and theoretical, yet so far-reaching and fundamental that it underlies many of the other benefits.

If you begin with a fundamental error, with a flawed and erroneous premise, then whatever you build on top of that error will necessarily and inevitably be flawed. The quality of output depends on the quality of input. As they say in computer science, "Garbage In, Garbage Out."

Suppose that the healthy selves model is closer to how things actually are, and the Single Self Assumption is erroneous. If we have built our lives—our ways of knowing and doing things, our ideas about what makes us tick and how we and others operate—on a flawed assumption, then a good deal of how we act may be suboptimal or flat out mistaken and ineffective. At the very least, if one of our fundamental psychological premises is wrong, then our lives will be continually colored by a variety of subtle (and not-so-subtle) distortions of reality.

What happens as we recognize that flawed assumption and begin to acknowledge a world of many selves? Many distortions fall away of their own accord. We find the world and our lives making more sense and experience an enhanced ability to sync with ourselves (and our selves) and others (and their selves).

Consider half a millennium ago when the Copernican view of the solar system—the planets revolving around the sun—supplanted the earlier church-supported Ptolemaic view of the Earth at the center. The Ptolemaic mistake had caused persistent unyielding difficulties for early scientists, mathematicians, and astronomers. Working with a fundamentally flawed model, they had to go to extraordinary lengths to come up with fixes to the existing system to make any sense of what they were observing.* Ultimately, it became clear that this system was unworkable. Imagine their sense of relief when early astronomers finally began working with a model—a new paradigm†—that allowed them to create more accurate descriptions of the world they saw.

Brief Philosophical Interlude: Which Way Does Occam's Razor Cut?

Occam's razor is a philosophical principle named after William of Occam, who lived about 1300 CE. Also called "the law of parsimony," it can be stated as follows:

> Do not unnecessarily multiply explanatory entities.

In other words, if you are looking for the best way of understanding or explaining something, the simplest and least convoluted answer is usually correct. For example, while early astronomers with their Ptolemaic epicycles could—after a fashion—make extremely complex models to account for planetary orbital data, putting the sun at the center led to much simpler explanations.

Part of why the healthy selves view is so compelling is that it easily and simply explains many things that we have all experienced about how our lives and the lives of other people actually work. As we consider many other situations and examples, please keep Occam's razor in mind.

As you open to your own relationship with healthy selves, you will better understand how you and other people operate. One major benefit has to do with how you react to inconsistent actions and statements made by others. As David Lester, author of *On Multiple Selves* (2016),

---

*To explain inconsistencies in observed data, pre-Copernican astronomers employed "Ptolemaic epicycles," an amazingly complex geometric model used to try to explain the variations in the direction, speed, and motion of the moon, sun, and other planets as they "circled" the Earth.

†The word *paradigm* and the idea of "paradigm shifts" were made famous by Thomas Kuhn in his seminal book *The Structure of Scientific Revolutions* (1962). We believe that the anomalies surrounding the Single Self Assumption have now built to the point where a paradigm shift into the healthy selves worldview has begun.

simply puts it: "Unless people accept that they have multiple selves, they will experience anxiety over their inconsistencies."[18]

Faced with a lifetime of experience and countless examples of people—both ourselves and others—acting inconsistently in a culture. with no ready means to explain this inconsistency, it is no wonder that many of us are saddled with ongoing mental stress and discomfort. As we begin to open to healthy selves awareness, this uncomfortable confusion starts to evaporate. Simultaneously, increasing compassion toward others naturally arises as we become aware that it was only a *part* of someone who said or did such-and-such, and that—like many of our own parts—it will respond better to recognition and support than to anger or condemnation.

BENEFIT: BEING KINDER TO YOUR SELF (AND YOUR SELVES)

One key to living a better life is whether all of your selves are working together as a team, or whether there is dissonance or even sabotage among the ranks. One place for everyone to start, then, is this:

Try being kinder to yourself (your selves)!

We all know what this advice means, but sometimes it is difficult to follow. You may have some selves that do not want you to be kinder to a self that is causing problems, and you may have some selves that do not want to be treated more kindly. No matter, go ahead and try being kinder to all of your selves anyway. In particular, try being kinder and evoking as much compassion as possible toward your most difficult and recalcitrant selves.

The problem is not so much that people lack insight: most everyone immediately understands the value that follows from being kinder to themselves. Instead, the problem is that since most people grow up under the Single Self Assumption, many have not developed the necessary inner teamwork and orchestration skills to in fact be kinder to themselves. Fortunately, *awareness heals,* which is why selves recognition, acceptance, and appreciation are such important first steps.

BENEFIT: GREATER SELF (SELVES) ACCEPTANCE AND APPRECIATION

One of the first benefits of opening to the healthy selves worldview is the feeling and experience of greater self-acceptance and appreciation. As you begin to acknowledge your selves and validate their importance, they will begin to relax, be happier, perform better, and be easier to get along with. We will consider how you can more readily learn to accept, appreciate, and work with your own selves and those of others in some detail later on.

But what about negative, disruptive, or otherwise unwelcome selves? Do you need to accept and appreciate even a self that is having thoughts and feelings of rage, as in Herschel Walker's case? The short answer is "yes." By accepting and appreciating each of your selves, you will generate an immediate sense of self-worth and validation not only in each of those selves but also in the totality of who you are. Moreover, you will come to better understand the needs of seemingly negative selves, setting the stage for working with each self so it can better satisfy its own needs in ways that also make sense for the totality of who you are.

BENEFIT: INCREASED PHYSICAL AND EMOTIONAL ENERGY

The Sufi teacher and writer Idries Shah* said of himself that when he was working at his desk and felt too tired to work anymore, he would go out into his garden. If he found he had enough energy for gardening, he knew he was not as tired as he thought he was. However, if he found he was too tired even for gardening, he knew it was time to get some rest.

As Shah's story illustrates, an awareness of our selves lets us work in ways that produce and give us more physical and emotional energy. One

---

*Shah himself had a distinct view on the idea of selves, titling his last book *The Commanding Self,* stating that "the Commanding Self . . . can be seen as a sort of parasite, which first complements the personality, then takes over certain parts of it, and masquerades as the personality itself."[19]

way of getting more energy is to live in a world that makes more sense and aligns with our ongoing experience. When you are not constantly swimming against the tide of distortions that flow from the Single Self Assumption—such as the notion that anyone who isn't 100 percent consistent 100 percent of the time is weak, flawed, or malevolent—you gain energy. Conversely, if you are swimming along in the wake of a more accurate worldview, it is easier to move forward.

Another way to free up more energy is by accepting our selves, being kinder and more compassionate to them, and learning to work with them in conscious and constructive ways. As Genie Laborde, an educator, author, filmmaker, and artist, put it, "by becoming aware of our internal conflicts, we can release the mental energy we have been using for repression, work out some internal negotiations, and use the released energy in our lives."[20]

As we become aware of our selves, we no longer spend so much energy repressing the parts of who we are that we don't approve of or want to admit to. As we come to acknowledge and appreciate our different selves, we learn to trust those selves within the totality of who we are. Knowing that we can trust our selves brings a certain type of freedom as well as an energetic opening to whatever might come next. As psychologist, therapist, author, and long-time advocate of "sub-personalities" John Rowan says:

> What we are talking about here is freedom. . . . Instead of finding ourselves pushed around by our own processes, we are free to choose among them. . . . Things which before may have seemed quite out of the question now seem within our reach, and within our world. . . . We can trust ourselves much more, and over a much wider range of decisions and possibilities. By doing justice to the one and the many, and being fully in the one and the many at one and the same time, we arrive at a new way of being.[21]

Similarly, to the degree we learn to conduct internal negotiations to work things out between selves that are in disagreement or do not get along, we are no longer drained by ongoing inner conflict. Such conflict may be below the level of consciousness, but it is still quite real and saps our strength.

BENEFIT: INCREASED ABILITY TO ACCESS SKILLS, TALENTS, AND CREATIVITY

Recognizing and learning to know, understand, and deal with the personalities that make up our selves can help us function to our fullest capacity in every endeavor.

RITA CARTER, *THE PEOPLE YOU ARE*

In each of us there may be an athlete, a scholar, a nurturing parent, and so on. Our facial musculature, gestures, vocabulary, accents, handwriting, phobias, and even our memories may be versatile in ways we've never dreamed of. Our stream of consciousness includes the stream of selves.

MARILYN FERGUSON, *AQUARIUS NOW*

Would you like to be able to do more things, and do the things you already do better than ever? Countless self-help books (including one Jim wrote)[22] begin by saying how they will address various deficits in your life so that you can get more of what you want. Our perspective here is quite different: we are suggesting that most people are not making full use of what they already possess—the various abilities of their selves—which is like not noticing that your pants have pockets, your smartphone has built-in apps, or your car has gears.

The healthy selves perspective explains how people can—through acknowledging and appreciating their different selves—access heightened skills, talents, and levels of creativity. Earlier, we saw how David Bowie intentionally created new personalities and learned to fully shift into them so he could (and did) rock the world. Another example is Herschel Walker, who, entering into his Warrior self, with guidance from his inner coach, was able to become a champion in multiple sports by consciously learning to invoke and utilize the part of him that could work with great pain (as we will soon see). Another example is Bob Dylan, who won the Nobel Prize in literature and will be discussed later and whose 2020 song "I Contain Multitudes" should not be missed.

Those who have studied pathological cases of multiplicity have long noticed the creativity, flexibility, and large skill sets of some of these individuals. For example, one self-help manual for those diagnosed with unhealthy multiplicity states that such people "are sometimes able to accomplish more than those who are integrated because of this ability to compartmentalize."[23] And if you have the chance to read Daniel Keyes's penetrating and often exhilarating account of *The Minds of Billy Milligan,* you will understand how Billy was able to become a highly sought after portrait and landscape painter, a Houdini-like escape artist, a fluent speaker of a language he never studied (Serbian), a demolitions expert, and someone who by consciously controlling his adrenaline could summon almost superhuman strength.

The ability to learn new skills, play new roles, and access profound creativity is clearly not limited to those diagnosed with pathological multiplicity. In fact, it seems that many highly talented and successful people have achieved success precisely *because* of their ability to access different parts of themselves. As Scott Barry Kaufman and Carolyn Gregoire write in their book *Wired to Create: Unraveling the Mysteries of the Creative Mind* (2015):

> Creative people . . . have at least some level of those varying characteristics within themselves, and they can chose to flexibly switch back and forth depending on what's most helpful in the moment. Creative people seem to be particularly good at operating within a broad spectrum of personality traits and behaviors. They are both introverted and extraverted, depending on the situation and environment, and learn to harness both mindfulness and mind wandering in their creative process.[24]

Along similar lines, Gretchen Sliker, a clinical psychologist, writes, "Although subpersonalities are present in all of us, and can be discerned directly through observation of their behavior, subpersonalities are most vivid in the complex personalities of talented people; they are evident in their life histories as well as in their varied behavior and production."[25] And as for creativity generally, Kaufman and Gregoire bring us the following wisdom—which echoes Walt Whitman's famous quote*—from famed psychologist Mihaly Csikszentmihalyi, who interviewed creative people for more than thirty years and originated the concept of "flow":

> If I had to express in one word what makes their personalities different from others, it's complexity. They show tendencies of thought and action that in most people are segregated. They contain contradictory extremes; instead of being an "individual," each of them is a "multitude."[26]

....

Reviewer Question:
Can You Choose a Younger Happier Self?

An early reader of this chapter posed an interesting question: "With this sort of idea would that mean that theoretically people could keep themselves younger for longer and increase their happiness simply by choosing a younger, happier, and wealthier you/self in each moment? I'm not sure if you were aware, but I'm a coach who speaks to individuals from disadvantaged backgrounds. This is something I'd love to share with them to see if it helps."

The reader's question reminds us of Harvard social psychologist Ellen Langer's reverse-aging study, described in her award-winning book *Counterclockwise: Mindful Health and the Power of Possibility* (2009). Bruce Grierson described the start of her experiment: "Eight men in their 70s stepped out of a van in front of a converted monastery in New Hampshire. They shuffled forward, a few of them arthritically stooped, a couple with canes. Then they passed through the door and entered a time warp. Perry Como crooned on a vintage radio. Ed Sullivan welcomed guests on a black-and-white TV. Everything

---

*"Do I contradict myself? Very well, then I contradict myself, I am large, I contain multitudes."

inside—including the books on the shelves and the magazines lying around—were designed to conjure 1959."[27]

After a week of being in the time warp, Langer reported that the experimental group showed improvements in manual dexterity, physical strength, posture, gait, perception, memory, cognition, taste sensitivity, hearing, and vision. Perhaps being immersed in the environment of their youth allowed these men to shift into younger and healthier selves, ones that started cooking meals for each other and that ended the study with an impromptu touch football game.

BENEFIT: INCREASED PHYSICAL HEALING AND PAIN MANAGEMENT ABILITIES

A good example of increased access to specific skills and talents can be seen in the way that some people learn to deal with pain or enhance their physical health and energy generally. For example, several years ago Jim was at a workshop being led in part by Chungliang Al Huang, founder and president of the Living Tao Foundation and a renowned master of t'ai chi. Jim's journal notes read as follows:

The first evening we worked with Al Huang. And I was there, thinking "Oh, gosh, it's Al again. So I am going to have to do t'ai chi again, and I am already tired. He has got incredible energy, and I don't; he never ages, and I do; and I feel bad." Well, at some point I began to be able to follow what he was doing, and the part of me that was so hungry to do what he was doing began to take control. At that point my thinking went, "I am not yet there. The part of me that is a boring, sober, middle-aged intellectual can kind of move, but it doesn't leave the ground."

But when I did find myself leaving the ground, there was this incredible pleasure, because the part of me that can leave the ground doesn't get out a lot. And I am sure it is one of the reasons that I love Al Huang so much, because he says to one of my parts, a part which is rarely given enough time, "This too is you!" As soon as I let that part out, it allowed me in the moment to experience a whole new level of health, and to then add that energy into and distribute it around the whole circle.

In this circumstance, by merely following along with someone who was deeply embodied and super healthy, Jim was able to access the part of himself that could easily follow along and achieve similar benefits.

In some cases, increased health—or less dysfunction—comes from being in one self but not another. For example, consider Timmy from chapter 1; in most selves, he cannot have orange juice without getting hives, but in one of his selves, orange juice is just fine. The literature contains similar stories of people who are allergic to cats or who experience terrible pain in one self but not in others.

As human beings, we all have to learn how to deal with pain. The conventional literature on pathological multiplicity points out that the creation of different selves* may be triggered by abuse that causes tremendous physical or emotional pain. As Daniel Keyes writes, in describing one self of Billy Milligan whose job it was to take on any physical pain that he experienced: "David, 8. The keeper of pain, or the empathy. Absorbs all the hurt and suffering of the other personalities."[28]

Herschel Walker provides a specific example of how he used a different self to deal with pain. While still in grade school, wishing to no longer be overweight, he determined he would become a dedicated runner. At a certain point, he experienced terrible pain in his knees and went with his mother to a doctor who told him that he could not run anymore.

Herschel's very supportive mother told him that he could run anyway if he wanted to—"You want to run. Go run."[29]—but this inevitably caused him a great deal of additional pain. "Without a doubt," Herschel writes, "the disciplined approach I took to my training helped me, but I can't emphasize enough how much pain my knees caused me when I first began to run after seeing Dr. Thomas. Somehow I was able to block out that pain and keep up with my training."[30] How did he do this?

---

*As discussed in detail later, not just negative, painful, and traumatic experiences create selves, but positive, affirming, joyful, and blissful ones can do so as well.

Only when I lay in bed at night did the pain set in, but when I closed my eyes, it seemed to go away. Now that I know about DID, and based on later experiences, I'm pretty sure that I developed an alter who was more or less impervious to pain—someone who was simply able to erase both the pain itself and any lasting memory of it. I mean, I'd feel the discomfort at first, but then something else would kick in, the Erase would kick in and I was able to go again at full speed. Unlike before, with my alters who helped me with my fear of the dark or to endure the teasing, when it came to dealing with pain, my switching, for lack of a better word, was closer to a truly conscious effort. I was aware that I was in pain, and I'd say to myself, "Okay. It's time to go. We've got to go. This isn't going to stop us. Push. Just push on through it." And I would.[31]

Later on in college, Herschel used his pain-handling alter to get through wisdom tooth surgery while foregoing anesthetics.[32]

For those of us who experience regular pain in our lives—which at some point in the arc of decades includes nearly everyone—it is not uncommon to have that pain let up or go away entirely while we are engaged in activities that we enjoy. For example, Jordan has sometimes experienced substantial stiffness and pain in his lower back and hips. However, when he practices the tae kwon do kicks he learned as a twenty-year-old—which he has done on and off for nearly forty years— he becomes much more flexible, and any pain usually disappears. One explanation is that by assuming and embodying the flexible positions needed to correctly execute a set of basic tae kwon do kicks, Jordan is stretching, moving, and somehow resetting his body in such a way that he automatically experiences hours or days of relief.

An alternative and complementary explanation is that by practicing something that he has been doing since he was a young man, he is literally "re-embodying"—bringing into physical focus—a younger, pain-free self. Ellen Langer's book *Counterclockwise,* as earlier described, considers how invoking younger, and healthier selves may provide innovative solutions to some of the challenges of aging. Similarly, in his book *Brain States,* in a chapter titled "Talking Heads and the Multiplicity of Selves,"

Tom Kenyon describes how he was able to get a severely disabled stroke victim to move his arm higher than his shoulder for the first time:

> I had Gerald raise his left arm as high as he could. He barely lifted it off his lap, perhaps two or three inches. It was then that a most amazing thing happened. I asked Gerald to recall a time when he felt he had been at his physical peak of vitality and strength. He closed his eyes for a moment and said "nineteen," when he had just gotten out of the Army.
>
> I had him return, in his imagination, to that time in his life. As I spoke, I put on some soft music to induce a deeper brain state and suggested to him that the nineteen-year-old youth was now some-how inexplicably inside his body. I asked him to allow the nineteen-year-old self to raise the left arm and just allow it to happen.
>
> Almost immediately his arm began to rise from his lap. He had reached up to just over his shoulder before he stopped. I happened to glance over at his wife, who was sitting literally on the edge of her seat, tears streaming down her face. "He's never been able to do that!" she said.[33]

BENEFIT: INCREASED ABILITY TO OVERCOME BAD HABITS AND ADDICTIONS

> *We've seen again and again that we are not one self, but multiple selves. Our human nature includes both the self that wants immediate gratification, and the self with a higher purpose. . . . Self control is a matter of understanding these different parts of ourselves, not fundamentally changing who we are. . . . People who have the greatest self-control aren't waging self-war. They have learned to accept and integrate these competing selves.*
> KELLY MCGONIGAL, *THE WILLPOWER INSTINCT*

An awareness of healthy selves can help you work with, limit, or even eliminate bad habits and addictions. Consider for a moment why traditional psychotherapy has a mixed or tarnished reputation for dealing with alcoholism compared with Alcoholics Anonymous,[34] which overall works quite well for those who stick with it. The crux of the matter may be this:

> **The part of a person that initially shows up to receive assistance from a psychotherapist is usually not the part or self that actually has the alcohol dependence or abuse issues.**

Alcoholics Anonymous engages the "drinking self" in a different and often more effective way. Before you share, you introduce yourself: "My name is John Doe, and I am an alcoholic." By explicitly stating this—and by being in a group setting and cultural milieu that encourages alcoholic selves to stay present—the problematic self can then be acknowledged, appreciated, counseled, and otherwise assisted in a peer setting.

Nearly everyone has some things in their life that they wish they did not do, or that they had more control over. As St. Paul famously puts it in Romans 7:15–19, "I do not understand what I do. For what I want to do I do not do, but what I hate, I do. . . . For I have the desire to do what is good, but I cannot carry it out. For I do not do the good I want to do, but the evil I do not want to do—this I keep on doing."[35]

The simplest explanation for not doing what we want to do, and for doing what we do not want to do, is that our different selves are not in agreement. One or more of our selves is perhaps indifferent to what might be better for the totality of our body and being. Whether we are talking about alcoholism, tobacco use, drug abuse, or overeating (or its opposite, anorexia), or other addictions like gambling, compulsive shopping, hoarding, or porn addiction, the first step is to recognize that there is a distinct part of you that initiates, engages in, and prioritizes this behavior.

That is, until you admit that there really is a part of you that is completely into and dedicated to doing whatever it takes to keep up your addiction—and unaware of or indifferent to the harm being caused—the totality of who you are has relatively little chance of successfully addressing the problem. On the other hand, once you do get clear that part of you is addicted to the behavior in question, you can begin to feel into, appreciate, negotiate with, and otherwise work with that part.

BENEFIT: BETTER RELATIONSHIPS

One remarkable thing about opening to the healthy selves perspective is that doing so will likely bring benefits not just to you, your selves, and your inner life overall, but it will likely also bring benefits to your inter-actions and relationships with *other people*. Just like you, other people are composed of more than one self or personality, which means that their different parts:

- will have different and sometimes unexpected needs,
- will operate in different ways and on different timetables, and
- will—from your perspective—sometimes act erratically or in ways that you do not approve of.

By becoming aware of this this, you open the door to experiencing the following benefits:

- becoming more accepting of inconsistencies and forgetfulness in others
- learning to be more patient and gentle with others both overall and in specific circumstances
- becoming more compassionate and empathetic and less righteous toward others overall, as you recognize that other people may have no idea that they have more than one self
- becoming less likely to "totalize" and label all of someone as being bad or unacceptable (that is, you may become increasingly able to see that while someone else has a part that you do not like, or that is sick or pathological, that is not *all* of who that person is); in any case, there are ways of working with that part of that person once you recognize that it is indeed a part of that person with its own needs (as in the above letter from Jim)

- learning to work well and harmonize with others as you situationally learn to sync your most appropriate or relevant self or selves with their most appropriate or relevant self or selves

Importantly, the personal benefits you receive naturally reinforce the benefits you will have vis-à-vis others, and vice versa, in a positive feedback loop (see fig. 2.3).

If you are feeling better about yourself—because you are aware of and perhaps acknowledging or even successfully working with your selves—it is easier to cut others some slack. As you remember that other people are working with more than one self, just like you are, your empathy and compassion naturally increase. To top it off, as you become more comfortable with yourself and more skilled in being around and working with other people, *other people will find you easier to spend time with as well.* Taken together, this adds up to three types of benefits:

- benefits that are *personal to you*
- benefits in *your* being able to deal better with *others*
- benefits in *others* being able to deal better with *you*

More good news: all of this can take place—and often does take place—without any special effort on your part. Remember "Awareness Heals," the last section of the first chapter? The more aware you become of your own healthy multiplicity, the more often you will naturally and

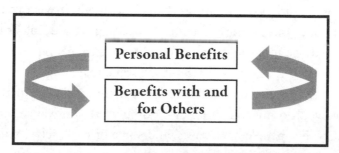

Fig. 2.3. The Virtuous Circle of Personal Benefits and
Benefits with and for Others

spontaneously shift the way you access and work with your own constellation of selves. This is true for benefits that are personal to you as well as benefits with and for others. Learning how to seamlessly shift into and out of different selves is a key skill that we will touch on many times throughout this book.

"DISADVANTAGES" OF THE HEALTHY SELVES PERSPECTIVE

The potential advantages of opening to the healthy selves point of view are many, but there are also some potential disadvantages. However, these disadvantages mainly relate to how difficult it is to let go of familiar and comfortable ways of looking at things, no matter how unrealistic, unhelpful, or off-base they may turn out to be.

One potential disadvantage is the need to own up to and take full responsibility for all of your selves. This may take a lot of work, and it is possible that one or more parts of you will not want to undertake the required effort or participate. Suppose you have an addiction or truly bad habit that originates in an unhappy or recalcitrant self. To the extent to which you can acknowledge, appreciate, and work with this self, you will free up energy and likely be happier. Other parts of you may be unhappy that this self exists and must be addressed. But it is precisely the effort that goes into working with selves that "have been feared, hated, and denied . . . [that] enlarges the realm of our consciousness."[36]

A related disadvantage is that you will need to let go of some unrealistic or magical thinking; that is, once you recognize that you have selves that are either doing things that you as a whole wish you did not do, or are not doing things that you wished you were doing, it becomes more unrealistic to wish for miraculous or magical changes in behavior. Instead, you need to get in there and do some real work.

This also applies to wanting other people to change if they have behaviors you do not like or are not doing what you want them to do. Like you, other people have selves, and some of their selves will consistently act in certain ways. Typically, those selves will not change their behaviors without some acknowledgment, appreciation, and work both on your part and on the part of the other person as well. And in certain cases, you may just have to accept that a certain part of someone is always going to do things that you don't necessarily prefer or agree with.

A final potential "disadvantage" is that you may find yourself unable to get or stay righteously angry at other people's selves as well as your own selves when they act in ways that are inconsistent or erratic, or even when they say or do things that you have explicitly gone over with them as being "not okay." Yes, part of the other person, or part of you, may have agreed to no longer do the offending behavior, but that may not be the self that is currently in charge.* The key here is to remember that you have one or more selves that can be more patient, more forgiving, and more willing to make peace than some of your other selves. If you can access a more forgiving and compassionate self, then everything will usually be better for everyone.

ADAPTING TO A RAPIDLY CHANGING POSTMODERN WORLD

In 1970 the futurist Alvin Toffler coined the term *future shock* in his book of the same name as a psychological state of individuals and entire societies wherein there is a personal perception of "too much change in too short a period of time."[37] There is little question that things are changing faster than they ever have before, and while it is hard to tell—as we are the fish in the ocean, barely if at all aware of changes in the water surrounding us—it seems that the pace of change continues to accelerate. From the interconnectedness fostered by the online milieu, with billions of people—including many people from whom you probably never thought you would hear—instantly reachable, to the unfolding of an astonishing variety of self-designated sexual identities (Facebook has dozens of gender options for users to choose from)[38] to the ability to custom create everything from clothing to technology

---

*There are important considerations as to personal, ethical, and legal responsibility, as well as the fear that some people might use healthy selves as a way to attempt to get out of trouble for things that a part of them may have done or forgotten. We will discuss these issues later.

(think 3-D printing), we are now living in a world rife with change, possibility, and alternatives.

As a result, we no longer live in the modern world; instead, we now live in a rapidly shifting postmodern world. Given the rapid changes and nearly unlimited possibilities before us, how can we best adapt and thrive? As Mick Cooper suggests, to maximize our potential and possibilities, we will want to be able to make use of a creative or adaptive plurality. He says:

> There may also be a form of self-plurality which allows the individual to maximize their potentialities—what we might call a "creative" or "adaptive" . . . plurality—in which the individual takes on different self-concepts primarily because *a singular self—however fluid—simply cannot make the most of the multiple opportunities that a postmodern world presents.* . . . In a sociocultural milieu . . . which celebrates heterogeneity and diversity, self-plurality may emerge as a potential means of maximizing one's possibility for actualization.[39] (Emphasis added.)

This brings us back to a critical point, one that Herschel Walker was aiming at, nicely restated by Rita Carter:

> What has conventionally been regarded as a potentially harmful pathology is actually a sign of inner diversity created by our species' wonderful ability to adapt to its changing circumstances. In our quick-changing and uncertain world, *the essential multiplicity of the human mind will I hope, come to be seen as a ubiquitous and precious faculty* rather than a curious and rare eccentricity.[40] (Emphasis added.)

When we acknowledge that we and other people have selves, and when we begin to appreciate and work with those selves, many areas of our lives rapidly make more sense and have better outcomes. The point, then, is not to fear or attempt to control the selves within us. Instead, accept the reality that they exist, and learn to take advantage of the incredible flexibility they offer.

In short, opening to an awareness of healthy selves—observing and affirming the "ubiquitous and precious faculty" found within all of us—can produce value in many ways, enabling individuals to come up with, reach for, and achieve bigger, better, healthier, and more useful goals.

For example, the goal of individual therapy might come to be seen as exposing the full range of skills and capacities that each of us has (or may develop) by encouraging and working with our selves. The goal of spiritual practice might be better described in terms of learning to harmonize and orchestrate our selves, rather than attempting to repress or integrate (or worse, annihilate) them. Emotional and mental fitness might come to be better described in terms of being better able to shift into the right mind at the right time. A great deal of thinking and revision will be needed to fully explore the potential scientific and cultural impact of the healthy selves perspective.

A VISUAL VIEW OF THE BENEFITS AND ADVANTAGES

As you begin to conceptualize, work with, and accept your selves, you'll see that not only are there benefits both to you and to others but also within each of these categories there are both inner benefits and outer real-world benefits. Consider the following idea.

Keep in mind: *a symphony of selves perpetually plays both within and without you.* Inside of you, it can be tuned in to through your thoughts, feelings, and emotions and is often reflected by the sense of harmony, coherence, and selves esteem that you are—or are not—currently experiencing.

Outside of you, it can be heard loud and clear in the congruence of your words and actions, the positive or negative habits that you reinforce, and the level of compassion you bring to your interactions with other people (and their selves).

As an alternative way to conceptualize and summarize the benefits and advantages that flow from opening to an awareness of healthy selves, please consider the following set of diagrams. The first, figure 2.4 on page 46, presents things from the 30,000-foot view, looking

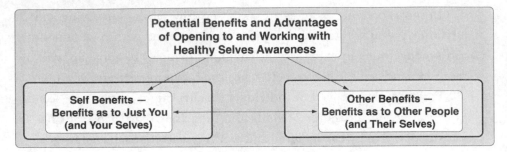

Fig. 2.4. Potential Benefits and Advantages:
30,000-Foot View

at personal benefits and benefits with others. Importantly, in what is called a "virtuous circle," each reinforces the other.

Let us now move in for a closer look. Figure 2.5 highlights another important distinction: benefits and advantages that you experience *inside* of yourself, and benefits and advantages that you experience *outside* of yourself. This is a reminder that the world of feelings, emotions, and energy within us is just as important as the outer world of physical objects and observable behaviors. Many modern authors have decried the "flattening" or de-sacralization of the world by only counting and considering surfaces and external, physically measurable, concrete aspects of reality while ignoring the vast inner landscape of meaning

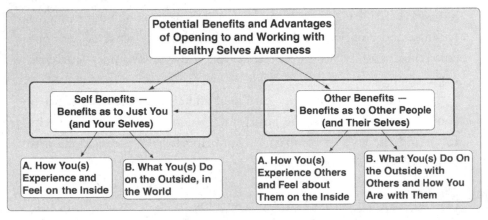

Fig. 2.5. Potential Benefits and Advantages:
Self Benefits and Other Benefits

and feeling that is our birthright. Long-time friends and fans of integral spiritual philosopher Ken Wilber may notice a similarity between figure 2.5 and Wilber's notion of "Four Quadrants."

Putting everything from this chapter together, figure 2.6, the most detailed, shows both the internal and the outer, or external, benefits with regard to both self benefits and other benefits. Fortunately, you don't have to start with contemplating all of these benefits! Instead, you can just start with attempting to be in the right mind at the right time more often, which we will discuss in detail in the next chapter.

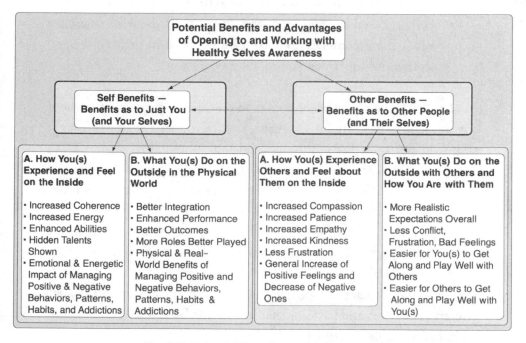

Fig. 2.6. Potential Benefits and Advantages:
Detailed Self and Other Benefits

BENEFITS AND ADVANTAGES OVER TIME

This chapter closes with a timetable of benefits; that is, how people usually tend to experience the benefits of the healthy selves perspective over time. We have mapped out three levels of increasing benefits. The ability to move through these levels is based on factors such as how familiar someone is with their own selves and the selves of others and how fully and easily they are able to question the Single Self Assumption (see fig. 2.7). The following list illustrates the three levels:

- Level 1 (*Implicit Awareness of Selves*): Benefits that you are likely already experiencing to some degree even before you become explicitly familiar with the healthy selves concept
- Level 2 (*Some Explicit Awareness of Selves*): Benefits that come to you easily and naturally once you have even a little bit of general awareness of the healthy selves worldview
- Level 3 (*Explicit Engaged Awareness of Selves*): Benefits that flow from a more complete understanding of the healthy selves perspective and for which you might have to work

Level 1 includes the benefits that you are already receiving, without any awareness or effort on your part, before you first read or thought about the possibility of healthy normal multiplicity. Even without any awareness, many people—especially successful, happy, balanced, and productive people—already benefit from an implicit awareness of selves as part of their existing social repertoire.

Put differently, as we are all actually living in a world of many selves, those of us who function reasonably well must already, to some extent, be effectively dealing with their own selves and the selves of others. If that is the case, then these people have probably learned and developed effective behaviors and patterns that reflect and beneficially leverage the reality of the existence of selves.

For example, consider the idea of a "teachable moment." When a child is not in the right frame of mind—not in a self that is grounded, reasonably patient, and respectful—there is a low likelihood of a productive conversation, especially one that involves learning something new or communicating difficult feedback. Without the right part of the child present, he or she will pay little attention, quickly tune out, or forget whatever is said. It obviously makes more sense to wait until the child is in a more suitable frame of mind.

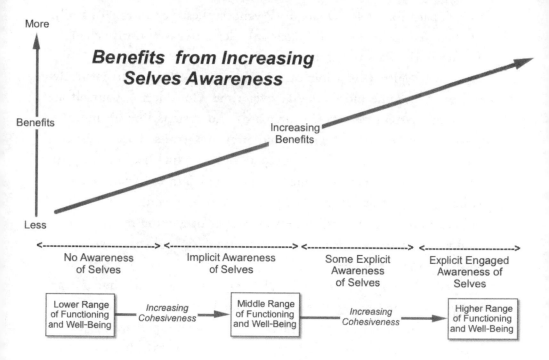

Fig. 2.7. Benefits from Increasing Selves Awareness

This simple principle—used by many effective schoolteachers, therapists, and parents—works so well because it leverages a real-world fact: children have markedly different parts or selves, and at any given moment some will be more amenable to certain types of tasks than others. Those who understand and make use of this principle with no explicit awareness of the reality of selves are experiencing and demonstrating Level 1 benefits.

Level 2 includes benefits that come naturally and easily as you gain some awareness of healthy multiplicity. Rather than powerful epiphanies and dramatic life-changing moments, most of the positive changes and benefits of Level 2 happen through small, natural, seamless, and spontaneous shifts in thinking, feeling, behavior, and speech; that is, in many cases, even just considering the possibility of healthy selves—whether it comes from reading a book like this, or studying Carl Jung's archetypes, or doing parts work in a seminar or as part of a personal growth path like Voice Dialogue, Psychosynthesis, or Internal Family Systems (all of which we will touch on)—leads to easy, positive changes in some of the ways you think, feel, and act.

So with just a little bit of awareness and effort, you naturally and easily become more *cohesive* over time. Considering yourself as an overall system of selves, your words and actions line up more—become more *congruent* with—your previous words, actions, intentions, and plans, and this helps you function more effectively in multiple domains. At the same time, others begin to experience you as being more *coherent* in what you say and how you say it, leading to better interactions with others as well as deepening relationships. And your *compassion* for others (and their selves) and your own selves naturally and easily increases.

Level 3 brings benefits and advantages that include, but go far beyond, those in the first two levels. As you become more familiar with and work through these ideas in terms of your own experience, you may become increasingly convinced—as others have—that the healthy selves perspective reflects the way that each of us really is. As part of this, you may find your selves becoming increasingly cohesive as you move up the scale of engagement from simply acknowledging that you and other people have selves, to actively appreciating your own and others' selves, to consciously and effectively learning to work with—collaborate and harmonize with—all these selves.

As you progress through these levels, the full spectrum of benefits and advantages described in this chapter become increasingly available to the totality of who you are. It may take some effort, but these benefits can make an extraordinary difference, both in your ongoing experience of life and in how others experience you.

DID WE FORGET ANYTHING?
ABSENTMINDEDNESS AND SELVES

A final benefit of the healthy selves perspective is that it throws light on many mystifying topics, including absentmindedness. We have all put something down—on a table, on the roof of a car, right in front of us—and not been able to find it, or started something (running hot water, turning on the stove) that we then walked away from when we should not have.

The simplest (and we believe correct) explanation is that the part of us that put the thing down is not the part that then has to look for it. We actually, really, truly have no present-time memory of where the object went, because the part of us that put it down is simply no longer present. Similarly, we forgot about the stove burner because the part of us that needed the stove departed or was distracted as we focused elsewhere.

THREE

Mental Health
Is Being in the Right Mind
at the Right Time

While chapter 1 focused on the "what" (healthy selves awareness) and chapter 2 on the "why" (likely potential benefits), this chapter suggests a simple way of working with the "how." We invite you to consider an important idea encapsulated in a short but powerful phrase:

Mental health is being in the right mind at the right time.

If, as human beings, each of us has different selves, there is value in being in the right, best, or most appropriate mind or self at any given moment and in any given circumstance. In this chapter we are defining mental and emotional health as being in the right mind—the right self-state or the right personality—at the right time. We will also discuss this concept's corollary, that mental illness or dysfunction can often be better described as being in the *wrong* mind at the *wrong* time.

How is being in the right mind at the right time the equivalent of mental health? Under this conception, when you are with your parents, your child emerges. When you are with your lover, your own lover comes forth. When you are having friends over for dinner, the part of you that enjoys social events, cooking, and taking care of other people will be present.

In the day-to-day world, when you are at work, the part of you that spent all those years in school—the part that knows how to work with others and add value—flourishes. When you need to do some serious financial planning or accounting, the part of you that is capable of doing that kind of focused, detailed work shows up and stays front and center. And somewhat more extremely, as Ray Grasse says, "When someone comes at your child with a butcher knife, it's time to activate the 'Inner Warrior' and take the sucker down, but when you are with your wife on a date, it's time to activate the 'Inner Lover.'"[1] (Note how similar this is to Herschel Walker's remark in the previous chapter that you would not want his Warrior self to be babysitting your children!)

Not only do you move into the right mind when needed, you find ways of keeping non-desirable selves from causing real damage. For example, when you are in a situation where you could easily make things much worse by being impatient or rude, the kind and grounded part of you comes to the fore instead.

Generally speaking, then, someone exemplifies mental and emotional health when they are cohesive enough to reliably manifest the right mind at the right time and then do the right thing to create better outcomes and desirable results.

Fig. 3.1. Dilbert: E-mail Personality vs. Gentle/Kind Real Time Personality.

THE VALUE OF BEING IN
THE RIGHT MIND
AT THE RIGHT TIME

Why should you aim to be in the right mind at the right time? First, and most obviously, as you expand your own healthy selves awareness, the array of potential benefits from chapter 2 become increasingly available to you. From greater self (and selves) appreciation to increased access to skills, talents, and the ability to work better with others, there is a lot to be gained from being in the right mind at the right time. As Celia Ramos puts it, "As a model, it can be said that optimal mental functioning is being able to switch easily and smoothly from sub-personality to sub-personality to gain the most productivity from a situation, plus the ability to access higher levels of problem-solving abilities."[2]

Second, consider the people you know who are relentlessly committed to remaining in the same frame of mind regardless of changing circumstances or situational needs. How successful and happy are such people, overall, and how close do they sometimes come to earning the moniker "single-minded fanatic"? Single-mindedness, of course, is sometimes necessary to accomplish certain types of tasks. However, in the medium and long run, nearly everyone benefits from having greater flexibility—the ability to see things from different perspectives when necessary or useful—in virtually every area of life.

Third, by learning how to steer or shift yourself into the right mind at the right time, you will be more aware that sometimes, inevitably, other people will be in—or will be moving toward—what for you will be the wrong mind at the wrong time. We will say more about this later, but the first key step here is to have an awareness that what is true about you—having selves—is true about others, which will enable you to more easily and compassionately create and nurture relationships.

THE RIGHT MIND: WHAT IS IT?
IS THERE MORE THAN ONE? IS IT ENOUGH?

Lucky people create, notice, and act upon the chance opportunities in their lives. Being in the right place at the right time is actually all about being in the right state of mind.

RICHARD WISEMAN

As a saying, "being in the right mind at the right time" is short, sweet, and, for the most part, completely self-explanatory. Nevertheless, here are a few definitions, clarifications, and answers to questions that may be useful.

Clarification: Don't "Mind" if We Do

The focus here is on being in the "right mind." But why use the word *mind* instead of *self, part,* or *personality*? Again, the exact word or term used to refer to your selves/minds/personalities/parts is just not that important. What is key, however, especially as you continue your journey into healthy selves awareness, is to *not* use words or terms that create resistance or dampen your desire to explore.

We have found that most people seem to have little trouble with *mind* as it is being used here. It's easy to understand and is commonly (if unconsciously) used by many people to refer to one or more of their own selves. The following expressions are ones you may have heard or used in your own life:

- I was (or wasn't) in the right frame of mind.
- I wasn't in my right mind.
- I need to get into a different mind frame.
- I'm going to give her a piece of my mind.
- I've got half a mind to go over there and do such-and-such.

If, however, you are bothered by the term *mind* here, then just substitute in the word *self*—"mental health is being in the right self at the right time."

Definition:
Being Pragmatically Right about "Right"

What do we mean by the "right" mind? The word *right* can be used and defined in many ways. To keep things simple, following our pragmatic orientation, we will define the word *right* as leading to positive practical outcomes. Thus, *right* means creating a favorable, desirable, or suitable outcome or result. If you are in the right mind at the right time, you should experience it as helping to create positive desired results.

Question:
Is There Only One Right Mind in Any Given Circumstance?

Why did we not define *right* in terms of producing the best possible or most optimal result? If each of us has selves, why not aim for having the "best possible mind" at the right time for any particular situation?

From the pragmatic perspective, we do not want to let the perfect become the enemy of the good; that is, we do not want to weigh ourselves down and hamstring ourselves with the struggle for perfection. There may be a "best" mind or self in a given circumstance, but aiming for being in *a good enough mind* is easy enough and still leads to very favorable outcomes.

As artist and writer Ari Annona said to us in a personal communication, "In any given interaction, we can never be sure of the part that we are actually playing—all we can do is show up and be fully who we are, in the given interaction, in the given moment."

In some circumstances more than one of your parts or selves may in effect form a coalition that serves as the right mind; that is, two (or more) minds or selves working together might function as the right mind. We will consider what it means to be working with more than one mind, and the value of forming coalitions, in section 3.

Clarification:
Is "the Right Mind at the Right Time" Enough?

The value that comes *both* from being in the right mind at the right time in a given circumstance *and* from saying or doing the right thing in that circumstance is substantial. Thus, we could have earlier used this formulation:

> **Mental health is being in the right mind at the right time (and doing the right thing).**

Fortunately, when you are in the right mind at the right time, you will—almost by definition—nearly always be doing the right thing, so we will be treating these (being in the right mind and the simultaneous saying/doing of the right thing) as one and the same.

Second, even if you are in the right mind (or minds) at the right time, and even if you do the right thing or things to create a favorable or desired outcome, that still might not be enough; that is, being in the right mind at the right time will not solve insoluble problems, create magic solutions when there are no good alternatives, or replace necessary hard work and effort. But all things being equal, as a general rule, when you are in the right mind (or minds) at the right time doing the right thing, what's left to be done will tend to become clear and then sort itself out pretty quickly.

PREPARATION AND PLANNING: INCREASING THE LIKELIHOOD OF BEING IN THE RIGHT MIND

Are there ways of moving or shifting into the right mind at the right time, or of substantially increasing the likelihood that this will reliably occur? Our goal throughout is to discuss just this dynamic. We have posited that we are all composed of selves and have invited you to question the Single Self Assumption in your own life and consider how viewing reality differently might regularly lead to beneficial outcomes. Later on we will distinguish between *switching*—the term used to describe how someone can be triggered to move abruptly from one self to another—and a healthier and more organic way of shifting or cohesively moving between selves.

In this chapter, our focus falls between a general call to raising awareness and a discussion of particular methods and mechanisms. To that end, we will set out three phases of using and benefiting from the right mind phrase, along with a couple of specific ways that some people successfully use it.

Please consider the following general principle:

> For more life energy and effectiveness generally, make
> sure that the part of you that is good at and wants to be
> doing something is currently present and in charge. If it is
> not, find a way to consciously call upon or shift into
> that part of you, or simply do something else until
> the right part can and does show up.

In your own life, can you think of times when being in the right or the wrong self made a substantial difference to your energy level, focus, and clarity? The next time you are not in the right mind at the right time, instead of forcing yourself to go forward with the task at hand, consider trying something else instead: take a walk, have a nap, meditate, stretch, play a round of Sudoku, listen to music, or do whatever else you ordinarily do to shift your frame of mind into a better place. A good illustration of how this works comes from Jim in a margin note to Jordan:

I intended to go over an early draft of this chapter one afternoon. However, late that morning I had news that I was going to be involved for some months in a lawsuit. I was a bystander and under no threat, but there was no doubt that it would take a lot of time, effort, and money, as I was once before in a long and ugly lawsuit. Upon hearing the news I immediately felt depressed, powerless, and barely able to think about anything else.

What I did at that point was take a nap and then go to a coffeehouse where I have successfully done prior editing. By changing my state and location, I was able to get back into my editing self and make real progress on the chapter. That this happened just as I was working on sections about how to shift successfully into the right mind is a puzzle best left unsolved.

THREE STAGES
OF AWARENESS AND BENEFITS

In the previous chapter we presented three phases of potential benefits that come from opening to an awareness of healthy selves. Similarly, there are three phases or levels of working with the right mind at the right time formula:

- Level 1: Without any conscious awareness of the healthy selves worldview or any effort on your part, throughout your life you have probably already navigated and moved yourself into being in the right mind at the right time on many occasions.
- Level 2: Here, after gaining some awareness of healthy selves—perhaps by working with the "right mind at the right time" idea—you increasingly find yourself considering whether you are (or are not) in the right mind and whether there is anything that you still can or should do about it.
- Level 3: Having experienced some of the benefits of consciously working with being in the right mind at the right time, you put in additional effort, working toward being in the right mind at the right time as often as is natural and helpful.

The more aware you are and the more effort you put in, the greater the rewards and benefits. Fortunately, it usually takes just one time—one circumstance in which you see the wrong self cutting in and thwart it, or one time when you create unexpectedly great results by shifting into a positive mindframe—to take notice and then want to expand your awareness even more.

A Driving Example:
Three Levels of Being in the Right Mind

As an example, consider a friend of ours who regularly commutes and is prone to experience anxiety about potentially being late, anxiety that on more than one occasion has turned into minor road rage. From countless experiences, he is well aware that when he is in a bad mood and looking for trouble, trouble is much more likely to find him. He also is well aware of his time anxiety and his potential for horn-honking, finger-giving road rage. From the perspective of his calm day-to-day self, he knows that it is never worth it to get into that frame of mind for reasons of health (blood pressure, stress hormones), accident prevention, and simple politeness.

But he wakes up a little late one morning, does not have any breakfast, and learns from his phone's traffic app that things will be congested once he leaves home. If he is in Level 1, he might be vaguely aware that he is heading for trouble. To ward off that trouble, perhaps he grabs some protein-rich food before he leaves the house, knowing that will help keep him grounded and let him make better choices. (Being "hangry"—hungry and angry—is very difficult for some people, and with its attendant blood sugar fluctuations this state can quickly lead to a less than optimal self being in charge.)

But what if he is in such a rush that he just gets into his car and heads into traffic without taking any food with him? If he is in Level 2—if he is starting to open to an awareness of healthy selves—he might be aware that he is heading toward being in the wrong mind at the wrong time. With *this* awareness, he might remember the importance of keeping his blood sugar level and search for and eat a granola bar that he keeps in his backpack. Or, he might simply remind himself that since it is about to be a tough drive, it is imperative for him to stay centered and remain in the right frame of mind. "This is going to be hard," he might say to himself, "but I'm ready, I'm determined to drive slowly and safely, and I'm not going to react to anyone no matter what they do."

And if he is in Level 3, he might have already made a plan ahead of time for when he is in such situations. Maybe he will put on some music that he loves that calms him down, or maybe he will consciously conjure up the right mind for that ride. Or maybe he will make use of an Odysseus Pact* that he has already set up, a plan that he has previously put into place that can be executed in just this kind of situation.

More generally, as someone in Level 3 he will simply be more likely to avoid ending up in a suboptimal or disastrous mind and more likely to end up in the right mind. This is because he is aware of both having different selves in the first place and the huge difference it

---

*In Homer's ancient Greek epic *The Odyssey,* Odysseus tells his crewmen ahead of time to *not* untie him from the prow of the ship when they hear the song of the Sirens, even though he will likely order them to do so; that is, he is ordering them in advance to *not* do what he says under certain circumstances—to ignore his subsequent real-time orders—no matter what.

makes to have the right self in charge. Clearly, driving oneself into road rage is an outcome to be avoided, and his Level 3 knowledge of healthy selves gives him the additional clarity and grounded focus he needs to find his way into (and stay in) the right mind for the situation he is in.

A STERN ADHERENCE TO MEDITATION

The exact ways of shifting into the right mind at the right time will differ for each and every human being—not only because we are each unique but also because real-world circumstances constantly change. Consider, for example, someone who finds himself tired and unhappy at the end of every workday, totally depleted of life energy and excitement. One means of shifting into the right self in this kind of scenario is through meditation, whether it be mindfulness, Zen, or another form. An example comes from a video conversation between comedian Jerry Seinfeld and radio shock jock Howard Stern. Stern describes how, after working hard producing radio shows for hours in a row, he reenergizes himself by meditating:

> In fact, to this day, after I do the radio show . . . my head is pounding so bad from the headphones and the noise and 5 hours of headphones and talking . . . I mean, it's exhausting. I go in and I meditate [voice becomes wistful] and I have the whole rest of my day. It's . . . I'm a new person! I don't think I could really live without it.[3]

Perhaps, when he meditates, a less tired part of him—a less tired self—steps in and then is energetically and joyfully able to do whatever it is that Howard Stern enjoys most for the rest of the day. This mind, or self-state, of Howard Stern—this autonomous complex or subpersonality—isn't tired at all.

What a valuable skill Howard Stern has: to know how to reliably shift gears and land in a happier and healthier frame of mind! Meditation, of course, may inherently bring more energy and recharge people on its own merits, but it may *also* give our selves the opportunity to recalibrate and do whatever is necessary to get the right part(s) of

Fig. 3.2. Howard Stern.
Photo by Bill Norton.

who we are on deck and fully engaged in whatever is coming next.

While the benefits of meditation have been exhaustively studied and proved, its ability to facilitate appropriate self-shifting has few mentions. Not surprisingly, there is to date no research on how long you have to meditate to enable a different and more appropriate self to step in. In Howard Stern's case, since he practices the specific type of meditation known as Transcendental Meditation (which involves repeating an individualized mantra), it is probably no longer than fifteen to twenty minutes. Shorter periods of time may also be effective. Jim reports that he has experienced this positive result, yet he never meditates for longer than ten minutes.

JUST IN THE NAP OF TIME

One way some people naturally shift between minds or selves is by going to sleep and waking up as a different self. Who among us has not gone to sleep feeling very emotional—whether it be positive or negative—and then woken up the next day feeling like a new, or at least a different, person? Taking advantage of this natural human proclivity, it is also possible to use short periods of sleep—naps—to help us shift into the right mind.*

Jordan, for example, sometimes describes himself as a champion "power napper," which is why he keeps a good-size beanbag chair in his downtown writing office. What he has noticed, however, is that while a longer nap is helpful to the extent that it rests and rejuvenates his body the way sleep normally does, taking even a short nap—even nodding off for a minute—can leave him much more alert, engaged, and focused than before he closed his eyes.

Writing, on occasion, can be very hard work, and if the "Writer" self is not present for Jordan—or is unhappy, tired, or bored—then sitting down at the keyboard is usually futile. But if he takes even a very short nap, he often wakes up in a completely different frame of mind—likely a different self—that is wide awake and raring to go.

Of course, even a micro-nap provides some much needed physical-level rest—like when you can only recharge your phone for five minutes, but it still takes it out of the low-power zone. But perhaps taking a short nap also in effect reboots the brain and allows a different self—one more appropriate to the task at hand—to take the helm.

Similar to napping, of course, is sleeping. Who among us hasn't felt refreshed—like a different person—after getting a good night's sleep? And who among us hasn't had to sleep off being inebriated or in a highly negative and toxic mindframe? Sleep enables a fresher and perhaps more appropriate self to become present.

MANY MORE WAYS OF SHIFTING

In *The Lord of the Rings: The Two Towers,* Gandalf knowingly says to Théoden King, "Your fingers would remember their old strength

---

*In *The Four-Hour Body,* exploratory journalist Tim Ferriss gives a detailed description of "polyphasic sleeping"—how to nap to increase effectiveness and reduce the total average number of hours you need to sleep.[4] Both Benjamin Franklin and Thomas Edison, for example, were renowned for their ability to nap and be extraordinarily inventive and productive.

Your fingers would remember their old strength better—

if they grasped your sword.

Fig. 3.3. Théoden King from *The Lord of the Rings: The Two Towers*.
Illustration by Ilana Gruber and used with permission.

better—if they grasped your sword." This is similar to Jordan's friend Tom McCook, who first thing every morning practices a thirty-one-movement aikido form, the Jo Kata, that uses a short staff. "As soon as my fingers grab the staff, I become awake, centered, and present, and ready to practice the form. I go from being partially asleep to being wide awake and focused." Physical objects can remind us of and revital-ize skills and selves with which we have otherwise lost touch.[5]

An important category to keep in your daily toolkit is movement and exercise of any kind. The idea that if you change the physiology, you change the psychology showcases the notion that any kind of movement of your body—changing positions, movement, exercise, walking, dance, yoga, biking—will enable you to better regulate your selves.

Another important category is what you do and do not put into your body. Many people have a marked tendency to switch into unpredictable and sometimes harmful selves when their blood sugar is too low or too high. Similarly—and this should go without saying—too much of any inebriant will make you more susceptible to unpredictable shifting and potential chaos in your constellation of selves. Sometimes, of course, a drink or two will enable you to more easily shift into a more confident or socially interactive mindframe or part of who you are.

There are many other ways to encourage or facilitate shifting yourself into the right mind for a given situation. Over time, we can become aware of the shifting mechanisms and levers we already have in place and develop new means by experimenting with our selves and learning from others. The following list is necessarily incomplete; its main purpose is to spur you to think about what has already worked—and what else might work that you have not yet tried—in your own life to help you shift into the right mind(s).

Some Ways of Shifting

- meditating
- napping
- sleeping
- changing blood sugar
- eating healthy food
- having sex
- microdosing*
- music—playing, making, singing, listening
- changing your physiology—in any substantial way—as a means to changing your psychology
- exercising, walking, any type of movement
- limiting unhealthy food
- changing bad habits and dysfunctional routines
- promoting positive and limiting negative self-talk
- asking other ally selves for help
- active imagination and daydreaming

*Microdosing refers to taking very small amounts of substances such as LSD or psilocybin. See James Fadiman, The Psychedelic Explorer's Guide (Park Street Press, 2011).

What you put into your mind(s) is also very important. If on top of everything else you run a negative internal dialogue—hearing voices or just thinking thoughts that involve how bad you are, or how often you make mistakes—then you are likely heading toward a self that is inappropriate or dysfunctional. Alternatively, if you tell yourself that you are increasingly aware of your symphony of selves and that you are working to bring about better outcomes for the totality of who you are, as well as for all the people in your life, you will be more likely to find yourself functioning optimally more often.

The last means of shifting that we will consider here is to learn to call upon another self as an ally when you feel you are about to shift into the wrong mind. Allison, a well-spoken friend of ours with two young children, told Jordan about how she had another of her many encounters with policemen giving her tickets for things she felt were unfair or unjust:

> After hiking the dish this morning I pulled out of my parking spot and turned left onto an empty street. A cop pulled me over and asked if I knew why. "I have no idea," I said. (I really didn't.) He told me a sign down the street said you can't turn left out of the parking stall. "I'm so sorry. I didn't see the sign and didn't know. I promise I will never do it again."
>
> "Please hand over your license and registration."
>
> After futilely begging for only a warning (I hadn't seen the sign!), he wrote up the ticket while I stewed myself into a full-fury indignant rage. In this state, I can become a gold medalist Lincoln-Douglas debater, all spitfire and tears, with everything being about ethics and morality. I kept thinking, "No, no, no, I do not want to let the part of me come out that mouths off at cops. It's not going to help, and I could end up in jail, or worse. I have to think of my children."
>
> But when the cop returned to hand me back my stuff, I completely lost it: "Why do you have to be an a-hole about it? If your job is about protection and safety, a warning would be sufficient!"
>
> I went on and on, sobbing about getting another ticket and my license being suspended. At times I paused, waiting for him to arrest me for insubordination—like being given a technical foul—but he just

stood there and listened. After about ten minutes I wore myself out and said, "Okay, I guess I'll go now."

"Well," he said, "I didn't actually give you the ticket. I'm going to do something I've never done before; I'm not allowed to void tickets once they've been written, but this time I'll figure out how to deal with it. I hope you have a good day."

"Thank you so much," was all I could say. "This is very redemptive for me. Thank you for listening. I respect you for doing this." And I drove off.

Allison had lucked out,* but she knew she was in trouble. Well aware of an obstreperous self that likes to scream lectures at policemen—a self that resists authority and has more than once gotten her into substantial trouble—she went the very next day to meet with her therapist, who, fortunately, was well versed in parts work.

Together, she and her therapist devised a strategy: in the future, when Allison felt the obstreperous self coming present, she would call on another one of her selves—as she put it, a self with a transpersonal orientation that always comes from the place of love—to help calm down and gently work with the agitated self. Creating an ally self that will become present in certain types of situations can be a very effective means of encouraging the best self for the circumstances to come forth. It takes planning to prepare such an ally self well before it is needed, and Allison's most recent report is that this strategy has already helped her more than once.

The Voice of Doubt

In chapter 9 we will discuss co-consciousness: when someone is actively aware of two selves at once, along with their independent thoughts, feelings, ideations, and so on. This is relatively rare, however, as most people experience being in one mind—one self-state—at a time.

What is more common, however, is for someone to notice that they often have a particular kind of "voice"—an ongoing and

---

*Or had she? Whether by luck, skill, or instinct, the self she turned to avoided the ticket.

repetitive stream of thoughts, feelings, or associations—that runs in the background, perhaps at a muted level. Some version of this "Voice of Doubt" is present for many people. In some cases, when this kind of voice becomes debilitating or paralyzing, therapy may be necessary or helpful.

However—once again and quite fortunately—awareness heals. If you can become aware of this or any other repetitive negative voice (or any pattern of negative or disabling thoughts regularly running in the background of your mind), you may find its effect diminishing as your ability to be in the right mind easily and naturally increases. Moreover, over time you may learn to identify this voice with a particular self that you can learn to appreciate, acknowledge, and work with. We will discuss hearing voices more generally in the next chapter.

COMPARTMENTALIZING AND EXPUNGING

Have you ever experienced yourself getting mad at something or someone, and then found that you stayed upset for hours on end, mainly to your own detriment? (Consider the metaphor of the hot poker: you pick it up in anger so you can jab someone else with it, but in the process of picking it up you are the one who gets burned.) As you become aware of having selves—as you begin to appreciate and consciously work with them—you will likely experience the value of learning to compartmentalize between them. Then, if a conflict occurs either within you or with another human being, the self that was engaged in that conflict—or the self that stepped into and then felt bad, guilty, or unhappy about the conflict—does not have to take root and take over.

For example, suppose you have an early morning disagreement over breakfast with your partner. If you can tune in to the part of you that is upset and let it know that you take it seriously and will work on the problem in the evening, then that part might not become the lens that colors everything else that happens throughout your day. In other words, if you can compartmentalize things and not get completely drawn into the unhappiness or upset associated with the self of the early morning disagreement, you will have a much better, more productive, and happier day.

One way of compartmentalizing things when you are unhappy, angry, or upset with someone else (or perhaps even with one of your own selves) is to either write down the things you are unhappy about, or tell them to someone else who is not involved. This is similar to writing an angry email to your boss, friend, or lover and not sending it. By getting things out in detail, the unhappy part of you can then more easily let things rest. Or by telling another trustworthy person what went on or what is wrong, the part of you that is unhappy will feel heard and then be more likely to relax and let go.

··

Reframing, Not Blaming

As a counselor, teacher, and—like all of us now—email correspondent, I (Jim) have long worked with people to help *reframe* whatever situations they have reported so they can then work with them in a different way. For example, something that is sad or painful can be reflected back to someone who then sees that very same circumstance as offering insight and leading to personal growth.

When someone suddenly sees his or her situation from the perspective of a different self, it can make much better sense, which often leads to a positive shift. For example, I have a close friend who calls me when she is quite upset to talk about her situation. The problem itself is almost always a real and difficult one. After hearing her out, I try out various kinds of reframing with her until I get to one that seems to work for her. At that point, her mood shifts almost entirely, and calls beginning with tears almost always end up with laughter.

When you are facing a difficult situation, or are feeling down, consider whether there is another way to see things, or whether there is a way to shift into another self that might see things differently or be better able to respond.

··

COROLLARY: WHAT MENTAL ILLNESS OR DYSFUNCTION IS

If mental health is loosely defined in terms of being in the right self-state, mood, or mindframe at the right time—the one most able to do the right thing—then what shall we say about being in the wrong mind at the wrong time? Much of what we call mental illness looks like (or can be described in terms of) having the wrong self in control at the wrong time; that is, being in the wrong mind at the wrong time and then doing the wrong thing.

For example, consider what happens when we fall apart or break down under stress. Very often, a childlike or younger self will have found its way onto center stage. There, it will do what it knows how to do best—throw a fit, cry, become incapacitated—regardless of whether doing so is appropriate or functional. Ultimately, then, the goal of much of psychotherapy might be reconceived of as teaching people how to shift into the right mind and away from dysfunctional self-states (rather than striving toward the unrealistic goal of being a single, unified, consistent self). Later on, we will consider current and potential future responses by psychology to healthy selves.

To keep things simple, then, we can state the corollary as follows:

> **Mental dysfunction (often) is being in the wrong mind at the wrong time.**

The earlier you become aware—the more preparation and planning you have done—and the sooner you move either into the right mind or out of the wrong mind, the better off (by far) you will be.

WHEN *SOMEBODY ELSE* IS IN THE WRONG MIND

What can you do when somebody else is in or obviously heading toward the wrong mind? What do you do if you see a train wreck of a situation—at least from your perspective—heading your way?

Fig. 3.4. "And to whom am I speaking? Mr. Pleasant Person
or Mr. Crabby Icky Man?"
Used with permission of Jerry Van Amerongen and Creators Syndicate, Inc.

Understanding that—from your perspective—others will not always be in the best self should provide you with more compassion, patience, and insight and enable you to either wait things out or find an even more appropriate mind or self of your own to shift into. If all you can manage is to remember that whenever someone is bothering, irritating, or annoying you that that is only *one* of their selves, then you will be way ahead of the game.

Remember that even if you see an undesirable situation unfolding or heading your way, *you will likely have little control over what happens within this other person*. If it is someone who has at least a rudimentary understanding of the healthy selves perspective, or someone who trusts you and with whom you communicate easily, then you might remind the person that he or she is moving into a frame of mind—a self-state—that could produce bad outcomes.

But this approach can easily backfire: depending on just how far the "wrong mind" self of the other person has come to the fore and settled into the situation, any attempt to ask it to leave or step down may just reinforce its determination. Timing is critical when attempting to move the right mind into the right place at the right time, or working with a wrong mind before it is in the wrong place at the wrong time. However you approach that other person, remember to look at things from their perspective.

THE DEGREES OF DIFFICULTY

How hard is it to get your currently in-charge self to relax its hold and allow another more appropriate or favorable self to step in? It depends both on the circumstances of the situation and on how well you get along with other people and among your own selves. A lot depends on timing and just when you become aware that it might be better to take a breath or two, come to center, and consider which self you might want to move in to. (The pivotal concept of coming to center will be discussed in detail later on.)

As already noted, overall it can be significantly easier to bring the right mind into play before it is immediately needed. By being aware of your situation and thinking things through, you can have a specific ally self ready to go once you see where things are heading. You may also have some experience to work from if you have previously worked through a response to this kind of situation, where the wrong mind or self has agreed not to force itself onto center stage.

Conversely, it can be substantially harder to get a self that has already taken charge to stand down and step away from a situation. Remember, you might not like something that this self does or wants to do, but for this self—from its perspective—its forthcoming action may be its very raison d'être; that is, among all of your selves, this self may believe that it has a specific duty to protect you or take some action in just this kind of situation. What this means is that it is much better to work at keeping the wrong self off center stage than it is to try to get it to not do what it always does or wants to do.

To return to a familiar example, suppose you are often impatient. Depending on the day, it will be much easier for you to have some leverage over your level of happiness by working toward not having that impatient self become the real-time dominant self. Once this anxious part of you is fully present, trying to talk it down from being impatient is a much tougher proposition.

In short, the best time to shift is before a behavioral episode has started—before one of your selves says or does something that is markedly dysfunctional or harmful. At this point, it is relatively easy to shift selves or at least have an impact on which selves are present. As an episode starts, it is not quite as easy, and once the wrong self has settled in and is in charge of what you are doing, it becomes hard to shift. And as the situation progresses—once the episode is actually happening, and immediately thereafter—it is often almost impossible to shift selves.

Sometimes, right after an event has happened, there will be remorse, sorrow, regret, and other emotions that will induce a more responsible self to shift back into control. Sometimes the self behind the episode will disappear almost immediately, in effect running away from the problem that it has caused, while another self takes over and has to deal with the consequences. As you become aware of your own patterns and those of (the selves of) the people in your life, you can help steer toward better outcomes and be prepared for whatever happens.

SECTION II

. . . .

Multiplicity All Around Us

Cultural and Intellectual Reflections

FOUR

Language, Voices,
and Popular Culture

There is an ongoing conversation among the different factions in your brain. . . . As a result, you can accomplish the strange feats of arguing with yourself, cursing at yourself, and cajoling yourself to do something. . . .

DAVID EAGLEMAN, *INCOGNITO*

In the first three chapters, we presented you with the what, the why, and the how of the healthy selves perspective. Now we invite you to take a step back and accompany us on a cultural tour of multiplicity. We will look at:

- *language itself*—how English and other languages demonstrate an awareness of multiplicity in what we say to ourselves and others;
- *the phenomenon of hearing voices*—what voices are under the healthy selves conception and what our culture says about voices, including those heard internally and those heard externally;
- *written representations* of more than one self in fiction (in books, stories, and comic books), in nonfiction (in biographies, autobiographies, and celebrity news accounts), and in a little bit of poetry; and
- *media representations* of multiplicity—in movies, television, and a number of songs and other musical treatments with a healthy selves theme.

In sorting through this material we were struck by just how prevalent the notion of multiplicity is throughout our culture, popping up not only in the language we speak but also in a wide variety of artistic treatments. With the pathological version of selves so often being presented as the *only* possible version, you can see why so many of us have never questioned the Single Self Assumption. While many of these cultural treatments of multiplicity may be misguided in their focus on pathology, there are still abundant insights to be gleaned from these artists and creative minds.

Obviously, this is not a comprehensive or definitive listing of every phrase, type of self-talk, book, comic book, play, movie, TV show, or song that addresses multiplicity. For those of you who want to further explore on your own, the box below provides a number of online lists and sources that address multiplicity—including the pathological variety—throughout culture.

....

Cultural References to Multiplicity

1. **Fictional Characters Generally:** Wikipedia has an extensive list of "Fictional characters with multiple personalities."

2. **Books:** Goodreads provides a list of more than 213 "Popular Multiple Personalities Books." Similarly, Goodreads has a list of "Popular Dissociative Disorder Books." This list includes nonfiction and fictional accounts.

3. **Comic Books:** The Marvel universe as well as other comic book series, television shows, and movies portray many characters thought to have dissociative identity disorder. Explore the Marvel Fandom Wikia and Heroes Fandom Wikia pages for characters with dual or multiple personalities.

4. **Movies:** Taste of Cinema provides a list of the fifteen "best" movies on multiple personality disorder. Infomory provides a list of "Famous Movie Characters Who Suffer from Dissociative Identity Disorder (Split Personality)." Ranker provides a list of the thirty-nine best movies "about split personalities," and TraumaDissociation.com provides a list of its top ten MPD/DID movies. Finally, Listal has a list of a few dozen "Multiple personality movies."

5. **TV and More:** TVtropes.org provides an extensive list of examples

of "Split Personality" in a wide variety of areas, including Anime & Manga, Comic Books, Fan Fiction, Film, Literature, Live Action TV, Music, Professional Wrestling, Roleplay, Tabletop Games, Video Games, Visual Novels, Web Only, Western Animation, and Real Life.

6. **Songs:** In addition to the TVtropes.org music list under "TV and More" above, Psych Forums has a user-created list of "Songs that remind us of DID," many with live links.

HOW THE ENGLISH LANGUAGE CARRIES THE CONCEPT

In many common phrases and metaphors, the English language shows a deep-in-the-bones awareness of the reality of many selves. Celia Ramos, in just two paragraphs from her graduate thesis, gives us a number of spot-on examples:

> The statement "I was beside myself" is said usually in times of anguish or worry. But how does one answer the question of the location of "I" in terms of "myself"? Another expression, "I don't know what got into me," is uttered when a person does not understand his/her own actions. What can get "into" a person such that the "I" would not know?
>
> The next expression is often used in situations where there is uncertainty: "I'm debating with myself whether to . . ." In this situation, there must be at least two conflicting viewpoints in order for there to be a debate. So one must ask, who is "Myself" such that "I" can have a difference of opinion?[1]

Similarly, focusing on the idea that we are consist of and often overtly speak about different parts of ourselves, Jay Noricks writes:

> We recognize our natural multiplicity in the ordinary language we used to express ourselves. A frustrated employee might say, "A part of me wants to tell my boss to go to hell, but the rational part of me says I need this job." Someone with marital issues might say, "A part of me

wants to leave, but another part is afraid to be alone." A friend with an addiction might say, "I can go for a few days without using, but then a part of me takes over and I find myself getting high all over again."[2]

Or consider Peter A. Baldwin, who spotlights a phrase covered in the previous chapter: "frame of mind."[3] Baldwin notes that people often acknowledge that it is better to put off talking to someone about something when they are in an agitated or nonreceptive frame of mind; instead, it is better to approach them later, when they are more open. Rita Carter similarly points out that being "in two, or more 'minds'" as to next steps is considered undesirable because it highlights "the discomfort of uncertainty and inner conflict."[4] Carter further asserts that using language to reflect the reality of many selves is something that we all commonly do: "Practically all of us do and feel contrary things from time to time. Afterwards we talk of 'not being ourselves.'"[5]

The combined use of *our* and *selves* in *ourselves* is also worth noting. Consider another use of these two words combined, in a phrase often found online attributed to self-help author Melody Beattie:

> **Choosing to take responsibility for ourselves and for the consequences our choices create looks like hard work, but it really sets us free.**

Try a little experiment: read the quote again, but this time, read or say aloud the word *ourselves* as two separate words:

> **Choosing to take responsibility for our selves and for the consequences our choices create looks like hard work, but it really sets us free.**

The second way—with "our selves" referring to our different selves—arguably makes more sense.

David Lester considers a different aspect, as described below:

Two terms are of special interest. In self-deception, we deceive ourselves. Yet this implies two parts of our self—the one who deceives and the one who is deceived. When we deceive others, at least the deceiver and the deceived are in two different bodies, but in self-deception, the two selves are in the same body! A similar dilemma exists when we say, "I am ashamed of myself." There seems to be two selves involved, the one who has behaved badly and the one who makes judgments about the behavior.

Consider the term which is very popular in psychological theory and research—the *false self.* The false self is the self that we present to others when we interact with them. What makes it false? It is our own self. If we act differently when we are with our children than when we are with our parents or colleagues, are all of these selves false?[6]

ON THE ONE HAND, ON THE OTHER HAND

Now let us turn to a common phrase used throughout the musical *Fiddler on the Roof.* In the story, Tevye, who is Jewish and lives with his wife and five daughters in a Russian village, finds that his traditions are continually challenged. First, his oldest daughter does not want to marry the man picked for her by the village matchmaker. But Tevye has already struck up a deal for this daughter's hand in marriage. And so Tevye goes through a mental wrestling match with himself, which Richard Ferris recounts like this:

> "On the one hand . . . I'm the papa, and I'm supposed to decide on the daughter's husband. But on the other hand . . . she doesn't love the man that I've arranged for her to marry."
>
> So on and on he [Tevye] goes, with "on the one hand this" and "on the other hand that" until he comes to a conclusion that "they love each other."[7]

Then Tevye's second daughter and a modern-thinking student announce that they, too, have become engaged. Tevye resumes his internal debate—weighing the sides of the issue first on the one hand and then on the other hand—until he convinces himself that maybe it's not all bad because after all, "they love each other."

On the one hand . . .

On the other hand!

Figure 4.1. Tevye from *Fiddler on the Roof* weighing both hands.
Illustration by Ilana Gruber and used with permission.

Ultimately, Tevye decides that with regard to his third daughter, "there is no other hand!" as he refuses to give his blessing and eventually disowns her entirely:

On the other hand, can I deny my own daughter?
On the other hand, how can I turn my back on my faith, my
    people?
If I try and bend that far, I'll break.
On the other hand . . .
No.
There is no other hand.[8]

What is all this "on the one hand" and "on the other hand"—Tevye's verbal formula and the animated gesticulations that accompany it—actually getting at? He is externalizing a conversation between his different selves to make explicit what those different parts are thinking and feeling.

Thinking aloud—talking to ourselves—can be a very effective strategy for making decisions. In Palo Alto, California, the Keeble &

Shuchat photography store closed down after fifty-one years in business, primarily because people would visit the store to see items and then buy them online. The owner, Terry Schuchat, "said he has considered closing for a couple of years. 'I would look in the mirror and say, "Self, what do you think?"' he said."[9]

Y'ALL NOW CONSIDER THIS

If you ever enjoyed the popular *Beverly Hillbillies* TV show, you know that the final line of the closing theme song was spoken by Jed Clampett (played by Buddy Ebsen): "Y'all come back now . . . ya hear?" Originating in the southern United States in the early nineteenth century, *y'all* is a contraction of *you* and *all* sometimes used to refer to a single individual. While there is a long-standing disagreement as to whether *y'all* is exclusively or only primarily a plural reference,[10] "strong counter evidence suggests that the word is also used with a singular reference, particularly amongst non-Southerners."[11]

Fig. 4.2. *The Beverly Hillbillies*:
Y'all Come Back Now . . . Ya Hear?

According to famed journalist and cultural critic H. L. Mencken, while *y'all* seemed to usually indicate an implicit plural, there are some cases when addressing a single person where it is *not* used as a plural term.[12] As writer Arika Okrent further amplifies:

There are documented cases of actual Southerners using "y'all" as a form of singular address that aren't easy to explain away with the implied plural principle. . . . A waitress, saying to a customer eating alone, "How are y'all's grits?" A shopgirl, saying to a lone customer, "Did y'all find some things to try on?" A student, saying to her professor, "Why don't y'all go home and get over that cold?"[13]

The *all* of *you-all*, then, could be an unconscious acknowledgment of inherent multiplicity. (Along similar lines, according to the American Dialect Society, the 2015 Word of the Year is *they*, used as a gender-neutral singular pronoun.[14] In 2019, Merriam-Webster proclaimed the singular *they* Word of the Year, and the American Psychological Association endorsed its use in scholarly writing.)

EXAMPLES FROM OTHER LANGUAGES SHOW MUCH THE SAME

Other languages also indicate an awareness of multiplicity. Here are a few examples.

In French, the phrase *Je suis hors de moi* roughly translates to "I am out of or beside myself [in anger]." *Ce n'est pas moi* means "that's not like me," and *Je ne me reconnais pas* is the equivalent of "I do not recognize myself."*

In Spanish, *¿Soy yo mismo o me paresco?* translates to "Did I do this, or is it someone like me?" *No supe lo que dije* means "I didn't know what I said," and *No estaba en mi mente* equates to "I was not in my right mind."†

In German, *Ich stehe neben mir* means "I stand next to myself," mostly in reference to anger, and *Ich bin außer mir* translates to "I am outside of myself," mostly in reference to worry.‡

---

*Thank you to Anne-Marie Lemonde for her translation.
†Thank you to Rocío Herbert for his translation.
‡Thank you to Tammy R. Coffee for her translation.

We also have some nice examples from Russian. Выходи́ть из себя́ (pronunciation: Vykhodit' iz sebya) translates as "to leave oneself" and means to lose one's temper, to lose control. Выводи́ть из себя́ (pronunciation: Vyvodit' iz sebya) translates as "to bring someone outside of himself or herself" and means to aggravate someone, to make someone lose control or their temper. Быть вне себя́ (pronunciation: Byt' vne sebya) translates as "to be outside of oneself" and is similar to the English expression about being beside oneself. One can be *vne sebya* with rage, joy, worry, or other strong emotion. Отдава́ть себе́ отчёт (pronunciation: Otdavat' sebye otchet) translates as "to account to oneself" and means to be aware, to realize. Сам не свой (pronunciation: Sam ne svoi) translates as "not belonging to oneself" and refers to behaving uncharacteristically, out of sorts, not oneself.[*]

Here is an example from Japanese: 我を失う (pronunciation: Ware o ushinau) translates as "to lose yourself" and is used to describe what happens after someone is overcome by rage and does something terrible. Afterward they might say, "I lost myself."[†]

We now turn from ordinary language that is written or spoken to the internal dialogues we have with our selves and the voices that some people say that they hear.

HEARING VOICES AND MAKING CHOICES

Starting in the late 1960s, on the popular TV show *Laugh In,* comedian Flip Wilson popularized a character named Geraldine, who often explained away her behavior by quipping, "The devil made me do it." In other words, the devil spoke to her and told her to buy that particularly bold dress, undertake sassy flirting with men, or just say outrageous things. St. Augustine, the early Christian theoretician (354–430 CE), would have had no problem understanding, if not agreeing with, Geraldine's contention:

---

[*]Thank you to Luba Schwartzman Chaffee, Yuri Koshkin, and Lisa Delan for their translation.
[†]Thank you to Conrad Chaffee, Luba Schwartzman Chaffee, Yuri Koshkin, and Lisa Delan for their translation.

Fig. 4.3. Flip Wilson's Geraldine, noted for her use of the phrase "The devil made me do it!"

Let them vanish from your sight, O God, as they do vanish, these vain babblers and seducers of the mind who because they have noticed that there are two wills in the act of deliberating conduce that there are in us two minds of two different natures—one good, the other evil. . . . For if there are as many contrary natures in man as there are conflicting wills, there would not only have to be two natures but many more.[15]

Maybe the hearing of voices—inside or outside our heads—demonstrates the existence of something like the devil, or maybe it just reflects the existence of more than one self.

Earlier, we asked whether you had ever argued with yourself and, if so, whose voice was on the other side of the argument. Nearly everyone argues with themselves from time to time, verbally "talking things through" or "working things out." (The Russian developmental psychologist Lev Vygotsky, as described in a RadioLab episode, suggested that thinking itself is dependent upon a child internalizing exterior dialogues with others—from thinking aloud with adults and other children to whispering to himself or herself to totally internalizing those voices.)[16] Even those who don't experience distinct back-and-forth arguments—like Tevye with his "on the one hand" and "on the other hand"—typically do in fact hear their own thoughts spoken internally as "inner speech."[17]

Although nearly all of us hear our own inner speech, the "hearing of voices"—as with multiplicity itself—is too often confused with mental illness. One estimate holds that between 5 percent and 28 percent of the general population hears voices that other people do not."[18] Importantly, "hearing voices is an auditory hallucination that may or may not be associated with a mental health problem . . . such as schizophrenia. However, a large number of otherwise healthy individuals have also reported hearing voices."[19] Perhaps when "otherwise healthy people" report hearing voices, it is simply a reflection of the give and take between selves.

MASTER'S MY FRIEND.
   You don't have any friends. Nobody likes you.
NOT LISTENING. NOT LISTENING.

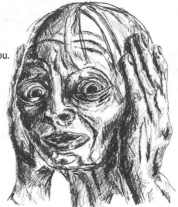

Fig. 4.4. Gollum and Sméagol from *The Lord of the Rings* in dialogue.
Illustration by Ilana Gruber and used with permission.

For some people, hearing and listening to inner voices has proved to be positive and motivating. Competitive athletes often talk aloud to themselves to get psyched up for a game, and it is not uncommon for someone to sort through mundane tasks—like what needs to be bought at the supermarket, or how to click through a layered menu to get to the right cable channel, or which street to turn down to get to an old friend's house—by speaking aloud. As we will specifically discuss shortly, speaking to oneself other than in the first person—like Gollum saying "we needs it"—seems to be particularly effective.

Even if it isn't a sign of mental illness, some say that hearing voices can reinforce dysfunctional behavior. As a Christian-based blogger recounted:

> But there is yet another take on this inner voice situation. . . . I have a nephew who has battled alcohol addiction for many years. Recently we were talking about this very topic and he enlightened me. . . . He said, *"When I'm sober I hear many inner voices telling me 'Great job!' 'Keep it up!' 'Don't take that first drink—it's a hard fall!' But I also have that one little voice that says, 'Come on, it's just one drink! You can handle one drink. No one will know. You're a big boy, you can make your own decisions.'"* But what he said next was most startling. He continued, *"But instead of listening to all the many positive voices, I CHOOSE to listen to the one small voice simply because it is telling me what I really want to hear."*[20]

This suggests the common image of shoulder angels (to which we will return later); that is, a devil sitting on one shoulder and an angel sitting on the other. Each tries to sway someone to do the right or the wrong thing; that is, to be in the right mind at the right time or the wrong mind at the wrong time. But the ultimate choice and responsibility to be in the right mind at the right time still comes back to the person as a whole, and to which voice—which self—one allows, encourages, or enables to win out.

Speaking to Yourself Aloud as Other Than "I"

> In this episode, we don't have any special guests, unless you count the multiple personalities in my own head.
> TIM FERRIS, SELF-HELP AUTHOR AND BLOGGER,
> AUTHOR OF *THE 4-HOUR WORK WEEK*

There is some intriguing research about people who talk to themselves aloud. An article by Laura Wiley—"Why Do People Talk to Themselves? It's Not What You Think"—discusses a study by Ethan

Kross of Columbia University. Wiley sums up some of what is now known about "private speech":

> In accordance with popular urban legend, talking to yourself is sup-posedly the first telltale sign of impending insanity. If this were true, most of us would have been declared clinically insane by the time we turned five, as this is the age by which the majority of people begin engaging in out loud, self-directed speech. . . .
>
> Within the last several decades, scientists and psychologists alike have come to understand talking to yourself, or "private speech," as a biological mechanism that better enables humans **to siphon off stress, solve problems, reason through difficult decisions, and concentrate with greater accuracy.**[21] (Emphasis in original.)

There are two important things to notice here. First, most people start talking to themselves aloud, in "self-directed speech," by the time they are five years old. Second, a consensus is arising that engaging in self-talk is good for us in terms of reducing stress, increasing focus, and so on.

Not only is constructive self-talk good for us in a variety of ways, but it also seems that people who use the term *I* in self-talk meant to boost confidence or give a competitive advantage do not do as well as people who refer to themselves in the second or third person! In one study where participants were asked to use self-talk to prep themselves for delivering a speech about their qualifications for a dream job, "those using second- and third-person pronouns were less emotionally dis-tressed both before and after the task than those who used first-person pronouns and they appraised future anxiety-provoking situations as more challenging than threatening."[22]

The first study mentioned in the previously quoted Wiley article agrees:

> People who speak to themselves in third person are more likely to have less anxiety, give better speeches and presentations, complete tasks with higher performance results, communicate more effec-tively, and maintain a deeper sense of self-advocacy than those who use the first person "I."

> Far from making you crazy, talking to yourself in the third person actually makes you smarter, more imaginative, and more confident. . . .
>
> Speaking in the third person lights up the brain's cerebral cortex, which is the outer layer of neural tissue linked to memory, perception, awareness, thought, language, and consciousness. The first person "I," on the other hand, lights up the brain's two amygdalae, which are located in the temporal lobes and associated with emotional reactions, anxiety, aggression, and fear.[23] (Emphasis in original.)

The biophysical correlation is clear: speaking to or with yourself, but not using the pronoun *I,* works better.[24] Another possible factor here is that speaking to yourself as "you," or by your given name, *enables you to be in better accord with and take advantage of there often being more than one self present during self-talk.* As we all have selves, it is only natural that from time to time they would talk to each other, and indeed, intrapersonal selves communication is often a necessary first step toward creating better outcomes.

Not Just for Dummies: The Wisdom of Inner Voices

Jean Houston's anecdote on the wisdom we sometimes find within provides a nice reframing of this discussion on voices. Jean, whose father Jack was a Hollywood comedy writer, loves to tell the following story:

> When I was eight years old . . . my dad was writing the Edgar Bergen and Charlie McCarthy show. We went to deliver the script and Edgar Bergen was sitting with his back towards us and talking to Charlie, his dummy. There was nothing unusual about that, I was used to seeing ventriloquists rehearsing with their dummies.
>
> But as we listened my father said, "I didn't write this." Edgar was asking Charlie ultimate questions. What is the nature of life? What does it mean to truly love? Where is the mind? Where is the soul? And this little block of wood with clacking jaws and head full of sawdust was answering with the wisdom of the finest thinkers of all

the millennia. Edgar himself was listening and you could see part of his mouth moving, but his eyes were in complete astonishment.

Finally my father, the agnostic Baptist, couldn't stand any more and he coughed loudly. Edgar turned around and his face went beet red. He said, "Hello Jack, hi Jean, you caught us." My dad said, "What in the world are you doing?" Edgar replied, "I sometimes talk to Charlie, he's the wisest person I know." My father was saying, "Hey Ed, that's you, that's *your* voice, you've just read a lot." Edgar replied, "Yes, I suppose ultimately it is, but you know, when I ask him these questions and he answers, I have no idea what he's going to say, and what he says *is so much more than I know.*"[25] (Emphasis in original.)

Fig. 4.5. Edgar Bergen and his
ventriloquist's dummy, Charlie McCarthy

One powerful means for facilitating channeled voices is hypnosis. In the context of the psychologists whose work we will look at later, hypnosis has often been used to enable or allow—or, according to critics, bring to life in the first place—the voices of other selves to have their say.

STORIES, NOVELS, BIOGRAPHIES, AND NEWS ACCOUNTS

Throughout, we refer to a wide variety of written sources. In this section, we highlight nonacademic written accounts, including fictional ones (short stories and novels) and nonfiction ones (biographies, autobiographies, popular science accounts and essays, and popular celebrity news accounts).

Two Centuries of Literary Doubles in Stories and Novels

In fiction, starting in the first half of the nineteenth century, there are many stories and full novels that fall into the "literary doubles" category. As James Grotstein explains, "In nineteenth-century literature the awareness of the 'stranger within' came even more to the fore, and many literary themes around the 'double' emerged. . . . Generally, the double seemed to connote one's darker, more sensuous, and less socially consonant self."[26] Grotstein then lists a number of "literary double" works by notable authors.

- Herman Melville, *Pierre; or, The Ambiguities* and "Bartleby the Scrivener"
- E. T. A. Hoffman, "The Story of the Lost Reflection" and "The Doubles"
- Charles Dickens, *The Mystery of Edwin Drood* and *A Christmas Carol*
- Dostoyevsky, *The Double, The Idiot, Crime and Punishment, The Possessed,* and *The Brothers Karamozov*
- Robert Louis Stevenson, *The Strange Case of Dr Jekyll and Mr Hyde*
- Joseph Conrad, *The Heart of Darkness* and "The Secret Sharer"
- Vladamir Nabokov, *Pale Fire*
- Edgar Allen Poe, "The Story of William Wilson"
- Henry James, "The Jolly Corner"
- Honoré de Balzac, *Peau de Chargin*
- Johann Wolfgang von Goethe, *Faust*
- Mary Shelley, *Frankenstein*
- Oscar Wilde, *The Picture of Dorian Gray*
- Thomas Mann, *Doctor Faustus*
- Flannery O'Conner, *The Violent Bear It Away*
- William Faulkner, *Sartoris, Go Down Moses,* and *Absalom, Absalom!*
- Jorge Luis Borges, "Borges and I" and "The Other"

Each of these works could merit further commentary. *Frankenstein,* for example, according to Matt Cardin, "may well be '*the* novel . . . about doubling, shadow selves, split personalities.'"[27]

Melville, Dostoyevsky, Stevenson,* Dickens, Poe, Faulkner, and the rest are a true who's who of fiction writers, as is Hermann Hesse, who gave us the Steppenwolf.

The Book within a Book:
Hesse's Steppenwolf "Treatise"

In 1927, Hermann Hesse, German-born Swiss poet, novelist, painter, and Nobel Prize winner, released the novel *Steppenwolf*. The narrator, Harry Haller, is a middle-aged man who "discovers" a small booklet called a *Treatise on the Steppenwolf*. (*Steppenwolf* is German for prairie wolf or coyote, literally, "wolf of the steppe.")

In the following excerpt, Hesse's *Treatise* explicitly describes several of the important themes from this book:

> There was once a man, Harry, called the Steppenwolf. He went on two legs, wore clothes and was a human being, but nevertheless he was in reality a wolf of the Steppes. . . . And so the Steppenwolf had two natures, a human and a wolfish one. . . .
>
> The division into wolf and man, flesh and spirit . . . is a very great simplification. . . . *For there is not a single human being . . . who is so conveniently simple that his being can be explained as the sum of two or three principal elements;* and to explain so complex a man as Harry by the artless division into wolf and man is a hopelessly childish attempt. . . .
>
> And if ever the suspicion of their manifold being dawns upon men of unusual powers and of unusually delicate perceptions, so that, *as all genius must, they break through the illusion of the unity of the personality and perceive that the self is made up of a bundle of selves.* . . .

*Morton Prince, one of the early psychological researchers of multiple personality, wrote the following about Robert Louis Stevenson: "After pondering much on the duality of man's nature and the alternations of good and evil, for a long time [he] cast about for a story to embody this central idea. Finally he wrote the wonderful story of double personality 'The Strange Case of Dr. Jekyll and Mr. Hyde.' It was meant to be only an allegory to present the two sidedness of human nature, good and evil. . . . Stevenson, in his imaginative creation, constructed better than he knew and anticipated the discoveries of psychological research."[28]

Fig. 4.6. Hermann Hesse's *Steppenwolf*

The delusion rests simply upon a false analogy. As a body everyone is single, as a soul never.[29] (Emphasis added.)

Hesse explicitly proposes the following themes:

- Every human being consists of a number—a bundle—of selves.
- There is an illusion (what we call the Single Self Assumption) of unity found throughout our culture.
- Once the illusion—or delusion—is broken through, it is incumbent upon each person to undertake the necessary effort and many steps required to create ideal harmony in their lives.

Writers' Reflections:
Novelists, Journalists, and Essayists

The test of a first-rate intelligence is the ability to hold two opposed ideas in the mind at the same time, and still retain the ability to function.

F. Scott Fitzgerald

As just described, two centuries of writers focused on doubles and other types of multiplicity in their stories and novels. Many other writers, from novelists to essayists to science journalists, have shared their thoughts and feelings on—or their personal experience of—selves and multiplicity. Here are some of their reflections (in alphabetical order, by first name):

Anaïs Nin, in *The Diaries of Anaïs Nin,* makes it quite clear that she has selves, although this troubles her:

> I have always been tormented by the image of multiplicity of selves. Some days I call it richness, and other days I see it as a disease, a proliferation as dangerous as cancer. My first concept about people around me was that all of them were coordinated into a WHOLE, whereas I was made up of a multitude of selves, of fragments. I know that I was upset as a child to discover that we had only one life. It seems to me that I wanted to compensate for this by multiplying experiences.[30]

She also wrote specifically about her own dual selves:

> We all have dual wishes, dual selves. A flashy side which wants to be noticed and famous, and a quiet side which only wants to be left alone in peace to work. My resolution was always: Do it all, they are all you, embrace them all. So now I do both—the public and the private. I must confess I prefer the quiet writing life to the public life, but the public life gives me the reason to be free, to move.[31]

Even clearer about the existence of selves was the physician and popular author Brugh Joy, whose book *Avalanche* has a chapter titled "One Body—Many Selves":

> One of the most powerful renovations of my consciousness occurred when I entered the almost taboo consideration that there simply may be no such thing as a single self, a single soul in a single body. This realization went on to include the possibility that the basis of

the human psyche . . . may be a collective of selves, independent and autonomous yet interrelating with one another, and mostly unknown to the outer awareness. Just as the body is a collective of well-defined patterns of energy identified as organ systems, the psyche, I realized, is a collective of well-defined patterns of forces discerned as selves. Each self has degrees of access to and control over the body. Each may seize not only the body but the consciousness as well, perhaps displacing the ordinary awareness of self or perhaps influencing the ordinary awareness to valorous degrees without overshadowing or displacing it.

The idea, that unknown to the outer mind, many selves utilize the same eyes and the same ears in each body is an awesome creative thought that has profoundly changed how I perceive myself and others.

Thus, as one engages larger and larger arenas of awareness, the *multiplicity of Beingness* begins to be recognized and appreciated.[32] (Emphasis in original.)

Joy succeeded with some of his medical patients by helping them to tune in to different selves with different resources, including the ability to heal. He generalizes the importance of cohesively making use of all of all of the resources of all of one's selves:

A fascinating aspect of recognizing and appreciating the multiplicity of Being is in coming to understand that each part of one's Beingness has particular resources. Then what's important is to begin the process of Self-Realization through the discovery of the various selves, which may involve far more than just a few selves, and to master the access to each one in appropriate circumstances. . . . Even using just one of the mature selves for all situations encountered in life would force that self to struggle with stages and circumstances it was never intended to handle! No single sense of self has access to all resources![33]

The English writer and novelist Colin Wilson wrote a great deal about true crime, mysticism, and the paranormal. He devoted a substantial essay called "How Many Me's Are There?" to the idea of selves in his book *Mysteries*. In the essay, Wilson provides up-close-and-personal accounts of some important early psychologists' reckonings on cases of "double personality" with hypnosis and other measures. Near the beginning of the essay Wilson writes:

> Yet the more we study cases of multiple personality, the less satisfactory this explanation seems. The "secondary personalities" so often appear to be distinct human beings with their own identity. If they are not really separate personalities—perhaps explainable by possession or reincarnation—then they suggest that personality has a definite and highly complex structure, quite different from what "common sense" has assumed in the past—like a crystal or a DNA molecule.[34]

Later on, after describing how Morton Prince worked with the famous case of Christine Beauchamp, he concludes:

> If that is true, the consequences would be, to say the least, of considerable interest for the science of psychology. It would imply that all of us are made up of a series of "selves," each complete and independent. These selves, it would seem, are already there, inside the new-born baby, as the caterpillar, the chrysalis and the butterfly are present in the new-born grub.[35]

He then adds that:

> One is almost tempted to assume that our bodies contain a multitude of different persons—like a boarding house—but that only the ground-floor-front tenant (who occupies the best rooms) can operate the body. But all the other tenants are anxious to move in, and may take advantage of periods of illness.[36]

David Carr was a well-known journalist and media professor who wrote for *The Atlantic Monthly* and *The New York Times*. Scott Barry

Kaufman and Carolyn Gregoire, in their book *Wired to Create,* describe him as being aware of his many selves:

> The brilliant journalist David Carr—a creature of many contradictions and a protean shapeshifter if there ever was one—said that he often reflected upon the many "selves" that he had possessed over his lifetime, from drug addict to media celebrity. "I spent time looking into my past to decide which of my selves I made up—the thug or the nice family man—and the answer turned out to be neither," he reflected. "Whitman was right. We contain multitudes."[37]

Kenneth Gergen is a science writer whose often-cited article "Multiple Identity: The Healthy, Happy Human Being Wears Many Masks" pushed the envelope for the early 1970s with the idea that we do indeed have selves, and that this was normal and healthy. He concludes:

> The individual has many potential selves. He carries with him the capacity to define himself as warm or cold, dominant or submissive, sexy or plain. The social conditions around him help determine which of these options are evoked.[38]

We already met Lewis Carroll in a plate taken from *Alice's Adventures in Wonderland.* Here, Alice considers who she is and exactly which one of her is real. As Gergen suggests a person is likely to do, Alice comes to grips with who she currently is based on her circumstances and surroundings:

> Alice took up the fan and gloves, and, as the hall was very hot, she kept fanning herself all the time she went on talking: "Dear, dear! How queer everything is to-day! And yesterday things went on just as usual. I wonder if I've been changed in the night? Let me think: was I the same when I got up this morning? I almost think I can remember feeling a little different. But if I'm not the same, the next question is, Who in the world am I? Ah, THAT'S the great puzzle!"

And she began thinking over all the children she knew that were of the same age as herself, to see if she could have been changed for any of them. . . .

"I'm sure those are not the right words," said poor Alice, and her eyes filled with tears again as she went on, "I must be Mabel after all, and I shall have to go and live in that poky little house, and have next to no toys to play with, and oh! ever so many lessons to learn! No, I've made up my mind about it; if I'm Mabel, I'll stay down here! It'll be no use their putting their heads down and saying 'Come up again, dear!' I shall only look up and say 'Who am I then? Tell me that first, and then, if I like being that person, I'll come up: if not, I'll stay down here till I'm somebody else.'"[39]

Lewis Thomas, an American physician and essayist, in his book *The Medusa and the Snail,* wrote a forward-thinking four-page essay, "The Selves," in which he discusses his personal experience of having several selves:

I am not sure that the number of different selves is in itself all that pathological; I hope not. Eight strikes me personally as a reasonably small and easily manageable number. It is the simultaneity of their appearance that is the real problem, and I should think psychiatry would do better by simply persuading them to queue up and wait their turn, as happens in the normal rest of us. . . .

Actually, it would embarrass me to be told that more than a single self is a kind of disease. I've had, in my time, more than I could possibly count or keep track of. The great difference, which keeps me feeling normal, is that mine (ours) have turned up one after the other, on an orderly schedule. . . . The only thing close to what you might call illness, in my experience, was in the gaps in the queue when one had finished and left the place before the next one was ready to start, and there was nobody around at all. Luckily, that has happened only three or four times that I can recall.[40]

Henri Ellenberger, a historian of psychology whom we will meet again later, summarizes the views of Marcel Proust:

What Marcel Proust indefatigably analyzed were the many manifestations of polypsychism, the multiple shades of personality within us. He considered the human ego as being composed of many little egos, distinct though side by side, and more or less closely connected. Our personality thus changes from moment to moment, depending on the circumstances, the place, the people we are with. Events touch certain parts of our personality and leave others out. . . . The sum of our past egos is generally a closed realm, but certain past egos may suddenly reappear, bringing forth a revival of the past. It is then one of our past egos that is in the foreground, living for us. Among our many egos, there are also hereditary elements. Others (our social ego, for instance) are a creation of the thoughts and influences of other people upon us. This explains the continuous fluidity of mind, which is due to these metamorphoses of personality.[41]

Marie Louise von Franz, a psychologist who wrote about fairy tales and collaborated with Carl Jung, was very clear that a multiplicity of selves lived within her:

I could give you a whole list of the persons I can be. I am an old peasant woman who thinks of cooking and of the house. I am a scholar who thinks about deciphering manuscripts. I am a psychotherapist who thinks about how to interpret people's dreams. I am a mischievous little boy who enjoys the company of a ten-year-old and playing mischievous tricks on adults, and so on. I could give you twenty more such characters. They suddenly enter you, but if you see what is happening you can keep them out of your system, play with them and put them aside again. But if you are possessed, they enter you involuntarily, and you act them out involuntarily.[42]

Note that one of her possible selves is male. At the end of the quote von Franz shares her all-or-nothing idea of being "possessed" by selves, something to avoid at all costs. She is referring not so much to demonic possession but to some kind of external trigger that abruptly triggers the experience of being switched into a less optimal self—a dynamic we turn to in detail later on.

Marilyn Ferguson, a New Age author who wrote *The Aquarian Conspiracy* (1987), spent a good deal of time promoting the idea of healthy selves in her book *Aquarius Now*. She gives us some context for the famous Ralph Waldo Emerson's quote:

> It's important to contend that we are all at least covertly multiple, and a good thing, too. Those who are doggedly the same day in and day out are probably as bored as they are boring. Ralph Waldo Emerson once remarked that "a foolish consistency is the hobgoblin of little minds." Our obliviousness to these selves, not our multiplicity, is the problem.[43]

For Ferguson, obliviousness to selves, not multiplicity itself, is the challenge we all must face.

Rita Carter is a British journalist and science writer whose book *The People You Are* agrees with many of our themes. In her preface she writes:

> I found that by thinking of each person as a group rather than as a single, unchanging personality many familiar but previously puzzling things made much more sense. . . . Multiplicity of mind is not some strange aberration but the natural state of human beings. Furthermore, our ability to shift and change has evolved because it is potentially useful—and today, more than ever, we need to make use of it.[44]

Near the end of her book, Carter reiterates that multiplicity is not a harmful pathology but rather an adaptive ability and states that she hopes that "in our quick-changing and uncertain world, the essential multiplicity of the human mind will . . . come to be seen as a ubiquitous and precious faculty rather than a curious and rare eccentricity.[45] We will discuss more of Carter's ideas later.

Salman Rushdie states that both characters in novels and people as a whole would be less interesting and alive if they were not able to move in and out of different selves:

> I think one of the great things that the novel has always known is that our identities are very plural. You know, "Do I contradict myself? / "Very well then I contradict myself." The idea [is] that we are not unitary selves, that we are very polymorphous. To make characters in the book interesting and alive they have to be like that—if they are only one thing, then they are dead. I tried to explore that over the years quite a lot. We all have this capacity to shift ourselves according to our circumstances. All the time. To say you've got to choose one of these things, to me, it's a straitjacket.[46]

Somerset Maugham, the British playwright, novelist, and short-story writer, gives us a clear and concise reflection on multiplicity. He reveals:

> There are times when I look over the various parts of my character with perplexity. I recognize that I am made up of several persons and that the person that at the moment has the upper hand will inevitably give place to another. But which is the real one? All of them or none?[47]

This question of "which is the real one" is as profound as it is recurring. The next time you find yourself deeply identified with a self that is not typically up front and in charge of things, ask that self whether it is every bit as real as any of the other selves that you embody. More than likely, the answer will be a resounding "Yes!"

Virginia Woolf had a strong sense of each of us having selves. In her experimental novel, *The Waves,* one of her characters clearly illustrates his own multiplicity: "I am not one person; I am many people; I do not altogether know who I am."[48] Earlier, in her 1928 novel, *Orlando: A Biography,* Woolf wrote:

> These selves of which we are built up, one on top of another, as plates are piled on a waiter's hand, have . . . little constitutions and rights

of their own. . . . One will only come if it is raining, another [will emerge only] in a room with green curtains, another when Mrs. Jones is not there, another if you can promise it a glass of wine—and so on. . . . Everybody can multiply from his own experience the different terms which his different selves have made with him—and some are too wildly ridiculous to be mentioned in print at all.[49]

Biographical and Autobiographical Accounts

> We all have numerous identities that shift with circumstances. The writing self is likely to be a highly private, conjured sort of being—you would not find it in a grocery store.
>
> JOYCE CAROL OATES

Perhaps the best-known cultural reflections of the existence of selves are the biographies and autobiographies of those with pathological versions of multiplicity. These books (and the movies that followed), sometimes co-written by all of an author's selves, typically go into great personal detail about the origins of the trauma that led to the splitting off of personalities.

As a primary purpose of such books is to sell as many copies as possible, there is always the question of how much things have been exaggerated, sensationalized, or just made up out of whole cloth. (This same problem is equally present if not more so in the way that Hollywood has made these pivotal books into movies.) As Bennett Braun, M.D., says in a volume he edited on treating multiple personality disorder or MPD, "Multiple personality also is a much-used—often misused— device in fiction, theater, and television. The phenomenology of MPD that emerges from scientific and clinical observation is not necessarily reflected accurately by the craft of the journalist or the art of the playwright."[50]

The first widely read book in this genre was *The Three Faces of Eve: A Case of Multiple Personality,* by Corbett H. Thigpen and Hervey M. Cleckley, published in 1957. "The book by Thigpen

Fig. 4.7. Thigpen and Cleckley's
The Three Faces of Eve

and Cleckley was rushed into publication, and the film rights were immediately sold to director Nunnally Johnson in 1957, apparently to capitalize on public interest in multiple personalities following the publication of Shirley Jackson's 1954 novel, *The Bird's Nest,* which was also made into a film in 1957 titled *Lizzie.*"[51] Following Shirley Jackson's novel *The Bird's Nest* by three years, both the *Three Faces of Eve* book and movie helped introduce many people to multiple selves.

The Three Faces of Eve focuses on a usually mild-mannered wife and mother who has terrible headaches and occasional blackouts. Her psychiatrist, Dr. Luther, discovers there is an Eve White (regular old Eve) and an Eve Black (her wild, flirtatious, fun-loving self; Eve Black knows all about Eve White, but Eve White doesn't know anything about Eve Black!). Later, a third personality named Jane emerges who eventually remembers everything about all of her parts and into whom the other two personalities are eventually merged.

Then in 1973 came *Sybil: The Classic True Story of a Woman Possessed by Sixteen Separate Personalities* by Flora Rheta Schreiber. Sybil, apparently the victim of extreme childhood abuse, experienced blackouts and memory loss. As part of her therapy, she was given amobarbital and interviewed while hypnotized. Eventually sixteen different

Fig. 4.8. Flora Schreiber's *Sybil*

personalities emerged, accompanied by changes in speech patterns and even physical appearance.

Sybil is often credited with the rapid increase in pathological diagnoses of patients with MPD after its publication. As one commentator stated: "When *Sybil* first came out in 1973, not only did it shoot to the top of the best-seller lists—it manufactured a psychiatric phenomenon. The book was billed as the true story of a woman who suffered from multiple personality disorder. Within a few years of its publication, reported cases of multiple personality disorder . . . leapt from fewer than 100 to thousands."[52]

Sybil has received so much publicity and has been attacked from so many quarters that at this point it is difficult to tell what was real and what was made up. For example, you can now read how the real Sybil, identified by two researchers as Shirley Mason in 1998, has subsequently admitted that her multiple personalities were made up in cahoots with the journalist-author of the book, Flora Rheta Schreiber.[53] Additionally, in 2011, journalist Debbie Nathan wrote *Sybil Exposed: The Extraordinary Story Behind the Famous Multiple Personality*. This book supposedly gives proof that Sybil's story was mainly made up by Shirley Mason, her ambitious psychotherapist, and an enterprising journalist, all of whom wanted to create and benefit from a bestseller.

If you were to read only *Sybil* and *Sybil Exposed,* and the many articles about whether the whole thing was intentionally made up by Shirley Mason with her therapist and the journalist, you might understandably doubt the reality of multiple selves. To put such doubt to rest, we invite you to read the finely written and detailed 1981 book, *The Minds of Billy Milligan,* by author Daniel Keyes (famous for writing *Flowers for Algernon*). Milligan was a young man who was not only a thief but also was found guilty of committing rape for which he was committed to a mental hospital. As it turns out, Milligan had twenty-four distinct personalities, each with its own name and unusual traits.

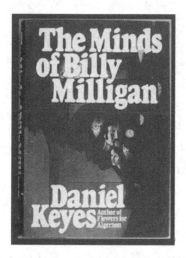

Fig. 4.9. Daniel Keyes's *The Minds of Billy Milligan*

Keyes, after extensively interviewing not just Billy Milligan but also the lawyers, doctors, psychiatrists, and orderlies who treated him, gives detailed portraits of Milligan's different selves and how they interacted with each other. The reality of Milligan having different selves becomes increasingly self-evident as you read the coherent illuminating details of this book.

Billy Milligan was able to access extraordinary abilities and potentials by fully being in his different selves (similar to Herschel Walker's inner coach, inner warrior, inner pain expert, and so on). For example, one of Billy's selves spoke fluent Serbo-Croatian; another one was a highly competent escape artist who could slip out of handcuffs and restraints; another was a gifted painter (even while he was in mental institutions, people paid Milligan hefty sums for his portraits). Another self had learned to directly manipulate his adrenaline, giving rise to the kind of super strength that once enabled him to punch a toilet bowl out of a wall. We will return to Billy Milligan later.

The final biographical account of note is *When Rabbit Howls* (1987). A collective autobiography whose authorship is attributed to "the Troops of Truddi Chase," Chase tells her story from the various perspectives of ninety-two personalities, some of whose different hand-writing styles you can see on the inner book jacket. Terribly sexually, physically, and emotionally abused (allegedly) by her stepfather (as well as allegedly mistreated by her mother), Chase would "go to sleep" as a different personality stepped in to help defend her or make sense of what was going on.

Many other biographical and autobiographical accounts of individuals with pathological multiplicity have also been written. However, these four biographies—*The Three Faces of Eve, Sybil, The Minds of Billy Milligan,* and *When Rabbit Howls*—are probably the most significant.

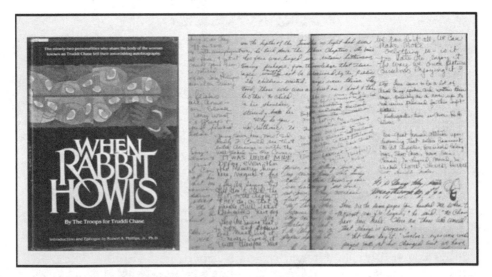

Fig. 4.10. Truddi Chase's *When Rabbit Howls*

Popular News and Entertainment Accounts of Celebrities Acting Strangely

> *No man, for any considerable period, can wear one face to himself, and another to the multitude, without* finally *getting bewildered as to which may be the true.*
>
> NATHANIEL HAWTHORNE

Finally, there are popular reports of celebrities, movie stars, politicians, or other public figures who act so bizarrely that reporters, bloggers, and even popular science writers attribute pathological multiplicity to them.

For example, early in his popular science book, *Incognito: The Secret Lives of the Brain* (2011), neuroscientist David Eagleman asks, "If the drunk Mel Gibson is an anti-Semite and the sober Mel Gibson is authentically apologetic, is there a real Mel Gibson?"[54] Eagleman then quotes Jewish film producer Dean Devlin as saying, "I have been with Mel when he has fallen off [the wagon], and he becomes a completely different person. It is pretty horrifying."[55] Eagleman's conclusion is quite clear:

> Many people prefer a view of human nature that includes a true side and a false side—in other words, humans have a single genuine aim and the rest is decoration, evasion, or cover-up. That's intuitive, but it's incomplete. A study of the brain necessitates a more nuanced view of human nature . . . we are made up of many neural subpopulations; as Whitman put it, we "contain multitudes." Even though Gibson's detractors will continue to insist that he is truly an anti-Semite, and his defenders will insist that he is not, both may be defending an incomplete story to support their own biases. *Is there any reason to believe that it's not possible to have both racist and non-racist parts of the brain?*[56] (Emphasis added.)

Indeed, we feel there is *every* reason to believe that the different parts of the human brain functionally and pragmatically equate to having, or give rise to, different selves.

"There is no excuse, nor should there be any tolerance, for anyone who thinks or expresses any kind of anti-Semetic remark. want to apologize specifically to everyone in the Jewish community for the vitriolic and harmful words I said to a law enforcement officer the night I was arrested on a DUI charge." — Mel Gibson

Fig. 4.11. Mel Gibson Apologizes for Anti-Semitism.
Photo by Georges Biard.

In other instances, celebrities make use of a popularized understanding of multiplicity to help make sense of the world. For example, Lindsay Lohan, well known for her own odd behavior, told the press that her fiancé, Russian business heir Egor Tarabasov, had abused and attacked her. Lohan then made this statement:

When we got home (from a night out) I went to bed and Egor went out. . . . A few hours later he came back and when I woke up he was standing over me. He wasn't himself, he was being very aggressive and he attacked me. . . . I've kept quiet for so long but now I'm scared of what Egor might do to me and to himself.[57]

Egor was likely a different one of his selves that night, an undesirable and violent one.

COMIC BOOKS AND COMIC STRIPS

The comic book industry has seen substantial growth in the past two decades.[58] With many independent companies as well as the major production houses (Marvel and DC) putting out new titles and reviving old ones, comics have always been a place to push limits and take the pulse of popular culture's imagination.

Fig. 4.12. Comic strips have long showcased
our "super" parts and selves

The resource list of references to multiplicity on page 77 contains two sources that list comic book heroes and villains who have multiple selves. The heroes sometimes have a secret identity, like Superman or Batman, but in some cases they completely transform into someone else who is not necessarily even human and who may not share any memories with them. A classic example of a fully transforming hero is Bruce Banner, who becomes the Hulk when he gets angry and loses control. Comic book villains—such as Batman's foe Two-Face or Spider-Man's opponent Norman Osborn (and then his son, Harry Osborn) who turns into the Green Goblin—tend to have fully incohesive pathological multiplicity, sometimes with an awareness of their normal selves, and sometimes not, often mixed in with elements of schizophrenia and other mental illness.[59]

In some cases, a comic book hero was directly modeled on the progressive understanding of multiple personality disorder that became popular in the 1980s and 1990s. As discussed later, this progressive view held that the creation, or splitting off, of new personalities by

Fig. 4.13. *Badger Berserk!* comic cover

someone (especially a child) who was exposed to horrific circumstances (e.g., sexual abuse, physical torture) was a positive, adaptive, evolutionary response. Thus, consider how one comic book blogger describes the Badger:

> Norbert Sykes is a Vietnam vet and suffered years of abuse as a child. The combination of these caused him to create a number of different psyches to deal with his emotional distress. The Badger is a martial arts master and defender of the weak and animals—calls everybody Larry; Emily is a 9-year-old girl that he created to escape the depravations of his father; Pierre, a homicidal Frenchman; Leroy, Norbert's childhood pet who was beaten to death by his a-hole father; Gastineau Grover Depaul, a black dude from the projects; and Max Swell, effete epicurean.[60]

In addition to comic books, there are newspaper comic strips and single-frame comics, some of which are reproduced in this book. From James Thurber's single frames in *The New Yorker* to Cathy Guisewite's *Cathy* strips, and from Scott Adams's *Dilbert* to J. C. Duffy's *Fusco Brothers,* there is an awareness among creators of comic strips that having selves is a regular—and often amusing or otherwise penetratingly informative—part of day-to-day experience.

MULTIPLICITY IN MOVIES AND TELEVISION

Not surprisingly, accounts of multiplicity—often pathological—have made it onto both the big and little screen; that is, major motion pictures as well as television series and even cartoons. In some cases, as with the "Evil Kermit" meme,* the internet is amplifying the concept of multiplicity. As you become more aware of the selves in your life, you will probably notice more characters working with or demonstrating their own selves in the movies and television shows you watch.

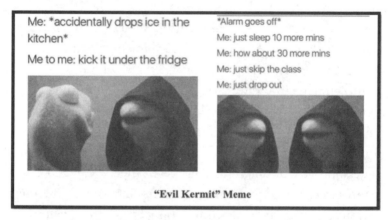

Fig. 4.14. Widespread "Evil Kermit" meme readily makes use of selves

Movies
Three of the four major biographical accounts of pathological multiplicity—*The Three Faces of Eve, Sybil,* and *When Rabbit Howls*—have already been made into major motion pictures (the movie of *When*

---

*"Evil Kermit plays off of a still taken from the 2014 film *Muppets Most Wanted,* in which pure and wholesome Kermit is chatting with his sinister doppelgänger, Constantine. In this meme's case, Kermit and Constantine are a stand-in for our socially acceptable selves warring with our asshole instincts." Megan Farokhmanesh, "What Makes a Kermit Goof Spread? Meme Thieves," The Verge website, November 17, 2016.

Rabbit Howls was called *Voices Within: The Lives of Truddi Chase*). As for *The Minds of Billy Milligan,* Leonardo DiCaprio has been working on it since 1997, intending to play Billy in the film version, *The Crowded Room.*

The compilation of "Cultural References to Multiplicity" at the beginning of this chapter (p. 77) provides several lists of movies about multiple personality disorder. One classic is *The Nutty Professor* (1963) starring Jerry Lewis as a college professor who drinks a potion to become a super-suave version of himself, a takeoff on Robert Louis Stevenson's Jekyll and Hyde. More recent movies include *Fight Club* (1996) with Brad Pitt and Jared Leto, *Me, Myself & Irene* (2000) with Jim Carrey, *The Lord of the Rings* franchise showing Sméagol/Gollum carrying on lengthy conversations among his selves, *Waking Madison* (2010), and *Frankie & Alice* (2010) with Halle Berry.

Two other movies bear special mention. First, in 2015, Pixar gave us *Inside Out,* which won the Academy Award for Best Animated Feature. The protagonist, Riley, is an eleven-year-old girl whose family abruptly moves, throwing her into the chaos of a new home and school. Based on the research of Paul Ekman,* the filmmakers take us inside Riley's head or mind, as well as back in time. We can see how, from the time she is a newborn infant (presumably this happens with all human beings), there are five personified emotions—Joy, Sadness, Anger, Fear, and Disgust—that are in effect actually running her deep emotional life and making decisions between them depending on who gets to a central control board and punches a button first.

These five emotions (depicted as distinct "personality islands" within Riley's brain) are not quite the same as the selves, parts, or minds we have been discussing—for one thing, as always, Hollywood intensifies each character for maximum dramatic effect. Still, there are some parallels and insights to be gleaned from this innovative film. The met-

---

*"They consulted Paul Ekman, a well-known psychologist who studies emotions, and Dacher Keltner, a professor of psychology at the University of California–Berkeley. Ekman had early in his career identified six core emotions—anger, fear, sadness, disgust, joy, and surprise. Keltner found surprise and fear to be too similar, which left him with five emotions to build characters around." See *Inside Out,* at Wikipedia.

aphor of the control panel that the personified emotional selves jockey for is an apt one, and Riley's ultimate epiphany—that sadness plays a key role in her life because it produces empathy within her—affirms the importance of acknowledging and appreciating one's selves and the selves of others.

Also worth noting is *I'm Not There,* a biographical musical drama focusing on Bob Dylan, with Dylan played by six different actors (including Cate Blanchett). Rita Carter states that "Dylan is a self-ascribed multiple; by his own description 'a different person every day.'"[61] According to movie producer Christine Vachon, "The thing about Dylan that's so fascinating is that he has completely and utterly changed his identity time and time again. . . . I think it's kind of the only way to look at him."[62] Explaining why six different actors were used in the movie, director Todd Haynes wrote:

> The minute you try to grab hold of Dylan, he's no longer where he was. He's like a flame: If you try to hold him in your hand you'll surely get burned. Dylan's life of change and constant disappearances and constant transformations makes you yearn to hold him, and to nail him down. And that's why his fan base is so

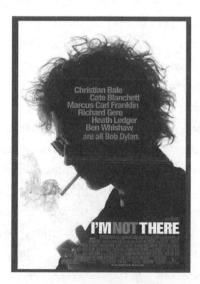

Fig. 4.15. The Bob Dylan biopic *I'm Not There*

obsessive, so desirous of finding the truth and the absolutes and the answers to him—things that Dylan will never provide and will only frustrate. . . . Dylan is difficult and mysterious and evasive and frustrating, and it only makes you identify with him all the more as he skirts identity.[63]

Television

Tommy Smothers often introduced *The Smothers Brothers Comedy Hour,* popular in the late 1960s, by mentioning "My brother and my selves." How about other television versions of multiplicity? Item 5 from the "Cultural References to Multiplicity" list at the beginning of this chapter (p. 77) provides a website with examples of multiple selves in TV programs and popular entertainment of many types, including cartoons.

An example of pathological multiplicity as the main theme of a television show is *United States of Tara,* a Showtime series where actress Toni Collette struggles with finding a way to be a mom and raise a family while dealing with four wildly divergent and often dysfunctional selves. This show highlights Tara's abrupt switching from one sub-personality into another, usually to the great distress of her family members (not to mention the people with whom she picks fights). According to Dr. Richard Kluft, "Tara is extremely real . . . but extremely unrealistic. What I mean to say is, everything that Tara demonstrates is real. I've seen it, many, many times over. What is unrealistic is that you see so much of it so [concentrated]."[64]

In addition to television shows that have directly focused on (usually pathological) multiplicity, some shows overtly address the subject just once but in a particularly memorable or creative way. The animated comedy *BoJack Horseman,* for example, includes a line that could serve as the summation for this entire book. A minor character (Alexi Brosefino) tries to convince a major character (Diane Nguyen) that he and his friends transcend their Casanova reputation: "But within each man lives a great multiplicity, right? Nobody is just one thing."

Another example is *The Big Bang Theory,* among the longest-running multi-camera sitcoms ever. Season 11, episode 3, "The Relaxation

Integration," presents us with the "Council of Sheldons," with many of Sheldon's different selves represented at the council he has in a dream. Earlier in the episode we are treated to the following dialogue between Penny and Sheldon:

> **Penny:** Is it possible that the sleep-talking is a part of your brain that's telling you everything's gonna be okay and you just need to relax a little?
>
> **Sheldon:** So you're proposing that the self is an illusion, and that we actually have multiple centers of consciousness that are communicating with one another?
>
> **Penny:** In laymen's terms, yeah.
>
> **Sheldon:** Huh. Interesting. So you don't believe there's a Cartesian self that underlies the flux of experience?
>
> **Penny:** Maybe in my twenties, not anymore.

A final example comes from the long-running show *Star Trek: The Next Generation,* which offered sci-fi fans a remarkable example of healthy multiplicity. In season 6, episode 20, "The Chase," Captain Jean-Luc Picard's old professor shows up on the *Enterprise* with an ancient but completely intact ceramic bowl—a "Kurlan *naiskos*"—that includes a set of figurines inside when the top is taken off. After lifting off the lid, Picard says, "You mean it's complete? . . . The Kirlan civilization believed that an individual was a community of individuals. Inside of us are many voices, each with its own desires, its own style, its own view of the world."

SELVES IN
POETRY, MUSIC, AND SONGS

Her name was Magill, and she called herself Lil, but everyone knew her as Nancy.

THE BEATLES, FROM "ROCKY RACCOON"

If the core idea behind this book is correct, and the Single Self Assumption is inadequate, then we would expect to find evidence for this throughout every area of culture. Many of the written and cinematic works described above focus on pathology. In other arenas, artists explore themselves more freely in a wide variety of mediums, including the poetry and music we next turn to. You will also find Pinterest boards categorized by "Multiple Personalities/Self Portraits" showing hundreds of different pinned images. Many of them seem to speak to the lives of individuals who leave behind a positive and complicated impression.

In Poetry
Given that issues of identity and self (if not selves) discovery have always been a focal point for many poets, there are no doubt many examples in addition to Walt Whitman's famous lines from "Song of Myself":

> *Do I contradict myself?*
> *Very well then I contradict myself,*
> *(I am large, I contain multitudes.)*

This is not the place—nor do we have the space—to work our way through the world of poetry. Here, though, are a few notable poems that speak directly to having, acknowledging, and working with selves.

First, from the Lebanese American writer, poet, and visual artist Kahlil Gibran (most famous for his bestselling book *The Prophet*), comes "The Seven Selves," an enigmatic poem from his book *The Madman—His Parables*:

> *In the stillest hour of the night, as I lay half asleep, my seven selves sat together and thus conversed in whisper:*
>
> *First Self: Here, in this madman, I have dwelt all these years, with naught to do but renew his pain by day and recreate his sorrow by night. I can bear my fate no longer, and now I rebel.*
>
> *Second Self: Yours is a better lot than mine, brother, for it is given to me to be this madman's joyous self. I laugh*

*his laughter and sing his happy hours, and with thrice
winged feet I dance his brighter thoughts. It is I that
would rebel against my weary existence.*

*Third Self: And what of me, the love-ridden self, the
flaming brand of wild passion and fantastic desires? It is
I the love-sick self who would rebel against this madman.*

*Fourth Self: I, amongst you all, am the most miserable,
for naught was given me but odious hatred and
destructive loathing. It is I, the tempest-like self, the one
born in the black caves of Hell, who would protest against
serving this madman.*

*Fifth Self: Nay, it is I, the thinking self, the fanciful self,
the self of hunger and thirst, the one doomed to wander
without rest in search of unknown things and things not
yet created; it is I, not you, who would rebel.*

*Sixth Self: And I, the working self, the pitiful labourer,
who, with patient hands, and longing eyes, fashion the
days into images and give the formless elements new and
eternal forms—it is I, the solitary one, who would rebel
against this restless madman.*

*Seventh Self: How strange that you all would rebel
against this man, because each and every one of you has a
preordained fate to fulfill. Ah! could I but be like one of
you, a self with a determined lot! But I have none, I am
the do-nothing self, the one who sits in the dumb, empty
nowhere and nowhen, while you are busy re-creating life.
Is it you or I, neighbours, who should rebel?*

*When the seventh self thus spake the other six selves
looked with pity upon him but said nothing more; and
as the night grew deeper one after the other went to sleep
enfolded with a new and happy submission.*[65]

From the thirteenth-century Persian and Sufi poet Jalaluddin Rumi we have the beginning of this clear and thought-provoking piece, "The Guest House," translated by Coleman Barks,[66] suggesting each self should be treated honorably:

> *This being human is a guest house.*
> *Every morning a new arrival.*
>
> *A joy, a depression, a meanness,*
> *some momentary awareness comes*
> *As an unexpected visitor.*
> *Welcome and entertain them all!*

Finally, the twentieth-century Polish poet Czesław Miłosz wrote:

> *The purpose of poetry is to remind us*
> *How difficult it is to remain just one person.*
> *For our house is open; there are no keys to the doors;*
> *And invisible guests come in and out at will.*[67]

Music and Songs

To end this tour through popular culture we will very briefly highlight a few relevant songs and some key lyrics:

- In the 1999 movie *Muse* (starring Albert Brooks), for example, the film score is composed and performed by Elton John and includes a light instrumental piece called "Multiple Personality."[68]
- Elton John's piano-playing peer and occasional touring partner, Billy Joel, gave us the hit song "The Stranger" from his 1977 album of the same name, wherein he tells us that "we all have a face that we hide away forever" and that all our faces are the faces of a stranger.
- David Crosby provides us with some selves-aware material in his song "In My Dreams," from the 1977 Crosby, Stills & Nash album *CSN*. He starts out by asking the listener who he sees and then tells us to "introduce yourself to whichever of me is nearby."

- Finally, consider The Pet Shop Boys song "Too Many People," from their 1993 album *Very,* which tells us that "the question of identity is one that's always haunted me; Whoever I decide to be depends on who is with me."

Before leaving music and songs, consider the many musicians—including David Bowie, whom we looked at in chapter 1—who seem to take on different personalities and create different types of songs and music in different selves. Jules Evans writes:

Many leading pop stars have alter-egos which they assume on stage or in different songs. The most famous is probably David Bowie's various alter egos . . . Beyonce also has an alter-ego, Sasha Fierce; Marshall Mathers has Eminem and Slim Shady; Lady Gaga has a male alter-ego, Jo Calderone (and Lady Gaga is itself something of an alter-ego); Prince has a female alter-ego, Camille; Bono invented three alter-egos for the Zoo TV tour; Tori Amos invented five for her "American Doll Posse" tour, and so on.

What's the point of these alter-egos? It often seems to give the artists permission to express an aspect of their personality which is somehow forbidden by their usual socially constructed self. It is ecstatic—it enables them to step out of their usual self and put on someone else. Beyonce says, "I've created an alter ego: things I do when performing that I would never do normally."[69]

THE FUTURE OF
SELVES-AWARE CULTURE

In short stories, novels, biographies, essays, popular science accounts, comics, news accounts, movies, television, paintings, poems, and songs—we have seen signs of selves both healthy and pathological. As a culture, as healthy selves become more visible, we will likely develop many new non-pathologically focused artistic reflections and interpretations. In the meantime, please join us for another tour in the next chapter, this one through the intellectual worlds of religion and Western philosophy.

FIVE

Souls and Selves
in Religion and Philosophy

Keen observers of themselves and others have long pondered the significance of multiplicity. Following the previous chapter's cultural tour, this chapter and the next two will review what some well-known and important thinkers—philosophers, theologians, psychologists, and scientists—have said about what it means for us to have selves.

This chapter starts by addressing the formative domain of religion, where multiplicity has long and often been some part of the picture. We then look into philosophy through the modern period. In chapter 6 we turn to what professional and academic psychologists have said about multiplicity. Chapter 7 extends this discussion by considering overlaps among certain aspects of postmodern thinking and philosophy, Buddhism, and contemporary scientific approaches.

Figure 5.1 shows some of the many volumes that were part of our research. Each of these volumes, in turn, cites dozens to hundreds of other authorities. By following the broad intellectual trail outlined by these citations, we soon found ourselves surveying and exploring a wide range of intellectual territory, from the religious and philosophical to the psychological and scientific, as well as the realm of inspirational teachers and spiritual systems. We are presenting overviews of these areas to make it easier for you to see beyond the Single Self Assumption.

Fig. 5.1. Books used in our research: each cites many sources

ANCIENT AND POLYTHEISTIC
RELIGIOUS SYSTEMS

Religious approaches to multiplicity go back at least to the beginnings of recorded history. As you will see, some religions have focused on the different parts or elements of human beings. Andrew Smith writes, "In many cultures it is believed that human beings may have more than one soul, reflecting the different aspects of the human being, which may include the rational intellect, the animal, the life force, the spark of divinity, the ego, the dreaming self, and so on."[1] Richard Schwartz and Robert Falconer write, "Anthropologists report that many indigenous cultures have, for centuries, been aware of an inner world in which they encounter parts of themselves. . . . For example, the Fijians, Algonkins, and Karens believe that people have two souls, while many North Asian peoples (such as the Chukchee and Yukagir) believe in three souls, as do the Ashanti and Dahomi in Africa. The Dakotas recognize four, and some Malays recognize seven."[2]

In other cases, polytheistic religions have embraced the existence and worship of many gods, suggesting ways for human beings to see themselves as naturally embodying multiplicity.

The Hmong: A Belief in Many Souls

The Hmong people, born in prehistory and surviving to the present day, are an ethnic group from mountainous areas in China, Vietnam, Laos, and Thailand. The Hmong have a vivid animistic spiritual worldview and religious system that sees human beings as having multiple souls:

> Human souls are differentiated from spirits and are the spiritual energy inside a person's body, believed to dwell in the physical world. It is said people have 12 souls—the three major ones are the reincarnation soul, the residing soul, and the wandering soul. The reincarnation soul leaves the body at death and is reborn in another being's body. The residing soul stays with the body as it breaks down and becomes the ancestral spirit that descendants revere and pay homage to. The wandering soul leaves the body during dreams or to play with other souls or spirits. If frightened, the wandering soul may be lost in the spirit world. At death, the wandering soul returns to the spirit world and continues to live life there much as it did in the physical world.[3]

Fig. 5.2. Hmong girls playing tug

For a person to remain healthy, his or her twelve main souls must be firmly attached to the body and work in harmony with one another. Unfortunately, "the souls of the living can fall into disharmony and may even leave the body," and the "loss of a soul or souls . . . can cause serious illness."[4] To this day, shamans actively practice within the Hmong community to help retrieve, integrate, and otherwise harmonize wayward souls:

> The Hmong religion is traditionally animist (animism is the belief in the spirit world and in the interconnectedness of all living things). At the center of Hmong culture is the *Txiv Neeb,* the shaman (literally, "father/master of spirits"). According to Hmong cosmology, the human body is the host for a number of souls. The isolation and separation of one or more of these souls from the body can cause disease, depression, and death. Curing rites are therefore referred to as "soul-calling rituals." Whether the soul became separated from the body because it was frightened away or kidnapped by an evil force, it must return in order to restore the integrity of life.[5]

This way of looking at the world originated in a culture where the Single Self Assumption never took root. To see what it is like for a Hmong family to struggle to reconcile the competing worldviews of Hmong multi-self healing and the American medical system, see Anne Fadiman's *The Spirit Catches You and You Fall Down: A Hmong Child, Her American Doctors, and the Collision of Two Cultures* (1997).

Ancient Egyptian Religion: A Panoply of Principles
The ancient Egyptians provide one of the best-known examples of a multi-part spiritual or religious system. Going back thousands of years, Egyptians divided the human being into distinct natural principles, or parts. "Ancient Egyptian belief referred to a number of souls that together constituted the individual. . . . These are sometimes translated as 'double,' 'soul' and 'spirit,' but these Western terms do not really give the full nuances of the concepts implied."[6]

To ensure eternal life, these various principles, or parts, had to be

Fig. 5.3. Ancient Egyptian funerary rites

properly aligned, prepared, and outfitted before death and final judgment. To illustrate the system's complexity, below is just one way of describing someone's different parts, principles, or souls.

- **Kha,** "the physical body" or corpse, which can be mummified
- **Ka,** the body's "double ego," wanders about, resides in statues, and eats and drinks
- **Ba,** "the soul," rises to the heavenly realms to enjoy eternity and returns to the deceased's tomb to partake in funerary offerings
- **Ab,** "the heart," the person's thinking and spiritual center, can separate or reunite with the body and move about freely
- **Khaibit,** "the shadow," also partakes of funerary offerings, moves about freely
- **Khu, Akhu,** "the spirit," the radiant shining one, is immortal and imperishable
- **Sekhem,** "power or form," the non-physical personification of a person's vital force
- **Ren,** "the name," exists in heaven and is essential on the journey through both life and the afterlife

- **Sahu,** "the spiritual body," springs from the material body, is where the soul lives, and can become incorruptible and dwell in heaven[7]

Upon death, Anubis would weigh the person's Ab (their spirit heart) against the Feather of Ma'at (the goddess of justice), and Thoth would record it. If the Ab—based on the person's bad behavior—was heavier than the feather, it would be eaten by Ammit, the devourer of souls; if lighter, the deceased would be allowed to travel into paradise.

Fig. 5.4. Anubis weighs a human heart against the Feather of Ma'at

For almost three thousand years, variants of this system formed the prevailing Egyptian worldview. The point here is not the details of this fascinating multi-leveled approach, or its parallels with modern conceptions of multiplicity. Instead, consider the likelihood that the inherent multiplicity of human beings may have given rise to detailed multi-part systems of thought and religious practice.

Polytheistic Pantheons Past and Present: Hindu, Greek, and Pagan Traditions

Polytheism is a belief in or worship of multiple deities who usually co-exist together in a pantheon of gods and goddesses.[8] For most of antiquity, through the Bronze and Iron Ages and up until the development of alternative forms of worship (primarily monotheism), polytheism was the world's dominant form of religion. In the modern world, polytheism is still practiced as part of Shintoism (Japanese traditional religion), Confucianism, Chinese folk religion,* Taoism,⁹ and the neo-pagan religions such as Thelema, Wicca, and modern Druidry.†

For brevity, this review will not include polytheistic religions of the Americas—the Incas, Aztecs, and Maya—or African tribal religions, Polynesian religions, or other indigenous and shamanic polytheistic systems. Instead, the pantheons of ancient Greece and Rome,‡ and the vivid and widely diverse manifestations of the gods and goddesses in Hindu religion,§ will serve to illustrate polytheism's reach, diversity, and relevance to multiplicity. We focus on the polytheistic elements of Hinduism—the world's third largest religion with about 900 million adherents—but it also contains elements of monotheism and pantheism (the belief that everything physically manifest is God).

Both the Greco-Roman and Hindu gods and goddess were conceived

---

*According to the Wikipedia entry "Ancestor Veneration in China" (accessed January 9, 2017), "in Chinese folk religion, a person is thought to have multiple souls, categorized as *hun* and *po,* commonly associated with yang and yin, respectively. Upon death, *hun* and *po* separate. Generally, the former ascends into heaven and the latter descends into the earth and/or resides within a spirit tablet; however, beliefs concerning the number and nature of souls vary."

†There are an estimated 200,000 to 1,000,000 contemporary pagans, or "neo-pagans," in the United States alone, and between 3 and 6 million adherents worldwide. See "Neopaganism in the United States," Wikipedia, and "Neopaganism Numbers by Country," Wikimedia Commons, both accessed January 9, 2017.

‡The Greco-Roman tradition brings us the gods and goddesses known as Zeus/Jupiter, Poseidon/Neptune, Hades/Pluto, Hestia/Vesta, Hera/Juno, Aries/Mars, Athena/Minerva, Apollo (the only god with the same name in both traditions), Aphrodite/Venus, Hermes/Mercury, Artemis/Diana, Hephaestus/Vulcan, Dionysus/Bacchus, Demeter/Ceres, and many more.

§Hinduism features Brahma (the Creator), Vishnu (the Preserver), Shiva (the Destroyer), Shakti (the primordial feminine force), Ganesha (the elephant-headed god, the Remover of Obstacles), the avatars or different forms of Vishnu on earth (including Rama and Kirshna), Saraswati (goddess of learning), Lakshmi (goddess of wealth and well-being), Hanuman (the Monkey King), and many more. Some versions of the Hindu pantheon state that there are 33 million gods and goddesses.

of as being like ordinary humans in many ways. They are attracted to and mate with each other, compete and squabble, and become involved with earthly affairs and the lives of human beings (especially in matters of love and war). In other ways, as divine or immortal beings, their powers and abilities (such as control over elemental forces or the ability to fly or shape-shift) make them far beyond regular human beings.

The gods and goddesses of the Greco-Roman, Hindu, and other polytheistic pantheons offer insight into the healthy selves model in at least three possible ways:

- *The reflection model:* some gods and goddesses are clearly multiple in nature, and thereby reflect the existence of selves in all of us.
- *The constituent model:* we are all physically composed of the essences of multiple gods and goddesses.
- *The participation model:* by identifying with, invoking, and embodying multiple gods and goddesses, we participate in and cultivate their qualities and abilities and avoid ignoring and thereby angering them.

First is the reflection model. Even a cursory glance at the Greek and Hindu pantheons reveals some gods and goddesses who seem to reflect the existence of multiple selves. Consider, for example, Janus, the two-headed god from Roman religion; the fifty-headed giants known as the Hekatonkheires or "Hundred-Handed Ones" from early Greek religion; or any number of multi-headed deities from Hinduism. (To signify their power, many demons also have multiple heads and arms.) An image that follows shows Brahma with four heads; apparently, once upon a time he had five, but then an angry Lord Shiva—for different reasons according to different stories—chopped one off.

By analogy, if the gods and goddesses have multiple faces or personas, it would make sense that ordinary humans—who are created by and in many ways reflect them—might also have multiple parts or elements. Or suppose that human beings envisioned the gods and goddesses in the first place through their worship and intention. If so, perhaps these worshippers projected their multiplicity onto their

Fig. 5.5. The multi-headed god Janus

Fig. 5.6. From the ancient Greek pantheon: Hekatonkheires, or
Hundred-Handed Ones.
Used with permission of Paizo Publishing.

Fig. 5.7. Dattatreya—the incarnation of Brahma, Vishnu, and Shiva

god forms so they could feel that those gods and goddesses correctly reflected how they already knew themselves to be.

Second, the constituent model—which helps us make sense of a number of later and generally lesser known religions or spiritual approaches including neo-Platonism and Swedenborgism*—holds that, as human beings, we are a microcosmic reflection of the entire universe and the divine realms. Thus, the gods and goddesses emanate their essences beyond time and beyond space, and those essences work their way down through many levels of reality into our ordinary terrestrial realm. It is these essences that give formless matter its form; that is, every characteristic of everything you can see, feel, touch, or otherwise know in any way only exists because it contains the essences of one or

---

*Emanuel Swedenborg was an influential eighteenth-century philosopher, scientist, and writer. In *Arcana Coelestia* he wrote, "Perfection and strength come from a harmonious gathering of many constituents, which act as one. . . . It is not just one community that flows in a given organ or member but many, and . . . there are many individuals in each community."[10]

more gods and goddesses. As a result, we manifestly have more than one part, or self, within us reflecting these different essences and influences.

Finally, we have the participation model, under which individuals choose to actively worship and identify with different gods and goddesses to receive their specific blessings and live a deeper, richer life that embodies their divine skills and qualities. Not only, for example, do "Hindus believe and worship many gods simultaneously in the hope of receiving blessings from many of them,"[11] but they also worship different aspects of different gods to develop those specific qualities and become more spiritually evolved. The doctrines of Spiritual Competence (*Adhikaara*) and that of the Chosen Deity (*Ishhta Devata*) in Hinduism recommend that the spiritual practices prescribed to a person should correspond to his or her spiritual competence:

> Each deity in Hinduism controls a particular energy. These energies, present in man as wild forces, must be controlled and canalized fruitfully to infuse a divine consciousness in him. For this, man has to gain the goodwill of different gods who stir up his consciousness accordingly to help him master the different forces of nature. In a person's path of spiritual progress, he or she needs to develop the various attributes of these godheads in him or her to attain all-round spiritual perfection.[12]

Sam Webster, a modern pagan, describes how and why he consciously evokes and embodies different deities to access and embody their wisdom:

> I sort out a deity whose nature is relevant to my life by identifying an arena that is important to me and in which I wish to improve my skills. A deity is in part the embodiment of competence in a given field. The deity also has a distinct character and can be experienced by what I call "looking through the eyes of the deity" or "wearing the form of the deity." To have this experience, I invoke the deity by its qualities and attributes. I begin with praise and description, calling to mind the image, the sound, the feel of the deity. By focus-

ing attention through words, gestures, or objects, the deity is felt or embodied. If you allow these symbols to affect you on a deep level, you may find that you "feel like" the deity or see the world from its point of view. You also take on its wisdom and associated skill.[13]

A related idea is to not anger any particular god or goddess through a lack of worship. Thus, Hal and Sidra Stone (formerly Sidra Winkelman)—whose Voice Dialogue system will be considered later—write:

> In ancient Greece there was an understanding that one was required to worship all the gods and goddesses. You might have your favorites, but none of the remaining deities could be ignored. The God or Goddess whom you ignored become the one who turned against you and destroyed you. . . . So it is with consciousness work. The energy pattern that we disown turns against us.[14]

If by worshipping multiple deities one can gain their blessings and skills and forgo their anger, then perhaps we can tune in to our own different parts—our own selves—for similar reasons.

MONOTHEISTIC RELIGIONS: ONE SELF WORSHIPPING ONE GOD (WITH EXCEPTIONS)

Where did the pervasive idea of one self—the Single Self Assumption—come from? In part, the idea is rooted in the world's monotheistic religious traditions. The next few subsections will consider Egyptian, Jewish, Christian, and Islamic monotheism.

As monotheism is the religious and cultural water in which we are all swimming, it strongly predisposes us toward the Single Self Assumption. If when looking *outside of ourselves* for religious authority we believe in a unitary God, then when we look *inside of ourselves* we will likely search for a single self. Another way of thinking about it is that if it is true that there is only one God, then oneness must permeate our own makeup as well. If there is one God, then we almost certainly only have one soul—and one self—each.*

The Single Self Assumption, therefore, flows right from and is reinforced by the Single God Assumption. While a few iconoclasts like psychologist James Hillman have explicitly questioned the assumed superiority of monotheistic religion, the culture-wide pervasiveness of monotheism—at least in the West—makes this an uphill battle. Since the evidence that underlies our ideas of monotheism seems functionally and structurally similar to the evidence that underlies our culture-wide predilection toward mono-selfism, we may be able to glean some important insights from this review.

Egyptian Monotheism:
Akhenaten's Short-Lived Attempt

Judaism is often considered the beginning of the Western monotheistic tradition. However, the Eighteenth Dynasty Egyptian Pharaoh Akhenaten, who lived around 1350 BCE, was the first to attempt to institute monotheism. Akhenaten promoted the worship of one God, the sun-disc Aten, and called himself "the son of the sole god: 'Thine only son that came forth from thy body.'"[15] But his program—for a variety of political, economic, and religious reasons—was short lived:

> Akhenaten's attempt to convert Egypt into a monotheistic nation during his lifetime led him to commit extreme acts. He had inscriptions that read "gods" changed to "god" and had the name Amun erased from temples and other public areas. Temples dedicated to other gods were closed or destroyed. . . . His efforts to institute monotheism in Egypt failed, and after his death, polytheistic worship reemerged throughout the country.[16]

---

*Douglas Hofstadter, referring to his "Twinwirld" fantasy, writes, "The real point . . . was to cast some doubt on a dogma, usually unquestioned in our world, which could be phrased as a slogan: 'One body, one soul.' (If you don't like the word *soul*, then feel free to substitute 'I,' 'person,' 'self,' or 'locus of consciousness.') This idea, although seldom verbalized, is so taken for granted that it seems utterly tautological to most people . . ."[17]

Fig. 5.8. Akhenaten and his family worship the sun disc.

Given the complexities of the ancient Egyptian conception of the human being, Akhenaten's failure to override tradition and enforce monotheism is not too surprising.

Judaism: No Other Gods before Me

Judaism is often considered the West's foundational monotheistic religion, but the early Hebrew tribes who would become the People of Israel were clearly not strictly monotheistic. There are multiple references to "gods" (*Elohim,* a grammatically plural form*) in the Hebrew Bible, and the focus throughout is more on not worshipping or making images of any gods as opposed to denying their existence outright. (For

---

*"As anyone who knows even a bit of Hebrew will recognize, *elohim* is a plural form; its primary meaning is 'gods.' There is a singular, *eloha,* but this form is almost never used in the Bible. When speaking about non-Israelite (or 'false') deities, *elohim* is treated as a full plural. . . . But when applied to the God of Israel, *elohim* is treated as though singular. . . . *Elohim* here is a collective form . . . meaning that all the multiple and diverse powers of godhood are now concentrated within this single personality."[18]

example, the Second Commandment states, "Thou shalt have no other *gods* before me.") It is not so much that other gods do not exist; it is that they must not be worshipped!

The Golden Calf episode near Mount Sinai shows just how difficult it was to be limited to just one God. Moreover, once the Jews conquered and settled the Land of Canaan, many people (especially women) may have continued to worship the prevailing pagan gods and especially agricultural goddesses.[19] Later on, during the Babylonian captivity, some Jews began to worship local divinities.

Over time, following the Babylonian exile (from around 597 to 538 BCE), Judaism did become truly monotheistic, probably in part influenced by an earlier monotheistic religion, Zoroastrianism:

> Many scholars believe that the Jewish religion was monolateral before the Babylonian Exile. Simply put, that means that the Jewish people acknowledged the existence of other gods, but believed that they should only worship the god of Israel. At the time the Persian Empire overthrew the Babylonians, many of the Persians practiced Zoroastrianism, a monotheistic religion that worshiped a [single] deity named Ahura-Mazda. Zoroastrianism went beyond monolateralism, insisting that only one god exists. Whether the concept came to Judaism through Zoroastrians or not, the teaching—known as monotheism—is now the central tenet of Judaism.[20] (Capitalization as given in the original.)

Even after monotheism became the central tenet of Judaism, hints of multiplicity and a recognition of the existence of selves remains visible in Jewish practice and tradition.

For example, in a way that is reminiscent of how the ancient Egyptians saw things, every Jew can be seen as having multiple souls.[21] According to Rabbi Ari Cartun,[22] there are up to five souls in each Jew:

1. the *nefesh,* the soul associated with the vegetable and root physiological operations of the body;
2. the *neshamah,* the animal soul associated with the body's activity;

3. the *ruach,* or breath,* that which animates one spiritually and intellectually;

4. the soul of whatever Jewish festival is being participated in, such as the Sabbath soul† (think of this as being similar to when you go to a sports stadium or concert venue and take on the "soul" or "spirit" of the event); and

5. a generalized *Yehudi,* or Jewish soul; for example, a secular Jew—someone who is of Jewish descent but who never practices Judaism to any degree—can be said to have not activated their Yehudi soul.

There are also some physical objects and associated gestures that may represent multiplicity in Judaism. For example, when Jews worship with their prayer shawls, or *tallit,* they gather up the fringes from the four corners before saying the quintessential Jewish prayer, the *Shema Yisrael.*‡ This can be seen as a unification of the physical, intellectual, emotional, and spiritual parts or elements of each worshipper.

More generally, "a major class of Jewish meditation practices are known as *unifications.* While the focus of these practices is on promoting the reunification of the divine, at a psychological level the practices may be conceived of as unifying diverse strands within the personality."[23]

Finally, the root of the Jewish Kabbalistic mystical tradition is the idea that God somehow fragmented into multiple interconnected *sephirot*—which can be thought of as spheres—in a tenfold pattern known as the *Etz Chayim,* or Tree of Life. As Professor Benjamin Sommer explains:

> The Kabbalistic doctrine of the *sephirot* in particular constitutes a highly complex version of the notion that the divine can fragment itself into multiple selves that nonetheless remain parts of a unified whole.[24]

---

*Rabbi Cartun notes that the *ruach,* or breath, can also be thought of as representing the most vegetative or root element of a human being.

†For more on this, see Kabbalah Online, "The Additional Shabbat Soul," translated by Simcha H. Benyosef from the teachings of Rafael Moshe Luria, available at Chabad.org.

‡The first lines of the prayer are "Hear, O Israel! The Lord is our God, the Lord is one!"

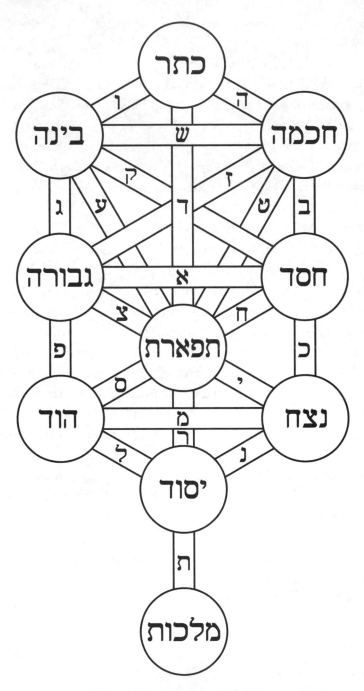

Fig. 5.9. Kabbalistic Tree of Life

Since the *sephirot* are conceived of as successively embodying very different kinds of energies and principles as the divine force flows downward, it seems that the most we can say is that the Kabbalah recognizes and even models a type of vertically oriented multiplicity but does not speak directly to the healthy selves model.

Christianity:
Two Millennia of Monotheism Plus

The Single Self Assumption has been reinforced by Christianity, long the Western world's dominant culture-shaping religion. But it is a very curious monotheism that has been promoted. While Christians have, from the very beginning, believed in the one monotheistic God whom they inherited from Judaism, they have always had a central focus on

Fig. 5.10. Catholic church window in Paris

Jesus, as the son of that same God, and on the trinity of Father, Son, and Holy Ghost. Additionally, since medieval times, there has been an emphasis on the worship and divine nature of Mary, Jesus's mother, as well as on a vast pantheon of saints. One God, that one God's son, the son's mother, the saints, and the Holy Ghost are all part of the core notion of this one God. This may be yet another reflection of the natural human need or desire to incorporate multiplicity into the currently dominant worldview.

Recall the words of St. Paul in Romans 7:15: "I do not understand what I do. For what I want to do I do not do, but what I hate, I do." Similarly, as we saw in the previous chapter, the formative Christian theologian St. Augustine (354–430 CE) asserted that "if there are as many contrary natures in man as there are conflicting wills, there would not only have to be two natures but many more."[25] Henri Ellenberger adds to our understanding of Augustine:

> Considering the change that had taken place in him since his conversion, Augustine remarked that his old pagan personality, of which nothing seemed to remain in his waking state, still must exist since it was revived at night and in his dreams. He wrote: "Am I not myself, o Lord, my God. And yet, there is so much difference betwixt myself and myself within the moment wherein I pass from waking to sleeping or return from sleeping to waking."[26]

Similarly, Schwartz and Falconer, citing Carl Jung, note that the early church theologian Origen "explicitly recognized multiplicity. 'Thou seest that he (man) who seemeth to be one is not one, but as many different persons appear in him as he hath [self-willed impulses].'"[27] Ultimately, it is not that far from the musings of St. Paul, St. Augustine, and Origen to the familiar "shoulder angel" trope.

Shoulder Angels: An Ancient and Widespread Trope

Fig. 5.11. Woman with angel and devil
advising her

The idea of shoulder angels originates with Greek mythology, "wherein each mortal has a pair of spirits, which are aspects of themselves, and represent good and evil and actually sit on the character's shoulders." However, the "angel/devil interpretation . . . originated with Islam in the form of *kiraman katibin* (literally, 'honorable recorders'—their job is to write down a person's good and evil thoughts and deeds)."[28]

Elizabeth O'Connor, author of *Our Many Selves: A Handbook for Self-Discovery,* says that she eventually came to the realization that the entire New Testament could be conceived of in terms of leading us to working with our selves:

> When I became aware that I was not one, I began to find in poetry and drama allusion to the multiplicity of selves. . . . And then in Scripture, I began to hear the same cry, "My name is Legion!" but in Scripture it was more than solitary utterance here and there. Parables and stories and teachings all concerned the possibility of man attaining to an inner unity. . . . "How long will you go limping with two different opinions?" was more than Elijah's question. It was the question of the whole New Testament. The early Church was confronting men with their inner division so that there might be a healing of it.[29]

O'Connor's recognition that she is "not one" and that most of the New Testament could, in theory, be interpreted in terms of people becoming aware of and learning to harmonize and work with their selves is helpful to her. But the dominance of the Single Self Assumption leads her to conceive of healing as the removal of divisions—as the removal of selves—within people. Later we will consider why forcing selves to become unified against their will is problematic and dysfunctional, and as far as we can tell, rarely if ever lasts or works well.

Many movie and TV versions of multiplicity include instances of supposed demonic possession and exorcism. It is likely that throughout Christian history cases of pathological multiplicity have been diagnosed and treated in terms of a demon—or the devil himself—possessing an individual. One contemporary Christian minister, Robert L., who accepts dissociation, pathological multiplicity, and the existence of alter personalities, writes:

> Other ministers who don't believe in alters, are failing miserably when working with people who have disassociated. As a matter of fact, the people are often walking away more bound and hurt than when they came in for ministry! This is because alters are surfacing and being treated like demons in a deliverance, which traumatizes them to go further down into that person, and carry even more hurt, trauma, and pain.[30]

Later we will discuss progressive ways for various institutions, including religious ones, to conceive of multiplicity and work with individuals with pathological selves.

Islam's Rigorous Monotheism and Sufism's Mystical Insights

> *Sufis teach that we first must battle and destroy the evil within ourselves by shining upon it the good within, and then we learn to battle the evil in others by helping their higher selves gain control of their lower selves.*
>
> FEISAL ABDUL RAUF, *WHAT'S RIGHT WITH ISLAM*

Islam is, in its view, the third and ultimate revelation of the monotheistic tradition, with the last true prophet, Mohammed, carrying on and completing the work of the previous prophets, including Abraham, Moses, and Jesus. Its "most fundamental concept is a rigorous monotheism. Muslims repudiate polytheism and idolatry . . . and reject the Christian doctrine of the Trinity and divinity of Jesus."[31] As in Christianity, there is a notion of possession by *Jinn,* a type of demon. Modern-leaning Muslim authors have recognized the harm that can be done to someone who has a legitimate case of pathological multiplicity—and who therefore likely needs clinical help for his or her most troubled part—who is thought to be possessed. As one Muslim commentator says:

> Ideas about Jinn and demons contribute to these illnesses to a small or a large degree. In the Christian societies the blame perhaps lies with the Bible, as the New Testament has countless mentions of demons and narrates several events, when Jesus, may peace be on him, took [the] demons out of others. In Muslim societies, the blame lies with the religious scholars, who in this day and age of information and scientific discovery, have not enlightened themselves with better paradigms and insist on interpreting some of the verses of the Holy Quran, in medieval ways.[32]

Alternatively, the mystical branch of Islam known as Sufism acknowledges the existence of different levels of the soul or different selves. Often translated as soul, ego, or self, the Sufis identify seven levels of *Nafs:* the tyrannical self, the regretful self, the inspired self, the serene self, the pleased self, the self pleasing to God, and the pure self.[33] Spiritual advancement requires working one's way up through these levels:

> In Sufi circles the concept of multiple selves is used in two different ways. In one these refer to the soul at its various levels of development: commanding, accusing, inspired, and illumined. . . .
>
> The second way of talking about multiple selves in Sufi circles is really a part of their methods of training. Here we sometimes hear or read that people have no self; they have selves; now this, now that.

Emphasis is laid on this, and the disciple is invited to observe himself or herself.[34]

Later, in our discussion of Buddhism, we will return to the recognition of selves as a "teaching method" for showing how our ordinary conceptions of self are limited.

....

Why Is Monotheism So Strong in the West?

Why is monotheism—and along with it, the Single Self Assumption—so strong in Western cultures? Celia Ramos offers her view that societies "in which the cultural dissociation barrier"—similar to this book's Single Self Assumption—"is inflexible and impermeable" are usually monotheistic, while societies without such firm dissociation barriers have more acceptance and awareness of multiplicity. Since monotheism more than other paradigms permits adherents to effectively make God in their own image, "the God of Western culture is a dissociated executive-self. . . . Monotheistic God is a rarefied, abstract, disembodied entity with greater awareness, power, and control than lesser beings like man. . . . The sole God, the ruling ego of the universe, is a mirroring or projection of the dissociated executive-self of the Western psyche."[35]

....

WESTERN PHILOSOPHY AND ITS UNITARY ESSENTIAL SELF

The mathematician, musician, and mystic Pythagoras of Samos inspired Socrates,* who in turn mentored his student and scribe, Plato. The bedrock of the Western philosophical tradition was then laid by Plato (who repeated and evolved what Socrates said and taught) and his student Aristotle (who, in turn, further refined Plato's ideas as well as tutored Alexander the Great). Both Plato and Aristotle were essentialists. "Essentialism . . . is the view that things have essences (the attribute, or set of attributes, that make an object or substance what it fundamen-

_____

*Socrates often spoke of being guided by a "daemon"—an inner oracle, voice, or nature spirit.

tally is). . . . An essence characterizes a permanent, unalterable and eternal substance, or a form (in the sense of the Forms or Ideas in Platonic Realism)."[36]

As another source further explains: "Essentialists believe true essences exist. In the *Metaphysics,* Aristotle (384–322 BCE) specifies the classic definition: an essence of a thing is that which it is said to be per se. It is that which is most irreducible, unchanging, and therefore constitutive of a thing. A thing's essence is that property without which the thing would cease to exist as itself."[37]

Under the essentialist view, the essence of an individual is, by definition, his or her unitary essential self. This root belief—that each individual has a single essential self at his or her core—remained at the core of Western philosophy through the classical and modern periods and is only now being challenged by postmodern philosophy (often in conjunction with feminist and race-related critiques). John A. Powell has given us a clear notion of just how deep this essentialist view runs in Western philosophy: "The dominant narrative of Western society . . . denies that we are or can be multiple and fractured and still remain 'normal' . . . its individualistic focus is one of the deeply rooted ideologies of Western society . . . [and] the individualistic norm . . . pervades our society."[38] Combined with and reinforced by the dominance of monotheism, the essentialist view provides a powerful philosophical foundation for the Single Self Assumption.

The Socratic Paradox: Resolved?

Still, along the way, there have always been a number of philosophers who have questioned the idea of a single essential self. For example, Plato himself gave us not just one, but two, three-part descriptions of the varied nature of human beings.* Peter McKellar sums up Plato's view:

> Many have made their attempts to map and label the subsystems of the normal personality. In ancient times Plato viewed it as a man

---

*The twentieth-century philosopher Alfred North Whitehead once quipped in his book *Process and Reality* (1979) that "the safest general characterization of the European philosophical tradition is that it consists of a series of footnotes to Plato."

(rationality), a lion (courage and spirit), and a many-headed monster (passions and appetites). Another of his famous metaphors likened it to a charioteer seeking to guide two powerful horses, the one spirited and noble, the other base and ignoble.[39]

A close look at Book IV of *The Republic* shows that Plato understood and even advocated the value of harmonizing one's parts or selves:

> Each of us also, in whom the several parts within him perform each their own task—he will be a just man. . . . Justice is . . . within and in the true sense concerns one's self, and the things of one's self. It means that a man must not suffer the principles in his soul to do each the work of some other and interfere and meddle with one another, but that he should dispose well of what in the true sense of the word is properly his own, and having first attained to self-mastery and beautiful order within himself, and having harmonized these three principles, the notes or intervals of three terms quite literally the lowest, the highest, and the mean, and all others there may be between them, and having linked and bound all three together and made of himself a unit, one man instead of many, self-controlled and in union, he should then and then only turn to practice . . . in political action or private business.[40]

Additionally, an important part of the legacy of Socrates and Plato has become known as "the Socratic Paradox":

> Plato in the second half of his dialogue *Protagoras* investigates Socrates's explanation of that aspect of his philosophy often termed "the Socratic Paradox." Socrates believed that we all seek what we think is most genuinely in our own interest. . . . On the one hand, if we act with knowledge, then we will obtain what is good for our soul because "knowledge" implies certainty in results.
> On the other hand, if the consequences of our action turn out not to be what is good for our soul (and hence what is genuinely not in our self-interest), then we had to have acted from ignorance

Fig. 5.12. Socrates.
Photo by Eric Gaba/Sting.

because we were unable to achieve what we desired. . . . Since we never intentionally harm ourselves, if harm happens to us, then, at some point, we had to have acted with a lack of knowledge.[41]

To rephrase the paradox, all human beings—at least occasionally and sometimes more frequently—do things that they know are bad or will likely produce suboptimal, dysfunctional, or even awful results. The ethical theory of Socrates and Plato is "to know the good is to do the good." Yet, based on our observations of ourselves and others, we know that virtually no one always does the good thing that they intend to do. How can this be explained?

If the Single Self Assumption is correct and each of us has one essential self, then we do indeed have a paradox. But if the self that engages in the "not doing the good" is an autonomous self with its own motivations and reasons, then this self may (a) not agree as to what is—or is not—good, or (b) may not care about the consequences of its actions, either for itself, or for the whole human being of whom it is part.

In short, if we have more than one self, and those selves are truly different and have distinct desires, needs, and ways of acting, then it becomes perfectly clear why we do not always "do the good"—why we sometimes do not refrain from eating too much sugar or drinking too much alcohol despite previous problems; why we get angry and curse out a driver who negligently cut us off; or why we gossip and say unkind things about others even though parts of us later regret having done so.

Not only does this explanation address the Socratic Paradox and the general problem of counter-intentionality, it is a *simple* explanation that intuitively makes sense.

SOME CHALLENGES TO THE SINGLE SELF ASSUMPTION

We are all made up of fragments, so shapelessly and strangely assembled that every moment, every piece plays its own game. And there is as much difference betwixt us and ourselves as betwixt us and others. Deem it a great achievement to act consistently, like one and the same man.

MICHEL DE MONTAIGNE,
FRENCH RENAISSANCE PHILOSOPHER (1533–1592)

Notwithstanding this quote from a well-known philosopher, it was not until the eighteenth century that a series of challenges to the Single Self Assumption began to arise. The English philosopher and theologian Bishop Joseph Butler (1692–1752) felt that instead of a single simple self, human beings had a complex psychology with multiple intersecting elements. Butler wrote:

For, as the form of the body is a composition of various parts; so likewise our inward structure is not simple or uniform, but a composition of various passions, appetites, affections, together with rationality; including in this last both the discernment of what is right, and a disposition to regulate ourselves by it. There is a greater variety of parts in what we call a character, than there are features in a face. . . . The principles in our mind may be contradictory, or checks and allays only, or incentives and assistants to each other.[42]

Weighing in as well was the influential Scottish philosopher and economist David Hume (1711–1776), who arrived at the "bundle theory" of personal identity. Bruce Hood, a modern developmental psychologist, summarizes Hume's process and agrees with his conclusions based on the findings of modern neuroscience:

He tried to describe his inner self and thought that there was no single entity, but rather bundles of sensations, perceptions, and thoughts piled on top of each other. He concluded that the self emerged out of the bundling together of these experiences. . . . Today . . . neuroscience . . . has found . . . much to support the bundle theory as opposed to the ego theory of the self.[43]

The notion of a bundle theory also bears similarities to Buddhist thought, which we consider later.

The German philosopher Immanuel Kant (1724–1804), among the central figures of modern philosophy and recognized as enormously influential, responded to Hume's bundle theory. As Daniel Bonevac puts it:

Kant argues against Hume's position. One argument is that my thoughts, feelings, and perceptions are mine. I think, I feel, I perceive; I can always append "I think" to anything in the mind. The thoughts are not free-floating; they presuppose a subject.[44]

Over the past few hundred years, Kant's view has generally prevailed in psychology. Kluft and Fine write:

Normal personality is a functionally integrated unit of many components, not an aggregate of components. Historically, this point has
been brilliantly argued in Immanuel Kant's reply to David Hume's
"bundle theory" of the self in Kant's masterpiece, *Critique of Pure
Reason*.[45]

Finally, it is worth briefly noting two thinkers who are often considered early existentialists. First, the German philosopher Friedrich
Nietzsche (1844–1900) referred to "useful 'underwills' or under-souls"
and stated that "our body is but a social structure composed of many
souls."[46] Second, the Danish philosopher Søren Kierkegaard (1813–1855)
"used pseudonyms in many of his works . . . [h]e assigned the 'authorship'
of parts of texts to different pseudonyms, and invented further pseudonyms to be the editors or compliers of these pseudonymous writings."[47]
Based on his use of pseudonyms, some have claimed that Kierkegaard was
among those who "offer critiques of the unitary conceptualization of selfhood and suggest alternative views of human selfhood in which the self is
viewed as more than one."[48]

We will return to the Western philosophical tradition later when
we look at postmodernism and its philosophical basis. For now, though,
we move from the mainly theoretical discourse of philosophy into the
experimentally grounded discipline of psychology, which over time has
had a great deal to say about multiple selves.

SIX

Many Minds on Many Minds

Psychologists and Multiplicity

"Do you think it would help if all the voices in my head came together and formed their own light-opera company?"

Fig. 6.1. "Do you think it would help if all the voices in my head came together and formed their own light-opera company?" by Jack Ziegler.
From *The New Yorker*, May 14, 2012. Used with permission of www.CartoonCollections.com.

The previous chapter's coverage of multiplicity in religion and Western philosophy was meant to highlight two things. First, throughout the historical development of religious practices worldwide and Western philosophy, there have been openings to, parallels with, and on occasion nearly full awareness of healthy selves. Second, however, the overall thrust over time has been to anchor and reinforce the Single Self Assumption, whether through the essentialist legacy of Plato, Aristotle, and Kant in Western philosophy up to postmodernism, or through monotheistic religion's reinforcement of the One God/One Self idea.

This chapter continues our intellectual tour through multiplicity, focusing on psychology. We will look at selves throughout the history of psychology, focusing on those thinkers* who advocated a multiple selves model or were at least aware that selves exist. Much of their thinking was about unhealthy or disturbed multiplicity, so that is where we will begin.

ACCOUNTS FROM
EARLY RESEARCHERS AND EXPLORERS

Psychology as an independent discipline is often said to have started in 1879 when the German scientist Wilhelm Wundt opened the first laboratory exclusively for psychological research in Leipzig, Germany. Before that, of course, human beings had been making thoughtful and in some cases detailed observations about the relationship between mind, thoughts, feelings, and behavior. Long before psychology became a science, unusual cases of identity and states of consciousness had been observed. As noted by Colin Ross, M.D.:

> Multiple personality is not a transient aberration, peculiar to twentieth-century North America. This can be shown by illustrations from ancient history: The fragmentation of self and the transformation of identity have been recognized by all races. Examples from different cultures give a sense of the university of these themes. [It] has gradually evolved from its prehistoric origins, through intermediate phenomena, to its modern form.[1]

---

*Psychology is defined as the study of the mind or the psyche, and all of those considered in this chapter focused their attention and careers on mental processes, the nature of consciousness, and mental illness and health. Even though they came from a variety of disciplines, as a matter of convenience we will generally refer to all of them as "psychologists."

From tribal elders and shamans during the Paleolithic period to religious and secular leaders of increasingly larger states throughout the last ten thousand years of the Neolithic, agrarian, and modern periods, leaders and healers have had similar experiences. They encountered and were responsible for individuals dealing with trance states, claims and experiences of seeming possession (by ancestors, helping spirits, demons, and the like), the effects of psychedelics and intoxicants on identity and memory, out-of-body experiences, and intentional shamanic transformations of identity.[2] MPD has been diagnosed very early in history:

> Some professionals believe that it was first "described" in the images of "shamans changed into animal forms" on cave walls during the Paleolithic Era. Throughout recorded history cases of demonic possession have been reported that many experts now believe are cases of multiple personality.[3]

Some sources state that Paracelsus (1493–1541), a Swiss German philosopher, physician, botanist, and occultist, was the first person to make at least a brief mention of an incidence of pathological multiplicity. More reliably, in the late 1500s, a detailed account of multiple personality was written down based on the experiences of a Dominican nun, Jeanne Fery (see fig. 6.2, p. 152). She had "an alter personality who stole her money"[4] and in 1584 and 1585 was subjected to an exorcism. According to one source:

> This is perhaps the earliest historical case in which DID can be diagnosed retrospectively with confidence. Jeanne Fery, a 25-year-old Dominican Nun, wrote her own account of her exorcism which took place in Mons, France, in 1584 and 1585. Her exorcists produced an even more detailed account describing both identity fragmentation and a past history of childhood trauma. . . . Jeanne's alters were at times visualized, at times heard arguing inside, and at times took over her body.[5]

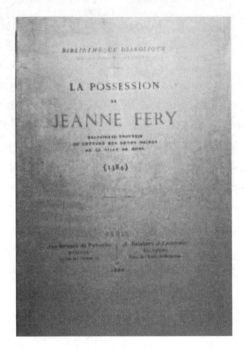

Fig. 6.2. Cover of *La Possession de Jeanne Fery*

In the late 1700s, American Dr. Benjamin Rush, chief surgeon of the Continental Army and the only man to sign both the Declaration of Independence (1776) and the Constitution (1789), began collecting accounts of multiplicity. As the "Father of American Psychiatry," Rush wrote *Medical Inquiries and Observations Upon Diseases of the Mind* published in 1812. According to Frank W. Putnam:

> Benjamin Rush . . . collected case histories of dissociation and multiple personality for his lectures and writings on physiological psychology. . . . Rush theorized that the mechanism responsible for the doubling of consciousness lay in a disconnection between the two hemispheres of the brain—the first of many such speculations on the subject of hemispheric laterality and multiple personality.[6]

We will mention just two more early cases from before psychology became its own science. The first, involving Mary Reynolds, who was born in England in 1785, was initially verified and written up in 1816 by Dr. Samuel Latham Mitchel as "A Double Consciousness, or a Duality of Person in the Same Individual." Later on her case was the subject of an article in *Harper's New Monthly Magazine* in 1860 and an autobiography by Mary Reynolds herself. Mary started having hysterical fits at age eighteen, and at age nineteen became deaf and blind for six weeks, after which a second personality emerged. "The original personality was melancholy and shy. The second personality . . . was 'witty' and 'fond of company.' After a period of alterations, the second personality became dominant. When Mary was thirty-six only the second personality remained, and it continued to be the only one until her death at sixty-one."[7]

Second, historian Henri F. Ellenberger states that the "truly objective study of multiple personality was inaugurated in France by the publication of the story of 'Estelle' by Despine Sr. in the form of a detailed account."[8] According to Frank Putnam:

In 1836, Despine undertook the treatment of an 11-year-old Swiss girl whose symptoms evolved over time from an initial paralysis and exquisite sensitivity to touch to an overt dual existence with a second personality who was able to walk, loved to play in the snow, and could not tolerate the presence of her mother. . . . The 60-year-old Despine developed a close rapport with his young patient and was able to effect a cure through psychotherapy implicitly in the variety of hydrotherapeutic and magnet treatments he employed. His detailed monograph, published in 1840, first set forth [treatment] principles that are recognized as valid today.[9]

What do these reports—as well as the many fictional accounts of literary doubles beginning in the first half of the nineteenth century—point to? Simply that multiplicity—like the concept of the unconscious—was part of the zeitgeist and soon to be the focus of more in-depth inquiry.

FOUNDATIONAL FRENCH PSYCHOLOGISTS: CHARCOT, JANET, AND BINET

Once the independent discipline of psychology got its start, occurrences of multiple selves or identities—usually as one symptom among others including hysteria, memory loss, physical disruptions, and other indications of pathology—became a significant research focus. From about 1880 to 1920, first in France and then soon in the United States, "a relatively large number of cases were reported. . . . Dissociation and multiple personality became subjects of intense interest for many of the great physicians, psychologists, and philosophers of the era."[10] As Colin Ross notes, "There was a great deal of clinical and experimental study of dissociation in the 19th century. Only in the last two decades have we started to repair a near complete discontinuity with that work."[11]

The men of the nineteenth century who gave these lectures, treated such patients (with hysteria or symptoms of pathological multiplicity), and wrote these reports, often had outsized personalities of their own. The history of their interests, breakthroughs, agreements and disagreements, and evolving alliances and schools of thought is complex and fascinating. In attempting to shed light on one small part of that history, we will do our best to bring all of these strands together later in this chapter in a single diagram, showing personal relationships and flows of influence. We will now turn to three pioneering French psychologists: Charcot, Janet, and Binet.

Jean-Martin Charcot: The "Great" Charcot

While any starting point is arguably somewhat arbitrary, we can comfortably say that sustained professional interest in multiplicity began with the pioneering French psychologist and neurologist Jean-Martin Charcot (1835–1893). As Ellenberger tells us, "the Salpêtrière school [Charcot's clinic] was strongly organized and headed by a powerful figure, that of the great teacher Jean-Martin Charcot (1835–1893), a neurologist who had come belatedly to the study of certain mental phenomena. During the years 1870–1893, Charcot was considered to be the greatest neurologist of his time. He was the consulting physician of kings and princes."[12]

Fig. 6.3. Jean-Martin Charcot

Charcot drew notable students from the United States and Europe, including Pierre Janet, William James, Alfred Binet, and Sigmund Freud. There can be little doubt that "the Charcot-Janet school, which formed from the work of Charcot and his student Janet, contributed greatly to knowledge of double and multiple personality."[13]

One caution that emerged regarding all psychological therapy came from Charcot's Polish student, Joseph Babinsky (1857–1932). At one point, Charcot thought he had discovered "hystereo-epilepsy," a new disease. But Babinsky, a skeptical student, felt the disease was an invented one:

> The patients had come to the hospital with vague complaints of distress and demoralization. Charcot had persuaded them that they were victims of hystereo-epilepsy and should join the others under his care. Babinsky eventually won the argument. In fact, he persuaded Charcot that doctors can induce a variety of physical and mental disorders.[14]

To counter this possibility of undue influence, Charcot and Babinsky put in place a successful two-step protocol. First, they separated patients so that they were not around anyone else with the same symptoms. Second, they used methods of suggestion (such as withdrawing interest from the patient's hysterical behavior) that encouraged the patients to focus on their recovery instead of their hystereo-epileptic symptoms.

The idea of the existence or presence of selves being induced by therapists remains one of the standard criticisms of multiplicity,* especially following Sybil's impact in the 1970s, as previously discussed. While it is certainly a good idea to make sure that psychiatrists, psychologists, physicians, and therapists do not talk patients into pathology, it makes little sense to expand this caution to somehow account for—and then make a wholesale denial of—the existence of ordinary and healthy selves in people.

Pierre Marie Félix Janet

If Charcot laid some of the theoretical basis for working with hypnosis and multiplicity, it was his student and successor, French psychiatrist Pierre Marie Félix Janet (1859–1947), who really moved things forward. Nephew of the philosopher Paul Janet, he focused his attention on those individuals who "appeared to be functioning autonomously from their normal consciousness: under hypnosis, spirit possession, and hysteria. He proposed that in these cases a separate consciousness had split off from the main personality, forming a new identity, and that they existed in isolation with no interaction between one another. Janet initially referred to this state as 'split personality,' although it later became known as 'dissociative disorder.'"[15]

Janet, who was asked by Charcot to become the director of the Salpêtrière hospital's psychological laboratory in 1899,[16] is an important figure for four reasons. First, he taught, met, and directly influenced a number of other key psychologists, including William James, Sigmund Freud, and Carl Jung. Second, Janet came up with innovative ideas and ways of working with patients to elicit different selves through the

---

*According to J. H. Van den Berg in his unique and stimulating *Divided Existence and Complex Society* (1974), Charcot actually hampered the development of knowledge of true multiplicity by inducing symptoms and selves in patients.[17]

Fig. 6.4. Pierre Marie Félix Janet

use of hypnosis, automatic writing, and other creative techniques. For example, William James tells us that:

> In his anesthetic somnambulist Lucie, [Janet] found that when this young woman's attention was absorbed in conversation with a third party, her anesthetic hand would write simple answers to questions whispered to her by himself. "'Do you hear?" he asked. "No," was the unconsciously written reply. "But to answer you must hear." "Yes, quite so." "Then how do you manage?" "I don't know." "There must be someone who hears these words I am speaking." "Yes." "Who?" "Someone other than Lucie."[18]

Colin Ross recounts how Janet treated a case of seeming possession as follows:

> Janet devised a treatment strategy derived from his knowledge of multiple personality and experimental work on automatic writing. . . . He allowed the demon to "rave and rant as he pleased" . . . and while standing behind him quietly ordered him to make certain movements. This is an experimental technique for eliciting dissociated

behavior that was used extensively in 19th-century French psychology. By automatic writing the demon entered into a conversation with Janet, during which he tricked the devil into cooperating with him. "To force the devil to obey me I attacked him through the sentiment which has always been the darling of devils—vanity."[19]

Third, Janet brought forth the concept of "dissociation" (see appendix). By the time of his death, it has been said, "Janet had described virtually everything known about dissociation today."[20] Janet felt that what we now typically think of as the adult ego is maintained by associative mechanisms in the mind. Usually there is enough energy or ego strength to bind the group of selves within us into an apparent unified entity. Those exhibiting unhealthy multiplicity, however, have found the stresses of life too strong and a separation between their selves is therefore maintained.

Fourth, Janet's ideas about the treatment of dissociation gone awry—that is, pathological multiplicity—were innovative, forward thinking (in the sense that he came up with roughly the same overall diagnosis and treatment paradigm that progressive post-Sybil therapists in the 1970s eventually rediscovered), and created a foundation for others to build on:

> Janet's studies of patients with amnesias, fugues, and "successive existences" (now known as alter personalities), convinced him that their symptoms were the effect of split-off parts of the personality which were capable of independent thoughts, actions, and identities. Further, he concluded that the dissociation which caused the symptoms was the result of past traumatic experiences, and that the symptoms could be alleviated by bringing the split-off memories and feelings into consciousness. Dr. Janet's contemporaries, both American and European, expanded upon his research and a model for the diagnosis and treatment of dissociation was soon built.[21]

Notwithstanding his contributions and influence, it is important to note that Janet was not—as we are—accepting of selves in someone as being normal or healthy. Contemporary researchers, unlike Janet, hold that "dissociative mechanisms are a pervasive feature of mental activity. While they contribute to certain pathological syndromes, they also serve important functions in ordinary life. Moreover, it appears that they may play an essential role in creativity, healthy and other exceptional abilities."[22]

Alfred Binet

Alfred Binet (1857–1911) was a French psychologist who is best remembered for creating the first practical intelligence test. (Even today, the fifth generation of the Stanford-Binet intelligence test is widely used.) Like Janet, Binet was initially associated with Charcot's Salpêtrière School.

Binet wrote in 1887 that "I believe it satisfactorily established, in a general way, that two states of consciousness, not known to each other, can co-exist in the mind of an hysterical patient" and that "the problem that I seek to solve is, to understand how and why, in hysterical patients, a division of consciousness takes place."[23]

In a succinct overview of his work and ideas, Colin Ross notes that Binet wrote two major treatises on dissociation. He also found that in highly hypnotizable subjects, experimental alters could be created,

Fig. 6.5. Alfred Binet

and that while such experimentally produced alters could only be summoned by whoever created them, anyone could call out auto- or self-hypnotic alters. Ross concludes that "the theoretical, experimental, and clinical study of dissociation in the 19th century is exemplified by Alfred Binet."[24]

Binet's own words provide additional insight into his views:

> One observes that in a large number of people, placed in the most diverse conditions, the normal unity of consciousness is disintegrated. Several distinct consciousnesses arise, each of which may have perceptions, a memory, and even a moral character, of its own. . . . Consequently, the limits of our personal and conscious memory are no more absolute limits than are those of our present consciousness. Beyond these lines there are memories, just as there are perceptions and reasoning processes, and what we know about ourselves is but a part, perhaps a very small part, of what we are.[25]

It is clear from this quote that the "the unconscious"—so often attributed to Freud—was very much on the minds of others by this point in time, as we will discuss later.

FOUNDATIONAL BRITISH AND AMERICAN PSYCHOLOGISTS: MYERS, PRINCE, AND SIDIS

We next consider the contributions of early British and American psychologists, including the Englishman Frederic W. H. Myers and the Americans Morton Prince and Boris Sidis.

Frederic W. H. Myers

The Englishman Frederic W. H. Myers (1843–1901) was best known as a founder of the Society for Psychical Research (for investigating paranormal or ESP-type phenomena). Myers corresponded with William James, and the two men were friends who influenced each other's ideas. Myers had a fairly sophisticated notion both of where

Fig. 6.6. Frederic W. H. Myers

selves came from and how they operated with respect to each other. This first summation of his views comes from Myers's 1885 article, "Human Personality":

> The cells of my body are mine in the sense that for their own comfort and security they have agreed to do a great many things at the bidding of my brain. But they are servants with a life of their own; they can get themselves hypertrophied, so to speak, in the kitchen, without my being able to stop them. Does my consciousness testify that I am a single entity? This only means that a stable cænesthesia exists in me just now; a sufficient number of my nervous centers are acting in unison; I am being governed by a good working majority. Give me a blow on the head which silences some leading centres, & the rest will split up into "parliamentary groups" & brawl in delirium or madness.[26]

William James repeated this next Myers quotation, from 1888, verbatim in his own 1896 lectures. It speaks to the value of different selves and to the kind of triggers that can bring about the abrupt and dysfunctional switching of selves.

The arrangement with which we habitually identify ourselves—what we call the normal or primary self—consists, in my view, of elements selected for us in the struggle for existence with special reference to the maintenance of ordinary physical needs, and is not necessarily superior in any other respect to the latent personalities which lie beside it—the fresh combination of our elements which may be evoked, by accident or design, in a variety to which we can at present assign no limit.[27]

To the degree that Myers and James influenced each other, Myers also influenced Morton Prince and Boris Sidis, two of James's closest students, associates, and friends.

Morton Prince

Morton Prince (1854–1929) is known to have said, "Is either side the real self? Or is one more real than the other? Would the individual himself know which he or she is? Certainly no one is more real than the other." A close friend of William James, this American physician and psychologist visited Charcot at the Salpêtrière in Paris.[28] David Lester, in his 2015 book, *On Multiple Selves,* describes Prince's historical role:

A multiple self theory of the mind has a long history. Although many scholars cite James (1890), Cooley (1902), and Mead (1934) as precursors to the concept of a multiple self, the true precursor is Morton Prince (1928). Prince devoted much of his research to the syndrome of multiple personality, and he generalized from that research to normal behavior. In his article "The Problem of Personality: How Many Selves Have We?" Prince noted that traditional theories of personality are inadequate and incomplete because they fail to take into account "normal everyday alterations of character." Prince used the term *personality* to refer to the sum total of our minds, and he proposed that people have many organized dispositions that compose the whole personality. Prince called these organized dispositions *selves, secondary units, characters, phases,* and

Fig. 6.7. Morton Prince

variants. . . . These different selves appear when there are changes in fatigue, illness, intoxication, mood, and situation. They can change from morning to evening, in adversity versus prosperity, happiness versus sorrow, sickness versus health, and in our different social relationships.[29]

Prince's awareness that switching or shifting in and out of various selves happens for a variety of reasons (fatigue, illness, and the like) is consonant with our previously stated notion that mental health is being in the right mind at the right time.

While Prince spent a good deal of time detailing accounts of pathological multiple personality, this next quotation from Prince himself shows that he understood that the pathological cases served to shine light on how multiplicity works in all of us:

No sound theory of personality can disregard, as is usually done, the data derived from the study of case of multiple personality. For the multiple nature of man, or to state it in a different form, the different selves, of which our minds and personalities are composites, may be most clearly recognized, as I have already intimated in the frankly abnormal cases of this kind observed in actual life. They are not uncommon and many have been studied. They are of interest, not because of the dramatic phenomena they exhibit, but because of the light they thus throw on the structure and mechanisms of the human mind, on the composite nature of man, and on the many little selves of which the mind is composed.[30]

Prince's recognition that a pathological version of something can be real without being the best or optimal point of focus make him a true precursor of the healthy selves perspective.

Boris Sidis

The last early psychologist to consider (before we get to William James himself) is Boris Sidis (1867–1923), who, along with his colleague Simon P. Goodhart, wrote the 1904 book *Multiple Personality*. The book, which Sidis wrote most of, was dedicated to William James,* his teacher and later close friend. (James wrote the introduction to Sidis's first published book, *The Psychology of Suggestion* (1898), in which he paid a generous tribute to its author's originality.)[31]

In addition to helping keep Janet's concept of dissociation alive[32]—one source even called Sidis "the Janet of the United States"[33]—and unabashedly titling their book *Multiple Personality,* Sidis and Goodhart "came out as saying [that] multiple personality was just an exaggerated expression of something which was actually quite normal in the human personality. Different selves are elicited by different situations."[34]

That is, like Prince, Sidis differentiated between multiplicity in normal people and the pathological cases of multiplicity—those from "abnormal psychology"—which were valuable in terms of how they shed light on things: "The formation of many personalities, their dramatic play, their dissociation, new associations, interrelations, and sense of familiarity can possibly be best brought home to the reader by concrete examples from the vast domain of abnormal psychology."[35]

---

*Sidis married a maternal aunt of Clifton Fadiman, who in turn is Jim Fadiman's uncle. Sidis was so close to William James that Sidis gave his son—who reportedly had one of the highest IQs ever—the name William James Sidis. And Jim Fadiman's father was named William James Fadiman.

Fig. 6.8. Boris Sidis

In *Multiple Personality,* Sidis first describes what most people think multiple personality is, and then he states that many of the characteristics found in pathological cases are equally applicable to the description of normal people:

> These cases may serve as good illustrations of the possible disaggregations and new aggregations of the mental systems that go to make up the warp and woof of human personality. Of course it remains yet to be shown how much of these phenomena is artificially induced and how much of this play is really spontaneous.
>
> In either case, however, *the fact of plural personalities stands out clear and distinct.* Training no doubt counts a good deal, but this in itself is insufficient to account for the independent personalities with their own characteristics, traits, intellectual and moral, and with their own trains of memories impenetrable to all other personalities, persisting in their existence once formed, persistently refusing to be merged into any of the other personalities, and resisting all efforts at fusion.[36] (Emphasis added.)

Note how, in the end of this passage, Sidis reaffirms the notion that selves exist independently—"persisting in their existence once formed"—and understandably resist efforts to be merged or fused out of existence.

WILLIAM JAMES:
FATHER OF AMERICAN PSYCHOLOGY

In certain persons, at least, the total possible consciousness may be split into parts which co-exist, but mutually ignore each other.

WILLIAM JAMES, *THE PRINCIPLES OF PSYCHOLOGY*

William James (1842–1910), the "Father of American Psychology," was a leading nineteenth-century thinker who remains among the most influential of all American philosophers. A co-founder of the philosophical school of Pragmatism and known as a "radical empiricist," James met Charcot in Paris 1882[37] and later heard Janet lecture and was deeply influenced by him. Then, "in January 1894 James read and reviewed with great admiration Pierre Janet's État mental *des Hystériques*. Janet's work, James told a friend, 'seems to outweigh in importance all the "exact" laboratory measurements put together' and had 'opened an entirely new chapter in human nature' . . . James was much struck with Janet's description of 'hidden selves' and discussed it in [James's] *The Principles of Psychology,* published the following year."[38]

According to Frank W. Putnam, "William James was clearly captured by Janet's ideas and discussed his work extensively in the 1896 Lowell Lectures . . . James summarized his first lecture with the statement that 'the mind seems to embrace a confederation of psychic entities.'"[39] Putnam further explains that James held the view that we are not a unitary single self—even if it sometimes initially looks that way—and instead "we are rather a multiplicity of selves, some segments connected in larger proportion than others. . . . James, himself, was an early pioneer in . . . studying cases of *multiple personality* . . . [and] subscribed to the spectrum of consciousness first articulated by F. W. H. Myers."[40]

In *William James on Exceptional Mental States: The 1896 Lowell*

Fig. 6.9. William James

Lectures (1982), Eugene Taylor worked from James's original lecture notes to put together running narratives of James's lectures. Following are some highlights from James's "Lecture IV: Multiple Personality" (some of which are direct quotes from James):

"We are by this time familiar with the notion that a man's consciousness need not be a fully integrated thing," James begins this fourth lecture. . . . "Of late years," he points out, "we have seen many cases of *alternating* personality." . . .

Up to this time James had presented his audience with cases of alternating personality where multiple selves appear in succession. But these new examples by Janet point to several simultaneously operating personalities within the same person. Such discrete personalities, James had said in 1890, "are proved by M. Janet not only to exist in successive forms in which we have seen them, but to *coexist,* to exist simultaneously." . . .

"The truth is," James acknowledges to his audience, "that we see here the complexity of Nature." Janet's formula, that these are merely split-off fragments of the primary personality, is "not descriptive" of such cases as these just mentioned. "Myers's is better."[41]

Despite his admiration for Janet, James felt that Frederic W. H. Myers had given a better overall explanation than Janet had, to wit, that what we are dealing with in multiplicity is not merely a split-off fragment from a main personality.

THE HIGH-WATER MARK OF EARLY INTEREST: JANET'S LECTURES AT HARVARD

We will now wrap up our look at the early period of experimental psychology in which favorably disposed French and American psychologists earnestly discussed the reality of multiple selves. Kluft and Fine (writing in 1993) recap the historical situation:

> A hundred years ago, French psychiatry and neurology were intensively focused on 1) hypnosis and hypnotic phenomena; 2) puzzling divisions of consciousness with amnesia; and 3) the quasi-neurologic anomalies of hysteria, led by Jean Martin Charcot and later by Pierre Janet. On the American shore stood William James and Morton Prince, both intensively interested in divided states of consciousness.[42]

This all led to a single event that brought Janet to America in 1906 when he was invited to speak at Harvard Medical School, thus solidifying the various strands of influence originating with Charcot and embracing many of the figures discussed in the previous few subsections. As Kluft and Fine further recount (referring to cases of multiple personality as "Gmelin's syndrome"*), "This was the first known transatlantic meeting on the subject of multiple personality."[43]

Janet's lectures were later published as *The Major Symptoms of*

---

*Eberhardt Gmelin is sometimes credited with first having written about multiple personality disorder. "In 1791, Eberhardt Gmelin reported the case of 'exchange personalities.' . . . He treated a 20-year-old German woman who would suddenly 'exchange' her personality, language, and manner with a personality who spoke perfect French and behaved like an aristocratic lady."[44] Moreover, Gmelin's work was so groundbreaking that some authorities have renamed multiple personality disorder as "Gmelin's syndrome."[45]

Hysteria in 1920. Janet's Lecture IV, "Double Personalities," begins with him saying that while he did not have the time to sum up existing theory, both Morton Prince and Boris Sidis (with Goodhart) had already written thorough treatments of the subject. Most of Janet's lecture consists of reports of individuals with two—"double"—personalities, one of which was often not very functional. He concludes that different selves really are different, not only in their ideas and feelings but also in their overall states of mental activity, an idea that foreshadows the later development of the term "self-state":

> The essential phenomenon that, in my opinion, is at the basis of these double existences, is a kind of *oscillation of mental activity,* which falls and rises suddenly. These sudden changes, without sufficient transition, bring about two different states of activity. . . . These two states separate from each other; they cease to be connected together, as with normal individuals, through gradations and remembrances. They become isolated from each other, and form these two separate existences. Here, again, there is a mental dissociation . . . not only of an idea, not only of a feeling, but of one mental state of activity.[46]

Within a decade, however, interest in multiplicity had greatly declined, mostly due to the influence of Sigmund Freud.

SIGMUND FREUD: REPUDIATION OF THE SEDUCTION THEORY (ALONG WITH SELVES)

Sigmund Freud is a towering figure who continues to dominate much psychological discussion even today. Indeed, Philip M. Bromberg starts his 2011 book, *Awakening the Dreamer: Clinical Journeys,* with the following story about two very influential men:

> In 1893, Freud published a memorial essay on Charcot, in which he recalled a verbal duel between them that Charcot won with a good-humored piece of repartee—a "one-liner." It was an incident

Fig. 6.10. Sigmund Freud

that Freud held in his memory with seemingly great fondness even though Charcot had the last word. Freud cited it frequently throughout his career:

"Charcot . . . never tired of defending the rights of purely clinical work, which consists in seeing and ordering things, against the encroachments of theoretical medicine. On one occasion there was a small group of us, all students from abroad, who, brought up on German academic physiology, were trying his patience with our doubts about his clinical innovations. 'But that can't be true,' one of us [in fact, Freud himself] objected; 'it contradicts the Young-Helmoltz theory.' Charcot did not reply by saying 'So much the worse for the theory, clinical facts come first' or words to that effect; but he did say something which made a great impression on us: *'Theory is good; but it doesn't prevent things from existing.'*"[47]

Unfortunately, given the direction he took his own theory, it seems that Freud (1856–1939) did not really take Charcot's point to heart.

Despite being open to multiplicity earlier in his career, his own well-known theory eventually led him to disavow the existence of selves.

There is no doubt as to Freud's cultural impact. His three-part division of the human psyche into id (impulsive, unconscious, instinctual), ego (rational consciousness), and superego (moral conscience) is widely influential.

Moreover, he is often credited with discovering, or bringing to public awareness, the notion that there are areas within our mind—perhaps very large areas—of which we are not conscious. However, the idea that Freud is responsible for bringing us the idea of the unconscious in the first place is a clear mistake. After mentioning Pierre Janet, Alfred Binet, and other authors on "double consciousness," Ernest Hilgard states that:

> Such divisions of consciousness were very much "in the air" when Freud began to write about the role of the unconscious in mental illness. The philosopher-psychologists of the early nineteenth century had prepared the way before the psychical researchers and hypnotists. Herbart, Kant's successor . . . had the concept that ideas could exist below the limin of consciousness in a state of inhibition as "tendencies," representing a kind of active unconscious. Later, in 1869, but in a more romantic vein, von Hartmann wrote his famous book *Philosophy of the Unconscious*. Freud did not "discover" the unconscious, though the brilliance of his clinical insights gave his views a special prominence.[48]

Freud did not discover the unconscious,* but he did put a particular spin on it that came to dominate psychology and psychiatry for decades.

---

*For those readers particularly interested in the history of psychology and the unconscious as it is bears on multiplicity and healthy selves, two books stand out. First, there is Henri F. Ellenberger's monumental *The Discovery of the Unconscious* (Basic Books, 1970). Binet, Charcot, Freud, James, Janet, Jung, Myers, Prince, Sidis—these and many other important figures are discussed, with major players given detailed treatments. The second, Lancelot Law Whyte's *The Unconscious before Freud* (Basic Books, 1960), briefly reviews two thousand years of thinking about the unconscious before Freud.

Fig. 6.11. Freud's mentor and early co-author, Josef Breuer

Somewhat ironically, Freud is often credited with having shown that the human mind, or psyche, has three different functional parts. These are "the id, ego and superego, all developing at different stages in our lives."[49]

It is important to note that although these aspects represent a theoretical division of the human being or his/her mind into multiple parts, the id, ego, and superego are much more different from each other—structurally, functionally, and in their core being—than are individual selves or personalities; that is, while our selves are unique, they are still recognizable as selves because they are roughly similar to each other.

At one point, Freud was very much open to the reality of selves. Early on in his career, in *Studies on Hysteria* (1895), co-written with Josef Breuer,* Freud had "introduced the concepts of psychoanalysis in the form of the case of Anna O.—herself clearly multiple [and] wrote

*In recent years the Austrian physician Josef Breuer has been increasingly acknowledged as perhaps being the "true father" of modern psychotherapy. He invited Freud into his home, gave him access to his patients (like Anna O.), shared his ideas and methods, and even loaned Freud money. Later, when the two had a break over Breuer not being in agreement with some of Freud's ideas around sexuality, Breuer simply withdrew into his medical practice and did not publicly criticize Freud.[50]

jointly with Breuer of the existence of a splitting of the personality to occur in a 'rudimentary degree in every hysteria.'"[51] Their exact words are well worth noting:

> We have become convinced that the splitting of consciousness which is so striking in the well-known classical cases under the form of "double conscience" is present in a rudimentary degree in every hysteria, and that a tendency to such a dissociation, and with it the emergence of abnormal states of consciousness . . . is the basic phenomena of this neurosis. *In these views we concur with Binet and the two Janets.*[52] (Emphasis added.)

Later, as part of an intellectual property dispute Freud had with Janet,* Freud himself said, "We followed his example when we took the splitting of the mind and dissociation of the personality as the centre of our position."[53] Moreover, while Janet thought that dissociation was a result of individual biological predisposition or weakness, Freud and Breuer essentially thought anyone could experience it. As Paul Kiritsis writes, "They differed from Janet in stressing that splitting was an inadvertent repercussion of the dissociative state rather than an individual propensity stemming from biological predisposition."[54]

What happened to shift Freud (with Breuer) from an early acceptance to a later dismissal of the reality of multiplicity? Mark L. Manning, Ph.D., and Rana L. Manning, Ph.D., whose own multiplicity meta-theory is called "Legion Theory," give a trenchant analysis of Freud's shift and its consequent impact.

---

*Pierre Janet's 1913 report on psychoanalysis claimed that many of Freud's psychoanalysis terms "were only old concepts renamed, even down to the way in which his own 'psychological analysis' preceded Freud's 'psychoanalysis.' This provoked angry attacks from Freud's followers. . . . The charge of plagiarism stung Freud especially. . . . [H]e denied firmly that he had plagiarized Janet, and as late as 1937, he refused to meet Janet on the grounds that 'when the libel was spread by French writers that I had listened to his lectures and stolen his ideas he could with a word have put an end to such talk,' but did not."[55] But Freud was no innocent in the back and forth polemics that went on for two decades and "became notorious for either downplaying or conveniently oversighting Janet's contributions every opportunity he got.[56]

The majority of patients in Josef Breuer and Sigmund Freud's book *Studies on Hysteria* were described as having been victims of sexual abuse and up until 1895 Freud considered that the majority of his patients were suffering from the aftermath of sexual abuse in childhood.

Freud then rejected this idea. There has been a great deal of speculation regarding this decision. Freud's biographer, Ernest Jones, proposed that given many of the fathers of his patients were part of his own social circle, it would have been difficult for Freud to publicly state that his patients had been sexually abused as children.

To then explain the symptoms of his patients, in the absence of any real trauma, Freud produced a socially acceptable theory that denied the reality of childhood sexual abuse. Once the memories of sexual abuse reported by personalities were rejected by Freud as not being memories of true events, then the interpretation of the nature of these additional, or "alter" personalities had to change. . . .

Despite the many great contributions made by Freud . . . the acceptance of his theory meant that many victims of sexual abuse were not believed and many patients with multiple personalities were to be misdiagnosed. For most of the twentieth-century the reality of many DID patient's condition was also rejected as their appearance did not fit accepted theory.[57]

Given Freud's influence, when he repudiated the seduction theory* he helped put an end to any further study of dissociation, hypnosis, doubles, or multiple personality.† As Colin Ross sums it up:

---

*Freud posited his seduction theory in the mid-1890s as the solution to the problem of the origins of hysteria and obsessional neurosis. According to the theory, repressing a memory of early childhood sexual abuse or molestation was the essential cause of hysterical or obsessional symptoms. But within a few years Freud abandoned his theory, concluding that the memories were nothing more than imaginary fantasies.

†Frederick Crews, *Freud: The Making of an Illusion* (Metropolitan Books, 2017), makes the case that Freud's repudiation of the seduction theory is more complicated than

In the 19th century and up until 1910 or so, the study of dissociation was in the mainstream of Western psychology and psychiatry and received attention from many of the major figures such as Freud, Jung, Charcot, Janet, Binet, James, and Prince. The study of dissociation had clinical, experimental and theoretical components. . . . MPD and dissociation fell into disrepute after 1910 because of Freud's repudiation of the seduction theory and the new diagnosis of schizophrenia.[58]

After Freud shifted gears, and his "theories were embraced by the psychiatric world, studies of dissociation declined. Renewal of interest among the professional community was not sparked again until the 1980s."[59]

Ultimately, then, Charcot's injunction was ignored by a Freud whose theory prevented him from seeing what was really there—selves—which he had initially acknowledged were quite real, based on his early clinical work.

....

Freud:
From Co-conscious or Subconscious to Unconscious

According to one source, "Whereas others, such as Morton Prince, had embraced the idea that there could be parallel rational conscious activity which could be described as 'subconscious' or 'co-conscious,' Freud rejected this idea and invented his unconscious. From this point onward Freud referred only to an unconscious. . . . The unconscious of Freud, therefore, was not able to hold accurate memories, assume rational control of the body, or to think as would a rational adult. If the sexual abuse [of the seduction hypothesis] was not seen to be true, then the alter personalities (or the 'unconscious' for Freud) must be irrational."[60]

....

(continued from page 174) previously thought. Still, there is no doubt that Freud was open to selves early in his career—again, he and Breuer *thanked* Pierre Janet and his uncle for their work in this area—and later on he was not. Another volume that yields nuanced insight into Freud's creation and then dismissal of the seduction theory is *Why Freud Was Wrong: Sin, Science, and Psychoanalysis* by Richard Webster (Basic Books, 1995).

EXPLORERS OF INTERIOR MULTIPLICITY: JUNG, ASSAGIOLI, AND HILLMAN

Freud's long-term impact was enormous. As Morton Prince wrote, "Freudian psychology had flooded the field like a rising tide, and the rest of us were left submerged like clams buried in the sands at low water." Moreover, Freud's theory of what was essentially an irrational or stupid unconscious dominated for many decades. Even so, even as his ideas became prevalent, others disagreed with him, including Carl Jung and his successors, to whom we now turn.

Carl Gustav Jung

Carl Gustav Jung (1875–1961) was an influential Swiss psychiatrist and psychotherapist whose works are as popular today as ever. Jung's awareness of multiplicity seems to have begun very early in life: "As a child, Jung already saw that he had two separate selves. 'I always knew that I was two persons.' He recognized one sub-personality as the nervous, difficult child that was in the world. The other sub-personality, which functioned initially only in his mind, was a prominent, intellectual man of the eighteenth century."[61]

As a university student at Basle, Jung was exposed to multiplicity as a medical student long before he met Freud:

> He was intrigued by the behavior of a female cousin aged fifteen and a half who began to exhibit signs of multiple personality. She would become suddenly pale, sink slowly to the ground (or a chair), then begin to speak in a manner completely unlike her everyday self. Instead of her usual Swiss dialect, she spoke literary German in a smooth and assured manner. Various spirits claimed to speak through her mouth,* and her mannerisms changed completely as different ones "took over."[62]

---

*Of the various spirits that spoke through her, Colin Wilson tells us: "One of them claimed to be her grandfather who had been a banal and sanctimonious clergyman. Another was an inane chatterer who flirted with the ladies who came to the 'séances.' Another, who claimed to be a nobleman, was an amusing gossip who spoke High German with a North German accent."[63]

Fig. 6.12. Carl Gustav Jung

Jung remarked that when his cousin held séances, contrary to her normal appearance and manner, "she could talk so seriously, so forcefully and convincingly, that one almost had to ask oneself: Is this really a girl of fifteen and a half? One had the impression that a mature woman was being acted out with considerable dramatic talent."[64] Jung took detailed notes at the séances and later—after studying with Pierre Janet in Paris in 1902—expanded them into his first published work, the doctoral thesis for his medical degree, "On the Psychology and Pathology of So-Called Occult Phenomena."[65]

Jung and Freud: A Close Then Broken Friendship

After getting married, starting a family, and lecturing in psychiatry at the University of Zurich, in 1906 Jung began an extensive letter correspondence by mail with Freud and traveled to Vienna to meet him in 1907. Jung was favorably impressed and "later described his initial impressions of Freud as '. . . extremely intelligent, shrewd, and altogether remarkable.'"[66] Freud was equally impressed.

The first conversation between Carl Jung and Sigmund Freud is reported to have lasted for over 13 hours. Freud, who was already established in his field, saw his younger, outspoken peer as a sort of protégé. Freud became a father figure to Jung, as if their relationship were its own psychological case study. In correspondences, Freud referred to Jung as "the Joshua to my Moses, fated to enter the Promised Land which I myself will not live to see." Again and again he speaks of Jung as his "heir," once as "my successor and crown prince," and even as "spirit of my spirit."[67]

Despite their initial positive mutual feelings and Jung's role as a prominent and vibrant proponent of Freud's ideas, the two men had a permanent break by 1913. Their break had personal, intellectual, and professional causes:

> This relationship and collaboration began to deteriorate as the years went on. While Freud had viewed Jung as the most innovative and original of his followers, he was unhappy with Jung's disagreement with some of the basic tenets of Freudian theory. For example, Jung believed that Freud was too focused on sexuality as a motivating force. He also felt that Freud's concept of the unconscious was limited and overly negative. Instead of simply being a reservoir of repressed thoughts and motivations, as Freud believed, Jung argued that the unconscious could also be a source of creativity.[68]

Jung then went his own way, bringing forth concepts like the collective unconscious (namely, that each of us has not only a personal unconscious but a collective unconscious that all of humanity participates in); his idea of meaningful coincidences or synchronicity; his fascination with myth, magic, and alchemy; and his overall theory of psychological development, which was that growth and integration continued throughout an individual's entire life and centered around a dominant archetype called the Self.[69]

Two ideas developed by Jung began to ever so slowly turn the psychological tide back toward a recognition of multiplicity. The first is

Fig. 6.13. At Clark University conference in 1909, Freud at lower left, Jung at lower right; William James, not in this picture, was also in attendance.

Jung's notion of "archetypes" (from the Greek *archein,* meaning "original or old," and *typos,* meaning "pattern, model, or type")—universal, instinctual, or mythic characters or forces that reside within the collective unconscious of all humanity. He felt that we all contain certain major archetypes within us that are fundamental to human experience and evoke deep emotion. As Carl Golden writes:

> Although there are many different archetypes, Jung defined twelve primary types that symbolize basic human motivations. Each type has its own set of values, meanings and personality traits. . . . Most, if not all, people have several archetypes at play in their personality construct; however, one archetype tends to dominate the personality in general. It can be helpful to know which archetypes are at play in oneself and others, especially loved ones, friends and co-workers, in order to gain personal insight into behaviors and motivations.[70]

Jung's archetypes included the Self, which represented the unity of the personality, the shadow (one's dark side), the anima (within men, the female principle), the animus (within women, the male principle), and many others. He also spoke of archetypal events, archetypal figures (great mother, father, child, devil, wise old man, the trickster, the hero), and archetypal motifs (the apocalypse, the deluge, the creation).[71]

The second crucial notion is Jung's idea of "complexes," or "autonomous complexes." Paul Levy contrasts archetypes and complexes:

> Archetypes are living entities, psychological instincts or informational fields of influence that pattern human perception and experience. . . . Archetypes are the structural forms that underlie consciousness, just as the crystal lattice underlies the crystallization process. . . . The complexes are the inner, psychological vehicles that flesh out the rich repository of contents of the underlying archetypes, giving the formless archetypes a specifically human face.[72]

Archetypes (such as the shadow, the anima, or animus), then, form the big picture background of human events and meaning, while autonomous complexes (such as the fool, lover, hero, magician) become their own type of independent entity and flesh out those archetypes in the ordinary world of daily lived life. David Lester writes that "Jung proposed that complexes exist within the psyche, autonomous partial systems that are organizations of psychic contents."[73] As Jung himself wrote about complexes:

> This image has a powerful inner coherence, it has its own wholeness and, in addition, a relatively high degree of autonomy, so that it is subject to the control of the conscious mind to only a limited extent, and therefore behaves like an animated foreign body in the sphere of consciousness. The complex can usually be suppressed with an effort of will, but not argued out of existence, and at the first suitable opportunity it reappears in all its original strength.[74]

Gretchen Sliker helps us see how Jung's vivid description of an unruly complex in many ways begins to resemble the selves we have been discussing:

> The qualities characteristic of this particular type of subpersonality are that (1) it appears as an image; (2) it has an emotional tone out of harmony with the preferred conscious emotional stance; (3) it has inner coherence and wholeness; (4) it operates with a high degree of autonomy; (5) it feels like a "foreign body" in the mind, at least in initial contact; (6) it takes an effort of will to suppress it; (7) it cannot be dismissed or argued out of existence; and (8) if suppressed, it returns in strength at the first opportunity.[75]

Is an autonomous complex, as a fleshed-out real-world form of an archetype, the same as the selves discussed throughout this book? Based on some of what Jung wrote about archetypes and complexes, it is not too great a stretch to say that he did indeed recognize selves, or sub-personalities, per se. For example, as to archetypes, he wrote, "It is not we who personify them; they have a personal nature from the very beginning."[76] And in *The Secret of the Golden Flower: The Chinese Book of Life,* where Jung collaborated with Richard Wilhelm, we read that "there are subtler, more complex emotional states which can no longer be described as affects pure and simple but which are complicated fragmentary psychic systems. The more complicated they are, the more they have the character of personalities. As constituent factors of the psychic personality, they necessarily have the character of 'persons.'"[77]

Ultimately, however, Jung promoted the Single Self Assumption by emphasizing the archetype of the Self, the ultimate archetype of unitary wholeness that he feels we all are—or should be—motivated by and moving toward. Still, Jung moved the dial quite a bit away from where Freud had set it—or perhaps more aptly, he tuned in to a different channel of inner possibility. Two of his students, Roberto Assagioli and James Hillman, more explicitly recognized and worked with selves.

Roberto Assagioli: Psychosynthesis and Sub-personalities

The Italian psychiatrist Roberto Assagioli (1888–1974) was a student and friend of Carl Jung's and a member of the Freud Society in Zurich. Assagioli founded Psychosynthesis, a holistic psychology movement, which to this day has practitioners and teaching institutes worldwide. A paper comparing Assagioli's and Jung's systems states:

> Roberto Assagioli . . . was the first in Italy to adhere to the Freudian movement, although he soon began to pursue his own course. A near-contemporary of Carl Gustav Jung, Assagioli embraced the emerging dynamic psychology of that period and developed it into a multi-level integrative vision of the human being, which he called "psychosynthesis." In developing both the theory and practice of psychosynthesis, Assagioli contributed to the history of psychology by showing how dynamic and analytical psychology on the one hand and humanistic and transpersonal psychology on the other might be brought into synthesis. He was, with Jung, a major pioneer and exponent of transpersonal psychology.[78]

Freud and Assagioli never met, but they did correspond. At first, Freud hoped that Assagioli would become the champion of his work in Italy. "Ultimately, however, both Jung and Assagioli saw Freud's theory as only a partial description of the dynamics of the psyche. Each set out in his own way to develop what they felt was a more accurate, complete theory."[79] As for the name "Psychosynthesis," it is clear that Assagioli was not the first to use it.[80] In fact, before Assagioli used the term, Carl Jung wrote, "If there is a 'psychoanalysis' there must also be a 'psycho-synthesis' which creates future events according to the same laws."[81]

As a comprehensive transpersonal system, much of Psychosynthesis is beyond our focus. But in his 2015 book, *On Multiple Selves,* David Lester makes a point that applies equally well to this book:

> What is relevant for the present book is that Assagioli proposed as one small part of his theory the existence of subpersonalities. Assagioli suggested that a therapist could ask a client, "Have you

Fig. 6.14. Roberto Assagioli

noticed that you behave differently in your office, at home, in social interplay, in solitude, at church, or as a member of a political party?" Assagioli proposed that each of us has different selves, based on the relationship we have with other people, surroundings, groups, etc.; that is, roles. We should not identify with any one of these selves. The goal is to become aware of the subpersonalities and immerse ourselves in each role, so that we can play consciously these various roles. The subpersonalities must be synthesized "into a larger organic whole without repressing any of the useful traits." Assagioli touched only briefly on the transitions from one subpersonality to another and to their organization. He also saw the value of having an *observing self* that monitors the different subpersonalities.[82]

Assagioli, then, understood very well that we all have selves, or as he called them, "subpersonalities."* He was quite clear that "we are

---

*In a recently available autobiographical interview, Assagioli said that early in his career, "I jumped on that and other cases by Boris Sidis, Janet and Myers, and emphasized the fact that there are multi-personalities. . . . But the main point of the discussion, the thing [others] could not swallow, was . . . that I adopted Morton Prince's terminology of the co-conscious. I said that each of these split personalities was co-conscious . . . that we had to admit that a sub-personality could be co-conscious, that is, it can have a split consciousness of its own. . . ."[83]

not unified; we often feel that we are, because we do not have many bodies and many limbs, and because one hand doesn't usually hit the other. But, metaphorically, that is exactly what does happen within us. Several subpersonalities are continually scuffling: impulses, desires, principles, aspirations are engaged in an unceasing struggle."[84]

Ultimately, however, Assagioli felt that getting to know and understand one's selves is merely a preliminary step to eventually integrating all those selves under a single Higher Self. As Gretchen Sliker puts it, extensively quoting Assagioli:

> [Assagioli] emphasizes the importance of knowledge of subpersonalities as an entry point in a systematic development process: understanding of subpersonalities is foundation work that precedes higher development. Of subpersonalities Assagioli said, "Everyone has different selves [subpersonalities]—it is normal." "It is imperative for each man and woman who wants to live consciously to be well aware of (the) elements or components of their personality—not a dim, passive awareness, but a deliberate assessment, valuation, understanding and control of them." "One should become clearly aware of these subpersonalities because this evokes a measure of understanding of the meaning of psychosynthesis, and how it is possible to synthesize these subpersonalities into a larger organic whole without repressing any of the useful traits."[85]

For Assagioli, working with sub-personalities liberates the individual. As his foremost pupil, the Italian psychologist Piero Ferrucci explains:

> Assagioli noticed several years ago that a great deal of psychological pain, imbalance, and meaninglessness are felt when our diverse inner elements exist unconnected, side by side, or clash with one another. But he also observed that when they merge in successively greater wholes, we experience a release of energy, a sense of well-being, and a great depth of meaning in our lives.[86]

Ferrucci further states that not only does awareness of sub-personalities liberate the individual but it automatically begins to integrate those very sub-personalities into a greater whole: "Before we work with them, sub-personalities are fairly distinct universes, ignoring or misunderstanding each other. But as soon as awareness penetrates them, their communication tends to increase. Awareness not only liberates, it also integrates."[87]

Assagioli's take on sub-personalities was an important development, but his ultimate stance—that they were little more than stepping-stones to be integrated on the way to the Higher Self—is made clear by Ferrucci:

> Subpersonalities, too, are degradations or distortions of timeless qualities existing in the higher levels of the psyche. . . . Subpersonalities are like the exiled gods—caricatures, degraded specimens of the original, luminous archetypes. . . . Instead of looking only at their surface aspects—at which no true unity is possible among them— we have to learn to look at them as *degraded expressions of the archetypes of higher qualities*. (Emphasis in original.)[88]

In the end, Assagioli contributed much, building on some of the insights and approaches of Jung's worldview while helping to further establish an alternative to Freud's ideas. As Sliker writes:

> Combined, the work of Jung and Assagioli presents the importance of subpersonalities. Jung focused on the inner experience of constellated psychic elements, whereas Assagioli was concerned with the conscious management and development of inner potential. . . . The writings of Assagioli and Jung are complementary. Assagioli sought to speak to the practical understanding of problem solving, while Jung presents the deep inner mystery of the psyche.[89]

James Hillman and the Return of Polytheistic Psychology

The American psychologist James Hillman (1926–2011) studied with Carl Jung at the Jung Institute in Zurich in the 1950s and later became the first director of studies there. After returning to the United States he taught at several major universities and wrote roughly twenty books. He was often cast as an iconoclast; that is, a breaker of idols and "a thorn in the side of respectable psychologists."[90] As Sanford Drob puts it, "vilified by some, he has been called brilliant, explosive and poetic by others."[91]

Hillman, well aware of events at the turn of the twentieth century, commented on what happened between the early enthusiasm of Charcot, Janet, James, Prince, Sidis, and Binet, and the ascendency of Freud's views: "Multiple personality was ending the rule of reason and so of course this phenomenon became the focus of the defenders of reason: psychiatrists."[92] Hillman makes it quite clear, however, that having selves should not be equated with being mentally ill:

> We conceive our psychological nature to be naturally divided into portions and phases, a composition of earlier and later historical levels, various zones and developmental strata, many complexes and archetypal persons. We are no longer single beings in the image of a single God, but are always constituted of multiple parts: impish child, hero or heroine, supervising authority, asocial psychopath, and so on. Because we have come to realize that each of us is normally a flux of figures, we no longer need to be menaced by the notion of multiple personality. I may see visions and hear voices; I may talk with them and they with each other without at all being insane.[93]

In fact, the early Hillman, who built on Jung's work as he re-visioned* psychology to create his own brand of archetypal psychology, was as close to an advocate of healthy multiplicity as anyone we have yet met. As John Rowan frames it:

> Most psychologists assume that, no matter how many subpersonalities we find, ultimately all has to be reduced to one. This is the most general conception of mental health. But [Mary] Watkins, and her

---

*Hillman's 1975 magnum opus, *Re-Visioning Psychology*, was nominated for the Pulitzer Prize.

Fig. 6.15. James Hillman

mentor James Hillman, ask the question "Why?" Would it not make more sense to live with multiplicity, to recognize more than one centre within ourselves? Hillman suggests that this quarrel is rather like the quarrel between monotheism and polytheism. Psychology, he says, is secretly monotheistic, and wants everything to be neatly hierarchical or bureaucratic. But could we not envisage a polytheist psychology, which admitted that there could be many gods and goddesses, many egos, many identities, many selves.[94]

Not only is Hillman aware of selves (sometimes addressed in Jungian terms as "complexes"), but his idea of a *polytheistic psychology* brings us back to some of the territory we covered earlier on selves and souls in religion. In 1971, near the beginning of his essay "Psychology: Monotheistic or Polytheistic," Hillman wrote:

The question "polytheism or monotheism" represents a basic ideational conflict in Jungian psychology today. Which fantasy governs our view of soul-making and the process of individual—the many or the one? The very sound of the question shows already to what extent we are ruled by a bias towards the one. Unity, integration and individuation seem an advance over multiplicity and diversity. As the self seems a further integration of anima/animus, so seems monotheism superior to polytheism. Placing the psychological part of the question to one side for the moment, let us first depose the ruling notion that in the history of religions or in the ethnology of peoples, monotheism is a further, higher development out of polytheism.[95]

Hillman further makes clear, in contrast to Jung, how and why a polytheistic psychology would be valuable:

Jung used a polycentric description for the objective psyche. [He envisioned it] as a multiplicity of partial consciousness, like stars or sparks or luminous fishes' eyes. A polytheistic psychology corresponds with this description and provides its imagistic formulation in the major traditional language of our civilization, i.e., classical mythology. By providing a divine background of personages and powers for each complex, polytheistic psychology would find place for each spark. It would aim less at gathering them into a unity and more at integrating each fragment according to its own principle, giving each god its due over that portion of consciousness, that symptom, complex, fantasy which calls for an archetypal background. It would accept the multiplicity of voices, the Babel of the anima and animus, without insisting upon unifying them into one figure, and accept too the dissolution process into diversity as equal in value to the coagulation process into unity. The pagan Gods and Goddesses would be restored to their psychological domain.[96]

He then concludes his essay with a clarion call for a return to acknowledging and harmonizing with all the parts of our psyche's "inherent polytheism":

We need adequate psychological models that give full credit to the psyche's inherent polytheism, thereby providing psychological vessels for the sparks. They may burst into religious conflagrations when left psychologically unattended or when forced into monotheistic integrations that simply do not work. The restoration of the Gods and Goddesses as psychic dominants . . . can give sacred differentiation to our psychic turmoil and can welcome its outlandish individuality in terms of classical patterns.[97]

With his amplification of Jung's ideas and his resurrection of polytheistic psychology, Hillman deserves a great deal of credit for raising awareness as to the importance of recognizing and valuing selves.

FLOWS OF INFLUENCE: JUST THREE DEGREES OF SEPARATION FROM CHARCOT TO HILLMAN

How important is it to understand the treatment of multiplicity throughout the history of psychology? In some ways, it is not that important at all. We were able to get through the previous five chapters—including chapter 3, with its pragmatic orientation on being in the right mind at the right time—without having mentioned any of this history. And in section 3, more practical advice and suggestions will be offered with little or no historical focus.

Still, the historical big picture can reveal significant trends and stimulate insight. We will, then, further summarize the history we have gone through and hopefully clarify a few points with the help of figure 6.16 on page 191: "Flows of Influence: Openness to Selves." The diagram is vertically oriented, top to bottom by time (labeled as the late 1800s, the early 1900s, and the mid-1900s). It also segments psychologists by country or region. The British and Americans are on the left, French psychologists are in the middle, and other Europeans are on the right. Arrows connecting thinkers show the direction of influence, and the thickness of lines indicates the strength of their relationship. We can see, for example, that the early Freud was influenced not only by Jean-Martin Charcot but also by Pierre Janet, who was powerfully influenced by Charcot.

The information in this diagram lets us do two things. First, we can marvel at how so many of these men knew and influenced each other, in a way reminiscent of the Six Degrees of Kevin Bacon parlor game. (Based on the "six degrees of separation" concept, this game relies on the premise that any two people on Earth are separated by only six or fewer acquaintance links.)

Second, we can begin to better see how the overall story of psychology and multiplicity unfolds by tracking their personal relationships and the flows of influence between these men. For example, we can start with Charcot, who was among the first psychologists open to the reality of multiplicity, and then his protégé, Janet, who became an open proponent as he developed his ideas of dissociation. Jung then clearly was influenced by Janet, with whom he studied, but Jung also had to metabolize the influence of his mentor Freud, who had gone from being open in his early days when he wrote about "double consciousness" (with Josef Breuer) and praised the influence of the Janets (Pierre and his philosopher uncle, Paul), to later not being open at all. So while Jung was open, his openness was about *internal* archetypes, not the reality of the existence of independent selves (pathological or otherwise) within people.

We can start at any number of different places in the diagram and derive useful insights.* Thus, starting with William James we can see multiple influences on him from Myers in America and Charcot, Binet, and Janet in France, and then see how this combined influence spread through James to his students, Prince and Sidis, both of whom influenced Roberto Assagioli. Tracing the relationships and flows of influence between and

---

*Another factor to consider is that, of these thinkers, only Charcot and Janet (and probably Freud) felt that selves occurred only as a symptom of pathological hysteria. Ann Taves, in the prestigious *Journal of the American Academy of Religion,* writes that "Janet, who followed his mentor, the neurologist Jean-Martin Charcot, on this point, viewed all manifestations of a secondary self as symptomatic of hysteria and, thus, as inherently pathological. He stood apart from Binet . . . Myers, and James, who . . . believed that secondary centers of consciousness could exist in healthy persons."[98] The journal article by Taves, which came to light just before this book went to press, makes clear both how powerful Myers's influence was (including his development of concepts like the "subliminal self," the "multiplex mind," and the "fissiparous self" that is able to divide into separate parts) and that another late-nineteenth century psychologist, Edmund Gurney, was regularly credited by James and Janet for his experimental work and arguably could have been included in the Flows of Influence diagram.

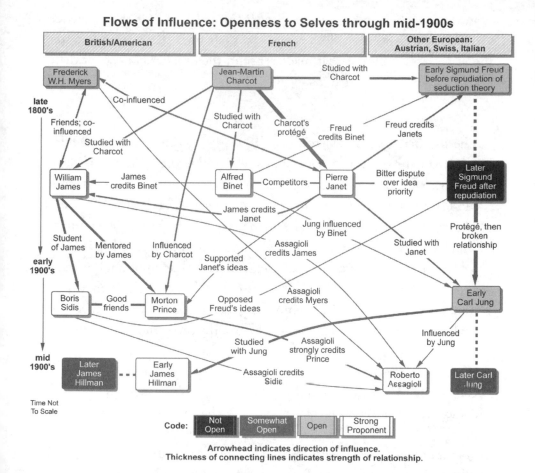

Fig. 6.16. Flows of influence as to openness to selves
through mid-nineteenth century. Arrows show the direction of influence while
thickness of lines shows strength of relationship.

among these thinkers help us unpack this deeply interpenetrated and evolving historical narrative that still influences us to this day.

OTHER NOTABLE TWENTIETH-CENTURY PSYCHOLOGISTS

We will briefly consider six other psychologists who had something interesting to say about multiplicity, or otherwise focused on selves or "parts psychology." These well-known thinkers had at least some awareness—and in some cases a well-formed idea—of the existence of selves, not necessarily as central to their own theories and strategies but as an adjunct that made sense in the broader context of their efforts.

Karl Menninger

The psychiatrist Karl Menninger (1893–1990), known as "the elder statesman and dean of American psychiatry,"[99] wrote, "Groups of ideas, together with their emotional concomitants, may become split off from the main personality . . . and continue a separate existence."[100] Well-known as a humanitarian and crusader for mental health, Menninger "emphasized creating a humane environment for patients to live in" and "contended that most crime was a stage of mental or emotional sickness and should be treated as such."[101] His core belief that the mentally ill were not all that different from other individuals,[102] and his focus on environmental triggers aligns with the healthy selves model.

Fritz Perls

German-born psychiatrist and psychotherapist Fritz Perls (1893–1970) coined the term *Gestalt therapy* to describe the approach he created with his wife, Laura. Peter A. Baldwin notes that Perls and other Gestalt practitioners experienced patients as being scattered, fragmented, and split-up due to frightening life experiences that made them take leave of the present moment, thereby "disappearing" parts of themselves. The goal of Gestalt therapy was to "facilitate persons becoming aware of their splits and fragments and lost parts, to re-own and reintegrate all of their parts into a functioning whole."[103]

John Rowan tells us that during Perls's therapy sessions, he would place an empty chair next to himself for the various members of our internal world to facilitate communication with them and even among themselves. In doing so a *topdog* and an *underdog* would often become apparent. According to Perls:

> The topdog is righteous and authoritarian; he knows best. He is sometimes right, but always righteous. . . . He manipulates with

Fig. 6.17. Karl Menninger   Fig. 6.18. Fritz Perlz

demands and threats of catastrophe. . . . The underdog manipulates with being defensive, apologetic, wheedling, playing the crybaby, and so on. . . . The underdog is the Mickey Mouse. The topdog is the Super Mouse.[104]

The emergence of conflicting parts or selves—such as topdog and underdog—is not uncommon for those first becoming aware of their entire roll call of selves and has been followed up on by a number of other writers as well.

Eric Berne

Eric Berne (1910–1970), a Canadian-born psychiatrist, made use of game theory to create a form of therapy called "Transactional Analysis" that achieved wide popularity based on his 1964 book, *Games People Play*. Berne, whose ideas in some ways resemble Freud's, argued that each of us has three people, or three "ego states," within us—Parent, Child, and Adult. For many people, these ideas gave them an entrée into considering the possibility that they really did have selves within. Elizabeth O'Conner writes of her own experience with Berne's book:

I did not have any new encounter with the concept of the many selves until I met it in the book *Games People Play* by Eric Berne.

Fig. 6.19. Eric Berne   Fig. 6.20. Milton H. Erickson

That book made a vast reading public aware of three psychological realities each person carries in him . . . the Parent, the Child, and the Adult. . . . This is a profound observation of psychological realities translated into terms easily grasped by lay readers, so that they are able to use them to observe these states in themselves and to note when the shift is made from one to the other.[105]

A similar book, *I'm Ok—You're Ok* by Thomas Anthony Harris (1967), was also a bestseller. Having people see themselves as playing one of three predetermined roles in most interactions (or social transactions) is a good start to the further recognition of the actual existence of selves within us.

Milton H. Erickson

American psychiatrist Milton H. Erickson (1901–1980) had an unconventional approach to individual and family therapy that made use of story, metaphor, and especially hypnosis. One author, focusing on "parallels between multiple personality, spirit mediumship, and hypnosis from historical, anthropological, and clinical perspectives," writes, "I emphasize Milton H. Erickson's view of multiple personalities as not necessarily pathological but as potential resources. He employed hypnosis to gain access to personalities and to transform their behavior from involuntary to voluntary actions."[106]

Celia Ramos makes the same point: "Milton Erickson was noted to remark that multiplicity could be looked upon as a potential resource. . . . He went further to state that it should not be looked upon as a distortion of reality, but as a kind of readiness to use one's abilities normally."[107] Finally, John and Helen Watkins sum up both Erickson's contributions:

> In his ingenious therapeutic strategies, Milton Erickson exhibited a genuine awareness of the fact that individuals can be multiplicities as well as unities. He communicated with his patients at more than one level. Yet he did this almost as an unconscious art, not one which he formulated into an easily transmitted science.[108]

Virginia Satir

Virginia Satir (1916–1988) was a social worker and therapist whose approach to family therapy—as described in her 1964 book, *Conjoint Family Therapy*—brought her wide recognition. One aspect of her work involved identifying and working with clients' body language to identify which of five different types of "stress responses" the person was embodying: the Placater, the Blamer, the Computer, the Distracter, and the Leveler.[109]

Fig. 6.21. Virginia Satir

In Satir's innovative approach to family therapy, selves were called the "parts" of a person:

> For one thing you probably have many parts that you have not yet discovered. All of these parts, whether you have owned them or not, are present in you. Becoming aware of them enables you to take charge of them rather than be enslaved by them. Each of your parts is a vital source of energy. Each has many uses, and can harmonize with many other parts in ways to add even more energy.[110]

John Rowan notes that Satir analogized people to a kind of spinning mobile that can only function well if all of its parts are recognized and then properly balanced.[111]

Mihaly Csikszentmihalyi

We close this subsection with a quote from the Hungarian-born psychologist Mihaly Csikszentmihalyi, best known for his work on "flow" and "flow states"—where someone becomes so fully absorbed in what they are doing that joyful timelessness occurs and exceptional performance becomes possible. Athletes, musicians, artists, and many others in wide-ranging contexts have experienced flow. Perhaps the real

Fig. 6.22. Mihaly Csikszentmihalyi

trick is to get into the right self—the one predisposed to flow—first. Csikszentmihalyi wrote, "If I had to express in one word what makes their personalities different from others, it's complexity. They show tendencies of thought and action that in most people are segregated. They contain contradictory extremes; instead of being an 'individual,' each of them is a 'multitude.'"[112]

PROGRESSIVE MPD THERAPISTS, THE RETURN OF HYPNOSIS, AND OTHER RECENT WORKS

As noted earlier, once Freud's influence became dominant, there was little work or interest along the lines of doubles, multiple personalities, dissociation, or hypnosis. From roughly 1915 or 1920 until the late 1970s and 1980s, very little if any progress in recognizing the existence and importance of selves was made, although there were some outliers and practitioners who continued their own work along these lines (including Jung, Assagioli, Hillman, and the other notable twentieth-century psychologists just described).

However, after *Sybil*—the book and then the movie—excited public consciousness in the 1970s, and after other cases of pathological multiplicity quickly emerged, things changed. A number of progressive psychiatrists and therapists took it upon themselves to write comprehensive books—essentially in-depth manuals for therapists—that coordinate, organize, and in some cases came up with new theories and intervention mechanisms for handling pathological cases of multiplicity.

These books tend to include sections on the history of multiple personality disorder, its diagnosis, and treatment modalities and techniques. Four of the better books along these lines include:

- *Treatment of Multiple Personality Disorder* by Bennett G. Braun, M.D., ed. (1986),
- *Diagnosis & Treatment of Multiple Personality Disorder* by Frank W. Putnam (1989),
- *Multiple Personality Disorder* by Colin Ross, M.D. (1989), and

- *Clinical Perspectives on Multiple Personality Disorder* by Richard P. Kluft and Catherine G. Fine, eds. (1993).

Also, there are two books on hypnosis worth considering:

- *Divided Consciousness: Multiple Controls in Human Thought and Action* by Ernest R. Hilgard, Ph.D. (1977), and
- *Unity and Multiplicity: Multilevel Consciousness of Self in Hypnosis, Psychiatric Disorder and Mental Health* by John O. Beahrs, M.D. (1982), with chapters contributed by other practitioners and theorists.

Ernest Hilgard and Hypnosis

Ernest Hilgard (1904–2001), in particular, is often credited with reestablishing the legitimacy and usefulness of hypnosis in the clinical setting. As Peter McKellar writes, "the psychologist E. R. Hilgard has pointed out that, in dreaming, one part of us IS 'spectator' to the drama which another part of us is staging.' . . . Hilgard argued that hypnosis provides a promising set of phenomena for the study of dissociative processes."[113] Perhaps more importantly, "Ernest Hilgard discovered through his work with hypnosis that forms of dissociation are clearly distributed along a continuum ranging from normal to pathological."[114]

Hilgard's breakthrough centered around a phenomenon called the "hidden observer," something William James had worked on in the late 1880s. The basic idea was that under hypnosis, one part of someone can be aware of some of what is physically happening while another part remains completely unaware. James had "reported on a hypnotic subject whose right hand commented in writing about pinpricks it had been given. When questioned about it, the subject was unaware of the physical sensations and, upon reading the writings of his own hand, dismissed them."[115]

Hilgard performed similar types of experiments "and reported apparent divided awareness—meaning that two parts of the personality, equally capable and intelligent, were unaware of each other."[116] In their foreword to *Unity And Multiplicity* by Beahrs, John G. Watkins and Helen H. Watkins, who work with the useful concept of ego states,

Fig. 6.23. Ernest Hilgard

spell out the importance of Hilgard's work on revitalizing hypnosis as they connect it to their own work:

> Ernest Hilgard . . . has demonstrated in his laboratory the existence of different cognitive structural systems indicating the presence of co-consciousness in relation to hearing and the perception of pain. And our own studies on ego states, as well as those by . . . [Beahrs], have shown quite clearly that *dissociation is not simply an "either-or" phenomenon, a few strange individuals being "multiple personalities" and everybody else constructed as a "unity."* . . . As therapists *we need much greater sophistication concerning the interaction of an entire person with his/her various facets of self* if we are to do better than fire therapeutic shotguns in the general right direction.[117] (Emphasis added.)

John and Helen Watkins further write:

> In working with research subjects under hypnosis, we have found that *individuals who show no sign of mental illness may nonetheless manifest segmented divisions in their personalities that may act like "covert" multiple personalities.* However, the boundaries that separate them from other such states are more permeable and are not necessarily maladaptive. These parts often have awareness for one another but retain their individual sense of identity. . . . In MPD, on the

other hand, the dissociated parts exist near the extreme end of the differentiation-dissociation continuum. There are often rigid, impermeable boundaries between the ego states, which permit little communication between them; they often possess no awareness of one another.[118] (Emphasis added.)

While these various therapists, theorists, and practitioners were close to recognizing that normal, healthy people have selves, the Single Self Assumption is discernable underneath much of their writing and theorizing. None of them conclude that multiple selves are normal and healthy, and the possibility that selves might come into being for other than traumatic reasons is rarely considered.

This is not too surprising given that almost all of these authors are therapists and have spent most of their professional lives working with unhealthy people. Based on their education, real-world experiences, and professional standing, it is often difficult for them to let go of and see beyond the Single Self Assumption.

Recent Contributions

Finally, these recent books (all of which we have quoted) add to our collective knowledge and appreciation of selves:

- *Embracing Ourselves: The Voice Dialogue Manual* by Hal Stone, Ph.D., and Sidra L. Winkelman, Ph.D. (1985) (This progressive book features "Voice Dialogue," a therapeutic and personal growth system we will return to later.)
- *Many Minds, One Self: Evidence for a Radical Shift in Paradigm* by Richard Schwartz and Robert Falconer (2017)
- *Mindsight* by Daniel J. Siegel, M.D. (2011)
- *Multiple Man: Explorations in Possession and Multiple Personality* by Adam Crabtree, Ph.D. (1985 and 1997)
- *Multiple Mind: Healing the Split in Psyche and World* by Gretchen Sliker, Ph.D. (1992)
- *On Multiple Selves* by David Lester, Ph.D. (2015) (This is a detailed book laden with dense but intriguing theoretical concepts.)

- *Parts Psychology: A Trauma-Based Self-State Therapy for Emotional Healing* by Jay Noricks, Ph.D. (2011)
- *The People You Are* by Rita Carter (2008)
- *Subpersonalities: The People Inside Us* by John Rowan (1990)
- *The Plural Self* by John Rowan and Mick Cooper eds. (1999)

....

"Our Multiple Selves" by Daniel J. Siegel, M.D.

"Our Multiple Selves" is chapter 10 of Siegel's 2011 book, *Mindsight*. Specifically making use of the self-state construct, he writes, "Healthy development involves coming to acknowledge, accept, and then to integrate one's various states: to discover how disparate states can link, and even collaborate as a unified whole composed of many parts." Some of his other points are that

- self-states are part of everyone's life, even if we have no history of trauma;
- we must accept our multiplicity, the fact that we can show up quite differently in our athletic, intellectual, sexual, spiritual—or many other—states (a heterogonous collection of states is completely normal in us humans);
- the key to well-being is collaboration across states, not some rigidly humongous unity—the notion that we can have a single, total consistent way of being is both idealistic and unhealthy; and
- unfortunately, that divide-and-destroy approach (to "integrating" selves against their will) simply does not work.[119]

....

As these books indicate, while the notion of healthy selves often begins to bubble up, it seems to stop short and fails to emerge into greater general public awareness. By questioning the Single Self Assumption from the get-go and by presenting a big-picture view of selves over time across many cultures, disciplines, and fields, we hope to raise general awareness of the healthy selves perspective so that it becomes a part of wider conversations that benefit us all.

SEVEN

At the Convergence
of Buddhism, Science, and
Postmodern Thinking

The more you realize there is no Self,
the more selves you can be.

KRISZTINA LAZAR,
VISUAL ARTIST

Something many neuroscientists, Buddhists, and postmodern philosophers have in common is that they do not support the Single Self Assumption. Whether based on thousands of years of religious contemplation, the application of the scientific method, or postmodernism's potent penetration of prior paradigms, the single self is seen to be a limited truth or an out-and-out error.

Consider the concept of negative space, the area between and around objects in a photo or painting used to render shapes and sizes more effectively. These three disciplines—neuroscience, Buddhism, and postmodern philosophy—and their practitioners have, in effect, created a series of overlapping negative spaces that, taken together, depict a subject by showing everything around the subject but not the subject itself. In this case, the subject itself—the single self—they conclude, was never really there in the first place.

BEHAVIORISM, AI, NEUROSCIENCE, COGNITIVE SCIENCE, AND ECONOMICS

We had been at the conference on Multiple Personality Disorder for two full days before someone made the inevitable joke: The problem with those who don't believe in MPD is they've got Single Personality Disorder.

NICHOLAS HUMPHREY AND DANIEL DENNETT,
"SPEAKING FOR OUR SELVES"

The last chapter looked at multiplicity from the perspective of those psychologies and psychologists who focused on the inner workings of the mind. But are other scientists, especially psychologists and scientists involved in "harder" sciences, open to the possibility and reality of selves?

B. F. Skinner: Radical Behaviorism and Selves as Explanatory Fictions

B. F. Skinner (1904–1990) was for decades the best-known psychologist in the United States. The effects of his work reached far beyond the confines of professional psychology. His distaste for and distrust of mental, subjective, intervening, or what he called "fictional"

Fig. 7.1. B. F. Skinner.
Photo modified by Esquilo.

explanations led him to focus on observable behavior and to formulate ways of observing, measuring, and predicting behavior.

Skinner felt that only behavior could be usefully studied and primarily worked with animals. As for human beings, he felt that "if observable behavior is the basis for defining the self, then to discuss the inner workings of the personality or the self becomes unnecessary."[1] Ultimately, Skinner felt that the term *self* was no more than an explanatory fiction:

> If we cannot show what is responsible for a man's behavior, we say that he himself is responsible for it. The precursors of physical science once followed the same practice, but the wind is no longer blown by Aeolus, nor is the rain cast down by Jupiter Pluvius. . . . A concept of self is not essential in an analysis of behavior.[2]

Moreover, he felt that if the idea of the self was allowed into psychological analysis, such an explanatory fiction would rapidly degrade the possibility of objectively and scientifically considering behavior. Louise McHugh and Ian Stewart amplify Skinner's notion that "the organism behaves, while the self initiates or directs behavior." They write that for Skinner:

> As with many hypothetical constructs that are inferred from behavior, the self as an entity or an agent is suspect, or worse, in behavior analysis because it denigrates or ignores the environment as the source of control over behavior. Considered as a hypothetical construct, self often is reified, becoming an entity. Once reified, it too often becomes the cause—the agent—of behavior. This in turn results in the all-too-familiar problem of circularity, and the creation of what Skinner . . . called an "explanatory fiction."[3]

Consider, then, twentieth-century psychology from the perspective of two of its most influential practitioners, Freud and Skinner. As explained in the previous chapter, Freud repudiated the consideration of selves as this book uses the term, substituting instead his vertical id/ego/superego model. Skinner, alternatively, sidestepped the workings of the interior entirely: no self, no selves, just behavior. Taken together, these two influential and defining giants of psychology made it difficult for any but a select few—like Assagioli and Hillman—to work with selves during most of the twentieth century.

Marvin Minsky, Artificial Intelligence, and the Society of Minds

Marvin Minsky (1927–2016) was a cognitive scientist who specialized in artificial intelligence. He co-founded the Massachusetts Institute of Technology's artificial intelligence laboratory and was also a founding member of MIT's media lab. David Eagleman, himself an important neuroscientist, gives us some valuable background on Minsky's work:

> Throughout the 1960s, artificial intelligence pioneers worked late nights to try to build simple robotic programs that could manipulate small blocks of wood: find them, fetch them, stack them in patterns. This was one of those apparently simple problems that turn out to be exceptionally difficult. . . . Confronting this difficult robotics problem . . . the computer scientist Marvin Minsky and his colleagues introduced a progressive idea: perhaps the robot

Fig. 7.2. Marvin Minsky.
Photo by Rama.

Fig. 7.3. David Eagleman.
Photo by Mark Clark. Used with permission.

could solve the problems by distributing the labor among specialized subagents—small computer programs that each bite off a small
piece of the problem. . . . These mindless subagents could be connected in a hierarchy just like a company, and they could report to
one another and to their bosses. . . .

This idea of subagents . . . brought into focus a new idea about the
working of biological brains. Minsky suggested that human minds
may be collections of enormous numbers of machine-like, connected
subagents. . . . The key idea is that a great number of small, specialized workers can give rise to something like a society, with all
its rich properties that no single subagent, alone, possesses. Minsky
wrote, "Each mental agent by itself can only do some simple thing
that needs no mind or thought at all. Yet when we join these agents
in societies—in certain very special ways—this leads to intelligence."
In this framework, thousands of little minds are better than one
large one.[4]

Minsky further wrote that:

All of this suggests that it can make sense to think there exists,
inside your brain, a society of different minds. Like members of a

family, the different minds can work together to help each other, each still having its own mental experiences that the others never know about. . . . Like tenants in a rooming house, the processes that share your brain need not share one another's mental lives.[5]

Note how Minsky is stating that our minds (our selves) may in effect be regularly working with—or at least cohabitating with—each other, even if we are not aware that that is what they are doing.

Along similar lines, Marilyn Ferguson wrote of Minsky that he "sees these subselves as a configuration of specialized brain functions— a society of agents capable of cooperating on our behalf. If we are ever to qualify intelligence shrewdly enough to detect qualitative differences between individuals, Minsky says, we may find that it correlates with how many of these agents an individual has vying for attention at the same time."[6]

Ornstein and Gazzaniga: Brain Science, Modulatory, and Small Minds

Now consider the work of two American psychologists with a special interest in the anatomy and functioning of the human brain. The first, Michael Gazzaniga (born 1939), is best known for expanding the research of his teacher Roger Sperry (1913–1994)* into what happens when the corpus callosum—which connects the right and left sides of the brain—has to be cut for medical reasons. The title of Gazzaniga's 1967 *Scientific American* article, "The Split Brain in Man," showcasing his and Sperry's work, is telling: "The human brain is actually two brains, each capable of advanced mental functions. When the cerebrum is divided surgically, it is as if the cranium contained two separate spheres of consciousness."[7]

Severing the corpus callosum can produce notable changes. As one source puts it:

---

*Gazzaniga was a Ph.D. student under Roger Sperry at CalTech in Pasadena. Sperry later was awarded the Nobel Prize in Physiology or Medicine in 1981 for his split-brain work.

Fig. 7.4a. Roger Wolcott Sperry

Fig. 7.4b. Michael Gazzaniga

Fig. 7.4c. Robert Ornstein

Did . . . split-brain patients now have two consciousnesses? There appears to be pretty good evidence that the answer to that question is yes. Its not simply a case of "the left hand not knowing what the right hand was doing," we appear to have a phenomenon of the left hand/ right brain not agreeing with what the right hand/left brain was doing.

This phenomenon was termed intermanual conflict. For example, one patient found that his right hand was struggling to pull up his pants, while his left hand struggled to push them down. On another occasion, this same patient's left hand attempted to strike his wife as his right hand grabbed it to stop it.

That is, *we* are a collective entity, composed of (at least) our left and right brains.[8]

This has also been termed Alien Hand Syndrome, a condition where someone experiences a limb (usually their non-dominant hand) moving of its own accord. As one research team wrote, "Alien hand syndrome is a phenomenon in which one hand is not under control of the mind. The person loses control of the hand, and it acts as if it has a mind of its own."[9]

Gazzaniga is important, in part, because his "contribution is to show that sub-personalities are not just a psychological concept, but have an objective anatomical basis."[10] In Gazzaniga's own words:

I think this notion of linear, unified conscious experience is dead wrong. In contrast, I argue that the human brain has a modular-type organization. By modularity I mean that the brain is organized into relatively independent functioning units that work in parallel. The mind is not an indivisible whole, operating in a single way to solve all problems. Rather, there are many specific and identifiably different units of the mind dealing with all the information they are exposed to. The vast and rich information impinging on our brain is broken up into parts, and many systems start at once to work on it. These modular activities frequently operate apart from our conscious verbal selves.[11]

Another psychologist whose research and writing has focused on the structure and workings of the physical brain is Robert Ornstein (born 1942). In *Multimind: A New Way of Looking at Human Behavior* (1986) he defines the human mind as a "bastard hybrid system."[12] As Ornstein tells us on his webpage:

We do not have a thoroughly modern mind although we live in a thoroughly modern world. *We do not have a single brain; we have a multiple one.* We have a complex and unorganized collection of special-purpose solutions to meet different circumstances. We have "small" minds for reacting to emergencies, for detecting sharp changes in the environment, and many "minds of the body" which control health. The brain contains several different and independent centers of action each of which has a "mind of its own." There are significant problems for the maintenance of our health when our separated small minds disagree.[13] (Emphasis added.)

Ornstein recognizes that our brains have autonomous parts—"minds of its own"—and that if our "small minds" are not working or cooperating, we can have significant health and other problems. Under his model, one "small mind" does its job, then exits as another takes its place, so the next job can get done. He says:

Instead of a single intellectual entity that can judge many different kinds of events equally, the mind is diverse and complex. The mind contains a changeable conglomeration of "small minds"—fixed reactions, talents, flexible thinking—and these different entities are temporarily employed—wheeled into consciousness—then usually discarded, returned to their place, after use. Which of the many small minds gets wheeled in depends on many factors, some within our control, others not.[14]

Ornstein's notion that we are not always in control over which of our small minds—which of our selves—gets wheeled in speaks to the question of how to increase the likelihood of being in the right mind at the right time. He notes, "We may well be able to decide how to behave in a situation when we are calm and can see many ways of acting, but that does not mean that it can be done. The small minds that we think we may choose from may be unavailable to consciousness when we need them."[15] Ultimately, Ornstein offers a positive perspective on working with our selves:

It is a question of who is running the show. In most people, at most times, the automatic system of the MOS [Mental Operating System] organizes which small mind gets wheeled in, most likely on that automatic basis of blind habit. But there is a point when a person can become conscious of the multiminds and begin to run them rather than hopelessly watch anger wheel in once again.[16]

Ornstein also made the connection that leaning into our different minds enables us to access the full spectrum of our talents and abilities. He explains that "the idea that we have one rational mind seriously undersells our diverse abilities. It oversells our consistency, and it emphasizes the very small rational islands in the mind at the expense of the vast archipelago of talents, opportunities, and abilities surrounding them."[17]

With regard to working harmoniously with other people, Ornstein astutely points out that they, too, always come with a variety of selves, not all of which you will necessarily prefer.

You may not like some parts, perhaps entire "subpersonalities," of someone, but there is a problem: people come in large and inconsistent packages, like other groups, teams, companies, and the like. These people may swing in different small minds at times, some of which you may find objectionable. . . . Considering others in the same way we consider groups or crowds, like our company, favourite team, or restaurant, might be the shift in understanding we need to make. "I like the food, but not the décor," neatly separate different functions, and we can decide whether to go to the restaurant again. The same approach could be used in marriage and in other close relationships.[18]

Douglas Hofstadter: Strange Loops of Inner Voices and Competing Selves

Consider Douglas Hofstadter (born 1945), whose 1979 book *Gödel, Escher, Bach: An Eternal Golden Braid* (1979) won the Pulitzer Prize for general nonfiction and the National/American Book Award for Science. In his 1985 anthology *Metamagical Themas,* in the chapter titled "The Tumult of Inner Voices," Hofstadter writes about the different voices within him and the conflicts his different parts have with each other:

The question is an intellectual, philosophical one: What is the meaning of the word "I"? Yet the question is also a pragmatic, real-life, soul-ripping issue: Which one of the many people who I am, the many inner voices inside me, will dominate? Who, or how, will I be? Which part of me decides? And can that part in turn have inner conflicts about how to decide which version of me it wants to let dominate? . . .

How can we understand the nature of our selves when we are composed of so many myriads of parts, none of which we understand? How are those parts put together? How does the total add up to, a self, a soul, a you or a me? . . .

Part of me was intending to read that dialogue to you tonight. One inner voice spoke for it. But another, more urgent inner voice

Fig. 7.5. Douglas Hofstadter.
Photo by Maurizio Codogno.

spoke eloquently against it. . . . Who was this other Doug Hofstadter that was so rudely intruding? And what did he want to say? Why was he fighting for control of my top level? What in him insisted that the story . . . was not appropriate?[19]

Hofstadter also writes about how "inner voices" or "competing subselves" must be allowed to be in control from time to time:

Competing subselves cannot be held in check indefinitely. They cannot be clamped down, forbidden to act. For each "inner voice" is in actuality composed of millions of smaller parts, each of which is active, and under the proper circumstances, those small activities will someday all "point in the same direction," and at that moment the inner voice will crystallize, will undergo what is called a phase transition, will emerge from obscurity and proclaim itself an active member of the community of selves.[20]

He concludes, however, that there must be a "governing personality" or "highest-level body" that ultimately makes choices about which self is in charge:

> I see it happening in me all the time. I have a "piano-playing subself," who, once he is given the floor, refuses to relinquish it for hours on end—until . . . until the phone rings or my watch beeps at me, telling me that some other facet of life must be attended to. And somehow, in such circumstances, there is a governing personality who can grab control away from the "hijacker." In fact, it is not at all hard to dislodge the piano-playing hijacker, or the [Rubik's] cubing hijacker, or any other subself, when a phone call comes. . . . Choices must be made, so there must be a highest-level body whose purpose is to make choices rapidly and reliably, one that sorts out the priority of subselves and allows only the one deemed most important to take charge.[21]

Hofstadter arrives at the conclusion that there *must* be a highest-level part or governing body seemingly without any evidence. Despite his detailed observations to the contrary, the Single Self Assumption wins out here as Hofstadter cannot help but conclude that we *must* have some kind of a hierarchically superior super-self that is ultimately in charge.

Daniel Kahneman:
Multiplicity and Behavioral Economics

In addition to the fields of behavioral science, cognitive science, anatomical brain science, and artificial intelligence, we also find multiplicity in economic theory, and in particular, "behavioral economics." In his book *Thinking, Fast and Slow* (2013), Daniel Kahneman, an Israeli American cognitive psychologist who won the Nobel Prize in Economics, tells us that there are two completely different systems within each of us that are best at making very different kind of decisions:

> The distinction between fast and slow thinking has been explored by many psychologists over the last twenty-five years. . . . I describe

Fig. 7.6. Daniel Kahneman

mental life by the metaphor of two agents, called System 1 and System 2, which respectively produce fast and slow thinking. I speak of the features of intuitive and deliberate thought as if they were traits and dispositions of two characters in your mind. In the picture that emerges from recent research, the intuitive System 1 is more influential than your experience tells you, and it is the secret author of many of the choices and judgments you make.[22]

Do we have here another Nobel Prize winner promoting the reality of different selves? Quite the opposite, because not too far into the book, in a section called "Useful Fictions," Kahneman makes it clear that Systems 1 and 2, despite his effort to get you to think of them as separate characters within you, are *not* real parts of who we are. He says:

You have been invited to think of the two systems as agents within the mind, with their individual personalities, abilities, and limitations. . . .

The use of such language is considered a sin in the professional circles in which I travel, because it seems to explain the thoughts and actions of a person by the thoughts and actions of little people inside the person's head. System 1 and System 2 are so central to the story I tell in this book that I must make it absolutely clear that they are fictitious characters. Systems 1 and 2 are not systems in the standard sense of entities with interacting aspects or parts. And there is no one part of the brain that either of the systems would call home.[23] (Emphasis added.)

After inviting us to focus on how we have two very different systems, which are both "so central to the story" and best suited for different kinds of decision making, Kahneman makes sure to emphasize that these systems are merely fictitious characters—that they are not really real. Why does he do this? He is very clear: in his professional circles, it does not pay to officially challenge the Single Self Assumption—even if the whole book he has written seems to do just that. With a nod to Shakespeare, it seems perhaps that the economist doth protest too much, we thinks.

Other important behavioral economists have been attracted to the explanatory power of a multiple self model. For example, Thomas Schelling (1921–2016), who won the 2005 Nobel Prize on his work in game theory, thought that "addicts have two selves, one keen for healthy lungs and another craving a smoke. Self-control strategies involve drawing battles lines between them."[24]

BUDDHISM AND
THE DOCTRINE OF NO SELF

A famous Buddhist story involves King Milinda, a Bactrian (Indo-Greek) king who lived about 150 BCE. One day the king met with the Buddhist sage Nagasena. Their dialogue was purportedly recorded in the *Milindapanha* ("The Questions of Milinda"), a book written in the Pali language about 100 BCE. Following is an abbreviated version of their encounter.

Fig. 7.7. Nagasena at the court of King Milinda

Nagasena and the Chariot

The story begins with King Milinda visiting the Sankheyya hermitage. . . . After traveling to the hermitage, he was greeted by Nagasena.

King Milinda: How is your reverence known and what is your name, sir?

Nagasena: I am known as Nagasena, great king, and everyone calls me Nagasena. Even though my parents named me Nagasena, the word Nagasena is just a name, a label, a series of sounds, a concept. It is just a name. There is no real person to be apprehended.

King: (addresses everyone) Listen up everyone, Nagasena tells me that he is not a real person. How can I agree to that? . . .

Nagasena: Your Majesty, I notice that you have been brought up in great comfort. If you walked here under the noon sun, on the sharp rocks and burning sands, then your feet would be hurt and you would be tired. So how did you come, on foot or on a horse?

King: I came on a chariot.

Nagasena: If you came on a chariot, please explain what a chariot is. Is the pole the chariot?

King: No, reverend sir.

Nagasena: Is it the wheels, or the frame, or the yoke, or any of the parts?

King: No, reverend sir.

Nagasena: Is it the combination of the parts? If we laid out the wheels and the frame and the yoke and all the parts, would that be a chariot?

King: No, reverend sir.

Nagasena: Then is it outside of this combination of parts?

King: No, reverend sir.

Nagasena: Then, ask as I do, I can't discover a chariot. Chariot seems to be just a mere sound. Where is this chariot? Your Majesty has told a lie!

Greeks: (applaud) How will you get out of this, Your Majesty?

King: Nagasena, I have not told a lie. It is in the dependency and interworking of all the parts that you have a chariot. A pile of parts isn't enough. It is when they all work together that you have this conceptual term, sound, and name of a chariot.

Nagasena: Your Majesty is exactly right about the chariot. It is just so with me. Nagasena is the working of all the parts of the body and the five skandhas that make me. But in ultimate reality, however, the person still isn't caught.[25]

Whether King Milinda and the sage Nagasena are looking at the individual named "Nagasena," the king's chariot, or the king himself, the thing or person being perceived is actually made up of many interdependent pieces or processes, none of which exists on its own. What is being questioned, then, is the notion that particular things ultimately have an independent, freestanding, essence.

The Doctrine of No Self

A central tenet of Buddhism, "nonself," can be can be better understood with the help of a useful analogy:

> Apart from those who have "lost their self," most of us believe sub-jectively that there is a "real me," a core self that is partially hidden by the facade selves that we erect in different social circumstances. However, that is a view primarily in the Western world. In the West, the analogy for the mind is a peach in which, after you have peeled away the flesh, you find the pit, the core self, at the center. In the Eastern world . . . there is no real self. In the East, the concept of the self is more like an onion. You peel layer and layer away, one after the other, but there is no central core, merely a final layer. How then, in the East, can there be a self? To use an analogy, the self is perhaps more like a river. The water flows along the river and the water in the river is always changing and never the same as it was a moment ago, yet the river exists.[26]

Let us look a bit deeper into what Buddhism has to say about the concept of nonself. *The Encyclopedia of Eastern Philosophy and Religion* has this entry for nonself under the Sanskrit term *anātman:*

> **Anātman** Skt. (Pali, anatta); nonself, nonessentiality; one of the three marks of everything existing. . . . The anātman doctrine is one of the central teachings of Buddhism; it says that no self exists in the sense of a permanent, eternal, integral, and independent substance within an individual existent. Thus the ego in Buddhism is no more than a transitory and changeable—and therefore a suffering-prone—empirical personality.[27]

There are several things to notice here. First, nonself (along with the allied notion of nonessentiality, which disagrees with the essential-ist position of Western philosophers from Plato and Aristotle to Kant, as described earlier) is one of Buddhism's central tenets. Thoughts, ideas, sensations, memories, projections, delusions, and emotions can be seen, felt, and detected, but there is no single consistent self underneath experiencing all of these. Second, for thousands of years, Buddhism has spoken directly about the error of assuming that a human being is comprised of a single self.

Third, the Buddha himself felt the question of whether there is a single self was inherently problematic. Thus:

> Buddha himself, in answer to the question of whether a self exists or not, never put forward a definite position so as not to cause new concepts to arise that would be irrelevant and obstructive for spiritual practice. Thus the teaching of no self is to be understood more as a fruitful pedagogical device than as a philosophical doctrine. Nevertheless in the course of the development of the Buddhist system of thought, this came more and more to be an unequivocal denial of the existence of a self.[28]

For Buddha and Buddhists, then, the question of whether there was a single self was mired in pitfalls and best avoided. The key point was to not end up believing in the reality of one's own single self, as doing so brought attachment and therefore, inevitably, suffering.

Complementing Buddhism's general focus on radical interdependence and the nonself doctrine, certain Tibetan Buddhist cultural rituals also reflect a worldview not bound by the Single Self Assumption. For example, in a video featuring the Dalai Lama and a Tibetan Buddhist official who goes into deep trance and prophesizes about the future, the narrator tell us this:

> Maybe this is the crux of the question of self that is raised by trance possession. If nothing exists with absolute independence, if things are only interdependent, then the whole notion of self changes from some fixed idea into something that is open and elastic, something that ultimately may be only provisional.[29]

NEUROSCIENCE AND BUDDHISM

According to Adam Gopnik, staff writer for *The New Yorker*:

[Vipassana teacher, Joseph Goldstein] believes that Buddhist doctrine and practice anticipate and affirm the "modular" view of the mind favored by much contemporary cognitive science. Instead of there being a single, consistent Cartesian self that monitors the world and makes decisions, we live in a kind of nineties-era Liberia of the mind, populated by warring independent armies implanted by evolution, representing themselves as a unified nation but unable to reconcile their differences, and, as one after another wins a brief battle for the capital, providing only the temporary illusion of control and decision. By accepting that the fixed self is an illusion imprinted by experience and reinforced by appetite, meditation parachutes in a kind of peacekeeping mission that, if it cannot demobilize the armies, lets us see their nature and temporarily disarms their still juvenile soldiers.[30]

The link between Buddhism's view of nonself and the work of some modern neuroscientists has not gone unnoticed. For example, consider Olivia Goldhill's article "You're Not the Same: Neuroscience Backs up the Buddhist Belief that 'The Self' Isn't Constant, but Ever-Changing":

While you may not remember life as a toddler, you most likely believe that your selfhood then—your essential being—was intrinsically the same as it is today. Buddhists, though, suggest that this is just an illusion—a philosophy that's increasingly supported by scientific research.

"Buddhists argue that nothing is constant, everything changes through time, you have a constantly changing stream of consciousness," Evan Thompson, a philosophy of mind professor at the University of British Columbia, tells Quartz. "And from a neuroscience perspective, the brain and body is constantly in flux. There's nothing that corresponds to the sense that there's an unchanging self."

Neuroscience and Buddhism came to these ideas independently, but some scientific researchers have recently started to reference and draw on the Eastern religion in their work and have come to accept theories that were first posited by Buddhist monks thousands of years ago.[31]

Given how well Buddhism and neuroscience blend, we now turn to postmodernism, where the cutting-edge of critical thinking, philosophy, and art frequently and explicitly embrace a healthy selves perspective.

POSTMODERN THINKING: DECONSTRUCTING THE SELF

Postmodernism is hard to define and can be difficult to understand. First, if we are all postmodernists now, what it is, exactly, becomes hard to discern. Second, some technical aspects of postmodernism—such as "deconstructing" narratives and meta-narratives—are complex and hard to follow, just as many of the movement's most important thinkers and writers, including Derrida, Eco, Foucault, Rorty, Lyotard, and Lacan, can be very intellectually demanding. Finally, postmodernism covers so much intellectual territory overall—from literary criticism and philosophy to architecture, painting, and other artistic movements—that it can be hard to see the big picture (or even become aware of all the parts).

Nonetheless, here is a very brief overview. If *modernism* is in part "founded upon the assumption of the autonomous individual as the sole source of meaning and truth," then *postmodernism* is in part founded on "a rejection of the autonomous individual with an emphasis upon anarchic, collective, anonymous experience."[32] The idea of deconstructing—of pulling apart, unpacking, and showing contradictions within—the concept of the single Western self is a recurrent topic among postmodern writers.

An informative overview law review article—"The Multiple Self: Exploring between and beyond Modernity and Postmodernity"—provides a great deal of background detail in philosophy and Buddhist theory. It notes that members of and advocates for oppressed groups—

including women, nonwhites, and those in the LBGTQ community—have made broad use of postmodern theory to help explain, ground, and legitimize their rights and perspectives. For example, the author writes, "Contemporary feminist theorists have made a significant contribution to the rejection of the modern unitary self by asserting that if such a separate and autonomous self exists, it is certainly not the female self."[33]

Consider the following from an abstract for a multi-author article called "Multiple Selves in Postmodern Theory: An Existential Integrative Critique":

> The self has come under considerable attack in postmodern times. Amidst many deconstructions and re-formulations of the self, various myths of self have lost their sustainability. . . . It is proposed that the self is a socially constructed entity which can be conceptualized from a variety of perspectives. . . .
>
> The self maintained a secure, even sacred place throughout the history of Western thought. Despite widespread disagreement about what constituted the self and the essential nature of the self, few questioned its existence. Contemporary times challenged this privileged place of the self. Technology and pluralism brought metaphors of multiple selves. Postmodern analyses quickly followed questioning whether a singular, essential self was a healthy construction. The influence of Eastern thought, in particularly Buddhist philosophy, introduced the ideal of no-self. Cultural analyses provided examples of cultures which did not have a conception of the self. In the end, the necessity of a self conception, so basic to Western psychology, is now in question.[34]

Another online article, "Identity and the Self," lays things out even more clearly, noting that the old modern idea of the self has already pretty much been replaced and that the new postmodern version of who we are is quite different:

> *The modern idea of individuality was replaced long ago. People have more than one way of being, and they have relationships and connec-*

tions with one another. They are also made up of many, often conflicting, parts. As they move in and out of different contexts, cultures, and sets of ideas (and/or between the different parts of themselves), they think differently, and behave differently in relation to others. They know that there are different rules of conduct in different contexts, that they are constructed—and can construct themselves— differently in these different contexts, and . . . perform better in some contexts than in others.

The postmodern person is thus a hybrid. They have, not one core, permanent self, but many selves. Their self—and their identity—are not fixed, but continually in process, as the boundaries between themselves and others, and between the different parts of themselves are negotiated.[35] (Emphasis added.)

Alfred North Whitehead:
Process Philosophy and Constructive Postmodernism

Alfred North Whitehead (1861–1947) was an English mathematician, logician, and philosopher. Moving away from his earlier work in logic and mathematics,* he developed a metaphysical system called "process philosophy," which holds that reality consists of processes rather than physical things.† Process philosophy posits that:

> The world, at its most fundamental level is made up of momentary events of experience rather than enduring material substances. Process philosophy speculates that these momentary events, called "actual occasions" or "actual entities," are essentially self-determining, experiential, and internally related to each other. . . . Actual occasions correspond to electrons and sub-atomic particles, but also to human persons. The human person is a society of billions

---

*This included collaborating with Bertrand Russell on *The Principia Mathematica* (1910–1913), one of the most important books ever written on logic and the foundation of mathematics.

†The pre-Socratic philosopher Heraclitus, famous for his dictum that we can never step into the same river twice, is probably the earliest Western philosopher with a process-theory-compatible perspective.

Fig. 7.8. Alfred North Whitehead

of these occasions (that is, the body), which is organized and coordinated by a single dominant occasion (that is, the mind).[36]

There is also a good deal of resonance between Whitehead's views and Eastern views:

In Eastern traditions, many Taoist and Buddhist doctrines can be classified as "process." For example, the Taoist admonition that one should be spontaneously receptive to the never ending flux of yin and yang emphasizes a process worldview, as do the Buddhist notions of pratyitya-samutpada (the inter-dependent origination of events) and anatma (the denial of a substantial or enduring self).[37]

Whitehead himself "spent far more time considering the dynamics of the individual than he did on the implications of these dynamics for societies of entities."[38] As for the little he did write directly on multiplicity, Whitehead seemed aware that process philosophy helped lay the ground for recognizing a healthy selves worldview: "What needs to be explained is not dissociation of personality but unifying control, by reason of which we not only have unified behavior, which can be observed by others, but also consciousness of a unified experience."[39]G. R. Lucas Jr. quotes Whitehead and sums up his position: "There are, moreover, limits to this unified control that 'indicate dissociation of personality, multiple personalities in successive alternations, and even multiple personalities in joint possession' of a physical location. . . . Whitehead's dissociation of personhood into . . . episodic experience, or Buddhist-like events, thus allows a discussion of many . . . features of identity, fission, and fusion of person-states."[40]

So while Whitehead himself was aware of multiple personalities as a philosopher—but not a psychologist—he did not go very far down these lines. But some of those who followed in his footsteps do take this on. For example, Russell and Suchocki conclude that:

> since the human self in Whitehead is not simply an actual entity, but a society of actual entities, this added complexity introduces a dimension of selfhood that is lost if only the dynamics of an entity are taken into account. . . .
>
> But even this does not sufficiently explore the multiplicity that is necessarily involved in human personhood. It reduces that multiplicity to unity too quickly, as if it did not contribute materially to the complexity of human selfhood. If we take that multiplicity seriously, we must explore the possibility that selfhood is not so easily reduced to the unitary sense of self—and that the unitary sense of experience may be in some sense illusory.[41]

The last statement here—that the unitary self *may* be in some sense illusory—shows the beginnings of an awareness that healthy multiplicity is worthy of serious study.

DIFFERENT WAYS OF SEEING THINGS

The mere fact that so many different types of selves have been considered shows how the idea of more than one self has spread throughout postmodern culture. On top of that, as the summary table on page 226 shows, (1) all of the approaches we have reviewed in this chapter say "no" to the question of whether there is *one* self, and (2) there is little agreement as to whether people have many selves.

Perspective or Approach	Is There One Self?	Are There Many Selves?
Buddhism	No	No
Certain Contemporary Scientific Approaches	No	Yes
Postmodernism: Deconstructing the Self	No	Yes
Postmodernism: Whitehead's Constructive Process Philosophy	No	Maybe
The Healthy Selves Worldview	No	Yes

A Fable about Seeing Things the Way They Are

To better show how the healthy selves worldview relates to the perspectives and approaches discussed in this chapter, we would like to present a fable.

In this fable, you find yourself uncertain about healthy selves because your cultural and religious training still has you worrying that there still might—or must—only be one self in human beings. You are aware that because of this, you have not yet been able to fully see beyond the Single Self Assumption. So, you decide to go for a treatment at the Full Selves Service Vision Clinic.

Doc, the ophthalmologist, sets you down in front of a phoropter (like the one shown in fig. 7.9), which helps determine someone's optimal eyeglasses prescription. Basically, this machine enables one to look through a wide variety of corrective lenses that are rotated in and out, as well as horizontally or vertically flipped, and that can be overlaid on one another, until an optimal prescription is determined.

After nestling your chin into a comfortable position and making sure you are comfortable, Doc says, "Some of the older worldviews you have been looking through seem to have distorted what you are seeing. This is quite common. Fortunately, with the availability of these new conceptual worldview lenses, your condition has become fairly easy to treat."

Doc rotates in the first filter, and suddenly you can see, very

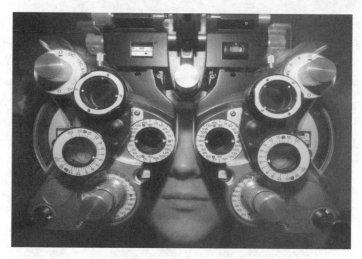

Fig. 7.9. A phoropter helps clarify
prescriptive assessments.

*clearly, that there is not just a single self in you or in others. "Doc,
this is great! What did you do?"*

*"I merely applied a very helpful 'dispelling' lens that comes with
all four of our clear-seeing packages, the Buddhism worldview, the
science worldview, and the two postmodern worldviews. When you look
through this lens, you no longer see what isn't there. Put differently, it
corrects the distortion caused by the Single Self Assumption."*

*"That's amazing, Doc. You are right: I no longer see a single self
anywhere. But still, I can't quite make out if there are actually many
selves in me and in other people. Can you help me with that, too?"*

"Why of course! Let me dial in the many selves corrective lens."

*Doc flips in a new lens, and suddenly you clearly see that there
are many selves, both in you and in other people as well. "Oh wow!
We all have selves! This makes everything clear. Thank you so much.
Are we done?"*

*"Yes," Doc says. "Now you are in alignment with several
cutting-edge scientific approaches, as well as with deconstructive
postmodernism, and possibly process philosophy as well. You are free
to go and see the world more clearly."*

Feeling great, you leave the clinic, ready, willing, and eager, as a first step, to get to know your own selves better.

The next chapter consists of a more detailed look at how selves are constellated in the first place; that is, what they may be made of, where they might come from, what their timeline is, and whether they are real.

SECTION III

· · · · · · · · · ·

Understanding, Acknowledging, and Working with Our Selves

EIGHT

Selves Explanations

Origins, Attributes, and Roles

Fig. 8.1. "I dunno, doc . . . sometimes it feels like there are all these other personalities inside me just waiting to get out." By Dave Blazek, December 4, 2016. Used with permission.

Readers this far in will tend to fall into one of two camps. First, as curious human beings, many of us want to know the facts. We yearn to discover "what is what" at the bottom of things and to determine what—if anything—is known for certain about selves:

- What are selves, really?
- Where do they come from?

- How many are there (usually)?
- Do they manifest in regular patterns?

We have often said that we do not have a formal theory. We do, however, have three premises and a few definitions. But we hold these premises and definitions very lightly, and only within a much larger context. This context includes the wide variety of explanations, facts, surmises, theories, speculations, and other approaches to selves discussed in this chapter.

Into the second camp fall readers who would rather get right to the practical techniques and tools related to working with selves. Fortunately, you do not need to understand more about biophysics or psychology to make immediate use of simple, low-effort, high-return ways to work with your selves. Gaining a deeper understanding of the exact nature and makeup of selves is not necessary to become more aware of the selves in your life.

There may be metaphysical, ontological, psychological, and physiological truths about selves, but for pragmatists those truths are only important or relevant if they have a practical advantage. Trying to determine the underlying truths behind selves can divert our attention away from learning to see and harmonize with those selves.* Despite this, we invite everyone to peruse this chapter. You may just find yourself putting various pieces together in a way that resonates well for you.

You have already been exposed to the ideas of many thinkers, writers, scientists, artists, and cultural makers-of-meaning with regard to what *they* think selves are. Similarly, we have supplied you with many personal stories and practical suggestions. As a result, you no doubt have uncovered or built up your own intuitions, feelings, and ideas about what selves are (and could probably tell us a story or two about the selves in your own life). To help things along, the rest of this chapter presents some possible answers to the following questions:

---

*We understand that some of you might *really* want to first nail down a coherent, comprehensive, and widely accepted theory of selves—but one does not currently exist. Given the many factors involved, and changing feelings, opinions, evidence, and even ways of doing science, it will be a while before a cohesive theory of healthy normal selves coalesces.

- What are selves?
- Where (from what source) do they arise?
- When are selves created?
- What types of selves are there?
- Are selves real?
- Why do we have selves?

As you read through these questions and answers, do your best to feel further into the parts of the various explanations that appeal to you. Which explanations make the most sense to you, and which might be the most useful?

If, for example, you are committed to the scientific notion that consciousness is an epiphenomenon generated from the physical body and its components—then you probably want to focus your understanding on physical-level explanations (such as those relating to the brain). If you are more comfortable with timeline or age-based models (with selves being created by traumatic events, positive events, or both), then perhaps you might want to frame your understanding around a time-driven psychological dynamic. Then again, part of you may be looking for a straightforward philosophical explanation. Or maybe you are more of an artist or spiritual warrior, someone who feels best embodying talented selves or successful archetypes. We suggest you use the constructs and explanatory factors that make the most sense to you.

WHAT'S IN A NAME?

I have come across no less than twenty-five different names for subpersonalities in the literature . . . and this means that if there is safety in numbers, then the idea of subpersonalities is a safe one.

JOHN ROWAN, *SUBPERSONALITIES*

This section presents many of the different names selves have been given over time.

Earlier we asked you to suspend your concerns about the exact terms or names we would use for selves. We did this because terminology changes over time, and many different terms and names have been used in many different contexts. Now, however, we thought you might benefit from seeing a list of many of these different terms and names.

....

Many Names for Selves

- actual entities
- alters
- alter egos
- alternate identities
- alternating personalities
- alter personality
- archetypes
- aspects
- autonomous complex
- characters
- complexes
- crew
- deeper potentials
- disaggregate self-state
- doubles or double personalities
- ego states
- facade selves
- facets
- fragments
- idée fixe
- imagos
- inner crew
- inside people
- inner self helpers
- internal self-state
- introjects
- headmates
- kids
- left brain/right brain
- little minds
- me's
- minds
- multiminds
- multiples
- multitudes
- mindframes
- parts
- part-selves
- personas
- personalities
- phases
- polyphrenia
- plural personalities
- plural selves
- programs
- protectors
- roles
- secondary units
- secret identity
- self-states
- selves
- shoulder angels
- sides
- small minds
- society of entities
- society of minds
- souls
- splits
- subagents
- sub identities
- subs
- sub-personalities
- subselves
- system 1 and system 2
- troops
- variants

....

We are not saying that all of the writers and sources that used these terms meant exactly the same thing. They most certainly did not. However, focusing on what is similar about these terms—the associations they conjure, the circumstances in which they arise, and the stories told using them—can help bring out a common core to which they all refer.

Definitions and assertions that we feel are necessary and self-evident include the following:

- Everyone has selves.
- While some people also have unhealthy or pathological selves, such pathological selves—while certainly needing and deserving specialized attention—provide a poor template and guide for understanding and working with healthy selves.
- Different selves are truly different—with different thoughts, characteristics, desires, and behaviors.
- Selves are autonomous; they can have their own preferences and agendas and can make behavioral choices that are different from or inconsistent with a person's typical or currently desired behavior.
- Pragmatically speaking, treating selves as real and inherently valuable—acknowledging them, appreciating them, and learning to work with them—leads to greater life satisfaction.
- Attempting to shut down, completely ignore, merge, or otherwise eliminate or "kill" particular selves is counterproductive and best avoided.
- Learning to be in the right mind at the right time pays huge real-world dividends.
- Becoming aware of and seeing beyond the Single Self Assumption is beneficial in a number of ways.

SELVES, SELF-STATES, AND RECURRING PHYSIOLOGICAL PATTERNS

Self-states arose from the concept of ego states. Sigmund Freud's associate Paul Federn (1871–1950) "first coined the term 'ego states' to describe personality segments."[1] Later, the term was picked up by Eric Berne, whose 1964 book, *Games People Play,* was previously discussed.

In the 1980s and 1990s, when progressive therapists began writing about multiple personality disorder, some of them, like John and Helen Watkins, picked up on the term and became advocates of ego state therapy, which "uses group and family therapy techniques to resolve conflicts between the various ego states, which in this model are understood to constitute a 'family of self' within a single individual."[2]

The idea of self-states also derives from the work on "altered states of consciousness" first put forth by Arnold Ludwig.[3] It was later developed and popularized by Charles Tart in his 1969 book, *Altered States of Consciousness.* Tart defines a "discrete state of consciousness" as:

> a unique *configuration* or *system* of psychological structures or subsystems. The parts or aspects of the mind that we can distinguish . . . are arranged in a certain kind of pattern or system. The pattern or system is the state of consciousness. A state of consciousness is a dynamic process; aspects of it are constantly changing in their particulars even while the overall pattern remains recognizably the same.[4]

Now we need to add in the body. Over the past few decades there has been an ever-broadening scientific recognition that the mind and body are not separate but instead deeply and ineluctably interconnected. Two examples of this increasing scientific awareness of mind-body interconnection are the widely acknowledged power of the placebo effect (better thought of as the "natural healing process") and studies that suggest that meditation can stop or reverse the shortening of telomeres (the end caps on genes that prevent chromosomes from fraying).[5] Put differently, the mind and body are in effect two sides of the same object or process.

Building on Tart, then, it is necessary to expand the definition of *states of consciousness* to include the body; that is, the chemical, neurological, hormonal, and overall physical situation of the body at any given moment. Tom Roberts does this by replacing *states of consciousness* with *mindbody states.*

Using Tart's definition of *state of consciousness,* mindbody states are overall patterns of cognitive and bodily functioning at any one time. They are composed of body plus mind considered as one unified whole. . . . By replacing *consciousness* with *mindbody,* the cognitive sciences can avoid ambiguity and specify the meanings they are using when they consider overall patterns of mind plus body functioning at any one time.[6]

Having moved from "ego states" and "states of consciousness" to "mindbody states," it is only a short step to substitute the term *self* for *mindbody* and arrive at *self-states.* Thus, in any given moment, our mindbody is constellated as a physiological, neurological, chemical, and hormonal pattern or situation, and a specific self manifests side-by-side with that pattern or situation. Thus, as Thomas Schelling stated, "the human being is not best modeled as a speculative individual but as several alternates according to the contemporary body chemistry."[7]

The last piece we need to bring into our definition is the idea of patterning—that selves are ongoing, long-lived patterns of self-states that recur on a regular basis.*

> **Selves are self-states, and self-states are recurring patterns of mindbody chemistry, energy, perception, and behavior in a human being.**

Philip Bromberg has put forward a "view of mental life as a nonlinear, self-organizing repatterning of self-state configurations that produce shifting representations of 'me.'"[8] Gregg Henriques has also written about the idea of multiple self-states as recurrent patterns of behavior:

Conceiving the "self" as patterns of behavior through time. Although we often think about the self as a "thing," it is also the case that one can think of the self as a pattern of behavior through

---

*The science of complex systems, which is beyond our scope, may shed light on the origins of selves and the nature of transitions from one self (one "attractive basin") to another.[9]

time. In this view, the "I" is synonymous with what I feel, think, and do feel across time. When examined in this light, then the idea that there are multiple self-states becomes clear in the sense that we do very different things across time. This basic insight frees us to think about the self in a much more dynamic way, as opposed to attempting to characterize it as a specific, fixed, and unchanging object.[10] (Emphasis in original.)

Peter Baldwin (employing the term *ego-states*) says something similar:

I propose that personality is invariably composed of multiple ego-states, i.e., personas, each of which represents a full subpersonality. . . . Each one of our selves, each one of our personas, amounts to the personification of a configuration of behavior patterns. Each persona as a pattern of behavior is recognizable and distinguished from other personas in terms of characteristic ways of thinking and performing.[11]

Circling back, is our proposed definition—"Selves are self-states, and self-states are recurring patterns of mindbody chemistry, energy, perception, and behavior in a human being"—sufficient? Selves themselves are not visible or scientifically measurable from the outside. But the recurrent behavior of specific selves is observable and measurable, and a self-state's physiological correlates—body chemistry, neurology, and brain activity as seen in brain scans, blood assays, hormonal levels, and the like)—are material and measurable. Our definition, then, provides at least two ways to assess the reality of selves—behavior and measurable physical correlates. Additional perspectives helpful in making this assessment will be provided throughout this chapter.

FROM WHERE MIGHT SELVES ARISE? MODELS AND METAPHORS

Our next question is "From where do selves arise?" This is not meant geographically, of course, but rather in terms of understanding where, exactly, or from what source, selves originate or arise. Note that when a possible source is listed, this means that selves *might, or possibly could, arise from this source.* Thus, any potential source is just *one of several possible sources* that might give rise to, or otherwise powerfully affect, the formation and existence of, selves.

Note, too, that while the potential sources vary widely from each other—starting in some very different places or realms of being—*they are not necessarily mutually exclusive.* For example, you might simultaneously hold that some selves have a natural or biophysical origin, while some are psychologically based in interactions with other human beings, and others are internally generated from archetypes:

Physical Level: Biological

Starting on the physical level, human beings are composed of both human cells and nonhuman cells.* A recent paper states:

> Psychologists and psychiatrists tend to be little aware that (a) microbes in our brains and guts are capable of altering our behavior; (b) viral DNA that was incorporated into our DNA millions of years ago is implicated in mental disorders; (c) many of us carry the cells of another human in our brains; and (d) under the regulation of viruslike elements, the paternally inherited and maternally inherited copies of some genes compete for domination in the offspring, on whom they have opposite physical and behavioral effects. . . . The overarching message is that we are not unitary individuals but superorganisms, built out of both human and nonhuman elements; it is their interaction that determines who we are.[12]

As for relative numbers, according to the National Institutes of Health, "the human body contains trillions of microorganisms—

---

*Although the focus here is mainly on bacteria and viruses, the human body also harbors or carries yeasts, mites, disease organisms, parasites, and other colonizers. Also, not only do mitochondria and cellular symbiotes possess non-human DNA, but a 2016 study shows that "eight percent of your DNA is alien, in that it's made up of non-human, viral fragments."[13]

outnumbering human cells by 10 to 1. Because of their small size, however, microorganisms make up only about 1 to 3 percent of the body's mass (in a 200-pound adult, that's 2 to 6 pounds of bacteria), but play a vital role in human health."[14] "Is Another Human Living Inside You?"—a BBC story from 2015—gives us some additional background and describes how one bacteria, *Toxoplasma gondii,* can seriously affect the behavior of rats and possibly also humans. Quoted in the article is Peter Kramer, who explains that "humans are not unitary individuals but superorganisms . . . a very large number of different human and non-human individuals are all incessantly struggling inside us for control." The article goes on to state:

> That may sound alarming, but it has long been known that our bodies are really a mishmash of many different organisms. Microbes in your gut can produce neurotransmitters that alter your mood; some scientists have even proposed that the microbes may sway your appetite, so that you crave their favourite food. An infection of a parasite called *Toxoplasma gondii,* meanwhile, might just lead you to your death. . . . The microbe seems to make someone risky, and increases the chance they will suffer from schizophrenia or suicidal depression.[15]

Increasing scientific attention is being paid to the connection between bacteria, our health, and how we think and feel.[16] David Kohn writes that:

> By now, the idea that gut bacteria affects a person's health is not revolutionary. Many people know that these microbes influence digestion, allergies, and metabolism. The trend has become almost commonplace: New books appear regularly detailing precisely which diet will lead to optimum bacterial health.
>
> But these microbes' reach may extend much further, into the human brain. A growing group of researchers around the world are investigating how the microbiome, as this bacterial ecosystem is known, regulates how people think and feel. Scientists have found

evidence that this assemblage—about a thousand different species of bacteria, trillions of cells that together weigh between one and three pounds—could play a crucial role in autism, anxiety, depression, and other disorders.[17]

Recently, as autism has risen globally, speculation that gut bacteria plays a role has increased, and it is thought that "behavioral symptoms of autism and gastrointestinal distress often go hand-in-hand."[18]

Moving to a more macro level, consider the notion that bodily cells and organs are implicated in consciousness. Emanuel Swedenborg, mentioned earlier, felt that cells and organs had a type of consciousness of their own. In Taoist philosophy, "positive and negative emotions are associated with the internal organs. One of the keys to good health is to become aware of the emotional energies that reside in the organs, and to transform the negative emotional energies into positive virtues."[19] Moreover, some bodyworkers report the distinct sense that different organs hold on to emotions. Liam Galleran writes:

> During my time as a body/energy (mind-body-spirit) worker, I became very aware on an energetic and physical level that memories, trauma, and unprocessed emotion can be stored or hidden throughout the body. When these sites on the body are focused on by touch, energy, or through the mind/spirit, the buried experience/emotion will be fully re-experienced to be processed with the assistance of a capable practitioner. So I have personal experiential knowledge that the tissues/nerves/organs do have memory, intelligence, and emotion, and have the capacity to communicate.[20]

Some philosophers and thinkers have directly stated that cells and organs are alive and conscious. A little more than a hundred years ago, Herbert Coryn wrote that:

> Every cell in the body as also every particle of any kind of matter is a life, a centre of conscious Force. Every such point of consciousness is capable of acting upon our human consciousness and of giving

rise to some kind of sensation on some plane. . . . Some of them awake passions; others awake pictures belonging to our own past, and this constitutes memory; some awake pictures of places and scenes belonging to remote areas of time and space; some engender spiritual ideation in our consciousness.[21]

Whether bacteria and microbes affect our moods or can cause dysfunctions like autism, and whether cells or organs are conscious and can impact us, the notions of the "mind in the gut" and the "mind in the heart" have a long history. "We have always expressed love and emotion from the heart and intuition from the gut; hence, the expressions *heartfelt* and *gut feeling*. Research suggests that they may have scientific explanations."[22] As Darin Stevenson puts it:

While your brain is "extremely interesting," your gut is a billionfold older, smarter, and more sophisticated in so many domains that it actually tells your brain what to become in many situations, much of the time. If you observe this process, that is, the feelings in your gut that become forms of brain or mind, you will be extremely surprised at the results.

Don't believe me? Watch what happens in your own gut during illness, intoxication (any form), and especially the "onset" of psychedelic or even dissociative experiences. Feel your gut during the onset of laughter, anger, frustration, arousal, or when feeling love. Feel your gut, and watch how "minds" and maybe even "other persons" just seem to start there.[23]

As for the human heart, there are many phrases and sayings that speak to the heart's ability to know things, like "trust your heart," the seventeenth-century mathematician Blaise Pascal's "the heart has its reasons that the mind will never know," and Noah Benshea's "my heart knows what my mind only thinks it knows."

Consider the scientific basis for the ability of the heart to know things. Recent studies have shown that the heart sends signals to the brain that are not only understood by it but also obeyed. Scientists have discovered neural pathways and mechanisms whereby inputs from the heart to the brain inhibit or facilitate the brain's electrical activity—just as the gut is capable of doing. Thus, both gut and heart-mind help in the thought process.[24]

There are two last possible biological-level sources of selves. The first is our individual genetic constitution. While everyone has selves, it very well may be the case that some people are genetically predisposed to the creation of more or different kinds of selves. Similarly, some of us may just naturally be more consciously in tune with our selves, more open to an awareness of them and thus better able to work with them.

The final potential source is whole body, or organismic, awareness. Sometimes, our bodies just seem to know what to do, even when we do not. Nietzsche wrote, "There is more wisdom in your body than in your deepest philosophy." Perhaps, like the hidden observer (previously described), we all have an organismic awareness that is always on and comes to our aid more often than we know. The experience of fully listening to, relying on, and trusting one's body comes into play in situations such as:

- getting into and sustaining flow states (creative, athletic, musical, sexual, and the like);
- dodging a car at faster-than-thought speed;
- catching something dropped before you are aware you have caught it; and
- heeding bodily signs of danger (feeling of dread, sick to one's stomach), especially in unfamiliar places and on long trips.

Physical Level: Brain Anatomy and the Default Mode Network

In 1874, William Carpenter, in his *Principles of Mental Physiology*, wrote, "Two distinct trains of Mental action are carried on simultaneously, one consciously, the other unconsciously." As Carpenter and many others have since posited, the brain's anatomy is a potential source of selves.

For example, consider the well-known triune brain concept first articulated by Paul MacLean in his book *The Triune Brain in Evolution*

(1990). MacLean laid out the differences between the oldest part of the brain that we share with reptiles (the reptilian complex); the paleo-mammalian complex, or limbic system, that mediates emotions; and the neocortex that is most closely associated with higher human thought and cognition. The reptile-related parts of our brain, according to MacLean, are responsible for species-wide instinctual behaviors like those involved in dominance, territoriality, and aggression.[25] Our paleomammalian complex, or limbic system, handles "the motivation and emotion involved in feeding, reproductive behavior, and parental behavior"; our neocortex is mainly involved in thinking, language, planning, and perception.[26] Marilyn Ferguson further describes MacLean's ideas and relevance:

> These three brains differ in structure, chemistry, and evolution-ary history. As Maclean puts it, we are obliged to look at the world through the eyes of three quite different mentalities. To compli-cate things further, two of the brains, the reptilian and the limbic, appear to lack the power of speech. One of our human biases it to imagine that that which is most recent is best. But the two older brains, although mute, are more conscious than we had imagined. They are very much present.[27]

Since MacLean first published, others have gone further in break-ing down the brain into more levels—for example, saying that the true seat of human language and reason is not just in the frontal lobes but in the prefrontal cortex. Diving into these debates is far beyond our scope. What is important here, however, is that anyone who has ever been triggered or switched into a reptilian level of attack or avoidance,* or anyone who has ever found their emotions positively surging toward another person, child, or a pet, is aware that there is a level of energy and intention that seems to completely bypass the ordinarily available thinking parts of the mind.

---

*A good deal of research and writing has been done on the role of the amygdala—brain structures located within the temporal lobes—in experiencing real-time emotional over-whelm. Daniel Goleman coined the term *amygdala hijack* to describe such intense emo-tional responses.

Another part of brain function beyond ordinary awareness is the default mode or "default mode network." Defined as "a network of interacting brain regions known to have activity highly correlated with each other and distinct from other networks in the brain,"[28] Lewis Mehl-Madrona suggests that the default mode renders "our storying brains . . . capable of generating multiple 'selves.'"[29] He further explains how selves might be generated by the default mode network:

> When we are at rest . . . this network is active; that means our minds are "wandering," or focused on internal cognitions such as remembering stories of our past, creating stories about ourselves in the future, and entertaining stories that show us how other people are thinking and feeling. The default network allows us to use the stories of our past to imagine possibilities that might emerge from our social interactions.[30]

Perhaps, then, the ongoing activity of the default mode network—where we are when our current up-front mind or self is not focused on anything in particular—at least in part represents the neuroanatomical location of where our different selves reside and operate; that is, where they think, feel, remember, and otherwise exist.*

Mehl-Madrona concludes with the following intriguing passage:

> We have internal . . . conversations with the characters or avatars that fill our minds. These imagined characters are mapped from real life people with whom we interact, have interacted, or wish to interact. They can be quite vivid visually, auditorally, and kinesthetically.

---

*Not only does the default mode network run nearly continuously, but conscious focus barely increases the total amount of energy used by the brain. Deep concentration causes the energy consumption in your brain to go up by only about 1 percent. Leonard Mlodinow writes, "No matter what you are doing with your conscious mind, it is your unconscious that dominates your mental activity and therefore uses up most of the energy consumed by the brain. Regardless of whether your conscious mind is idle or engaged, your unconscious mind is hard at work doing the mental equivalent of push-ups, squats, and wind sprints."[31]

We can have such powerful internal experiences that our hearts race and our faces turn red. More importantly, when the medial frontal lobe . . . is damaged, we become a multitude of seemingly separate voices and characters, each struggling to be heard and to achieve primacy over the others. In my experience, *most people can experience this when they reflect on how their minds actually operate, but in ordinary life, we are trained to minimize this dialogue and to view ourselves as autonomous, single selves.*[32] (Emphasis added.)

Intense Events and Interactions with Other People

Selves are often thought to come from—be generated by—interactions with other people and the external world; that is, in contrast with the biological and anatomical sources already discussed, and also in contrast with the internal psychospiritual sources we turn to next, here selves are created when an individual has certain types of real-world experiences, with other people often but not always at the center of the experience.

When the progressive therapists and psychiatrists tackled the burgeoning number of cases of multiple personality disorder in the 1970s, the consensus quickly arose that dissociation was essentially an adaptive response to horrific circumstances—physical abuse, sexual abuse, torture, and so on. In other words, they felt that it was *intense negative interactions with other people* acting as a self-preservation mechanism that gave rise to selves.

For those who assumed that only mentally ill people had selves, and who saw the association between abusive behavior and the creation of selves, the idea that most or all selves are formed in this negative manner made perfect sense. However, it is a very narrow and limited perspective that does not take into account the fact that both happy, joyful times as well as simply new, different, or intense experiences can also foster the appearance or creation of selves.

For example, a few years ago Jordan vacationed in the small town of Cape Charles, Virginia. There he had the opportunity to float in an inner tube, for hours at a time, in the quiet waters of the Chesapeake Bay on two successive warm days. Lazily and contentedly floating about for two or three hours on both occasions, he was brought back to his childhood. As a young boy, he would spend hours and hours many days of each summer playing in the ocean, much of it floating on a canvas raft. So, the particular self Jordan re-experienced coming present on vacation in the Chesapeake Bay was very familiar and certainly the result of happy times.

Similarly, after a bike accident, Jordan stopped riding for nearly three years. The moment he got back on, he was flooded with feelings, memories, and a felt presence of how much he has loved bike riding since his father and sister taught him at age five. Getting back onto the bike instantly transported Jordan back into a part of himself that felt freedom, joy, and a deep-seated satisfaction at being able to quickly and powerfully propel himself through the physical world.

If negative interactions with other people—sexual and physical abuse, physical and emotional torture, and so on—can spur the formation of selves, and if positive ones can do this as well, then what about mixed negative/positive interactions with other people? It seems likely that nearly *any* unique, intense, or prolonged experience with others could also give rise to selves; that is, the hallmark of what generates selves is not necessarily the positivity or negativity associated with an experience but the fact that a different part of who we are is being called to respond and react to the circumstances before us. If so, it may also be that unique, intense, or prolonged experiences where one is not with other people—a solitary vision quest, hiding in a city under bombardment, or being a shut-in—could also give rise to selves.

Interactions with others can also lead to selves in two other previously mentioned ways. First, Lev Vygotsky (discussed in chapter 4) suggests that thinking itself may be dependent upon a child's capacity to internalize and model exterior dialogues with others.

Second, as a more general proposition, to some extent we all model the behavior—from ways of walking and talking to ways of thinking and feeling—of those in our environment. If a child has musical parents and family members and regularly observes the playing of instruments and the singing of songs, then it would not be surprising if a part of that child models this behavior and evolves a strong musical self. The same holds for children whose parents go boating or hunting, or attend concerts or religious services. As humans, we necessarily model those in our environment, and depending on context and circumstances, this can lead to the rise of one or more selves.

Psychospiritual Sources

A proposed source of selves is suggested by those who feel that materialism is an incomplete worldview. For these people, there are trans-ordinary or psychospiritual realms of human existence that may be the very source of meaning in our lives. Whether one thinks in terms of biological instincts or Carl Jung's archetypes, or instead believes in something like the mobile principles, or souls, characteristic of ancient Egyptian religion or the Hmong, we find non-physical, spiritual, or supernatural beings in most cultures, languages, and religious systems. Here, a large cast of inner characters can play a wide variety of inner roles and identities.

- angels
- aliens
- demons/daemons
- ancestors
- reincarnated souls
- essences

- future selves
- past selves
- dream selves
- higher selves
- inner helpers
- teacher selves

Also belonging to the psychospiritually generated category are selves that derive from what might be called our "energy anatomy." For example, some writers have described selves as being related to *chakras*—the seven-fold Eastern system of bodily energy centers—or to *sephirot,* the ten different energy centers, attributes, or emanations rooted in the study of Jewish Kabbalah (as previously discussed). Ray Grasse writes:

Perhaps most individuals might be seen as expressing a complex blend of different chakras simultaneously, with their own unique constellation of inner energies representing the overall state of their personality. Rather than being a static, unchanging pattern, however, this constellation of chakric or sephirotic centers should be viewed as constantly changing in accord with one's varying dynamics of mood or thoughts.

Questions of scientific verifiability aside, what may be most interesting about such systems is their depiction of human nature as essentially *multiple* in nature, as a constellation of different sub-states in relation to one another. Could it be that within these ancient philosophical ideas we are in fact encountering early intuitions into the deeper multiplicity of human personality which modern investigators are now only discovering? . . . For both the modern MPD theorist and the traditional esotericist, healthy personalities could be described as ones in which all of an individual's sub-personalities (or energy centers) have become harmoniously integrated within a balanced whole.[33]

Three Theories
Embracing Multiple Sources of Selves

This section presents three summaries of potential sources of selves, one by Adam Crabtree, one by John Rowan, and then our own.

For Crabtree, who thinks of multiple selves as tools for living in the world, there are four potential sources:

1. *Social multiplicity:* interactive personalities that manifest in daily life and that for the most part enhance functioning
2. *Inner multiplicity:* personalities that are discovered through an inner search process and that may enhance or inhibit functioning
3. *Pathological multiplicity:* personalities that manifest in daily life but that (although they may have been fashioned to aid functioning) for the most part interfere with it
4. *Expressive multiplicity:* personalities formed to give expression to creative drives[34]

As for social multiplicity, Crabtree states, "In many ways a personality-tool of this type corresponds to the 'persona' of Carl Jung's psychology, which he defined as 'the individuals system of adaption to, or the manner he assumes in dealing with, the world.'"[35] Inner multiplicity selves, which may include a "rescuer" or "inner self helper," can arise to handle some inner need or crisis, can be discovered by therapeutic search, can arise from spiritual searching, can be a past-life personality, can be a "hidden observer," or can be a "fictive personality," meaning something made up from the unconscious.[36] As for pathological multiplicity, "this includes everything from momentary manifestations of split-off fragments of the psyche to full-blown multiple personality disorder and the possession syndrome. Split-off fragments or dissociated elements of the unconscious may occasionally break through as personalities or partial personalities."[37]

Crabtree's last category is expressive multiplicity, or "personalities of the creative type, where the function is not so much to respond to expectations from the social environment as to construct a useful vehicle to carry out a personal inner drive to accomplish something."[38] Recall Herschel Walker's successful attempts to construct new specialized selves to handle particular challenges, or some of the previous discussion about the necessity of having different types of selves to be able to survive and thrive in a postmodern world.

Alternatively, for John Rowan there are at least six sources of sub-personalities:

1. The collective unconscious—if Jung is right, this is where the archetypes come from.
2. The cultural unconscious.
3. The personal unconscious—the complex and internal objects described by Jung . . . and others.
4. Conflicts or problems—sometimes the two or more sides of an internal conflict or problem situation may become vivid enough and frequent enough to seem to require an identity each.
5. Roles the way we appear to one group may be quite different from the ways we appear to another, and each role may bring out a different sub-personality.
6. Fantasy images—we may identify with a hero or heroine, or with an admired group, and take on some of their characteristics; perhaps sometimes two or more heroes or heroines may merge. And these fantasy images may come from the past or future, as well as from the present. They may even be constructed to order.[39]

Both Crabtree and Rowan's systems overlap the material presented in this chapter, as summarized in figure 8.2 below. That selves seem to arise from a multitude of different potential sources should not surprise us: just as there is more than one self in each of us, there is likely more than one source from which they arise.

Where Might Selves Originate or Come From?		
Physical Level: Biological & Anatomical	Intense Interactions with Others & World	Internally Psychospiritually Generated

• Bacteria: Humans as Superorganisms
• Organs
• "Mind in the Gut"
• Heart Awareness
• Vertical Brain Structures
• Horizontal Brain Structures
• Overall Genetic Predisposition
• Whole Body Awareness
	• Negative and Traumatic
	• Positive and Joyful
	• Mixed: Negative and Positive
	• Thinking Modeled on Others' Speaking
	• Modeled on Overall Interactions with Others
		• Instincts
		• Archetypes and Autonomous Complexes
		• Reincarnation
		• Incorporeal Entities:
		  • Angels & Demons
		  • Souls
		  • "Teachers"
		  • Higher Selves
		  • Inner Helpers

Fig. 8.2. Where might selves originate or come from?

Different Languages, Different Selves?

Multilingual people often experience themselves as being a different person depending on which of their languages they are speaking. Alice Robb wrote about senior editor Noam Scheiber in the online *New Republic*. "Scheiber—who grew up speaking both Hebrew and English—explains why he stopped speaking only Hebrew to his three-year-old daughter. 'My Hebrew self turns out to be much colder, more earnest, and, let's face it, less articulate,' he writes. 'In English, my natural sensibility is patient and understated. My style in Hebrew was hectoring and prosecutorial.'"

I understand the feeling. My not-so-fluent French self is most comfortable talking about classroom supplies. It's surprising, though, that people who are actually fluent in two languages also feel their personality shifting as they switch between languages. Yet researchers have confirmed this: Between 2001 and 2003, linguists Jean-Marc Dewaele and Aneta Pavlenko asked more than a thousand bilinguals whether they "feel like a different person" when they speak different languages. Nearly two-thirds said they did.[40]

WHEN DO SELVES APPEAR?

Colin Wilson, referring to "Janet's staircase" (which we will come to shortly), has stated, "All of us are made up of a series of 'selves,' each complete and independent. These selves, it would seem, are *already there,* inside the new-born baby, as the caterpillar, the chrysalis and the butterfly are present in the new-born grub."[41] (Emphasis in original.) Instead, if this assumption about all of our selves having always been present within us is not entirely correct, then a whole series of "when" questions present themselves:

"O.K., we're all here. Let's synchronise our inner selves."

Fig. 8.3. "Let's synchronise our inner selves," by BART.
Used with permission of Cartoonstock.com.

- When do selves show up in a person's life?
- When do selves usually first appear?
- What does the many selves timeline look like for most people?
- Is there a time *before which* most people do not experience new or different selves?
- Is there a time *after which* most people do not experience new selves, or the return of earlier selves?

To answer these questions, it makes sense to start by thinking through the previously discussed sources of selves—from whence they might arise. Thus, if biology or brain anatomy turns out to be a significant source of selves, notwithstanding maturational changes that occur over time, most potential biological bases of selves would have had to have been in place from a very early age.

Alternatively, if you consider intense formative interactions with the world and other people—whether negative, positive, or mixed— these are not in place at birth and can play a role at nearly any age. Similarly, internally psychospiritually generated selves—like archetypes or higher selves—can manifest at virtually any point after birth. If we work through Crabtree's above-stated summary of the sources of selves—social, inner, pathological, or expressive—these could all play a role at nearly any point in someone's life.

Saying that some or most of the sources of selves we have already identified can come into play at any age does not, however, mean that there are no patterns as to when selves form. For example, under any of these explanatory frameworks, what we called interactions with the world plays a key role in the timing of selves formation.

If social interactions are key, then those experienced during someone's formative years will play a large role in creating their constellation of selves. Negative developmental challenges and disruption—including disruptions from moving; poverty; school changes; personal illness; death of a parent, sibling, or other family member; and all too often, bullying and abuse of many types—might be easiest to track and would likely tell us a good deal about when, how, and why different selves emerge in individuals.

Of course, not only intense negative experiences but also other intense experiences often play a role, especially for children. Extended family get-togethers, religious gatherings, vacations, summer camp, hiking and camping, watching media together, singing, playing, wrestling, making art together—whatever the day-to-day warp and woof of life is like, within it intense moments and experiences inevitably arise. Any of these might be fertile ground for the formation of new selves.

Time and Again: A Well-Known Metaphor

The element of time also plays a familiar role in most people's perception of who they are now and how they got to be that way, even if they have never thought in terms of multiplicity. Statements like "I am not the same person I used to be" and "I was a very different person when I was younger" are commonplace in literature and ordinary conversation. There is widespread acceptance of the idea that at different stages of our life, we are—or can be (or have needed to become)—different people.

When recounting difficult periods from the past, people sometimes say, "I just had to grow up." Similarly, there is an idea of certain types of experiences "turning boys into men" (like military service), "robbing someone of their childhood" (the child whose parent dies and who has to mature fast to take care of him-/herself or the family), or teaching young adults to "grow up" (getting that first job and apartment). Similarly, many people speak of pivotal events that changed them or helped them become a new, better, or stronger person, or that harmed them and resulted in their becoming a lesser or discouraged person. And anyone who has been through an intense professional, athletic, academic, or other training regimen—especially boot-camp style—understands the dynamics by which new selves can rapidly emerge.

Think back to your childhood or early adulthood. Take ten or fifteen seconds to tune in to any particularly vivid memory you have. If you can remember how you felt then, and then think of yourself today, you may be able to get a firm fix on how you have transitioned and evolved to get to who you are today. Colin Wilson's personal attempt to go back in time and describe the transitions between his various selves is instructive. He recalls:

If I open our family photograph album, I see a picture of me at the age of eighteen months, sitting on my grandfather's shoulders. A later one shows me as an awkward looking ten-year-old, with his head on one side and a hesitant smile. If I try hard, I can remember what *that* Colin Wilson was like, because he had just been given a chemistry set and had started to read science fiction. A few pages later I see myself in an RAF uniform. I can remember *him* all right. I still have a lot of the stuff he wrote. And I can remember how awkward he felt with pretty girls. By reading his work and recalling some of his embarrassments . . . I can just about put myself inside his skin. Was he "me"? No, he certainly wasn't. Am I him? That is harder to get into mental focus; but when I succeed I see that the answer is a qualified yes. He is a bit of me. Not too badly integrated, I hope.[42]

Based on the dimension of time, then, many if not most people understand that they have already experienced a wide variety of selves.

Janet's Staircase

Colin Wilson's chapter "How Many Me's Are There?" in his previously mentioned 1978 book, *Mysteries,* gives us some wonderfully detailed accounts of the early clinical work on multiplicity done by Carl Jung, Morton Prince, and especially, Pierre Janet. Building mainly on Janet's ideas, Wilson develops "Janet's Staircase" as a metaphor for a time-centric selves creation mechanism:

Janet's studies led him to believe that he could distinguish nine distinct levels of consciousness in living creatures. First the reflex level. . . . Finally there comes the "progressive level" [that] Maslow called . . . "self-actualisation," the consciousness striving to evolve. . . . It is a fairly accurate picture of *a hierarchy of levels* in man. Each one, Janet was convinced, is as distinct as a step in a flight of steps. . . .

Think of Janet's "hierarchy of consciousness" as a flight of stairs. You and I and practically everyone we know has had to climb that flight from the time we emerged from the womb; we have all gone through a compressed version of human evolution. What was wrong with [individuals in famous clinical cases] was that they had become arrested; they had *ceased to climb*.[43] (Emphasis in original.)

Colin Wilson then further explains Janet's staircase: selves are like seeds within us, planted at different depths of our lives:

> We can think of a human being as a small garden containing a number of seeds at various depths. If all goes well, and the human being strives for self-actualization, for the realization of his or her potentialities, then the "seeds" awaken one by one, and quietly integrate with those that have already started to germinate. But if the human being becomes severely discouraged and refuses to climb Janet's "staircase," the whole personality becomes static. The seeds start to germinate, put out a few buds, then "freeze."[44]

Janet's staircase, as developed by Wilson, builds around the concept of timely maturation and integration of selves. If a self becomes frustrated— if it ceases to climb to the next level of the developmental staircase hierarchy—then that part of us can later emerge as a distinct self.

WHO'S IN THERE?
TYPES, ROLES, AND NUMBERS

Those who wish to diagram or constellate the big picture of their own personal system of selves will likely get different results by doing so at different times and by using different methods. Still, to get an idea of the different types of selves and the roles they play, it can be useful to review how others have organized selves. Rita Carter, for starters, groups selves into majors, minors, and micros:

> A major is a fully fleshed out character with thoughts, desires, intentions, emotions, ambitions and beliefs. Minors are less complex (though often very strong) personalities which "come out" in particular situations. Micros are the building blocks of personalities— individual responses, thoughts, ideas, habits. . . .

Compatible micros tend to get attached to one another to form minors, which in turn coalesce into majors. . . . Some people have one major and several minors . . . while others have varying numbers of minors. . . . A few have just one almost wholly integrated major. . . .

A major is built up from a dense web of experiences that have bound together over a very long period. . . . Major personalities are more often in evidence than minors—indeed it is the greater range of experience they accumulate by being "on stage" most of the time that makes them major. Because a person's major is the one that other people usually see it tends to be regarded, both by itself and by others, as the person's "real" self.[45]

Early into the process of writing this book, Jordan found Carter's concept of "free-floating micros" useful when working on some of his own habits and patterns. He realized that he could isolate, identify, acknowledge, appreciate, and then learn to work with specific dysfunctional patterns and habits without having to specifically identify the selves involved. His takeaway: even if a troublesome self is seemingly not all that well-formed or long lasting, it is still possible to work wonders by processing what Carter has termed *micros* or *fragments* on a one-off, real-time basis.

Role Call

The *different kinds of roles* that selves may play is a large subject that we have been covering on an ongoing basis throughout this book. Not surprisingly, writers on multiplicity (many focused on pathological multiplicity) have set out their own systems of roles for selves. Thus, Rita Carter follows up on her majors/minors/micros system with a typology of selves in a chapter called "Meet the Family," where she tells us:

Every "family" of personalities is unique, but they are created in brains that are put together in much the same way and from experiences and needs that are pretty much common to us all. Hence each of us tends to have an inner family which has a broadly similar structure. For example, we all have personalities whose main purpose is to protect us. Others can be regarded as "controllers"—there to drive and steer our behavior. . . . We make personalities to deal with particular roles: school, dating, work, parenthood. And most of us carry around old versions of ourselves which once had a use but are now redundant.[46]

Ultimately, Carter proposes the following typology and notes that while most people have one or two personalities from each group, some do not fall into any of the following categories:

- *Defenders:* protect and guard us against threats, both real and imagined
- *Controllers:* drive and steer our behavior
- *Punishers:* controllers or defenders whose energy has become misdirected
- *Role players:* personalities created for a particular situation or purpose
- *Relics:* old minors that no longer have a useful function
- *Creatives:* originate new ideas, aims, visions[47]

Stewart Shapiro, who expanded on Eric Berne's previously discussed work, proposes another typology. John Rowan summarizes Shapiro's selves, and then gives examples of each:

1. *Nurturing parent selves:* protecting parent and guardian angel
2. *Evaluative parent selves:* prosecuting attorney, slave driver, or big shot
3. *Central organizing selves:* executive self, chairman self, or coordinating self
4. *Good, socialized, adapted child subselves:* obedient child self or performer
5. *Natural child selves, creative selves:* the original child or creative self[48]

Another comprehensive role typology is found on the TraumaDissociation.com webpage. Focused on pathological multiplicity, the term *alters* is used throughout for selves. The types of alters from the website are listed on the next page.

- animal alters
- abuser alter
- baby and infant alters
- caretaker/soother
- child alters, littles
- core/original
- dead alter
- demon, demonic, and "evil" alters
- disabled alter
- famous people (introjects)
- fictional characters
- fragment
- gatekeeper alter
- host, presenting part, front person, or fronter
- insiders
- internal self-helper
- introject/copy alter
- manager alter/system
- military and political alters
- opposite-sex alters
- nonhuman alters
- object alter
- persecutor
- protector
- psychotic alter
- robot or machine alter
- sexual alter
- shell
- spirit, ghosts, supernatural beings, and "possession" alters
- sub-parts
- suicidal alter, internal homicide
- teen alters
- twin alters[49]

One type of self regularly appearing in the literature is the Inner Self Helper. Ray Grasse provides the following description:

Of the many kinds of sub-personalities exhibited in MPD cases, one in particular has gained increasing attention for its potentially constructive aspects. Termed the "Inner Self Helper" (or ISH for short) by Ralph Allison, this is a unique form of alter which appears to assess the characteristics of a spiritual, ever transcendent observer. In contrast with most conventional sub-personalities, which usually possess elaborate personal histories and distinct ages, the ISH is frequently ageless, and often serves as a guide to both the MPD individual and the therapist. This has even led to speculation by some researchers that the ISH might be synonymous with the "Higher Self" or "Inner Guru" described in many esoteric traditions.[50]

In addition to the ones just reviewed, other specific systems have set out their own role typologies. We will discuss some of these later.

Number of Selves

How *many* selves do most people have? Each person who conducts this inquiry on themselves (or on someone else) will likely come up with a different number. Moreover, most people will get different results based on *when* they are asking and *what methodology* they are using to separate out and identify their selves.

When multiple personality disorder was regularly being written about by the progressive therapists and psychiatrists in the 1980s and 1990s, the generally accepted rule of thumb—for pathological cases—was that most patients had between two and fifteen alters. In recent years there has been little focus on reporting the number or characteristics of alters in clinical research. Likewise, the number of alters is not mentioned in the DSM-5.[51]

What about the number of selves found in most of us who experience ordinary healthy multiplicity? Depending on what method or system you use, you would likely come up with significantly different answers. The number of selves each of us has is unimportant; what is important is their willingness and ability to acknowledge and cooperate with each other.

Animals Seemingly Have Selves

What about pets and animals generally? Do they have selves? During the writing of this book, your authors have indeed observed their pets as having selves.

For example, Jim's wife, the filmmaker Dorothy Fadiman, in reference to their small dog, Adam, said, "I was thinking of our two Adams . . . one affectionately domesticated bestowing kisses beyond measure, the other a wild growling—and, if not heeded—snarling teeth-bared menace." Jim reflects that since Adam is a rescue dog, his fear/aggression response suggests he was hit—or worse—as a puppy.

Similarly, Jordan's cat Rafiki, also a rescue pet, displays distinctly different behavior patterns—perhaps self-states—sometimes rapidly switching back and forth between different selves. She is:

- a cat who freaks out and runs at the slightest noise or disturbance;
- an incredibly affectionate, relaxed, dive-into-your-lap and sleep-across-your-chest for hours on end sweetheart of a cat;
- a playful, happy hunter who enthusiastically enjoys other cats (wrestling) and cat toys (chasing and reliably fetching!) or exploring the world; and
- a cat who regularly positions himself in sinks to lick a dripping faucet for extended periods of time, even with a full bowl of water nearby.

Some of the possible sources of human selves described earlier might apply to animals. We cannot know if pets and other nonhuman animals have selves, but it is possible and, experientially, seems likely.

HOW REAL ARE SELVES?

We come back now to a question that has been with us since the very beginning: Just how "real" are selves? We will consider four perspectives:

- a behavioral perspective
- a physiological perspective
- a subjective perspective
- a pragmatic perspective

....

Robert Anton Wilson on T. S. Eliot:
They're Real Enough

Jordan Gruber: *Seeming* entities? Are the entities real?

R. A. Wilson: I haven't made up my mind yet.

Jordan: Really?

R. A. Wilson: Well, it's like a famous story about T. S. Eliot. He was on a ship coming back from France to England and as they approached the White Cliffs of Dover somebody said, "They're so beautiful it's hard to believe they're real." And Eliot said, "Oh, they're real enough." A literary critic pointed out that because Eliot said it, we can read it about five different ways—we're so used to ambiguity in his poetry, we attribute it to his ordinary speech. They're real enough compared to us. Were they real *enough*, or were they *real* enough? How real do you have to be to be really real?[52]

The Reality of Selves: A Behavioral Perspective

To the degree that human behavior can be initiated, seen, and experienced by the person doing the behavior, as well as by others, that behavior is real. Near the very beginning of this book we asked a set of questions about whether you could recall a time when you did some surprising things. Ever since, we have been pointing to inconsistent, surprising, and sometimes dysfunctional behavioral instances and patterns that can be readily explained through the recognition that we all have selves.

In this sense, you can see how real your own selves are when you do something that is counter-intentional, especially something that is part of a pattern that you cannot stop. Consider the following incident that Jim wishes he never had to recall:

> I was having breakfast during a conference with a wonderful young man, a medical researcher in a loving marriage, whose life worked very well. However, during the entire breakfast I found myself attacking his psychological training, spiritual beliefs, and ongoing research . . . thank goodness I didn't go after his marriage.
>
> The entire time, part of me was saying, "What on earth is going on?" But the part of me that could see that this was a rude, vicious, and unnecessary set of attacks wasn't in control. And the person who was *doing all those things* happens to have been a nasty, heady being whom I know all too well.
>
> My friendship with the medical researcher recovered and is still ongoing, but it certainly was a shock to recognize how differently this other self of mine was capable of behaving. In fact, until the final draft of this book, I was unwilling to acknowledge that such an unattractive

self was part of my whole being; I even originally wrote this story as if it happened to a friend. Not only is honesty the best policy, but I also feel a bit more complete for having acknowledged this part of me and might not be so surprised and unable to work with it should it arise again.

There are, no doubt, many examples that each of us can think of in our own lives. From struggling with overeating or substance abuse, to speaking out or sending an angry email when we know we should not, to being less patient or kind than we had hoped we would be, almost all of us sometimes act in ways that are contradictory to—and at cross-purposes with—our stated intentions, desired outcomes, and well-being.

Moreover, sometimes our behavior changes simply because *we* have changed internally; that is, we have "changed our minds" and a new self is present. For example, a friend of the authors was staying with Jordan, and at around 9:30 in the morning was asked whether he wanted to go to a Father's Day brunch with some family relatives he did not know that well. "No," he said, "I don't think so. Why would I want to do that?" But an hour later when someone else asked him, without missing a beat, the friend looked up and said, "Sounds good to me."

Having overheard this, a somewhat puzzled Jordan approached him: "I'm surprised that you want to go out now, because when I asked you before, you distinctly said you weren't interested." The friend replied, "Well, when you asked before, I wasn't hungry. When I was asked again, I *was* hungry, and it sounded good."

Change of mind? Change of self? Hunger—or gut bacteria—driving the friend to change which part of him was in charge? There are no simple answers, but the next time you find yourself doing something that surprises you—or that goes against what you think you want to do or said you would do—try feeling into the possibility that beyond a simple, inexplicable anomaly or a mood shift, you have indeed moved into a different self.

The Reality of Selves: A Subjective Perspective

A common assertion is that reality is subjective. Perhaps reality is not *only* subjective, but it seems clear that each of us, in any given self-state, has a unique and personal point of view. As has been noted throughout, while co-consciousness of more than one self does occur, most people experience only one self at a time.

What we invite you to do, then, is to get in touch with the subjectivity of more than one of your own selves, either one you have experienced recently or one from longer ago. Later, even if you cannot remember just what it was like to be in any other particular self, you may still be able to hold on to the feeling that this is indeed what actually happened, and that from inside that self, things looked and felt substantially different.

There are a couple of ways to do this. One is to think back to a time when you "were not yourself" and did something surprising. (Such events are usually easy to remember.) Recall that moment as vividly (and with as many senses) as you can, and see if you can get in touch with what it was like, on the inside, to be that self. Alternatively (and this may be easier for starters), you can pick a happy, exultant moment from your life—from sports to relationships to vacations to making art to whatever you love most—and then dive in to the self that was then present.

Another way, going forward, is to remember to place attention on just how "you" are feeling the next time the self that is up front for you changes. You can do this when an external or internal trigger switches you into an unwelcome, suboptimal, or dysfunctional self, or when you consciously choose to proactively shift yourself ahead of time. As you practice placing attention on what it feels like to be on the inside of different selves, it becomes easier to notice what it feels like as you move from one self to another.

Following is a story of how Jordan became aware of how he had unconsciously switched from one self to another:

Having been called for dinner, I briskly walked out of my downstairs office and in the process switched off the bathroom light. But I hadn't. Instead of turning one light off, I had actually turned a second one on. I knew I had done that—in fact, I quickly looked back and saw I had also left on two other lights, including the big one in my office and one in the hallway. Nonetheless, I continued accelerating my stride so I could bustle up the staircase two at a time and not be late.

Well, in that moment, the other parts of me became aware of the self that knew that—despite my original overall intention—it had actually made things worse by turning on more lights. The other parts of me heard that self chuckling—"look what I'm getting away with!"—and in that moment the rest of me had its own collective insight: "We don't really want to leave all those lights on, do we? Who's in charge here, anyway?"

So I turned around, switched off all the lights, and felt better for it. The working principle I extracted is that if I hear part of me laughing about how I'm getting away with something in real time, that's an excellent opportunity to pause, assess, center . . . and then decide on the best thing to do overall. Perhaps, it could be said that I merely had a "pang of conscience," but that begs the question as to where such pangs come from.

However you do it—either through vividly recalling past self-states or by placing attention on the internally felt dynamics of your selves shifting and switching during everyday life—the experience of your different selves from their perspective, *from inside the subjectivity of each of those selves,* is a compelling indication that they are real.

The Lover Who Leaves, the Partner Who Cheats

Have you ever spent the night with someone for the first time, only to wake up early in the morning and abruptly—even covertly—leave? Or have you ever been the person to whom this has happened?

How can it be that in the night you—or your partner—was totally turned on and fascinated, but by the morning not only has that experience been forgotten, but it also has been replaced by an opposite feeling?

Possible explanations include that hormones and brain chemistry have shifted, sexual charges have been spent, or perhaps there never really was much going on between the two of you. Or, it could be that on the previous night, at least one of you was coming from a very different self.

"Which version of yourself was the one who sabotaged the relationship?"

Fig. 8.4. "Which version of yourself was the one who sabotaged
the relationship?" by Drew Dernavich.
Used with permission of www.CartoonCollections.com.

If you were the one who abruptly left, see if you can go back in time and remember what it felt like when you were smitten. Then compare that to how you feel now. If you were the one who was left, see if you can accept the possibility that both you and the person who left you have different selves, and that by the morning, a self that no longer wished to stay, or that might have even regretted what happened, was now present. Either way it went, see if this perspective allows you to have more acceptance and compassion for what happened.

A related dynamic concerning why people have affairs and otherwise cheat has been observed by Esther Perel, author of *Mating in Captivity* (2007) and *The State of Affairs: Rethinking Infidelity* (2017): "Affairs [can be] a form of self-discovery, a quest for a new (or lost) identity. For these seekers, infidelity is less likely to be a symptom of a problem, and more likely an expansive experience that involves growth, exploration, and transformation. . . . Sometimes when we seek the gaze of another, it's not our partner we are turning away from, but the person we have become. We are not looking for another lover so much as another version of ourselves. . . . So often, the most intoxicating 'other' that people discover in an affair is not a new partner; it's a new self."[53]

The Reality of Selves:
A Physiological Perspective

Something can be said to be real if it actually, objectively, exists in the physical world and can be measured; that is, it has to extend in space-time and be capable of external, objective measurement. Suppose selves are self-states, and self-states each have their own unique combination of bodymind attributes, many of which are measurable. If some of those measurable attributes reliably differ substantially among selves, then, in that sense, different selves would be really, substantially, different.

Remember Timmy who liked orange juice from chapter 1? Most of his selves could not tolerate orange juice, but for the one younger self known as Timmy, there was no problem. As it turns out, there are many reported cases—both controlled scientific studies and real-world, real-time incidents—of individuals manifesting very different physiological parameters in different selves.* These reports include Billy Milligan having control over his adrenaline, Herschel Walker turning off pain, and others, as previously discussed.

Proving the bona fides of any reports or experiments along these lines is beyond our scope, especially because no laboratory research (to our knowledge) has yet been done comparing healthy, normal people in their different self-states. Even though such research has to date only been undertaken looking at pathological cases of multiplicity, ask yourself what it would mean if some of these reports are accurate. Here are three summary analyses or reports to consider:

- *Scientific American:* "Differences among alters can be nothing short of astonishing . . . some [therapeutic] practitioners claim

---

*The 2016 horror movie *Split* is in part based upon this premise, but, as usual, Hollywood magnifies, distorts, and sensationalizes. The movie quickly devolves into a supernatural psychopathic horror story.

that alters can be identified by objective characteristics, including distinct handwriting, voice patterns, eyeglass prescriptions and allergies. Proponents of the idea of multiple personalities have also performed controlled studies of biological differences among alters, revealing that they may differ in respiration rate, brain-wave patterns and skin conductance, the last being an accepted measure of arousal."[54]

- **Adam Crabtree on Billy Milligan and the NIMH:** "From the first identification of the condition called 'dual personality' or 'multiple personality,' there have been those who consider it a deliberate deception on the part of the subject. Even Billy Milligan was thought to be a clever deceiver by some of his caretakers. However, the evidence gathered from clinical work and psychological testing over the last one hundred years only serves to confirm that the phenomenon is genuine. Most recently, research done at the U.S. government's National Institute of Mental Health . . . has provided further proof in that direction."[55]

- **Trauma and Dissociation Focused Website:** "Alters may have . . . psychobiological difference to others, e.g., different vision, medication responses, allergies, plasma glucose levels in diabetic patients, heart rate, blood pressure readings, galvanic skin response, muscle tension, laterality, immune function, EEG readings, etc. [followed by five citations to different sources]. . . . Different alters have shown different results in neuroimaging tests, including functional magnetic resonance imaging activation, and brain activation and regional blood flow and differences in PET scans [followed by citations to two sources]."[56]

There is no question that in different selves we have more or less energy and social drive. We also have more or less ability to concentrate, tolerate hunger or physical discomfort, move into and execute our professional and artistic capacities, and succeed at sustained creative endeavors. It really should not be such a big surprise, then, when even discrete physical measurements differ significantly depending on which of our selves is present.

....

Brain-Wave Patterns as Evidence of Selves

In 1982, *Science News* published a small article on "The Three Brains of Eve: EEG Data," reporting both the work of Frank Putnam and a follow-up study by Collin Pitblado, finding that "each of a multiple's personalities is associated with a distinct pattern of brain waves and suggest, furthermore, that such neurophysiological variability cannot be faked."[57] Perhaps the most detailed subsequent discussions of both Putnam's and Pitblado's research comes from the philosopher Martin Heidegger in his essay "Possession's Many Faces."[58]

....

The Reality of Selves:
A Pragmatic Perspective

From a pragmatic perspective, the world makes more sense if selves are real. If we experience certain recurring bodymind patterns over time, then, pragmatically speaking, this is very useful to acknowledge. For William James, co-founder of the philosophical school of Pragmatism, the test of truth is to first suppose an idea or belief to be true and then ask if that truth makes your life better. As you experience the reality of the selves in your own being, consider whether doing so makes your life work better. As Dan Millman has suggested, ask yourself: "'What would the strongest, bravest, most loving part of my personality do now?' And then do it. Do it with all your heart. And do it now."[59]

WHY DO WE HAVE SELVES?

We have saved the "why" question for last, because in many ways it is the most difficult. "Why" questions often lead to nebulous or hard to assess spiritual answers and may presuppose the existence of "ultimate ends." Despite the research that does exist regarding selves, an ultimate conclusion has not yet been reached, and opinions regarding selves remain split.

Flexible Selfhood

Instead of moving into purely metaphysical territory, we would like to propose three simple answers for why we have selves, any one of which may be sufficient:

1. Selves are an emergent property of our human-animal bodymind biochemistry.
2. Selves are an evolutionarily adaptation and solution to trauma.
3. Selves are a generalized evolutionary adaptation.

First, selves can be seen to be an "emergent property" of our complex human bodyminds. An emergent property is something that you cannot predict based on an object's elements or parts. Thus, water is an emergent property that results from combining hydrogen and oxygen in the right proportions. Life itself is an emergent property of the chemicals that existed on our planet and the circumstances in which they were found. In the same way, we can say that selves, or self-states, naturally and spontaneously arise from the complexity of evolving as the kind of big-brained biological entities we happen to be.

Second, selves can be seen as an evolutionary necessity to handle and take maximum advantage of intense negative interactions with the outside world, especially physical and sexual trauma and abuse. Under this well-known adaptive dissociation view, first seen in the brutal backgrounds of multiple personality disorder cases, the splitting off of different personalities was necessary for psychological and perhaps physical survival; that is, to stay sane and healthy, we have to have the ability to create and move into new selves when necessary.

A third answer takes this adaptive dissociation notion and expands it, so that selves are created during intense interactions with the external world and other people, positive, negative, or mixed, to enable us to take care of the many opportunities and challenges we face. Bromberg, for example, states that "through the creative use of dissociation, the mind selects whichever self-state configuration is most adaptive at a given moment without compromising affective safety."[60] Noricks sums up this overall "why" answer:

Parts appear in our lives naturally, as the results of a universal, developmental process. When we need to adjust to something new in our lives, whether it is something in our own development, such as puberty, or something in our external environment, such as the way we are parented, additional subpersonalities spontaneously appear, enabling us to adjust to our changed situation. Thus as we grow and develop, new parts appear whenever our existing parts cannot easily deal with a new challenge. Parts Psychology holds that subpersonalities are the natural building blocks of the mind, and without their development, we would lack the essential human flexibility that has allowed us to adjust to virtually every social and physical environment our planet has to offer.[61]

We invite you to consider the "why" question on your own. You might be impressed and surprised with what your selves come up with.

NINE

How Selves Cooperate
Metaphors and Models

Imagine that we are each complex and diverse. Imagine all the selves within us as divergent and wondrous species co-existing in a particular ecological niche bearing our own name. Imagine that multiple selves are a natural and healthy phenomenon. . . .

DEENA METZGER, FLYER FOR
"ALL THE VOICES WITHIN US" WORKSHOP

Everyone can learn to increase their ability to communicate with and harmonize with their selves. We have helped enhance your skills in this domain by engaging you in a progressive, step-by-step journey, first as to the reality of selves and then as to the value of working with them.

This chapter is purely pragmatic. We start by reviewing a few subjective written accounts of the experience of selves and then turn to the value of having selves work together. The rest of the chapter lays out a variety of metaphors and models that describe how selves can cooperate and function together. These metaphors and models lay the groundwork for next chapter's specific focus on tools, techniques, and strategies for selves work.

EXPERIENCING SELVES:
A FEW ACCOUNTS

By now, you have been exposed to dozens of examples and written renditions of what the experience of selves is like. Also, you have probably observed the day-to-day behavior of the selves of others as well as subjectively felt and sensed your own selves. Following are a number of illustrative accounts to compare against your own experience.

Please keep in mind that *there is no one right way to experience your selves.* Some of these accounts suggest that having a sense of one's selves is not very different from what most people already experience. For these authors, there is nothing particularly remarkable about noticing that different parts or voices have a say within them. They generally remain unaware of their selves as they move in and out of them.

Alternatively, some accounts emphasize the direct awareness of selves, experienced sequentially. And finally, some people experience co-consciousness as well—the ability or state of being simultaneously conscious of multiple selves and what those selves are saying, feeling, or wanting.

On the "experiencing selves is no big deal" side of things, let us begin with Philip Bromberg, who writes:

> A human being's ability to live a life with both authenticity and self awareness depends on the presence of an ongoing dialectic between separateness and unity of one's self-states, allowing each self to function optimally without foreclosing communication and negotiation between them. When all goes well developmentally, a person is only dimly or momentarily aware of the existence of individual self-states and their respective realities, because each functions as part of a healthy illusion of cohesive personal identity—an overarching cognitive and experiential state felt as "me." Each self-state is a piece of a functional whole, informed by a process of internal negotiation with the realities, values, affects, and perspectives of the others. Despite collisions and even enmity . . . it is unusual for any one self-state to function totally outside of the sense of "me-ness"—that is, without the participation of the other parts of self.[1]

Similarly, Jay Noricks writes that we are generally unaware of how our parts blend together in normal day-to-day life:

> The self is an agglomeration of many selves, and whichever self speaks as the I on any given occasion may be different from the selves or group of selves that speaks as the I on another occasion. . . . Generally, a person is unaware of a part's blending, and whether the person is feeling anger, sadness, joy or some other emotion, the blending is so seamless the person owns the experience entirely. She would say, for example, "I am angry," without any sense that the anger originated with a blended subpersonality.[2]

For Lewis Thomas, alternatively, there is an explicit awareness of his selves, which usually show up in an "orderly schedule," and sometimes they "are all there at once":

> I've had, in my time, more [selves] than I could possibly count or keep track of. [What] keeps me feeling normal, is that mine (ours) have turned up one after the other, on an orderly schedule . . . they have waited turns and emerged on cue ready to take over, sometimes breathless and needling last-minute briefing but nonetheless steady enough to go on. . . .
>
> To be truthful there have been a few times when they were all there at once, like those girls on television, clamoring for attention, whole committees of them. . . . No chairman, ever, certainly not me. At the most, I'm a sort of administrative assistant. There's never an agenda. At the end I bring in the refreshments.[3]

David Quigley goes even further with these insights into his decision-making process:

> Each of us at one time or another has entertained the illusion that he or she is one person, with discrete ideas and feelings, with the ability to make decisions and follow through from a strong sense of inner purpose.

Most of us, however, discover sooner or later that nothing could be further from the truth. When it comes to any major or even minor decision, we have such a raging tangle of inner conflicts of feeling and intention that it's a wonder any decisions *ever* get made! Indeed, usually a decision is made only because one or another of these inner voices happens to take over at a key moment and blurt out its own message, while other aspects of the personality are shoved under. Often this temporarily dominant *Sub-personality* will use manipulative feelings (guilt, fear, anger, greed) to push us into a decision which may be hasty or senseless. Then when other sub-personalities emerge, they are angry at being stuck with a decision which seems to them to have been made by someone else. How many have heard that familiar phrase: "Why would I *do* a thing like that?"[4]

Why *would* you, indeed, how *could* you, if there was only a single you, do things that were counter-intentional and against your best interests? Once again, the simplest answer is that there is not just a single you.

SELVES WORKING TOGETHER

Paul Bloom, in his "First Person Plural" essay in *The Atlantic,* focuses on how a new and improved conception of what "I" means might lead people to greater happiness:

> What's more exciting . . . is the emergence of a different perspective on happiness itself. We used to think that the hard part of the question "How can I be happy?" had to do with nailing down the definition of happy. But it may have more to do with the definition of *I*. Many researchers now believe, to varying degrees, that each of us is a community of competing selves, with the happiness of one often causing the misery of another. This theory might explain certain puzzles of everyday life, such as why addictions and compulsions are so hard to shake off.[5]

Bloom acknowledges the paramount importance of appreciating the reality of the self caught up in addictive and compulsive behavior. He also understands that happiness itself requires that we deal with our own inner community. But what can we do to prevent happiness from turning into a zero-sum game, where in Bloom's concept selves are competing with each other with the happiness of one often causing the misery of another? Perhaps we might instead embrace Donald Capps's idea: "the ultimate goal of the healthy personality is to sustain a sense of camaraderie between the *several selves* that constitute the composite Self or sense of *I*."[6] Can such camaraderie be created and sustained? What processes are involved? Terms for the many ways that selves can work well together include the list below:

- agreeing
- amalgamating
- attuning
- assembling
- banding together
- blending
- building rapport
- coalescing
- cohering
- coming together
- concording
- cooperating
- coordinating
- harmonizing
- huddling
- integrating
- joining forces
- meeting of minds
- melding
- meshing
- optimizing
- orchestrating
- playing well
- pulling together
- symphonizing
- synergizing
- synthesizing
- teaming up
- throwing in with
- working with

When selves experience camaraderie and consistently work well together, the positive pragmatic impact is obvious and potent. Unfortunately, the opposite is also true: consider what happens to a sports team or an orchestra when there is a lack of cooperation, or worse, intentional disruption.

Alternatively, when our selves cooperate with each other, things can go much better. Earlier, we reviewed the general benefits from having selves work well with each other.* There is, however, something more: a self-actualized state of being that comes from having harmonious selves and being committed to selves-conscious work. Peg Boyles writes:

> The most important lesson I have learned in forty years of living is that I am not a unitary person, but rather a motley collection of fairly disconnected selves, each with its own pressing agenda. . . . For me, the fundamental task of life is to track down these various inner selves, observe them, get them to acknowledge one another's presence, establish communication networks among them, assign appropriate work to each, and finally achieve consensus regarding our mutual direction.[7]

For Boyles, selves-conscious work is "the fundamental task of life." And this fundamental task is carried out not just by acknowledging our selves but also by having them acknowledge one another so "mutual direction" can be achieved. As the Cheshire cat said to Alice (and as George Harrison repeated in his song "Any Road"), "If you don't know where you're going, any road will take you there." Not only will selves-conscious work likely help your whole life run better, but it will also help you—as the entirety of who you are—determine what direction to head.

FORGET FORGING
A "SUPER-SELF" CAPTAIN

Rather than framing selves-conscious work positively—as "the fundamental task of life" as Peg Boyles did, or as a significant piece in the

---

*As a quick review, these overall benefits include a world that increasingly makes more sense; greater self (selves) acceptance and appreciation; increased physical and emotional energy; increased skills, talents, and creativity; increased physical healing and pain management abilities; increased ability to limit and work with bad habits and addictions; and better relationships from accepting and appreciating others.

happiness puzzle as Paul Bloom did—Verlaine Crawford focuses on preventing outright *mutiny:*

> An angry word, an accident, any number of events or experiences may trigger a change within us and suddenly the captain is different. Who is this new captain taking control of our lives? There seems to be a battle on board the ship, deep inside, tearing apart our minds and hearts.
>
> Yes, we are captain of our own ships. And the way I see it, these are pirate ships. Each of our crews are made up of the many sub-personalities living with us. And the crew is planning mutiny.
>
> [You can] stop the battle, the war raging within you. . . . By learning more about your many sub-personalities, you can chart a course which satisfies all parts of you.[8]

Crawford's idea here, that it is necessary or essential to find a single "captain," echoes the views of a number of thinkers on—and systems for—working with selves. For example, two systems that we will turn to later, Roberto Assagioli's Psychosynthesis and G. I. Gurdjieff's Fourth Way, ask or even demand that you find, access, or forge a kind of spiritual super-self to be in charge.

Similarly, Peter Baldwin presents the notion of the commanding "vincular self":

> The activity attending to and attempting to manage one's various personas with more or less command is vincular activity. The vinculum, or vincular self, is the persona that arises as leader among equals, absorbed in a very special task/role: the pathfinder, participating in that which is being observed and facilitated. Depending upon its strength, it binds together the various facets of an individual's personality. . . . Leaders who are either excessively permissive or excessively controlling. The ideal calls for a vinculum or meta-self team captain who inspires colorful idiosyncratic initiative by team members capable of playing together.[9]

The possibility of Baldwin's meta-self team captain is an appealing notion. Many people assert that they have a super-self, a Higher Self, or a small, still voice within that directly and personally hears the voice of God, spirit, or some divine being or force.

Sometimes there does seem to be a Higher Self or the equivalent in someone's selves repertoire, but even when such selves come with remarkable abilities or levels of awareness, they are far from infallible or omnipotent. Daniel Keyes tells us early on that Billy Milligan had a twenty-six-year-old super-self known as "the Teacher":

> *The Teacher, 26.* The sum of all twenty-three alter egos fused into one. Taught the others everything they've learned. Brilliant, sensitive, with a fine sense of humor. He says, "I am Billy all in one piece." . . . The Teacher has almost total recall, and his emergence and cooperation made this book possible.[10]

But there is a very telling moment, deep into the book, where facing a certain level of chaos, noise, and uncertainty, the Teacher abdicates "the spot." Overwhelmed and unable to cope, the Teacher completely withdraws as another self takes over.

Another potentially more serious problem with any super-self oriented system is that by elevating a single self in this way, the reality and needs of other selves are likely to be questioned or even ignored. This can sometimes lead to the highly questionable practice of forced merging or integration (death) of selves.

Learning to work with one's own selves and the selves of others is a skill developed over time with patience, practice, and awareness. Imagining a single super-self may be, at best, a distraction, and at worst a movement away from cultivating personal harmony.

An Instructive Struggle with Hierarchy

John Rowan has doubts about a hierarchy of selves with a super-self on top. He says, "There is no particular reason to suppose that a hierarchy is the only way of looking at the matter. . . . My own tentative view is that subpersonalities are for the most part rather poorly organized, as one might expect when they are in such inadequate communication with one another. As they become more connected up, through the process of self-knowledge, they seem to adopt various formations, depending on the person involved, and become more like communes (if the person is of a democratic disposition) or like committees (if the person is more hierarchically inclined)."[11]

He concludes that we really don't know if there is a super-self under it all, and ultimately—pragmatically—it doesn't really matter: "We have left it ambiguous as to whether there is such a thing as the Real Self, or the Higher Self (Transpersonal Self, Greater Self, Deeper Self, Inner Self, Self with a big *S,* and so on). . . . In a way this is not a particularly important issue. There is plenty of work to be done . . . regardless of how we may wish to answer this question."[12]

METAPHORS FOR GROUPS OF SELVES

Rather than thinking of ourselves as unique, discrete individuals, we need to shift to understand ourselves as a complexity of our relationships, memories, culture, inventions, and experiences, moving through time. We need to think of ourselves in a way that is less literal.

LEWIS MEHL-MADRONA, *REMAPPING YOUR MIND,*
CITING PSYCHOLOGIST PAUL ROBERTS

While metaphors can mislead—rarely is one thing *exactly* like another—they also help us see in new ways. By comparing the unfamiliar with the familiar, we gain conceptual comfort and can better see how things function. Not only do the big-picture comparisons facilitated by metaphors offer other perspectives, but in many cases they directly illuminate what is being looked at as well. Since we are interested in how selves can work better with each other, we will turn to some useful and prevalent metaphors for cooperating groups of selves:

- symphonies, orchestras, and bands
- sports teams

- tools in a toolkit
- the braided self
- actors in plays and theater companies
- discussion groups, task groups, and boards of directors
- families and democracies
- flocks and herds
- constellations

Sound Metaphors

Among the most prevalent metaphors addressing healthy multiplicity is the idea of the harmonious, well-coordinated symphony or symphony orchestra. Baldwin writes:

> To be selves-possessed is to be able to be aware of where one is coming from, and to be able to direct the act in the moment, to be able to compose and play. I am woodwind and I am percussion. I am brass and I am strings. I am at times like many musicians warming up their instruments, with an ear for my instrument only, before a concert. A cacophony of sounds, of noise, and not disturbing to my ears as I am at home with my sounds. I know the difference between warm-up and performance. And, when the conductor, who I am as well, directs the attention of the players to the piece we are able to play as many-in-one, we gather into an integrated body of players.[13]

A *New York Times* science reporter discusses the metaphor's solid neurological basis:

> The more you learn about the brain's architecture, the more you recognize that what happens in your head is more like an orchestra than a soloist, with dozens of players contributing to the overall mix. You can hear the symphony as a unified wash of sound, but you can also distinguish the trombones from the timpani, the violins from the cellos.[14]

Progressive therapists and psychiatrists also tuned in to this metaphor. John O. Beahrs, for example, states:

> My favorite metaphor for understanding and working with human behavior is to liken the human mind to a symphony orchestra. Like the overall Self, the orchestra is a complex whole with a personality of its own. . . . Like any multicellular organism or social group, it is composed of many component parts or orchestra members, each with its own sense of identity and unique personality, but all of which function together in a coordinated cooperative endeavor to the advantage not only of the whole, but of all the parts. . . . It is held together and organized by the leadership of an executive, the conductor. Although he makes none of the actual music, the conductor is in charge—at one level a fundamental paradox, at another simple commonsense knowledge available to all of us. . . . It is this collective of all our component parts which I liken to the orchestra, that which actually makes the music of life.[15]

Historical context may be useful here. Up through the early nineteenth century, rather than there being a dedicated conductor, a member of the orchestral ensemble would conduct. Moreover, the idea of a conductorless orchestra is still commonplace, although typically only with smaller-size ensembles. Note how Beahrs struggles with the need for having a conductor when there does not seem to actually be one, which he refers to as a paradox. Celia Ramos reflects further on this paradox: "While the music is made entirely by the composite of its parts, it is held together and organized by the leadership of the conductor. Although this leader makes none of the actual music, the conductor is in charge of tone level, and on another level is being guided to conduct by the music itself."[16]

Ray Grasse similarly struggles with the question of whether a dedicated conductor is necessary. Grasse states, "one could theoretically learn to activate one's inner centers . . . in increasingly complex and interrelated ways, with a degree of skill comparable to that exhibited by a concert pianist drawing melodies from a keyboard."[17]

This exact question—whether we must have a dedicated conductor inside of us if we are in fact constituted of selves and the symphony orchestra metaphor holds—was considered more than two decades ago by Jim in a series of back-and-forth psychology journal letters with Willard B. Frick:

> *Frick's position is that we are an orchestra, of different sounds and skill sets. If so, and it sounds eminently reasonable, then there must a conductor—one who works with every part so that the overall effect is as if a single being with a hundred hands plays the symphony of our lives. One might wonder where the composer fits into this analogy. . . .*
>
> *I no sooner write this than the members of my inner orchestra begin to argue over who is best suited to lead. . . . Worse, some of my more radical elements clamor for a more democratic procedure, like a rotating chairperson's job in an academic department or like geese in flight where the leadership constantly revolves, or like a basketball team where each player is responsible for being aware of all the other players once the ball is in motion.*
>
> *In the world political arena, we see state after state trying to move away from top-down forms of government. In our ideologies we are trying to withdraw from a Patriarchal view of divinity. Yet the argument for a conductor is a seductive one. It is plausible, as Frick avers, that inside our own personal chaos, we still would like to have an elected-for-life leader who knows what is best for all of us. Some of the most fully described multiples aspire for a conductor, but end up discovering that having the right person in the right job at the right time is a more effective, realistic, and elegant alternative.*[18]

We will come back to the "who conducts" question when we consider the notions of "presence" and "returning to center" later in this chapter.

Stepping down in size from a symphony orchestra is the idea of a band, which Dictionary.com defines generally as "a company of persons or, sometimes, animals or things, joined, acting, or functioning together; aggregation; party; troop," and more specifically for our purposes here, as "a group of instrumentalists playing music of a specialized type: rock band; calypso band; mariachi band."[19]

Many bands and other groups of "teamwork artists"* rotate or shift their leadership ongoingly. Jazz bands and ensembles, for instance, are famous for their trading back and forth solos. Or consider the Beatles: while it was usually McCartney or Lennon in the songwriting and singing leads, sometimes George, and on occasion even Ringo, got some of the limelight. Indeed, the case has been made that Ringo was actually indispensable to the group's success.[†]

Moreover, there have been many famous rock bands in which different functions were performed by different members, including the original Pink Floyd, The Rolling Stones, and Fleetwood Mac. An article by John O'Leary—"Who's the Leader of the Band?"—offers some useful insights and perspectives:

> Rock bands do have leaders, but the leadership is rarely: (1) authoritarian; and (2) from just one individual. The creative nature of music just doesn't lend itself to a command-and-control model. And given their defiant individualism, most rock & rollers just won't put up with autocratic leadership.
>
> . . . [M]ost of the best bands have had more than one leader, even at the same time!
>
> Bands often have different leaders for different functions. . . . This matches my own experience from playing in a dozen bands: there were different leaders for different aspects of the job, instead of one all-encompassing leader. One might be the creative director at rehearsals; another might take charge on stage and call out the songs; another might be the technical expert who made decisions on

---

*This term was suggested by musician and aikido student Jeramy Hale, our good friend.
†"The Lennon–McCartney songwriting machine was well oiled by the supple, moody musicality of George Harrison. But so it was by an unerring Starr. In the past two decades, nerdy concentration on precisely who wrote what, and which Beatle was most important, has often occluded a more basic truth: the Beatles were great only because of the greatness of four men composing and playing together. Without Starr in the mix, they would have sounded quite different, and probably not as wonderful."[20]

equipment purchases; another might be the organizational or business leader whose job was to deal with club owners or agents and
distribute the pay.[21]

So, if you think of yourself as being like a rock band, it makes
sense to let the different players—your different selves—do what they
do best. The more you trust your selves, the more different selves can
lead when it is their turn and follow when it is not. There is a strong
resonance here with motivational speaker John C. Maxwell's "Law of
the Niche": "All players have a place where they add the most value.
Essentially, when the right team member is in the right place, everyone
benefits. To be able to put people in their proper places and fully utilize
their talents and maximize potential, you need to know your players
and the team situation."[22]

Finally, let us consider a military combat band, as in a troop, company, or band of brothers. In their 2017 book, *Stealing Fire,* Steven
Kotler and Jamie Wheal state that according to the commander they
interviewed, the real secret to being a SEAL—the one thing above all
else that makes SEAL Team Six function so well in times of great danger and stress—was the ability of the men to merge, act cohesively, and
enter into a type of group flow. They write:

> The Greeks had a word for this merger . . . *ecstasis*—the act of
> "stepping beyond oneself." [The commander] had his own word
> as well. He called it "the switch," the moment they stopped being
> separate men. . . . Plato described ecstasis as an altered state where
> our normal waking consciousness vanishes completely, replaced
> by an intense euphoria and a powerful connection to a great
> intelligence.
>
>   Whatever the description, for the SEALs, once that switch was
> flipped, the experience was unmistakable. Their awareness shifted.
> They stopped acting like individuals, and they started operating
> as one—a single entity, a hive mind. . . . As isolated individuals,
> with fingers on the trigger, someone was bound to twitch. But as a
> team, thinking and moving together? Intelligence got multiplied,

fear divided. The whole wasn't just greater than the sum of its parts; it was smarter and braver too.[23]

The Whole Is Greater

Almost as useful as the symphony/orchestra/band sound metaphor, then, is the metaphor of the team, including but not limited to members of a sports team. Think of the way a football team works. The players have different skills, different body types, different strengths, different levels of activity, and can do different things. The clearer the sense of why they are there and how each can best support the others, the healthier and more successful the team.

Peter Baldwin gives us an idea of why the team metaphor is so valuable, contrasting personas who are out of step with those who act as members of an integrated team:

> Each persona reflects an aspect of one's true self. Each functions to protect and enhance the well-being and potentials of the elemental humanness of each individual. Each in his or her own fashion alerts to peril and opportunity. Unintegrated with the others and acting out willy nilly, the individual is scattered and impulsive. Reactive rather than responsive to every circumstance. When unbridled, when playing loner, personas tend to overplay their errand. . . . In contrast, when integrated together, the personas act like a team composed of different sorts of players so that they enjoy one another's special natures and work well on the field. . . . Every strength is essential.[24]

Similarly, for Gretchen Sliker, sub-personalities ideally function best when each one of them does what it does best. In addition to the teammate metaphor, she raises the toolkit analogy:

> Like the tools of a carpenter's kit, each has its function, and its skills are honored in view of the goal to be attained; one would never use a saw to hammer, or a hammer to saw. Indeed, the highest acts of creativity and productivity necessitate the presence of balance,

developed subpersonalities operating as a single talent or as a team.[25]

Celia Ramos says something very similar in her reference to selves as tools. "The healthy personality is a balanced set of subpersonalities in which each subpersonality is robust and its particular talents fully developed."[26]

Adam Crabtree also provides a rationale for thinking of personalities as tools:

I believe the whole of our social and emotional lives are also centered around the invention and utilization of tools: the tools we call "personalities." And I believe we have a remarkable ability to create these personality-tools as the need arises. What this implies, of course, is that we are all multiple, that we all can and do create various personalities to accomplish life's tasks.[27]

The teammates and tool-in-a-toolkit metaphors resonate nicely with another metaphor: "the braided self." Marilyn Ferguson tells us that "human beings are multiplex—literally, braided from many strands. The idea of a single self may be little more than a useful convention, necessary for the purpose of formal agreements and Rolodex cards."[28] Importantly, just like when teammates work in sync with each other, the different strands of a rope or hair, when woven together, are much stronger than any individual strand. Pamela Cooper-White agrees:

So what does hold each of us together as healthy "multiples"? If we are not, as we once imagined bound by the gravity of an inner core, what keeps us from flying to pieces? What keeps our healthy multiplicity from dissolving into unhealthy splitting, or even fragmentation? . . . There is a thread, or threads, holding together the fabric of our mental lives. . . . Rather than identifying this thread as a singular conscious identity formation, I proposed a metaphor for the multiple self as *braid,* whose strength derives precisely from the interweaving of its disparate conscious and unconscious threads. . . . This web or net of threads, taken together, constitutes a "whole"—

but a whole whose very coherence and binding power is made up of our multiple subjective experiences and states of being-in-relation.[29]

Actors as Selves

Most are familiar with the words of Shakespeare: "All the world's a stage, / And all the men and women merely players; / They have their exits and their entrances, / And one man in his time plays many parts" (*As You Like It,* act II, scene VII, lines 139–42). Even the Bard, it seems, was on to multiplicity. Working backward from "sub-personality" to "personality" to "persona"—a term that often comes up when discussing multiplicity—Adam Crabtree gives us a good starting point for the metaphor of selves as actors:

> The Latin word from which "personality" derives is, of course, "persona." The first and original definition of this term is "a mask worn by actors." Now the interesting thing about the actor's mask of ancient times was that it was used not to conceal, but to reveal. Placed over the face of the actor, if allowed him to put aside his own identity and give expression to the character of the play. For that reason, the second meaning of persona was "a character in a play, a dramatic role," and the third meaning was "the parts played by a person in life."[30]

Peter Baldwin notes that our personas enable us to become all of who we are and to develop fully as human beings: "We can characterize human existence as performance in a world in which everyone is engaged in living theater, in which all the world is a stage. . . . Over the course of our lives, there emerges in each one of us a cast of male and/or female psychodramatic character selves which we call personae, or personas. The manner in which any of us portrays social roles is 'seasoned' by features of one or another of our personas."[31]

For those who study method acting, John Rowan notes that Stanislavski's well-known book, *An Actor Prepares* (1936), can be seen as giving frequent instructions for setting up a sub-personality that mirrors the character to be played. "One of the definitions of Method acting might be, that form of acting which depends upon sub-personalities for its success."[32] The entire theater environment also comes up as a metaphor. Consider what French historian and cultural critic Hippolyte Taine wrote more than a century ago:

> One can . . . compare the mind of a man to a theater of indefinite depth whose apron is very narrow but whose stage becomes larger away from the apron. On this lighted apron there is room for one actor only. He enters, gestures for a moment, and leaves; another arrives, then another, and so on. Among the scenery and on the far-off backstage there are multitudes of obscure forms whom a summons can bring onto the stage . . . and unknown evolutions take place incessantly among this crowd of actors.[33]

Families and Society Metaphors

Groups of selves can also be compared to families or society as a whole. As to the former, Stewart Shapiro writes, "In this model, the person is seen as an inner family, with parents, children, adolescents, adults, etc. The inner family has the usual joys and problems, fights, loves, attachments, tragedies, and common fate of many of our families in modern society."[34] In a sense, just as both individual and group therapy might benefit someone, internal "family therapy" can be very helpful for acknowledging and appreciating our selves.

As for comparisons to groups larger than the family, Peter Baldwin offers a few options for how an inner "town meeting of the mind" can be run:

> Engaging in Self responsibility thus calls for community action. And the "town meeting of the mind" may be conducted acceding to Parliamentary Procedure, the dictates of the mightiest, or the way practiced by Friends [Quakers]. . . . As personas vary in regard to moral development and values perspectives, attention to and effective work within the community of the mind invites patient and careful process, processes rarely implemented effectively by the might of the one or the might of the majority.[35]

Ultimately, we agree with Baldwin that many of the ideals of traditional liberal democracy—such as the unique value and worth of each human being—apply to our selves as well, and that autocratic models of organization simply do not work as well.

Selves as Colleagues

Discussion groups make a good metaphor; that is, talking to and among our selves. Similarly, the idea of listening to—and positively and productively engaging with—our inner voices is, by now, very familiar territory. Shapiro writes that the discussion group model "emphasizes talk, discussion, conversation; i.e., the voices of the subselves."[36]

Similar to the discussion group is the task group, about which Shapiro says, "Here the politics, communications, power, coalitions, and conflicts are stressed . . . there is much attention to objectives or purposes and getting the job done or functioning effectively. This model emphasizes action and behavior of the subselves and effective self-management."[37]

Think back to a time when you successfully sat down with a working group of others to discuss and implement important mutual goals. From family life to sports teams to musical groups to businesses to military units, we all know what it is like when a group is working well together. If a *work group* can be defined as "two or more individuals [or selves] who routinely function like a team, are interdependent in achievement of a common goal, and may or may not work next to one another or in the same department,"[38] then learning how to create ad hoc or long-running work groups within ourselves, for our selves, may prove quite useful.

Flocks, Herds, and Schools

> *If I tell a man to do what he does not want to do, I am no longer chief.*
>
> WANADI, FROM THE MOVIE *EMERALD FOREST* (1985)

Consider how a flock of birds turns all at once, without there being any obvious leader. Have you ever wondered who is calling the shots? Or how leadership changes from one bird to another? Or how a herd of wildebeests knows where to go and how to move? Or how a highly coordinated school of fish swims in and out of a rocky shoal? As a subset of "complex systems behavior," many scientists have studied the leadership of groups of animals.

With the help of multiple high-speed cameras, one scientist explored whether there was really rotating leadership in flocks, or "if a fearless feathered leader" would emerge. Frank Heppner determined that "the flock maintained a state of dynamic equilibrium, with different birds briefly finding themselves at the flock's leading edge at different times."[39]

Scientists working with homing pigeons arrived at similar conclusions. They suggest that there are beneficial evolutionary reasons for having all members of a flock, herd, or school participate in decision making:

> Researchers have found that a flock follows several leaders at any given time in flight. But the flock's leadership can change so that even low-ranking birds sometimes get a chance to command. . . . The leaders weren't always the same, even within a single flight. And sometimes, even the birds at the bottom of the pecking order would lead the flock for brief periods.
>
> The arrangement made each flight more egalitarian, but the researchers think the reason might be more evolutionarily than politically driven. It's possible that this type of group decision making is more accurate or beneficial than others. . . . Perhaps the individuals in the flocks stand a better chance of survival if they sometimes participate in guiding the group rather than constantly submitting to a single leader.[40]

We will return to collective behavior later when we discuss complex systems behavior in terms of center, presence, and "swarm intelligence."

The Constellation of Selves: A Stellar Double Metaphor

The last metaphor to consider is that of the constellation. The stars we see in the pattern of a constellation like the Big Dipper are at vastly different distances from the Earth, and their "proper motions"—the speed and angular direction with which they are actually moving—vary widely.

Like the constellations in the night sky, the constellation of selves in your own particular case might look and feel very different, depending on the technique, system, or theory you are using and which of your selves is observing. Whatever constellation of selves you map out will potentially be valuable to you. However, just like the constellations in the sky, your own personal pattern will essentially be a reflection of how you were looking at things and the inner material you brought to the table at that moment.

Why is this important? Just as the constellations in the sky aren't real in an objective sense, any constellation of selves that you map out will not be fixed. You could have easily named and grouped them differently. However, if we take our stellar metaphor to the next step, we realize that just as the stars behind constellations are themselves very real—hot, powerful, long-lived radiant furnaces converting hydrogen into helium for most of their lives—the selves comprising each human being's constellations of selves—as autonomous, independent, and recurring patterns of mindbody chemistry, energy, perception, and behavior—are also quite real and powerful.

> The constellation of selves never ceases,
> with new patterns and arrangements of who we are
> ever blossoming into existence.

A Final Bit of Advice

About halfway through Michael Murphy's 1977 novel, *Jacob Atabet— A Speculative Fiction,* the following passage appears:

> He went back to the stove and rubbed his hands for warmth.
> "A city," I said. "Yes, it looked like a city. And just before that

there was a sense of something shuttling back and forth behind a curtain. It reminds me of something I've read. . . ."

"Now wait," he broke in. "Don't compare it, to science fiction or fairy tales or anything else. *Try to see what it was.*"

"But it did look like something from science fiction stories. Remember those old Flash Gordon comic strips?"

"It might've *seemed* like that. But don't compare!" He made a blade with his palm, as if he were cutting away anything I brought from the world of ordinary memory. "Don't compare," he said. "Just see it."[41]

The lesson is obvious: each of us, an individual human being, must learn to *see* our selves for who they are, as they are. As interesting, useful, and powerful as they can be, models and metaphors are just maps—not the actual territory—of your selves. Glean what value you can from the metaphors and models presented in this chapter. Visualize your selves as an effective team and give John Maxwell's law of the niche a go, or feel into the possibilities of seamlessly shifting in and out of the right selves at the right time like a well-honed jazz combo, or pick another metaphor. As always, experiment with what works for you.

Metaphors and models will go only so far. As a human being, you are *already* a constellation of selves, and the totality of who you are has already established many working protocols to get you this far through life. If you can see into how and why you—as the collective you—already tick, you can home in on what is already working and simply do more of that. Or, you can consider what might not be working so well and experiment with toning that down a notch or two. All of which brings us to our next chapter on specific tools, techniques, and strategies for selves work.

TEN

Tools, Techniques, and Strategies for Selves Work

Learning the possibilities of the co-existence and co-extension of our inner selves teaches us that conflict, competition, power struggle and territoriality are not the inevitable responses to multiplicity and difference, that we have the opportunity to make surprising alliances with the sometimes fearsome diversity and complexity of ourselves and of contemporary life.

DEENA METZGER, FLYER FOR
"ALL THE VOICES WITHIN US" WORKSHOP

As noted earlier, awareness heals. Simply acknowledging the reality of selves often produces positive benefits. The next proactive and intentional steps take more work but can bring substantial additional benefits. Building on the previous chapter's review of metaphors and models for how selves can cooperate, we now drill down to consider a variety of useful tools, techniques, and strategies.

After gaining an awareness of and accepting the reality of selves, the next stage is learning to appreciate and harmoniously work with—or pull together with—all of our selves. Positive outcomes can occur quickly and easily, or take some effort. Using her previously discussed majors language, Rita Carter frames this issue with the following words:

Acknowledging we are not alone does not itself create responsibility where there was none. Once our personalities realize there are others sharing their mind, however, they can start to get to know each other, explore their strengths and weaknesses, discover what situations bring each of them to life, and allow each its moment in the sun. Majors [strong regularly present selves] can learn to give way on occasion to those who are more retiring, imaginative or patient. Fearful, pessimistic and distrustful personalities might learn to come out only when they are really useful. Over-conscientious majors can agree to give ne'er do wells and shopping queens their lie-ins and indulgences.[1]

Let us now turn to how to create more awareness of, and have better outcomes with, your selves.

FROM ONE TO TWO TO MORE OF YOU

Pierro Ferrucci wrote, "Working on each of our sub-personalities, one by one, is the first, essential step. Later we may become aware of the dynamic interplay between them."[2] We agree with Ferrucci: it is generally good to start simply. You may find it easiest and most effective to begin by identifying and working with just one part of you.

How do you do this? If you consistently place at least some attention on which self you are in, you might notice one or more selves fairly quickly. For example, you may find yourself in another self upon waking up in the morning, or you may come to realize *after* you have been triggered by some intense experience—pleasant or unpleasant—that you have been switched out of the self you were a little while ago. The very first step, then, is to become aware of at least one distinct different self as being present, palpable, and real.

The next step is to acknowledge and work with two parts of who you are at the same time. As Miller Mair writes, "Perhaps it is easiest to introduce the idea of 'self as a community of selves' by referring to the smallest form of community, namely a community of two persons."[3] Fortunately, merely identifying and acknowledging two or more selves often opens up dialogue and communication among them. Pierro Ferrucci states, "Before we work with them, sub-personalities are fairly distinct universes, ignoring or misunderstanding each other. But as soon as awareness penetrates them, their communication tends to increase."[4]

If you want to be even more proactive, at some point it will likely become apparent to you that two parts of you are making themselves known at the same time—two feelings, two trains of thought, two sets of desires in opposition. This can happen with respect to how much to eat or drink, how late to stay up, which movie or TV show to watch, whether you should bring up that difficult conversational topic right now, or in nearly any situation when there are multiple choices, options, and outcomes clearly pulling different parts of you in different directions. Once you have a present sense of these two opposing selves, you can experiment a little bit and bring these parts of yourself into dialogue. This is an opportunity to proactively practice shifting into or out of a different mind as a way of reaching a resolution to the disagreement. Take some breaths, maybe try to see things from both sides, and look for the best decision or compromise.

As for the perceived tension or disagreement, you might learn that there is—or is not—an actual conflict between these two parts of yourselves. And if there is an actual conflict, you may realize that it is perfectly fine that it is that way—on top of it being the way things actually are. Consider Jim's experience with a well-known Japanese-trained teacher of Soto Zen Buddhism:

Kennet Roshi, an early British Zen teacher, was visiting at my home many years ago. We were talking about high spiritual things before dinner, and then she began speaking about how much she hated her brother. Not her "brothers," but her own biological brother. I listened, thinking it was a good opportunity to learn something about how Roshis sometimes behave.

A little while later, without missing a beat, she mentioned that there was nothing on earth that she would not do to help her brother. Kennet Roshi was able to move comfortably between the parts of herself, including parts that were either underdeveloped or in opposition. But when she needed to become the wise teacher, she could become that part of herself in an instant. Also, I learned that it was all right, even for a master teacher, to sometimes feel negatively about one's brother.

Once you have identified two or more selves and experienced their interplay and dynamics, you can introduce more selves into the equation. As you do this, things can rapidly become more complex energetically and emotionally. Since there is no rush—some constellation of your selves will always be in place—it may make sense to adopt a curious and measured approach. Take your time to really feel into how things change as you notice where complexity arises and opportunities for growth appear.

TALKING TO AND WITH OUR SELVES

It is a common error to think that if you talk to yourself, you're ready for a mental institution. The fact is, it's really the other way around. People who never talk to themselves—and who don't know how to talk to themselves—are more likely to have a breakdown. Talking to yourself is a healthy thing to do.

STEWART SHAPIRO, *THE SELVES INSIDE YOU*

Talking to, with, and among our selves has been a central theme of this book, with everyone from philosophers and religious figures to scientists, artists, athletes, and writers engaging in selves dialogue. We saw earlier that there are different ways of talking to or hearing our selves— from the dramatic use of "on the one hand . . . but on the other hand" by Tevye in *Fiddler on the Roof,* to our own subvocal or inner speech, where we are lightly hearing words, thoughts, and conversational streams in some manner somewhere in our heads.

We also learned that nearly everyone talks to themselves. For many people, doing so is a reliable way of staying focused and working through a problem or issue, even if (especially if) no other human being is around. And we saw that different ways of talking to ourselves can be especially effective. For example, Jordan's close friend Andy was the residential college tabletop foosball champion. Whenever the fortunes of Andy's team started faltering, he would start exhorting himself aloud: "You can do better than that, Andy. Come on, let's stay focused. Andy, you're better than that!" Once this self-directed talk started, Andy would inevitably reassert himself and his team would do much better. As discussed earlier, scientific brain scans have shown that using a word other than *I* when talking aloud to ourselves brings newer, more evolved, and less emotionally reactive parts of the brain into play, with better performance typically following.

We are once again circling back to selves talk because it is such an effective, familiar, and readily available tool. Rowan and Cooper explain the key importance of selves dialogue:

> The functionality of self-plurality is fundamentally related to the level of dialogue between the different selves. Where there is a lack of communication, where selves disown each other or where one self dominates to the exclusion of all others, then the result tends toward a cacophony of monologues—a discordant wail which will always be less than the sum of the individual parts. But where selves talk to selves, where there is an acceptance and understanding between the different voices and an appreciation of diversity and difference, then there is the potential for working together and co-operation— an interwoven harmony of voices which may transcend the sum of the parts alone.[5]

The real key here is not talking per se, but *communication*. You might, for example, have a self that does not like to talk much or that is very young or otherwise cannot talk. This self will still be able to communicate in other ways: through body language, nonverbal and subverbal utterances and exclamations, and other ways of expressing or signaling feelings, visceral sensations, or recalled sense memories.

As Carl Jung and others have pointed out, selves that are disowned or shut down will eventually turn against us, one way or another. Recall chapter 5's comment from Hal and Sidra Stone (*Embracing Our Selves*) that in ancient Greece it was believed that the god or goddess you ignored became the one who turned against you and destroyed you. The same dynamic appears in many European fairy tales. The fairy or spirit not invited to a christening or wedding arrives angry and vengeful, cursing the child or the couple. The opposite happens when selves that are talked to or otherwise communicated with feel acknowledged and appreciated. They are generally much more open to harmonizing with other selves, finding appropriate outlets for their energy, and assisting with your overall efforts

Accepting and Taking Counsel from All My Selves

Visual artist Kristina Lazar once shared the following reflection with Jordan.

When I was younger—even in middle and high school—I knew there were a lot of people "in there," a lot of different personalities that came out at different times. I would always think, "This isn't cool. I'm disjointed and unfocused: I have to pick just one." So I'd deem some of them bad or good, passed a lot of judgment on which one I should be, and even practiced squelching some of my inner people more than others.

I felt that way until fairly recently. But as part of learning to be OK with myself, I realized I am all of those inner people. I learned to recognize each of my personalities as their own person, and to value what they could offer and give to me as a whole.

Now it is OK for me to be with my selves. Instead of trying to squelch, hide, or get rid of certain ones, I honor them all for who they are and what they have to say to me. I love whiskey, art, science, sales, working out, fashion, and jewelry, and I love to make things and teach. All of these things and so much more are me. One of these things without the rest is not me. So I've been learning, working with, and sitting with each of them to see how they fit into the multifaceted overall totality of who I am.

What a relief. Now I don't have to stress myself out anymore that I am a bad person for not picking one thing and sticking to it my whole

life. Now they can all talk to each other and they have even become a kind of counsel for me to utilize.

Depending on the situation, I have everybody sit and listen to just the one voice that is talking. I have been doing a lot of healing of my past traumas, and the personality that was most affected had a lot to say about what occurred at that time in my life. I have everybody else just sit there and listen to that one voice and offer either words of comfort and healing, or just acceptance.

But for selves talk or dialogue to be effective, a genuine conversation must occur. This requires acknowledging and accepting that the selves that are involved are real and have valuable things to communicate and perspectives that must be taken seriously. In *The Minds of Billy Milligan* (1981), one of Billy's selves posits this reality argument very explicitly to a treating psychiatrist:

Dr. George explained his approach to Allen [one of Billy's alters] during the therapy session by pointing out that the other patients on the unit became confused when they heard the various names of [Billy's] personalities.

"Some people call themselves Napoleon or Jesus Christ," Allen said.

"But it's different if I and the staff do it—call you Danny one day and Arthur or Ragen or Tommy or Allen another time. I suggest that to the staff and to the patients, all your personalities answer to the name of Billy, while in—"

"They're not 'personalities,' Dr. George. They're people."

"Why do you make the distinction?"

"When you call them personalities, it's as if you don't think they're real."[6]

John Rowan makes the same essential point, that "one must be willing to engage in real dialogue with the subpersonality. We have to be genuinely open and listening."[7] Similarly, Robert A. Johnson, Jungian analyst and popular writer on archetypes, asks us to actively call out and listen to our selves as described here:

One must be willing to say: "Who are you? What do you have to say? I will listen to you. You may have the floor for the entire hour if you want; you may use any language you want. I am here to listen." This requires a formidable realignment of attitude for most of us. If there is something in yourself that you see as a weakness, a defect, a terrible obstruction to a productive life, you nevertheless have to stop approaching that part of yourself as "the bad guy."[8]

Johnson's focus on appreciating each self for what and how they contribute may also be the most effective way to treat someone with an addiction. Instead of excoriating an addicted self, a better first step may be to find a way to acknowledge and even appreciate it. Similarly, when you begin talking to or with any one self, doing so with kindness, gentleness, and an open non-judgmental attitude goes a long way.

If you want to start actively engaging in selves dialogue, one way to begin is to identify some of your selves. Rowan writes, "Each sub-personality is a distinct energy pattern. Each has a distinct facial expression, posture, tone of voice, and each creates a different set of energetic vibrations in its surroundings."[9] He then provides a number of starter questions, listed below, for those wishing to actively engage in selves dialogue.

- What do you look like?
- How old are you?
- What situations bring you out?
- What is your approach to the world?
- What do you want?
- What do you need?
- What have you got to offer?
- Where did you come from?
- What is your basic motive for being there [in the world]?
- What are your blocks to full functioning?
- What helps you to grow?
- How do you relate to men, women, and children?[10]

This kind of structured or organized approach is certainly not for everyone. What is important, though, is that from time to time you slow down enough to feel whichever of your selves is currently most present or most needs to be seen and experienced. Then, you can begin to get comfortable with the reality that this self exists, along with the fact that it is not your only self. In a relaxed setting, asking simple questions, like "What does this self want?" and "What does it offer?" can lead to little informal discussions and optimized ways of doing things that are good for all of you.

NAMING OUR SELVES

Another structured approach—again, certainly not for everyone—is to name some or all of our selves. John Rowan is of two minds about giving the sub-personality a name. He feels that this would be helpful "if we want to go back to it later, and also makes it seem more human and more approachable. Such names can be very variable. For example, one person had these subpersonalities: Galaxy; Mighty Dam; Train; . . . and Bomb. Another had these: Adventurer One; Adventurer Two; Honourable Felicity Flippant-Gregarious; . . . and Miss Crumble."[11] But then he quickly heads in the other direction, telling us that some people just can't work with names—perhaps because such names feel inappropriate, silly, or forced—and concludes that "it is clear that this way of working is not for everyone."[12]

One potential problem with naming is that a name can function as a *negative label* that serves mainly to limit and constrict a self; that is, to make it feel bad and even perpetuate dysfunctional behavior. Jordan, for example, thought he had (but had not) lost a pocketknife and worked through his feelings like this:

As someone who used to lose a lot of things, I had built up a kind of "last minute look around" self so that wherever I am—a coffee shop, hiking, a car—I take one last look before I leave. As a result, I lose many less things, but obviously, I didn't look around before I came home last night.

So, part of me was pretty worried, obsessing even. Then I had a talk with my selves, and let the worried part know that whatever had happened with the knife, it wasn't really its fault.

"Oh no?" the worried part asked. "No," another part of me continued, "and in fact, we know how hard you have been working on not losing things, and if it is anyone's fault, it's some of the rest of us, not you, who is responsible, so you don't need to be so upset and unhappy. In fact, we know how much you care, and you've done great. If anyone lost the knife, it wasn't you, so you really can relax now. Plus, it's only a pocketknife; not only can we get another, we already have another one waiting just in case we need it."

So far, so good, except that when Jordan communicated this story to Jim, he described the worried part as "Larry the Loser." Jim's eyebrows shot up: "What was the name you gave him?" That was all Jim had to say for Jordan to realize that naming can be hurtful, which he does far less now, especially with selves that need work or support.

Avoid naming or labeling parts of your selves in such a way that those parts feel belittled, constricted, or "less than." If a name shows up unbidden, or becomes clear to you, and it is positive, fun, interesting, archetypally resonant, or generally affirming, then you can go ahead and use it, but be very careful of any name or label that, *from the perspective of that self,* would be perceived of as negative or belittling. A similar dynamic applies to labeling some selves as majors and others as minors or fragments, which is recommended by some writers on working with selves (as already discussed). Doing so can impede cooperation with selves so designated, as almost no one likes to be told they are small or unimportant.

TWO MAIN APPROACHES: VOLUNTARY SHIFTING VERSUS WORKING WITH SELVES IN PLACE

The two main approaches to working with selves are quite distinct. The difference between them revolves around a central question: Are you working to make sure that the right self is in place, or are you working with a self that is already firmly in place to change its thoughts, feelings, or behavior?

Voluntary Shifting—Not Triggered Switching

> *Contemporary psychology speaks of the disorders of the self.*
> *In the work we are presenting, we suggest instead that one*
> *of the selves is mismatched from the relationship he, she, or*
> *it is supposed to be managing and needs to be swapped out*
> *for a more appropriate self for the task.*
>
> LEWIS MEHL-MADRONA, *REMAPPING YOUR MIND*

Chapter 3 focused on the importance of being in the right mind at the right time. By shifting or guiding ourselves so that the right self is available and in charge,* our lives are likely to work much better. The opposite happens when we are switched from one self to another—often without our knowledge or awareness—based on an external trigger that far too often brings forward the wrong self for the circumstances.

A trigger is anything that causes you to move from one self to another, especially involuntarily. Colin Ross wrote, "examples of triggers for switching [between selves] include a color, touch, sexual arousal, the need to perform a specific function, the company of certain people, a specific emotion such as fear or anger, looking in the mirror, hearing a baby cry, a phone call from a past abuser, physical pain, having a bath, and a psychotherapy appointment."[13]

For a recovering alcoholic, it can be as simple as being offered a drink. For someone with romantic heartbreak, it might be listening to an old song that triggers a feeling linked to when and where you heard the song. A word or look from someone you know well (or a stranger) can act as a trigger, as can bad or unexpected news. And, of course, various circumstances piling up on top of each other can trigger us from

---

*Different terms have been used for the self that is currently in charge or up front, including "being on stage," "being on the spot," "driving," "fronting," and "being in executive control."

stress, exhaustion, or overwhelm. Nearly anything can serve as a trigger or involuntary switch if it "re-minds" us—is associated with—past experiences, current worries, or future fears, and thereby shifts us into a suboptimal self for that situation.*

The greatest benefits come to us when we learn to both consciously and intentionally practice voluntary shifting *and* when we learn to recognize—or better yet, completely avoid, or at least dampen the effect of—involuntary switches and triggers whenever possible. The late transpersonal psychologist Ralph Metzner spells out how these two dynamics work together; that is, the benefits of avoiding triggers and learning to proactively shift into desired selves:

> If we can identify the transitions or trigger points when the mode of consciousness changes, we can learn to utilize the positive states according to our conscious intention: for example, a musician or other artist might find that a period of meditation facilitates accessing the flow state that heightens creative expression. Perhaps even more important for our well-being, we must learn to navigate out of negative, destructive states: for example, learning to recognize the verbal triggers for an altered stage of rage is an important aspect of anger management in interpersonal relationships.
>
> The transitions between different states are intersection points of different time lines, where we can consciously choose to move along another time line into a more expansive space, pregnant with new possibilities. If we don't choose consciously, then we will be shunted into a different state according to the prevailing winds of karma, or our habitual reactions.[14]

But choosing consciously—voluntarily shifting—takes time and practice to learn. It also requires that we be gentle and kind with our own selves and the selves of others.

---

*Triggers are seen as being at the heart of post-traumatic stress disorder. Someone who is triggered by a traumatic memory moves into the self dominated by those memories, and that self—since it has just re-experienced the traumatic memory, perhaps quite vividly— finds it very difficult to calm down or have another self take its place.

Pierro Ferrucci sums up the advantages of learning to voluntarily shift instead of being unconsciously triggered:

> We need gradually to develop a steering ability to keep ourselves from slipping mechanically into this or that subpersonality. Thus we become able to identify with each part of our being as we wish. We can have more choice. It is the difference between being impotently transported by a roller coaster and, instead, driving a car and being able to choose which way to go and for what purpose to make the journey.[15]

Dialogue, Negotiation, and Healing

Earlier we noted that once the wrong mind has settled in, it often becomes very difficult to dislodge it. Proactive shifting is usually more effective and desirable than trying to get a self in place to change, but that's not always possible.

Instead, sometimes we just have to deal with a situationally negative or dysfunctional self that is already in place. Much of what has already been suggested then applies, from acknowledging and validating the reality of that self in place, to learning how to gently, kindly, and non-judgmentally talk to and dialogue with it. There are three helpful action steps you can take:

1. Talking to
2. Negotiating
3. Working to heal the self already in place

Action step one is talking to a difficult or non-desirable self and finding a way to dialogue with it. As Rowan puts it, "the first step is always, of course, simply to get to know the sub-personality, by getting it to talk and interact."[16] If you simply try to override the self in place, you will likely make things worse, so opening up a communications channel as soon as you can makes great sense. This does not imply that you will be having an internal or external dialogue with whole sentences and carefully constructed arguments. That can happen, but there are many different ways of establishing communication through feeling tones, visualizations, and simply tuning in to the different parts that are involved.

Action step two is negotiation. For example, in a recent letter to someone with a shopping addiction, Jim suggested negotiating with the addicted self to slowly but steadily reduce excessive spending, still allowing the involved self a reasonable amount of new purchases monthly. With Jordan's self who was worried about being labeled "Larry the *Loser*," a discussion about how it was not really that self's fault was helpful. In some cases, when it is clear that there will be a challenging upcoming event, the previously discussed Odysseus Pact, or some other kind of up-front agreement where a challenged self agrees to abide by certain rules or unfailingly do certain things, can be very helpful.

Action step three is to work to heal the self already in place. Healing can take place through dialogue with other selves (similar to the "talking cure" of psychoanalysis pioneered by Janet and then Breuer and Freud, among others), or through the general deployment of proven self-soothing and relaxation techniques. The self in place may have its own favorite ways of calming down, engaging in dialogue, seeing things from more than one perspective, and relaxing into cooperating with the rest of who you are.

Sometimes, however, a self is so disturbed or dysfunctional that an external therapeutic intervention may be required. We have said all along that we all have selves and that recognizing this and committing to work with them is a hallmark of health, rather than illness. However, none of this negates the reality that sometimes individuals have selves that are mentally ill. When Herschel Walker was playing Russian roulette, a deeply disturbed self was in charge that benefited from therapeutic intervention. We will turn to a number of therapeutic interventions when we later discuss the responses and reactions of organized groups and disciplines to the existence of multiplicity.

A word of caution: Working with a self in place—especially directly negotiating with that self, or proposing the first steps toward healing—may necessitate an abrupt, intense confrontation with that self. As Rowan puts it, one way of "approaching the question of change . . . is to challenge the structure or content of a sub-personality directly, by confronting it in some way."[17]

The problem with confrontation, however, is that it can serve to make things worse by locking in the self that is already in place, thereby worsening the situation. Moreover, disowning, acting against, or attempting to directly harm a self can backfire and go terribly wrong, so confrontations should be handled as consciously and carefully as possible.

This is why it makes sense to start with proactive shifting to get the right self into place. If it is too late for that, start first with dialogue and then negotiate with the self that is in place. If, ultimately, only an intense confrontation will suffice, then it may be best if that happens within the kinds of therapeutic milieus we will consider in the next chapter.

COLLECTIVE APPROACHES IN NATURE

Science writer Ed Yong and NPR Talk of the Nation host, Neal Conan discuss swarm intelligence in a 2013 interview:

> **Yong:** "So while the individual fish aren't tracking the darkness . . . just by moving together [they] can unlock this new ability to seek out shade and follow it.
>
> **Conan:** And that suggests that, as a collective, there is an intelligence that does not apply to any of the individuals or even the aggregate of the individuals.
>
> **Yong:** That's exactly right. It's the idea that there is this swarm intelligence, this ability to make decisions, to carry out computations that exists only at the level of the group. The individual fish don't have it. They can't—they fundamentally cannot do this thing that the group of them can manage.
>
> **Conan:** And there are, of course, other things that can form swarms, including human beings.[18]

There is another approach that, over time, may help you to both seamlessly shift selves and work better with selves in place. This approach begins with some ideas and possibilities about how we can, as biological organisms and living animals, work with our selves on the collective level. Once we recognize that we are a collection—a complex system or community of selves—we can better access the intelligence of the whole of who we are.

For example, earlier we spoke about how music in certain types of situations seems, in effect, to begin to play itself, even without a discernable permanent leader. Also many types of animals have ways of optimally engaging in vital types of behaviors without requiring or benefiting from having a single leader. One way to describe this is "swarm intelligence," which is applicable to the behavior of insect colonies, animal herds, schools of fish, bird flocks, and even human communities. "Serving as an advantage to the whole community and to the individuals that make up the whole, swarm intelligence is a different order of thinking. . . . Like any intelligence, conscious choices are involved. But swarm intelligence is emergent, with choices distributed across the actions of multiple agents."[19]

Kevin Kelly further describes the swarm model:

We find many systems ordered as a patchwork of parallel operations, very much as in the neural network of a brain or in a colony of ants. Action in these systems proceeds in a messy cascade of interdependent events. Instead of the discrete ticks of cause and effect that run a clock, a thousand clock springs try to simultaneously run a parallel system. Since there is no chain of command, the particular action of any single spring diffuses into the whole, making it easier for the sum of the whole to overwhelm the parts of the whole. What emerges from the collective is not a series of critical individual actions but a multitude of simultaneous actions whose collective pattern is far more important. This is the swarm model.[20]

Paul Miller adds that "a single ant or bee isn't smart, but their colonies are."[21] When the complex system we are trying to manage is our own set of selves—or the selves of others—the swarm model provides a few key insights:

1. No single individual is or can be in charge of everything we do. *Truly effective leadership must rotate,* in part because no single self knows everything or contains all of our capacities.
2. Each of our selves has something valuable to contribute to our collective intelligence and ability to make wise choices.
3. Whatever our collective intelligence looks like, it will belong to the entirety of who we are, not to any individual self or subset of selves. If we want to be as smart, effective, and happy as possible, it seems that we are going to need to take all of our selves—and the collective wisdom and behavioral capacities generated from them at a meta-level—seriously.

What does this emergent process look like? One model involves establishing or returning to a kind of place within us that we can think of as "center." Center is not a self; as Gretchen Sliker writes, "center is the executive branch of the psyche; it is never a subpersonality."[22] Instead, it is more like the ground or space within, where selves stand and gather. When we return to or touch into center, it becomes easier to work with all of our selves and, given our real-time context and needs, to shift into the right mind or out of the wrong one. As Erica Ariel Fox of the Harvard Negotiation project writes:

> The key to a good outcome, whether around a conference room table or the dining room table, is to undertake a negotiation within ourselves . . . ultimately the ability to achieve mastery over how we lead and live with each other comes from a place within, what I call "center of well-being," or our "center." When we anchor ourselves in our center, we are mindfully aware of our reactions and choices. The actions we then take produce better results, stronger relationships, and more of life's deeper rewards.[23]

Going further, orthomuscular therapist Liz Elms makes the critical point that when we are in center, we can choose which self to use, rather than finding ourselves being used by a particular—and situationally less than ideal—self. John Rowan makes much the same point: "My hypothesis would be that different leaders would be able to come forward at different times, in quite a healthy way—the person would be able to use the subpersonalities, rather than being used by them."[24]

Liz Elms also noted, conversely, that when we are doing something—anything—that is hurtful or detrimental to the body (which can be as simple as sitting slumped over or overeating, or as detrimental as self-mutilation or alcohol/drug abuse), then that is a clear sign of *not* being in center. While many of our selves do not necessarily care that much about what is happening with our bodies, when we are in center, we will always find our selves taking care of our bodies.

Gretchen Sliker, in her book *Multiple Mind* (1992), further develops the notion of "Center" and "Centering." She tells us that when she begins working with a client's sub-personalities, the client is asked to learn to take a step back and observe all of their parts from a space called "Center." She feels that learning this skill "is important in the development of subpersonalities. Moving back and forth between the subpersonalities and Center, using Center as an observation point, results in the skill to instantly recognize characteristic subpersonality behavior patterns. Recognition initiates modification. Appraisal is inevitably followed by choice for change."[25]

Sliker then further elaborates the critical importance of center:

> Ideally, individuals initiate all life function from Center, which is immediate, focused on the present, and uncluttered by past history and future anticipation. From Center the world is perceived accurately. The healthy psyche is "managed" by a well-developed Center, and it is from Center, the director's chair, so to speak, that the appropriate subpersonality to act in a situation is selected. The transformed subpersonalities are the well-polished tools that bring about effective action.[26]

Pierro Ferrucci, whom Sliker approvingly quotes, says much the same thing of the center, where "we can get into this subpersonality or that, we can regulate them, correct them, care for them. The knack to be learned is flexibility, so as not to be dominated by our subpersonalities, not to suffocate their expression and ignore their needs—in other words, to have a sense of compassionate, playful mastery."[27]

A final metaphor that may be helpful here is the notion of presence. *Presence* can be defined as "a noteworthy quality of poise and effectiveness."[28] Like center, presence is not a self or sub-personality. But unlike center—which connotes a distinct place or space, albeit an internal, psychological, or energetic one—presence implies a wise essence or quality of being.* Cultivating presence and learning to move to and act from center are distinct but positively reinforcing dynamics. Ongoing practice focused on becoming increasingly selves aware seems to develop both.

ADDITIONAL TECHNIQUES AND STRATEGIES FOR WORKING WITH SELVES (ALPHABETICALLY)

In addition to the various approaches outlined above, there are many other ways to work with selves. For example, earlier in the book we presented a list of "Some Ways of Shifting" (p. 65).

Alphabetically listed, following are more techniques and strategies for you to try.

Act as If—The idea of "act as if," or "fake it until you make it," is well known in pop psychology and law of attraction circles. Simply, if you act as if a specific self has been proactively shifted into or away from, it becomes much more likely that will indeed happen, especially if you make use of multiple sensory modalities; that is, if you are hoping for a specific self to be present and in charge, do what you can to pretend you are *already* in that self, such as talking, walking, or gesturing with your hands the way that self does, or even using your senses (sights, smell, and so on) the way that self typically does. Similarly, you can consciously start acting in ways that are unlike the self you hope to move away from.

---

*One current coaching model includes: (1) parts (or selves); (2) process (how selves interact and do things); (3) center (a neutral place to operate from); and (4) presence (the feeling or quality that builds in center).[29] A fifth "nondual" element is sometimes added.

Active Imagination—Active imagination, "a cognitive methodology that uses the imagination as an organ of understanding," was originally used by various Western esoteric traditions and then developed by Carl Jung as "a meditation technique wherein the contents of one's unconscious are translated into images, narrative or personified as separate entities."[30] As Mary Watkins notes, "The Jungian practice of active imagination is another means to enter into the imaginal realm and engage in dialogue between parts of the self, for the self and others, or to observe dialogue between multiple others."[31]

Allies with which to Collaborate—Consider developing allies among your selves. Recall our friend who successfully scolds police officers in real time. Peter Baldwin frames this from a therapeutic perspective where a front, head-on assault on a self or its behavior is likely to trigger defensive resistance. To get around this, we can work with another cooperative one of our selves to communicate with a troubled one. As Baldwin puts it, "personas vary in their collaborative and trusting responsiveness to the therapist's ideas. Hence, one does well to engage the persona or personas least uneasy in regard to a particular issue" as a way of supporting and aiding less comfortable or cooperative selves in dealing with problems.[32]

Alternative Plans Practiced and at the Ready—Earlier we discussed Odysseus Pacts: making an agreement with a part or parts of yourself that no matter what happens or how things are going, *this* is what you—as a whole—are going to do in *this* potential future circumstance, no matter what any one part of you says or asserts later. These agreements, and other kinds of alternative plans that require voluntary shifting, are much more likely to succeed if you mentally rehearse and practice the necessary shifts ahead of time.

One approach is to feel into the self or constellation of selves that you will have had to have shifted into so as to have successfully carried through the plan you had practiced. This brings us right back to "Act as If": imagine and experience what it will be like from the perspective of that self, and how happy and satisfied you will feel when you succeed.

For example, consider an emergency fire rescue team that has every member mentally rehearse likely eventualities ahead of time so that it can unhesitatingly plunge into extreme danger. Or, if you always defer to your boss but *this* time you really need to speak up, do your best to feel into and experience what it will feel like when the brave part of you steps in. Doing so makes it a lot more likely that you will actually be able to advocate on your own behalf. If you know that when you are running late your impatient driver emerges, imagine how much better off you will be if you keep the patient, wiser part of yourself literally in the driver's seat. The more you practice, the more control you will have, and the happier you will be.

Anonymous Microshifting—Proactively shifting into the right self at the right time or away from the wrong self at the wrong time does not have to be a formal big deal. You can make small shifts—microshifts—without knowing which selves are involved, or without putting too much elaborate conscious thought into it. Essentially, you can begin to intuit what would benefit the totality of who you are and gently edge yourself in the right direction, without having to think very much about it or stop the rest of what you are doing. (*See also* **Dynamic Subordination.**)

Becoming Aware of Others' Selves First—If acknowledging the reality of your own selves initially proves difficult for you, then first bring your attention to others and see whether their behavior makes sense in terms of them having selves. If the idea of others having selves proves to be a useful and valuable way of seeing things, then you can go ahead and turn your observational efforts in your own direction.

Couples Selves Retreat—We know of a couple, Sally and Albert, who have very busy ordinary lives, except when they "go upstairs together." Following is Sally's account:

> *Albert and I have a weekly ritual. We clear an afternoon, light a candle, and go upstairs. Whatever chaos, demands, pettiness, or irritations have built up in us immediately dissipate, and what's left is the best of both of us. Within minutes we become smarter, funnier, sexier, and infinitely more interesting than the two bores we left downstairs. They pay the rent, make the money, and pick up the*

kids from school on time. They put our money in IRAs and health insurance every year. But let's face it, under normal circumstances, they are basically only slightly above average, dull-but-well-meaning, middle-aged white folks.

We appreciate all they do to keep it together for us, but more and more, we're trying to come out. It's true, the upstairs Sal and Al are slobs. We eat a lot, make messes for the others to clean up, and cancel appointments we really should keep. But it was the upstairs Sal and Al who came up with our first big success, with all its warmth and wit, and who were the ones who decided to write it in the first place. The downstairs couple would never have quit their day jobs and gone for it. Our goal is to let our brightest selves inform our straight selves so that the door separating us from each other can open and stay open.[33]

Dis-Identification: Having versus Being a Bad Dog—Even if one or more of your selves is bad or dysfunctional, always keep in mind that is not all of who you are. Even when such a self is up front—even if it is acting out—it is crucial to keep some distance and not over-identify with it. According to Howard Sasportas:

Diana Whitmore uses this analogy to explain the difference between being a subpersonality and *having* a subpersonality. She says that if you are a dog that bites, then you bite. But if you have a dog that bites, then you can choose to let it bite, or choose to put a muzzle on the dog, or teach it not to bite. If you are totally identified with a subpersonality, then you just act it out. But if you realize a subpersonality is something you have operating in you, then you can do something to change, alter or transform it.[34]

Elizabeth O'Connor elsewhere offers a similar example concerning a jealous self:

If I say, "I am jealous," it describes the whole of me, and I am overwhelmed by its implications. The completeness of the statement makes me feel contemptuous of myself. . . . But suppose that each of us understood the multiplicity of his life. What if it were such common knowledge that only an ignorant person would ever be heard to say, "Well, if he is that way, I want nothing to do with him," as though the "way" of a person could be known just because one of his selves was glimpsed for a moment. If I respect the plurality in myself, and no longer see my jealous self as the whole of me, then I have gained the distance I need to observe it, listen to it, and let it acquaint me with a piece of my own lost history.[35]

Dynamic Subordination—As discussed in the previous chapter, Navy SEALs learn to rapidly shift leadership back and forth among whichever member of the group is best suited to lead in that moment. A protocol called "dynamic subordination" is used, "where leadership is fluid and defined by conditions on the ground [and] is the foundation of accessing the performance gains of group flow."[36] According to one Navy commander:

> When SEALs sweep a building . . . slow is dangerous. We want to move as fast as possible. To do this, there are only two rules. The first is do the exact opposite of what the guy in front of you is doing—so if he looks left, then you look right. The second is trickier: the person who knows what to do next is the leader. We're entirely non-hierarchical in that way. But in a combat environment, when split-seconds make all the difference, there's no time for second-guessing. When someone steps up to become the new leader, everyone, immediately, automatically, moves with him. It's the only way we win.[37]

Modeling on Navy SEALs, we can begin to practice dynamic subordination with our own selves. By doing so, not only will we become better at freely trading or passing off leadership to the part of who we are that makes most sense in the moment, but over time this interaction style can become a well-practiced and effective personal protocol.

Fully Embrace Each Self to Get Back Gratitude, Nourishment, Cooperation—Squelching your selves does not work well; eventually, their energy always comes out in dysfunctional ways. The alternative is to consciously, fully, embrace one self at a time. Let your artist create for as long as it (reasonably) wants; let your drummer drum and your dancer dance to exhaustion; let your TV-binger watch the entirety of *Game of Thrones* in a weekend; treat your overeater to an occasional multi-course buffet. When you fully embrace any one self—as long as it is not too destructive or dysfunctional—that self becomes satisfied, happier, and more able to fully cooperate with other selves going forward. Most of us have one or more parts that we rarely let out; when we do allow those selves to be present, they are grateful, energized, and better team players.

Loving Them into the Whole—Kintla Striker, a yoga teacher and speaker who works with her local criminal justice system to assist trauma victims, helps her clients practice a simple but powerful technique. She explains:

> One aspect of my work is giving clients the space to notice their parts, recognize them, begin to have a conversation with them, and ultimately, to "love them into the whole." If a part of a client is stuck in anxiety or panic, they can begin to recognize that part and then start a conversation such as, "I hear you, would you like to say more?" or "I feel you; how about we do a breathing exercise together?" But they can't always just scoop up all their parts and love them into the whole right away, because other selves may not like them or sometimes will even hate them. While it can be a very slow process, in the long run, it is a very powerful one. Compassion from another human being while on this journey is imperative.[38]

Requesting Cooperation Politely and Simply—A self-help (selves-help) pamphlet by "Willow, for all the folks, the Team, & the Little Ones" provides some good ideas and testable advice:

> When I have insomnia, I say inside: "OK. I need to go to sleep now. Could those who want to stay awake, go somewhere else now? . . .

Great! I'm sleepy now. Thank you! Thank you! Thank you!" . . . *When I can't see clearly: "I need those who can see through these glasses . . . Thank you! Thank you! Thank you! That's great!" Any time: "Those who don't want to be here, if I don't need you, you can go somewhere else."*

Before we developed this way to cooperate, I had thought I could never develop any system management until I identified who was who. . . . Now we have a great system of cooperation going! Requesting, not dictatorship. They can make the decision whether to cooperate or not. Here is how I/We do it:

Always thank them as soon as I can.

I don't ever ask any "who?" questions, because that scares them. I say, "Those who . . ."—Those who can drive, those who know how to use the computer, those who remember about this, etc. They know who they are, and they make the decisions.

I always word the request in the positive—without using not or don't or any negative words, because they get confused by negative words.

I ask for them to come (or tell them they can leave) right at the time they are needed, not an hour ahead or a day ahead, because they don't understand anything except present.

I tell them how long I need them by telling them "as long as the body" or "until the body" statements.[39]

Seeing Your Selves through the Eyes of Others—Endeavor to see how you speak, act, and behave—when you are in different selves (and selves constellations)—from the perspective of others. Over time, this enables you to experience how—from the "outside"— you really do act like different people at different times. If it is someone who has an unfounded negative view of you, there may still be value in seeing things from their perspective, at least for a moment.*

---

*Thanks to John Nadler for his clear formulation of this concept in conversation with Jordan Gruber.

Strengthening or Weakening Particular Selves—If one of your selves tends to be too dominant or problematic, John Rowan suggests strengthening one or more sub-personalities to take over some or all of the dominant or problematic self's functionality. Over time, the overblown self can "sink into the background"[40] and become less of a problem.

HOW HELPFUL ARE THESE TOOLS AND TECHNIQUES?

Anyone who has ever had even the slightest opportunity to examine himself has come to realize that, far from being unified, coherent beings, we are an unruly republic of more or less independent entities, some of which obey the rules set for them, some of which do not. And, like the bad child in a family, the disorderly parts generally win the most attention.

RICHARD SMOLEY, BOOK REVIEW
OF *DEMONS OF THE INNER WORLD* IN
GNOSIS MAGAZINE, NO. 19 (SPRING 1991)

How useful and necessary is the material presented in this chapter? Again, a simple awareness that you and the other people in your life have selves is all you really need to get going. That awareness alone begins to open you up to many of the benefits previously described and discussed.

If you want to step things up a notch, you can work with the catchphrase from chapter 3—"mental health is being in the right mind at the right time"—and its variants. This simple idea, applied just occasionally in real life, can enable you to avoid conflict with others and remain focused on whatever you are doing or aiming at.

After that, the more you become aware of the healthy selves model, the more benefits you (and the other people in your life) are likely to receive. Indeed, many of Jim's and Jordan's personal friends and family members who have heard us describe the contents of this book in general ways have reported benefits in their lives.

Going further, you can focus on the distinctions between the two major approaches, voluntary shifting and working with selves in place. Then, you can add in the third meta-level practices of centering and developing presence.

Over time, considering things from the perspective of healthy selves will more frequently lead you to situations in which you successfully apply the techniques and strategies we have described.

SECTION IV

• • • • • • • • • •

Healthy Normal Selves in the Twenty-First Century

ELEVEN

Spiritual, Therapeutic, and Sociocultural Responses

> *Man is not made up of one piece but of many pieces and each part of him has a personality of its own. That is a thing which people yet have not sufficiently realized— the psychologists have begun to glimpse it, but recognize only when there is a marked case of double or multiple personality. But all men are like that, in reality.*
> SRI AUROBINDO, *LETTERS ON YOGA,* VOLUME 1

"Healthy Normal Selves in the Twenty-First Century," our final section, starts with a look at some systematic responses to the existence of selves. First, we will consider some nineteenth- and twentieth-century spiritual teachers who created systems in which cultivating selves played a central role. Then, we will briefly review a number of therapeutic systems and approaches, including some contemporary ones. Next, we will touch on how societal and cultural institutions in law, religion, and medicine may be impacted by healthy multiplicity. The chapter will then close with a brief look at the existing and potential future impact of technology on healthy selves.

SPIRITUAL TEACHINGS AND TEACHERS

Some spiritual teachers have incorporated the reality of selves into their practices and writings. Following are three notable examples.

Sri Aurobindo: Many Parts and Personalities

Sri Aurobindo (1872–1950), born Aurobindo Ghose, was an Indian nationalist, philosopher, yogi, poet, and spiritual reformer. Educated in England, he returned to India to politically oppose British rule and then became a yogi and guru. The ashram he founded in Pondicherry, India, is still active. His "integral yoga" writings remain influential, and a worldwide society of followers actively discuss his writings, poetry, and other insights.

Aurobindo wrote that "we are composed of many parts each of which contributes something to the total movement of our consciousness, our thought, will, sensation, feeling, action."[1] In a book chapter titled "The Parts of the Being—Men Do Not Know Themselves," Aurobindo sets out his ideas in a section titled "Many Parts, Many Personalities."

Fig. 11.1. Sri Aurobindo

The being is made up of many parts. One part may know, the other may not care for the knowledge or act according to it. . . .

The consciousness has in it many parts and many movements and in different conditions and different activities it changes position and arranges its activities in a different way so as to suit what it is doing—but most people are not aware of this because they live only on the surface and do not look into themselves. . . .

Everybody is an amalgamation not of two but of many personalities. It is a part of the Yogic perfection in this Yoga to accord and transmute them so as to "integrate" the personality. . . . The aim should be in Yoga to develop (if one has it not already) a strong central being and harmonise under it all the rest, changing what has to be changed.[2]

The book *Our Many Selves* collects relevant writings from both Aurobindo and his disciple, the ashram's French-born co-founder, Mirra Alfassa (1878–1973), also known as "the Mother." As you read through these introductory passages, notice:

- how natural and obvious it is for this integral yoga system to declare that we all have parts or personalities, even if most people are unaware of this;
- how some of the language used—involving orienting around a divine center and creating presence—is not dissimilar from the third general approach to working with selves previously outlined;
- that while there is a focus on a spiritual Self—a kind of super-self—that Self is not the same as the personalities or selves otherwise discussed, and therefore, even if a kind of "unification" under the supreme spiritual Self is the goal, this may be quite different than dubious attempts at forced integration or unification of selves, which we will return to later; and
- it is directly suggested that learning to recognize and work with one's selves makes one far more effective as a person, in effect putting an army of selves at our disposal.

The introduction of *Our Many Selves* begins by quoting Aurobindo:

"Man is in his self a unique Person, but he is also in his manifestation of self a multiperson . . ." In this statement Sri Aurobindo makes a distinction which is fundamental . . . the distinction between the Person and its many personalities. This distinction is far from apparent to us in our ordinary consciousness.

"The ordinary mind knows itself only as an ego with all the movements of the nature in a jumble and, identifying itself with these movements, thinks 'I am doing this, feeling that, thinking, in joy or in sorrow etc.' The first beginning of real self-knowledge is when you feel yourself separate from the nature in you and its movements and then you see that there are many parts of your being, many personalities each acting on its own behalf and in its own way."[3]

This next passage from *Our Many Selves* is by the Mother:

There are beings who carry in themselves thousands of different personalities, and then each one has its own rhythm and alternation, and there is a kind of combination; sometimes there are inner conflicts, and there is a play of activities which are rhythmic and with alternations of certain parts which come to the front and then go back and again come to the front. . . .

But there are people truly like a multitude, and so that gives them a plasticity, a fluidity of action and an extraordinary complexity of perception, and these people are capable of understanding a considerable number of things, as though they had at their disposal a veritable army which they move according to circumstance and need; and all this is inside them.[4]

Notice how close some of this sounds to others quoted earlier, including Lewis Thomas, Colin Wilson, Douglas Hofstadter, and Billy Milligan.

G. I. Gurdjieff: The Absence of Unity

G. I. Gurdjieff (1866?–1949) was of Armenian and Greek descent. Born under Russian rule, he eventually settled in France. A mystic, philosopher, and spiritual teacher, he attracted students from around the world because of the method he created, called "The Work" or "the Fourth Way," so they could stop being functionally "asleep" and "wake up." (The first three ways were the way of the fakir, the way of the monk, and the way of the yogi.[5]) Today there are Gurdjieff groups around the world offering training, practices, and group experience of "The Work."

Gurdjieff's own writings are often difficult to understand. Many of his ideas have come down to us through his disciples, including Pyotr Ouspensky, who makes Gurdjieff's position clear beginning with what he called the "absence of unity in man":

> A man is never the same for long. He is continually changing. He seldom remains the same even for half an hour. We think that if

Fig. 11.2. G. I. Gurdjieff

a man is called Ivan he is always Ivan. Nothing of the kind. Now he is Ivan, in another minute he is Peter, and a minute later he is Nicholas, Sergius, Matthew, Simon. And all of you think he is Ivan. You know that Ivan cannot do a certain thing. He cannot tell a lie, for instance. Then you find he has told a lie and you are surprised he could have done so. And, indeed, Ivan cannot lie; it is Nicholas who lied. . . . You will be astonished when you realize what a multitude of these Ivans and Nicholases live in one man. If you learn to observe them there is no need to go to a cinema.

 . . . These Ivans, Peters, and Nicholases . . . all call themselves 'I.' That is, they consider themselves masters and none want to recognize another. Each of them is caliph for an hour, does what he likes regardless of everything, and, later on, the others have to pay for it.[6]

Not only is there an absence of unity in human beings, but consider how the part of someone (Ivan) who cannot have done something has, in fact, been supplanted by a different self (Nicholas)—who has no trouble doing it at all. This is close to how we have been describing human behavior throughout this book. Another familiar theme is that the part of you that does something (for example, the part that drinks too much alcohol) is likely not the part of you that pays the consequences (waking up with a hangover).

 This next Ouspensky passage, ending with an example about how and why people do not follow through on their decisions, should by now sound familiar:

Man such as we know him . . . cannot have a permanent and single I. His I changes as quickly as his thoughts, feelings, and moods, and he makes a profound mistake in considering himself always one and the same person. . . .

 Man has no individuality. He has no single, big I. Man is divided into a multiplicity of small I's.

 And each separate small I is able to call itself by the name of the Whole, to act in the name of the Whole, to agree or disagree, to give promises, to make decisions, with which another I or the Whole will have to deal. This explains why people so often make decisions and so seldom carry them out.[7]

Another well-known Gurdjieff disciple, Maurice Nicoll, focuses on the difficulty some people have in admitting that they are not just one single unified self:

> For a long time the illusion that he is always one and the same person will struggle with his attempt to observe himself uncritically and make it difficult for him to realize the significance of his observations. He will find excuses and justify himself and so cling to the idea that he is really one and has a permanent individuality.[8]

Gurdjieff's response to the "problem" of having multiple selves or minds was similar to Sri Aurobindo's. As David Lester puts it, "The ultimate solution for Gurdjieff was for the person to develop a true master, a higher self who could control all of the lesser selves."[9] While some of Gurdjieff's ideas are precisely on point, and his descriptions of conflicting selves are quite illuminating, we find little evidence of success behind his "ultimate solution" of forging a single super-self to oversee the rest of one's selves.

Jean Houston: Polyphrenia and Your "Inner Crew"

The writings and workshops of Jean Houston (born 1937), an American author and human-potential-movement leader, fully incorporate the healthy selves perspective. A flyer for one of her workshops states that you will "develop some of the personalities of your inner crew in order to increase your intellectual and writing skills and resources." In another program, participants are told they will discover "the different kinds of intelligence that you have within you, such as emotional intelligence, different states of consciousness, accessing creative states, and orchestrating various members of your 'inner crew' or extended personalities as needed to help you achieve things you literally had no idea you could do."[10] Participants would also learn "how to access 'inner experts,'

Fig. 11.3. Jean Houston

willing helpers or personas that will help you navigate the complexity of life with confidence."[11]

Houston coined the term *polyphrenia* "to describe a high-functioning, multi-leveled consciousness that is well-organized and synergistic within its levels."[12] Douglas Eby, who interviewed Houston, further explains that "Houston believes people are essentially polyphrenic. 'Polyphrenia—the orchestration of our many selves—is our extended health. We have a vast crew within, that used to be called sub-personalities.'"[13]

Houston takes a pragmatic approach with regard to embracing her own polyphrenia. When asked about how she has done so much—from writing dozens of books to traveling millions of miles worldwide giving workshops to experiencing political notoriety*—she responded as follows:

People always ask me, how have I been able to do so much in my life? I say it's very simple. I have subscribed to the belief that we are not schizophrenic—that's our pathology—instead, we are polyphrenic. We contain so many, many persons in us. For instance, I am a teacher, a dog person, a traveler, a meditator, a cook (that is a serious part of

---

*In 1996, Jean Houston helped First Lady Hillary Clinton get in touch with any advice that Eleanor Roosevelt might have for her through an imaginative exercise undertaken in the White House.

myself), wild woman. I could probably name you twenty different people I am within myself. I realize little local Jean, or the egoic self, is only one small part of me; ego is but one image among the multiple images of the psyche. When I need to do something that I don't particularly feel skillful about, I tap into another part.

For example, I dislike writing. Intensely! . . . In order to write, I have to tap into the part of myself who is a cook. I am a very good cook. I have no blocks whatsoever, full of galloping chutzpah. I get into my cook self to be able to write, to stir the mélange of ideas, to add a little pepper sauce, if I need something really vital, add the herbs of energy there, and so as a cook I can write. But as Jean I cannot write.[14]

PSYCHOLOGICAL AND THERAPEUTIC APPROACHES

It's not just a question of remaining positive, it's also a question of asking who we are in this time and space . . . these challenges are evoking people to use domains and levels of themselves—multiple ways of being—that have never been used before.

JEAN HOUSTON,
INTERVIEW WITH ENLIGHTENMENT.COM

As earlier discussed, the discipline of psychology was put off from understanding selves by the combined influence of Freud and the rise of behaviorism in the beginning of the twentieth century. It took several decades for psychology to come around for another look, inspired by and focused on tales of pathological multiplicity (then called multiple personality disorder, or MPD). This started with the books and movies *The Three Faces of Eve* and *Sybil* and eventually resulted in advances in thinking by progressive therapists and psychiatrists. They recognized that the dissociation part of the disorder was in fact an adaptive, evolutionary mechanism that helped abused individuals hold things together as well as possible.

Through nearly the whole twentieth century, however, there were some pioneering psychologists and therapists who not only thought and wrote about selves in one form or another (including Carl Jung and James Hillman, both discussed earlier) but who also produced organized systems or therapeutic approaches specifically for working with selves. This section will briefly cover a few of the most important of these—Psychosynthesis, psychodrama, Voice Dialogue, and Internal Family Systems—all of which are actively practiced today.

We will then take a quick look at the contemporary scene and the rise of parts work in many different professional and therapeutic settings. As for psychotherapy itself, we will consider a number of techniques and strategies that mainstream psychologists and other therapists can use to work with those who have a disturbed or unhealthy self. Finally, we will take one last look at the question of forced unification.

Psychosynthesis and Assagioli

Roberto Assagioli, covered in some detail earlier, was an Italian psychiatrist who founded a holistic or transpersonal psychological movement known as Psychosynthesis.* A friend of Carl Jung's (who introduced him into the Freud Society of Zurich), Assagioli began developing and disseminating his own ideas in the years after 1910, and in 1926 he founded what would become the Institute of Psychosynthesis.

The idea of sub-personalities—multiple personalities that are often in conflict—is "a central strand in Psychosynthesis thinking."[15] Assagioli wrote:

> We are not unified. We often feel we are because we do not have many bodies and many limbs, and because one hand doesn't usually hit the other. But, metaphorically, that is exactly what does happen within us. Several subpersonalities are continually scuffling: impulses, desires, principles, aspirations are engaged in an unceasing struggle.[16]

---

*James Jackson Putnam, Carl Jung, and A. R. Orage all used the term *psychosynthesis* before Assagioli did.[17] For example, Jung had written, "If there is a 'psychoanalysis' there must also be a 'psychosynthesis' which creates future events according to the same laws."[18]

Psychosynthesis developed a five-phase process for dealing with selves, from "recognition" to "acceptance" to "coordination" to "integration" to "synthesis." The ultimate payoff in getting to the synthesis phase was that it "leads to the discovery of the Transpersonal Self, and the realization that this is the final truth of the person, not the subpersonalities."[19] For Assagioli, the focus is moved away from selves and toward a super-self.

Psychodrama and Jacob Moreno

Psychodrama was developed by Jacob Moreno, an Austrian American psychiatrist who came to New York City in 1925 and began experimenting with group therapy (which he pioneered) and "psychodramatics."[20] Moreno's psychodrama "is an action method, often used in psychotherapy, in which clients use spontaneous dramatization, role playing, and dramatic self-presentation to investigate and gain insight into their lives."[21]

According to Rowan, "[Moreno] never used the term [psychodrama], but he did use the approach, very freely and individually."[22] One of psychodrama's techniques, as described by Zerka Moreno, cofounder of psychodrama and wife of Jacob Moreno, is the "multiple double technique" in which "the patient is on the stage with several doubles of himself. Each portrays part of the patient. One auxiliary ego acts as he is now, while the patient acts himself as he was when he was little. . . . The masks of the patient are simultaneously present and each acts in turn."[23] Rowan concludes that "what happens in psychodrama, of course, is that the protagonist (client, patient) takes all the roles sooner or later, and experiences each of these parts, from the inside, as that person. . . . We have to get to know the subpersonalities from the inside, by playing them, and not from the outside by observing or describing them."[24]

Psychodrama makes active use of selves or sub-personalities in role playing but does not recognize them as such. It is, therefore, not written about very often in the literature on selves and sub-personalities. Rowan writes, "in a way it is absurd to say so little about psychodrama, because in a way psychodrama has a better grasp of how to work with subpersonalities than anyone else, but . . . pscyhodramatists do not talk very much in these terms."[25]

Voice Dialogue and Hal and Sidra Stone

Hal and Sidra Stone invented Voice Dialogue, which their website tells us is "the basic method for contacting, learning about, and working with the many selves that make up each of us."[26] In *Embracing Our Selves* (1998), they write:

> We have referred to the fact that we are made up of many selves. . . . They have been known as the many I's, selves or partial selves, complexes, multiple personalities, and more recently, as energy patterns. . . . Some people object to this idea, arguing that such a theory fragments the personality. We feel that it is already "fragmented," and our task is to become aware of this fragmentation or multiplicity of selves so that we can make valid choices in our lives.[27]

Voice Dialogue places a special emphasis on not dishonoring or rejecting selves; doing so pushes these "disowned selves" into the unconscious, yet strengthens them, enabling them to "grow inside of us in unconscious ways, gaining power and authority."[28] The Stones write:

> Most of us have a surgeon's mentality when it comes to those selves we dislike. We try so hard to get rid of our temper, our rage, jealousy, pettiness, shyness, feelings of inadequacy . . . the list is endless. . . . If we can learn to step back and allow our awareness to operate, we will not only encounter these selves, we will also realize that our wish to eradicate these patterns is actually the voice of yet another self.[29]

The Stones feel that "each subpersonality is a distinct energy pattern—each has a distinct facial expression, posture, and tone of voice, and each creates a different set of energetic vibrations in its surroundings."[30] They also recognize that sub-personalities "are like people: They like to feel that they have our undivided attention as well as plenty of time to express themselves."[31]

In recent years, the Stones have recast Voice Dialogue as being only one aspect of the broader system that they now call the "Psychology of Selves," which "provides a clear explanation of how these selves operate in your life and how they keep you from realizing your full potential."[32] Thus, you can "learn how these selves determine the way you see the world, control your behavior, and limit your choices."[33]

Internal Family Systems and Richard Schwartz

The Internal Family Systems model is a psychotherapeutic approach developed by Richard Schwartz. It recognizes the existence of sub-personalities and then applies some of the insights and dynamics from family therapy or family counseling to working with these sub-personalities.[34] Following are the basic assumptions of Internal Family Systems:

- It is the nature of the mind to be subdivided into an indeterminate number of subpersonalities or parts.
- Everyone has a Self, and the Self can and should lead the individual's internal system.
- The non-extreme intention of each part is something positive for the individual. There are no bad parts, and the goal of therapy is not to eliminate parts but instead to help them find their non-extreme roles.
- As we develop, our parts develop and form a complex system of interactions among themselves; therefore, systems theory can be applied to the internal system. When the system is reorganized, parts can change rapidly.
- Changes in the internal system will affect changes in the external system and vice versa. The implication of this assumption is that both the internal and external levels of system should be assessed.

The overall goals of Internal Family Systems therapy include:

- to achieve balance and harmony within the internal system;
- to differentiate and elevate the Self so it can be an effective leader in the system;

- when the Self is in the lead, the parts will provide input to the Self but will respect the leadership and ultimate decision making of the Self; and
- all parts will exist and lend talents that reflect their non-extreme intentions.[35]

Schwartz's root understanding is that the human mind is naturally constituted of sub-personalities. He also emphasizes that there are no bad sub-personalities and no need to eliminate any of them through forced unification. Repeating a familiar pattern, Schwartz then places a major emphasis on developing the essential Self, with a capital S, as the ultimate lynchpin of his system.

For example, the 2017 book Schwartz wrote with Richard Falconer, *Many Minds, One Self,* covers some of the same cultural, psychological, and neurological territory that we do but concludes with such a strong return to the Single Self Assumption it even makes the title. After Schwartz and Falconer establish the existence of many minds in all of us, they then tell us that the way to work with those minds is to develop a single essential spiritual Self.

....

A Singular Apology

Many of the systems covered in this chapter have a great deal in common with how this book has described selves. Each system may have its own proponents, trainings, years of working with clients, and even a journal. In most cases, each system begins by describing its own observations about selves—what they are like, how they are created, how they can be accessed, and so on. Each system then turns to how to best work with selves, focusing on the effectiveness of its own therapeutic interventions.

Many of the systems then suggest that above and beyond these separate and observable selves there is—or must be—something else: a higher, wiser, special, or morally superior being, perhaps one of an entirely different order, a super-self or supra-self that sits behind or above all of our other selves.

We part ways with these supra-self systems, not because we

necessarily disagree or say it can't be so—we do not quarrel with the possibility of a supra-self—but simply because we have not found enough compelling evidence. What we have found, though, is that people who acknowledge, appreciate, and harmonize their selves consistently find their lives improved. We are aware that by not having a position on the existence of a supra-self, we may offend adherents of existing and well-established approaches to multiplicity. For this we apologize in advance, but we have almost always tried to limit ourselves to the obvious and observable and not speculate about the merely possible.

Contemporary Examples

Selves, parts, or sub-personalities are frequently used in many current treatment and support modalities. For example, all four of the approaches in the previous section—Psychosynthesis, psychodrama, Voice Dialogue, and Internal Family Systems—are actively practiced today around the world. Additionally, the gestalt techniques pioneered by Fritz Perls (previously described), along with role playing and role reversal, are widely used in therapy, counseling, and coaching of all kinds. For a good overview of the use of parts and selves in a wide range of therapeutic approaches, see the article "Parts Integration and Psychotherapy" by Richard Bolstad.

There are many other contemporary teachers, teachings, techniques, and self-improvement tools that, in one way or another, recognize and work with the existence of parts, or selves. While we cannot name them all, here are some worth noting:

- **Neuro-Linguistic Programming:** NLP, created by Richard Bandler and John Grinder, often refers to "a part of you" and has some explicit parts-related techniques including "6-step reframing," which involves negotiating between one's parts.[36] Virginia Satir, discussed earlier, is credited with having introduced parts work into NLP. Bolstad notes that that as early as 1976, Bandler and Grinder put together a number of ways of working with conflicting parts, such as Satir's "Parts Party" and Gestalt psychology's "empty chair process." In regard to "six step reframing," an early model that incorporated parts work, Bandler and Grinder explained its rationale, saying, "This only makes sense if you have a belief system that says 'Look. If he had conscious control over this behavior it would have changed already.' So some part of him which is not conscious is running this pattern of behavior."[37]

- **The Hoffman Quadrinity Process** separates out and makes use of the Physical Self, Emotional Self, Intellectual Self, and Spiritual Self.[38]

- **Process Work** as developed and taught by Arnold and Amy Mindell makes use of role playing and role switching, as "all the various parts in a conflict or discussion are actually roles that everyone has within themselves to a lesser or greater extent."[39]

- **The Inside Team,** a business coaching process created by Cynthia Loy Darst, makes direct use of selves. The process helps bring into awareness what it calls "Inside Team Players," defined as a "collection of voices, beliefs, [and] aspects of our personality." Participants then consciously redesign their inner alliances with themselves to make choices and take actions that move them forward in their lives.[40] There are resonances here with Ariel Erica Fox's previously mentioned work, which also focuses on internal negotiations between selves.[41]

- **The Hakomi Process,** a kind of body-centered psychotherapy, contains a "Unity principle" that "assumes that, as people, we are living, organic systems that are integral wholes, composed of parts, which also participate in larger systems. The interdependency of all levels of the system, including the physical/metabolic, intrapsychic, interpersonal, family, cultural, and spiritual are recognized in Hakomi."[42] The Re-Creation of the Self Model of Human Systems (R-CS), developed by Hakomi practitioner Jon Eisman, "describes the method by which we fragment our consciousness into a collection of various sub-selves, or self-states. . . . Each self-state is a distinct state of consciousness, or trance, and each holds a specific perspective and set of truths about the nature of ourselves and the world."[43]

SOME SELVES MAY NEED REAL HELP, BUT NOT "FORCED UNIFICATION"

We have said this before, but it is an important point and we want to be absolutely clear: having selves is normal. The healthiest way of being that we know of is to acknowledge the reality of our own selves and the selves of others and learn to work together effectively. Having selves is normal—BUT—many people have one or more selves that may be disturbed, dysfunctional, depressed, or deeply unhappy and need help. You or someone you know may, then, very well have a self that needs or could benefit from therapy, counseling, coaching, or other interventions. Again, *having selves is not inherently unhealthy—quite the opposite, in fact—but having a disturbed self that does not get proper treatment and assistance can be very unhealthy.*

Suppose you have one or more selves that act out, or that are chronically unhappy and dissatisfied. Obviously, it is critically important to find a way to address those selves. Many mainstream therapies may also prove helpful once a conventional therapist recognizes that parts or selves are involved. Thus, cognitive behavioral therapy, conventional psychotherapy, or any one of many potential therapeutic approaches, when addressed to a particularly problematic self, might prove very helpful.

What is almost always a mistake, however, is forced integration, or "fusion," which amounts to killing or destroying a self. Colin Ross gives us some historical background to and analysis of why this approach is a mistake:

> Morton Prince . . . made the other major error in the field, one repeated by Thigpen and Cleckley in *The Three Faces of Eve* (1957). He decided that the best way to treat MPD is to force the disappearance of most alters, and to back the ascendancy of one. Such treatment consists of trying to get rid of the "bad" alters and keep the "good" or "real" ones. This does not work because the bad alters have a function, only appear to be bad when not understood, and are a necessary part of the whole. This kind of treatment is a secular

version of exorcism that does not heal the pain, resolve the conflicts, or lead to integration.[44]

Susan C. Roberts (embracing the orchestra metaphor) further explains as follows:

The goal is not to get the split-off parts to fuse—a word that sounds threateningly like annihilation for parts of the self that are full of life and energy—but to practice "time-sharing of the psyche," as one psychiatrist puts it. The image of wholeness arrived at after a successful treatment thus is not likely to be of a solid unit so much as of a functioning plurality—an orchestra, say, or a collegiate rowing team—where the various selves cooperate in working toward an agreed-upon goal.[45]

And C. W. Duncan, who notes a historical movement in the right direction, puts it this way:

Today knowledgeable therapists would never designate a "real" personality and play God by "sacrificing" an alter. Since the whole personality is made up of all the alter parts, each must be honored and involved if the treatment process is to be successful. Unfortunately some therapists are still practicing nineteenth century therapy by trying to exorcise MPD alters rather than to heal the MPD system.[46]

As Ross, Roberts, and Duncan all indicate, therapeutic interventions aimed at fusion or forced integration are in effect attempts to kill, destroy, or annihilate one or more undesirable selves. Attempts to quash the energy of a part of ourselves—a real and autonomous part that is inherently valuable and that has its own energy and life force—almost never work. The suppressed energy finds a way to bubble up, boomerang, or otherwise come back. Even in cases where severe pathological multiplicity has been treated, forced unification rarely lasts or results in a stable configuration of selves. Indeed, patients often revert back to their previous selves and problematic behaviors.

DISTINGUISHING SCHIZOPHRENIA
FROM MULTIPLICITY

The U.S. National Institute of Mental Health defines *schizophrenia* as "a chronic and severe mental disorder that affects how a person thinks, feels, and behaves. People with schizophrenia may seem like they have lost touch with reality . . . the symptoms can be very disabling."[47] It can also be defined as "a long-term mental disorder of a type involving a breakdown in the relation between thought, emotion, and behavior, leading to faulty perception, inappropriate actions and feelings, withdrawal from reality and personal relationships into fantasy and delusion, and a sense of mental fragmentation."[48]

Both in the popular mind and in the minds of some mental health professionals, there has been an unfortunate tendency to confuse pathological multiplicity with schizophrenia. Bennett Braun writes that "Rosenbaum . . . speculated that Bleuler's introduction of the term *schizophrenia* around 1911 led to misdiagnosis of many MPD patients as schizophrenic. Indeed, in their recent study of 100 consecutive MPD cases, Putnam et al. . . . reported that some were previously misdiagnosed as schizophrenic."[49] Colin Ross makes the same point about widespread confusion and misdiagnoses:* "Schizophrenia is almost undoubtedly a disease of the brain requiring physical treatment. There is no evidence that there is anything structurally or physiologically wrong with the MPD brain."[50]

Ken Wilber describes how this terminological misunderstanding has been amplified in contemporary culture by filmmakers:

Notice, then, something that movies always get wrong: Schizophrenia, which is a form of psychosis . . . is taken by almost

---

*Ross also provides the etymological background of *schizophrenia,* which was called *dementia praecox* until the term *schizophrenia* was introduced by Bleuler. He tells us that *schizophrenia* means "split mind," from the Greek *schizo* (or split) and *phren* (or mind), but "it is actually MPD that is characterized by a split mind. This confused terminology has given rise to popular confusion about schizophrenia, which is often thought to be the same as split personality."[51]

all films as something usually called a "split personality" (which is what "schizo" seems to mean)—that is, somebody with multiple personality disorder—for example, the lead character in *The Three Faces of Eve*. In films, the character's psyche is fractured into several subpersonalities, one of which is usually portrayed as a cold-blooded serial murderer. Such an individual is labeled as totally "schizo" or as a "split personality." But [in] real multiple personality disorder (a genuine "split psyche" condition) . . . each of the personalities is fully in touch with conventional reality—there are no hallucinations or waking-dream fragments.[52]

This kind of terminological confusion—as well as the inevitable serial killer plot—still happens, as seen clearly in the 2016 horror film *Split*.

This book has addressed the distinction between having selves—which we all do—and having one or more pathological selves or a dysfunctional selves-system that needs assistance or treatment of some kind. Schizophrenia is real, of course, but isn't directly relevant to our understanding of healthy normal multiplicity.

SOCIETAL AND CULTURAL RESPONSES

If the main thesis of this book is correct—that human beings have selves that are real, inherently valuable, and autonomous, and that by learning to recognize and appreciate those selves it becomes much easier and more effective to work with them—then there is substantial work ahead for many major societal and cultural institutions. Our very baseline for total mental and psychological health will need to shift substantially.

Many discussions and conversations will be needed in a wide variety of cultural, social, and institutional settings to digest and incorporate this revised conception. In this section we will consider:

1. The legal system and questions of responsibility
2. Psychiatry, psychology, and mental health systems as a whole
3. Questions of wellness, healing, and happiness

The Legal System and Selves Responsibility

The idea that we all have selves can be seen as a potential threat to notions of ethics and responsibility and systems of law and order. As Peter Baldwin put it, "What of law and order? Doesn't this way of thinking offer people license to say: 'I can't be held responsible for what one of my own personas did!"[53] Rita Carter writes, "One reason, perhaps, why people are reluctant to acknowledge human multiplicity is the fear that to do so would be to undermine the principle of personal responsibility. If everyone started blaming their less acceptable behavior on someone else there would be chaos, so it is safer to hang onto the illusion of singularity."[54] John O. Beahrs says much the same thing, "that there might lie within our self entities which we do not experience as 'me' and over whose actions we may not have control . . . threatens man's view of ethical responsibility. Moreover, if a single 'person' cannot be completely equated with a single 'body,' if it is possible that we do not always know with whom we are dealing, then our entire system of jurisprudence is threatened."[55]

In American criminal law (based on traditional common law), someone can typically only be found guilty if they both performed the physical act in question (the *actus reus*) and possessed the required mental state while performing the act (the *mens rea*).[56] While exceptions exist based on strict liability statutes, a criminal conviction generally requires *both* a bad act *and* a bad actor; that is, someone who had a guilty mind or wrongful purpose.

If we have selves—and we do!—then what happens when a part of us that is no longer present has committed a crime? Even if the actus reus is still attributed to the same human being (since he or she only has one body), what about the mens rea? If the part, or parts, of the person that is usually present did not have a guilty mind or wrongful purpose, should the person be convicted? How does the idea of "not guilty by reason of insanity" fit in here, and how *should* it fit in?

Billy Milligan, whom we have referred to frequently, was found not guilty of rape based on his MPD diagnosis and then spent years in secure psychiatric hospitals before finally being released.[57] However, in the case of the Hillside Strangler, Ken Bianchi's DID defense was found to be contrived, and he was sentenced to life in prison.[58]

A related kind of defense has brought to life a new discipline called "neuro-law." Among other things, neuro-law makes use of brain scans to compare different self-states in situations where someone has taken a medication or substance of some kind that has altered their brain chemistry so substantially that they claim they are not responsible for their actions or the crimes or torts they have committed. As David Eagleman wrote in *The Atlantic,* "Advances in brain science are calling into question the volition behind many criminal acts."[59] This can come up in cases where someone was on prescribed medication, or was taking over-the-counter or illegally obtained painkillers (especially opiates), or even because they ate the wrong kind of food. (Consider the "Twinkie defense" posited by Dan White's attorneys with respect to his murdering San Francisco city supervisor Harvey Milk and Mayor George Moscone.[60])

Some writers, like psychiatrist Seymour Halleck in his article "Dissociative Phenomena and the Question of Responsibility," contrast "the case for minimizing attribution of responsibility" (because of the kind of negative life experiences often associated with pathological multiplicity) with "the case for maximizing attribution of responsibility" (because it is better in the long run for both the patient and society as a whole).[61] Overall, there seems to be wide agreement that the existence of selves does not—and should not—change our basic notions of responsibility and legal approaches. John Rowan writes:

> There is one warning which should be given here, however, and that is that I do not believe that subpersonalities should be understood as taking away the responsibility of the social person. There have been attempts to say that if the idea of subpersonalities holds water, then it could be said that if one subpersonality committed a crime, another subpersonality could not be held responsible. This has actually been tried. . . .
>
> But even in the case of true [pathological] multiple personality . . . it would be wrong to diminish the responsibility of the social person who is visible to all, or the legal person who signs cheques, owns property, enters into contracts, and so forth. . . .

So the warning is: don't run away with the idea that the concept of subpersonalities can be used to diminish any of our human responsibility for all of our actions, no matter how partial or one-sided or inadequate the impulse behind it may be.[62]

The legal system will—and probably should be—very slow to change with regard to these sort of issues. Those in the DID-diagnosed self-help community seem for the most part to be clear that if any personality or self has committed a crime, the entire person will be seen as being responsible for that. As James Vargiu puts it, "We are responsible for our sub-personalities, just as we're responsible for our children, our pets and our car. We certainly need to see that they don't cause trouble to ourselves or others."[63]

Psychiatry, Psychology, and the Mental Health System as a Whole

We would like to offer an invitation to the practitioners of psychiatry and psychology and to all allied mental health professionals. The invitation has two parts: first, acknowledge or recognize the reality of selves and multiplicity in human beings generally; second, rethink the goals and methods of your discipline in this light.

The recognition and understanding that the healthiest among us not only have selves, but also have found ways to harmonize and work with their own selves and the selves of others, will call for fundamentally reconceiving many aspects of psychiatry, psychology, and allied mental health professions. If our take on optimal human functioning and happiness is correct, then many mental health professionals and practitioners will need to adapt.

Cases of pathological multiplicity will still have to be dealt with—as suggested earlier in this chapter—but within a larger framework that holds the existence of selves as an undeniable pragmatic fact. For those within ordinary parameters of unhappiness, depression, or other reasons for entering therapy, the goal for patients will be to get to know their selves and learn to work well with all of them.

If you are a mainstream therapist and are for the first time working with someone who has become aware of having selves through this book or otherwise, there are a few different ways for you to move forward. Resources you can make use of include the following:

- any of the approaches or techniques described and discussed early in the book
- approaches and techniques that you can borrow from currently practicing selves-aware modalities, like Psychosynthesis or Voice Dialogue
- the following two protocols, one of which is simpler and the other more complex

Simple Protocol

Jay Noricks recommends a four-part approach for dealing with troubled selves and their behaviors:

> The procedures for healing through work with the inner world are straightforward. First, find the part that carries the problem behavior, while remaining aware that sometimes more than a single part may be involved. Second, elicit the problem memories held by the part. Third, neutralize the energy attached to the problem memories. Finally, help the new flexible part adjust to a newly defined role when necessary.[64]

Multi-step Protocol

Peter Baldwin uses the term *persona* to lay out the following steps that can be undertaken in a psychotherapeutic encounter:

- identifying each persona
- identifying introjected compatriots, antagonists, and introjected audiences
- externalizing each persona through costuming her or him and assigning each a chair in the therapeutic setting
- facilitating the capacity of the subject to identify behaviors produced by each persona, as important issues and life situations are processed

- developing appreciation of the assets and liabilities of each persona
- increasing the capacity of personas to recognize their collusions with one another and the capacity to strive for problem-solving bargains
- keeping ever alert to the subtle or swift "hit and run" emergence of latent personas
- inspiring a gradual release of the subject from overly conscious preoccupation with problem solving through contrived "group sessions" of personas
- through the introduction of hypnotic story, accessing deep (unconscious) and conscious assessment and reassessment of the story or stories inspiring and/or crippling the unfolding drama of a person's living[65]

If you are a psychiatrist, psychologist, or any other kind of therapist, counselor, or coach, and someone wants you to help them with one or more of their selves, acknowledging the potential reality of their selves is a great place to start. Once you personally experience the reality of selves and the value of appreciating and working with them, you will be in a much better position to help clients who require or desire selves-aware assistance.

Wellness, Healing, and Happiness

Earlier we discussed the work of psychiatrist Ellen Langer, who placed a group of men in their seventies into an environment from their youth. In just a matter of weeks, she observed that these men were doing much better on many physical and psychological measures. It seems likely that the progress of these men was at least partly due to Langer having called out and brought present a variety of their younger and healthier selves by making it seem like they were living in 1959, when they were much younger and healthier.

The different parts of who we are share some common needs and goals, but they are also their own autonomous centers of experience and expression. Some of our selves need very specific things to make them happy and healthy. One self might need to paint; another might desire long, solo, moonlit walks; and another might crave a gallon of ice cream. Consider the story of Dr. B. J. Miller, a triple amputee and executive director of the Zen Hospice Project:

> Miller described languishing in a windowless, antiseptic burn unit after his amputations. He heard there was a blizzard outside but couldn't see it himself. Then a nurse smuggled him a snowball and allowed him to hold it. This was against hospital regulations, and this was Miller's point: *There are parts of ourselves that the conventional health care system isn't equipped to heal or nourish, adding to our suffering.*
>
> He described holding that snowball as "a stolen moment," and said, "But I cannot tell you the rapture I felt holding that in my hand, and the coldness dripping onto my burning skin, the miracle of it all, the fascination as I watched it melt and turn into water. In that moment, just being any part of this planet, in this universe, mattered more to me than whether I lived or died." Miller's talk has been watched more than five million times.[66] (Emphasis added.)

Whether it concerns the healing of the body or optimization of psychological states such as flow, as whole human beings we are unlikely to be as engaged, healthy, and well as we can be unless our selves are as engaged, healthy, and well as they can reasonably be supported to be. There must, of course, be compromises, but compromises can only come after recognizing the existence of our selves and learning what each needs and wants. For example, suppose a part of us likes to spend a whole morning in bed every now and again. If we allow that self to occasionally get what it wants, we are likely to be surprised by how good it feels to that self and be rewarded by an upsurge of energy and inspiration that comes back to us once we have scratched that itch.

There is of course a way of exaggerating this argument—what philosophers call a *reductio ad absurdum*—wherein someone might say, "Well, then, I guess the part of me that wants to smash into the guy who cut me off should get to do that from time to time" or "A very small part of me has always wanted to ride my bicycle on the street for five minutes with my eyes closed."

Of course, we are not suggesting that you should do anything and everything that any of your selves wants, requests, or demands! However, requests and desires that are reasonable—or just not too outlandish or dangerous—should be earnestly considered and, when possible, occasionally accommodated. For many of our selves, a little bit of self love goes a long way.

TECHNOLOGICAL IMPACTS AND OPPORTUNITIES

The continued upsurge of communications technology and social networking brings forth many important questions related to the healthy selves model and worldview. We will limit ourselves to a few brief comments and questions.

On the one hand, technology and social networking in particular seems to offer many opportunities for role playing and the exploration of different selves. For example, with regard to the popular online site Second Life, one blogger writes:

> Avid Second Life users seem to understand that the virtual world gives people the opportunity to express facets of who they are (or would like to be) in a new context. Many Second Life users are not just tinkering around—they are expressing one of their identities. Whether that identity is very similar or very different from their "real" world identity matters very little—a Second Life identity is a valid part of the whole picture of a person.[67]

Moreover, regardless of how obscure something is that any part of you is interested in, you can now find and interact with other people who are also interested in it. From formal online role playing games to simply playing different roles with different people online, there seems to be almost no limit to how we can explore the different needs and wants of our different selves.

On the other hand, there are concerns that the rapid rise of social networking, especially in the ubiquitous form of Facebook, is now limiting the ability of individuals to be different selves in different contexts. If everyone from your relatives to your work crowd to your old friends to people you have just met can see what you are up to and are interested in, it becomes more difficult to become—to authentically shift in to—your different selves in different contexts through the ordinary course of your life.

Artist and professor Benjamin Grosser has written an analysis of this dynamic.* He writes:

> Ever since its inception, people have used the technology of the Internet to represent themselves to the world. Sometimes this representation is a construction based on who they are outside the network, such as with a personal webpage or blog. Other times people use the built-in anonymity of the Internet to explore and engage alternative identities. This identity tourism . . . takes place within game spaces (e.g., MUDs, MMORPGs), chat rooms, or forums, as well as within those spaces already mentioned such as webpages and blogs. . . . This paper explores how the technological design of Facebook homogenizes identity and limits personal representation. . . .
>
> According to Facebook CEO and founder Mark Zuckerberg, "having two identities for yourself is an example of a lack of integrity. . . ." The design and operation of Facebook expects and enforces that users will only craft profiles based on their "real" identities, using real names and accurate personal details (Facebook, 2011). This ideological position of singular identity permeates the technological design of Facebook, and is partially enforced by the culture of transparency the site promotes.[68]

It seems, then, that technology, and social networking in particular, is a double-edged sword. It can help bring about a greater understanding

---

*Thanks to Giséle Bisson for alerting us to these issues and to Benjamin Grosser's work.

and implementation of healthy selves, but it may also inherently move us toward homogenization and a reinforcement of the Single Self Assumption.

Similar dynamics may apply to two of the "next big things": AR (augmented reality) and VR (virtual reality). Augmented reality, which made its big splash with Pokémon Go, and virtual reality, which continues to become better and less expensive, enable individuals to explore sides of themselves that might otherwise be difficult to access. Is there a sword-fighting you, an opera-singing you, a mountain-climbing you? Or perhaps there is a you that is raising a family in another century or on another planet? As these sorts of experiences become more readily available, they will likely intersect with a growing general interest in healthy selves in ways that will be surprising, challenging, and illuminating.

TWELVE

From the Traditional Continuum to the Expanded Full Spectrum

This short chapter presents an easily accessible visual metaphor, "the full spectrum of selves." The full spectrum shows healthy human development as embracing not just the *possibility* but also the *desirability and necessity* of knowing all of our selves. In doing so, the full spectrum reframes the conventional view of what optimal functioning and health look like.

We will build up to the expanded full spectrum of selves in a series of steps:

1. First, we will consider **the traditional continuum of dissociation,** which helped explain and make sense of pathological multiplicity. This traditional continuum arose in earlier writings on MPD starting in the 1970s and then continued to be popular in writings on DID once the latter became the new official DSM diagnosis.
2. We then come to the **full spectrum of selves,** first articulated (under a different name) by Dr. Colin Ross. The full spectrum in effect doubles the traditional continuum.
3. We then pause for a **definitional interlude** to explain how and why we are substituting in the term *cohesiveness* for *dissociation*.
4. **The expanded full spectrum** *adds happiness and well-being as an*

additional dimension of inquiry and assessment. Doing so enables us to clearly connect a person's overall cohesiveness and their level of happiness and life satisfaction.

THE TRADITIONAL CONTINUUM OF DISSOCIATION

A *continuum* is "something that changes in character gradually or in very slight stages without any clear dividing points,"[1] or "a continuous sequence in which adjacent elements are not perceptibly different from each other, but the extremes are quite distinct."[2] When the progressive therapists and psychiatrists looking at MPD began writing books and manuals in the late 1970s and 1980s, dissociation began to be viewed

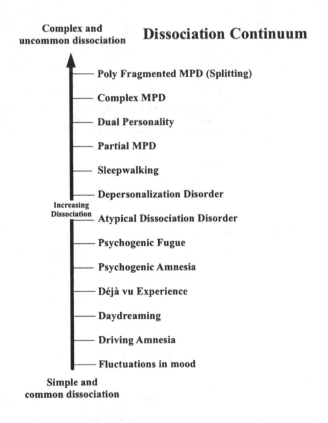

Fig. 12.1. The traditional continuum of dissociation, derived from Celia Ramos

as existing on a continuum.* (The traditional continuum shown in fig. 12.1 derives from Ramos, who in turn credits multiple sources.[3]) Uri Bergmann writes:

> It is proposed, therefore, in keeping with the work of John Watkins and Helen Watkins, that dissociation be viewed as another developmental line. . . . Accordingly, as in the other developmental lines, dissociation will be viewed as a dynamic continuum, from healthy/adaptive to pathological.[4]

Similarly, John Rowan writes:

Dissociation is not an either/or phenomenon, but exists along a dissociative continuum. At one end of the continuum are fluctuations in mood. . . . Further along . . . but still well within the range of normal experience, are the roles and ego states and sub-personalities within which individuals perform state-specific tasks and life activities. Further along . . . outside the range of normality are . . . states of possession. . . . At the far end of this continuum are the very dissociated states, characterized by fugue and amnesia.[5]

Representing dissociation on a continuum became popular for two reasons. First, it helped bring together—in one easily understood graphical representation—a variety of states of consciousness. Fluctuations in mood, problems with functionality and memory, feelings of depersonalization and derealization, and experiencing more than one identity—these could all be represented in a single diagram. The diagram shown at the beginning of this section makes clear how different states of consciousness and experience can readily be made to fit into a linear continuum.

Second, by showing that we all experience some degree of these states—whether it is tuning out of a boring conversation, experiencing "highway hypnosis," or forgetting things we have said or agreed to—the

---

*For a detailed discussion of dissociation—definitions, usages, problems, alternatives—see the appendix.

continuum began to normalize and take the stigma away from dissociation in general. It thus helped contribute to rehabilitating the standing of those suffering from pathological multiplicity: such individuals had simply taken a built-in mechanism of the human mind to an extreme to protect themselves in an adaptive (and even evolutionary) move geared to self-preservation. Dissociation per se was no longer seen as primarily maladaptive or inherently pathological. However, incorporating the idea of multiple, normal, healthy selves was not generally considered or discussed.

THE FULL SPECTRUM OF SELVES

Consider Rita Carter's description of the traditional continuum of dissociation (which she calls a "spectrum"):

> The best way to view dissociation, then, is as a spectrum. At one end there is the everyday, entirely normal neglect of background distractions. Then there are states such as daydreaming and fantasy. The teenager who doesn't hear the call to dinner . . . concentrating on a computer game, the film-goer who weeps at a sentimental ending, the child who doesn't hear the teacher because she is lost in a daydream . . . these people are all dissociating. . . .
>
> Beyond here on the spectrum dissociation becomes pathological. This is the realm of the Dissociative Disorders, which include MPD. . . . There is a thin and moving line between adaptive dissociation—a healthy and useful trick of the brain that gives us mental flexibility and maintains a degree of separation between our personalities—and the disorders.[6]

Despite Carter being a popular advocate of healthy multiplicity, she still presents the same limited continuum that only goes between so-called normal and fully pathological. Instead, what was needed for a more complete picture was a representation of the full continuum, or spectrum, of selves,*

---

*Carter uses the term *spectrum* rather than *continuum* to present her ideas. For our purposes, a *continuum* will mean a graded sequence with continuous values, usually presented in a single linear dimension. Alternatively, a *spectrum* will refer to the entire possible range in which a value or a quality can occur.

including healthy, normal, multiplicity. We are fortunate to have been given just that by Dr. Colin Ross.

Specifically, in a chapter in a 1999 anthology,[7] Ross presents a simple but profound visual reconceptualization of what is to be included in the spectrum.

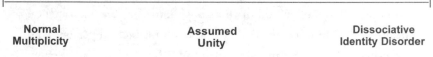

| Normal Multiplicity | Assumed Unity | Dissociative Identity Disorder |

Fig. 12.2. Colin Ross's reconfigured
continuum of dissociation

Ross, who refers to it as the "reconfigured continuum,"* writes:

The solution to the conundrum of DID . . . is to reconfigure the continuum of dissociation. Rather than to posit a continuum of dissociation with normal dissociation at one end and DID at the other, I propose the following. What we call normal in our culture is actually [assumed unity]. . . . The left-hand of the reconfigured continuum is normal multiplicity . . . the middle is [assumed unity], and the right-hand end is DID. . . . We need a psychotherapy that can take us from [assumed unity] to normal multiplicity.[8]

Peter Baldwin, who also offers an alternative version of the full spectrum, places truly healthy multifaceted people in the middle.

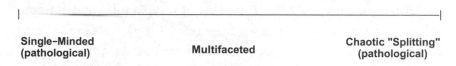

| Single-Minded (pathological) | Multifaceted | Chaotic "Splitting" (pathological) |

Fig. 12.3. Peter Baldwin's reconfigured
continuum of dissociation

---

*For purposes of clarity, we have taken the liberty of replacing Colin Ross's term *pathological pseudounity* with *assumed unity* throughout this section.

Baldwin writes:

> The way these personas work and play together defines a
> −10 . . . 0 . . . +10 mental health continuum. Persons evidencing
> extreme single-mindedness characterize pathology at one end of this
> continuum. Floridly chaotic splitting among personas characterizes
> pathology at the other end of this continuum. . . . Optimal mental
> health is therefore characterized by clearly multifaceted persons who
> experience themselves and are experienced by others as interesting,
> productive, and fundamentally happy.[9]

We will make use of and extend Ross's diagram, not Baldwin's,
because it more easily enables us to describe the full spectrum and
expanded full spectrum; that is, while it is possible to represent the
full spectrum as Baldwin did—with those experiencing healthy, multifaceted multiplicity in the middle position—by using Ross's conception
we can more easily show a clear progressive development from (a) those
characterized by unhealthy multiplicity to (b) those who (like many
people) adopt the position of assumed unity to (c) the healthiest people
of all, those who embrace and leverage healthy multiplicity.

DEFINITIONAL SUBSTITUTION:
COHESIVENESS FOR DISSOCIATION

Just as the previous chapter's discussion of schizophrenia was the first
time we directly focused on that important and relevant term, this chapter is the first time we will spend any significant time on the construct of
dissociation per se. In part, this is because of the inconsistent definitions
and generally problematic nature of the term—as we describe in detail
in the appendix. We also realized that the term was not really needed or
desirable for elaborating on the healthy selves worldview in its entirety.

In the remainder of this chapter's diagrams we will substitute in
a familiar term that will prove generally useful for anyone discussing
multiplicity.

Thus, we redefine dissociation by substituting in the term *cohe-*

siveness. As suggested earlier in the book, *cohesiveness* can be defined in terms of *whether a human being is functioning and presenting in an effective and well-integrated manner.* Just how effective they are, in turn, is substantially based on:

1. how *congruent* their words, actions, and overall behaviors are with their previous words, actions, intentions, and plans;
2. how *coherent*—how understandable and sensible—they are in their interactions, communications, and relationships with others; and
3. how *compassionate*—how kind, patient, and understanding—they are with their own selves and the selves of others.

This definition of cohesiveness not only covers the most important aspects of what has traditionally been referred to as dissociation, but also helps us see the full picture in a positive way; that is, this definition sheds the pathological focus that has for so long dominated most thinking about selves. Instead, it helps us move forward toward increasing congruence, coherence, and compassion.

With cohesiveness used in this way, the traditional continuum of dissociation can then be recast as shown in figure 12.4; that is, starting from pathological selves on the far left, cohesiveness increases overall until assumed unity is reached on the far right.

The full spectrum of selves, then, now looks as presented in figure 12.5. Here, we move from dysfunctional selves on the far left to assumed unity in the middle to healthy normal multiplicity on the far right, with cohesiveness increasing all along the way.

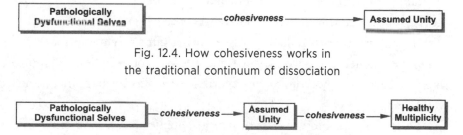

Fig. 12.4. How cohesiveness works in
the traditional continuum of dissociation

Fig. 12.5. How cohesiveness works
in the full spectrum of selves

THE EXPANDED FULL SPECTRUM OF SELVES

So far, the two representations we have looked at—the traditional continuum of dissociation and the full spectrum of selves—both use the horizontal axis to represent how cohesive someone's selves are and how well they both function.

But we can see more by adding in *happiness and well-being.* Thus, the expanded full spectrum shows both (1) cohesiveness and (2) happiness and well-being (including health and satisfaction).

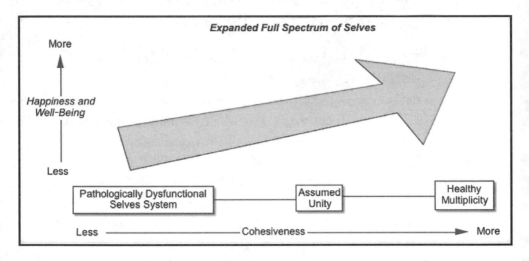

Fig. 12.6. How cohesiveness and health and well-being work
in the expanded full spectrum of selves

The broad gray arrow in figure 12.6, the expanded full spectrum diagram, represents our observation that the more cohesive you are, the more happiness and well-being you are likely to experience. Specifically, with regard to the constellation of selves that currently composes each of us, the further along we move toward healthy multiplicity, the more likely we are, on the whole, to experience increasing happiness and well-being.

The happiness and wellness dimension applies not just to our overall system of selves but also to our individual selves as well; that is, each of our different selves *also* has a place somewhere along the vertical happiness and well-being dimension. It is important to see how cohesive each self is—how well it works with other selves—but it's also important to be aware of the well-being and happiness of each self.

Some of your selves may be very functional and happy, others less so, and still others may need help, assistance, or educational and developmental options. Remember when we spoke about how happy a self that rarely gets to come out or be on the spot feels when it has an opportunity to contribute? Similarly, consider how much better you as a whole human being will feel and function as you begin to address and assist your least happy or well selves.

THE HEALTHY NEW NORMAL
BEYOND THE SINGLE SELF ASSUMPTION

It is easiest to see the overall scope of our inquiry by viewing the progression to the expanded full spectrum in a single diagram (see fig. 12.7, p. 360).

As the expanded full spectrum makes clear, by stepping beyond assumed unity we enter into new territory. As stated throughout the book, there are many people who have already figured out—in one way or another—that they and other people have selves and that acknowledging and working with this reality, even to a small degree, increases cohesiveness and produces dramatic positive results.

This territory, where people consciously acknowledge and work with their own selves and the selves of others—will, we believe, over time become thought of as the "healthy new normal." It will be healthy because it embraces healthy multiplicity in conscious and effective ways; it will be new because previous attempts at embracing and understanding multiplicity have almost always focused only on pathological versions and manifestations; and it will be or become normal in the sense that it will eventually come to be seen as something that characterizes all human beings.

Yes, the societal and cultural responses—from the legal system to psychiatry, psychology, and the mental health system as a whole—will take some time to catch up and recognize healthy multiplicity for what

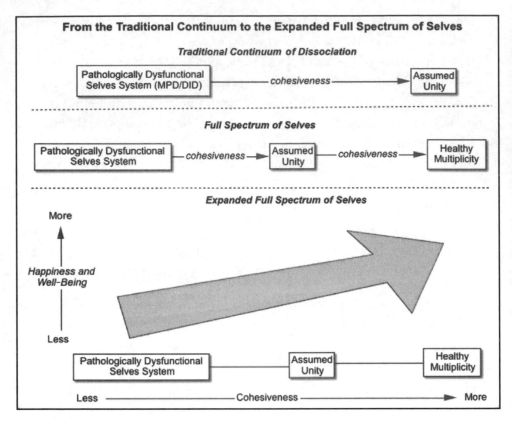

Fig. 12.7. Cohesiveness from the traditional continuum of dissociation (top) to the expanded full spectrum of selves (bottom)

it is. But if we are correct that assuming and working with the reality of healthy multiplicity does indeed produce positive results and outcomes, then more and more people will inevitably embrace these ideas and practices.

As increasing numbers of people come to understand and embrace the healthy selves worldview, it will become not just much more common but de facto will become normalized. The more normalized and common it becomes, the more additional people will find themselves letting go of assumed unity. In this way, we hope that saner, healthier, and more effective individuals who better know how to access their capacities will help make a better world for all of us.

THIRTEEN

Recaps, Reflections, Reminders

The idea that we all have multiple personalities—but not a disorder of personalities—may at first be shocking. But the evidence for this normal multiplicity . . . is so powerful that even the most skeptical of readers may change their minds.

JAY NORICKS, *PARTS PSYCHOLOGY*

A brief recap of the book's major points begins with three central premises:

- We all have selves.
- Different selves are truly different and inherently valuable.
- Ultimately, it is easy to see beyond the Single Self Assumption.

We first described potential benefits and advantages: living in a world that makes more sense; increased physical and emotional energy; increased skills, talents, and creativity; better relationships; and a greater ability to heal and manage pain and more easily overcome bad habits and addictions. Next, we expanded on a simple phrase: "Mental health is being in the right mind at the right time."

In the second section we presented examples of cultural and intellectual multiplicity all around us. We took a tour through language, hearing voices, and popular culture. We then turned to selves, souls, and multiplicity in worldwide religions and Western philosophy. Next, we described selves from the perspective of psychology, with a special emphasis on the evolution of the idea through the works and relationships of significant psychological theorists and practitioners. Finally, we noted that a convergence of ideas in psychology, modern science, Buddhism, and postmodern thinking all pointed to selves.

In the third section we offered speculations for the origins, attributes, and roles of selves. We looked at what selves are, how they might arise, and how people experience them. We turned to models and metaphors for how selves can cooperate, including symphonies, rock bands, actors, groupings of animals, and more. Next, we presented some tools, techniques, and strategies for selves work.

The final section looked at organized responses, reactions, and approaches to working with selves, including those offered by spiritual teachers and by a number of current psychological and therapeutic approaches. We then turned to the possible disruptive effects of recognizing selves on religious institutions, the criminal justice system, and the health care system. Last, we described what an expanded view of personal health might look like given a proper appreciation of selves. The book closes with an appendix on the term *dissociation*.

AN ALTERNATIVE
METHODOLOGICAL RECAP

An alternative recap of this book derives from our overall approach and method; that is, *what* have we done and *why* have we done it? We have tried hard to make this clear from the very beginning, as illustrated by the following anecdote.

One day, Jim observed several colorful pinwheels spinning energetically in Jordan's front yard. Jim noted that what was making them spin might have been a little electric motor in each one (battery or solar powered). Or, it might have been leprechauns, or the spirits of dead relatives. But probably it was just the wind. First, Jim simply observed what was there: spinning pinwheels. Second, he used common sense and prior experience to begin to figure things out, discarding explanations as he went.

From the very start, then, our main goal has been primarily to point to what we ourselves have seen and experienced—that people have selves and that understanding and applying this realization provides a wide range of benefits. To back up our observations, we also presented examples from religion, philosophy, psychology, neuroscience, computer science, economics, literature, movies, comic books, and more. And we included many stories—about ourselves and people we know—about the benefits of recognizing, encouraging, and working with healthy selves.

All of this was done so that you would be spurred to notice your own selves, and the selves of others. We wanted to make it increasingly easy for you to observe selves in action, test things out, and take appropriate action.

Some Personal Reflections: Jim

When Jordan suggested that, for the conclusion, each of us write about how this book has changed our own behavior and awareness, I wasn't sure what to say, since I have already been thinking along these lines for many years.

Handing me drafts of the last two chapters and the appendix, plus that request, he left on a short family vacation, knowing that I would quickly get to work with suggestions and revisions. More than a week passed, and I had not touched the materials. I wondered (and worried) about my inaction. Then, sitting down in the same coffeehouse in Santa Cruz, California, where I'd edited before, almost immediately I became immersed in the editing.

Laughing at myself, the obviousness hit me. I had shifted into the self that was fully invested in the book being as clear and well written as possible. That self was capable of—even enjoyed—serious editing (staying in flow with a tight focus and not being distracted by the other issues I was dealing with that day).

Later, as the coffeehouse closed around me, I felt relief and pleasure as I finished the last page of one chapter. I've edited enough books and articles to know when it is going well. I have an equal number of memories of avoiding editing and doing all kinds of other tasks instead. The difference that day was that I observed my own self-shift—what was new was that I now had an accurate word for it—and saw that it was voluntary. I'd moved into "the right mind at the right time." Writing this book has greatly enhanced my ability to notice when others and I move among selves.

When we began this book, Jordan and I were coming from very different realms of experience. I have been mulling over these ideas for more than thirty years, written short articles, done workshops, given speeches, collected examples, spoken about it with friends and family— even laid out possible books. While Jordan had intuitively grasped the idea of healthy multiplicity, he had, to begin with, no knowledge of its many manifestations or potential positive influence. When we first decided to work together, I said to Jordan, "Let me give you my files." I handed him a very large and very full file box. A few weeks later I called to tell him, "I've found more files," and heard a soft groan on the other end of the phone. The second box was, if anything, larger than the first.

However, because Jordan is so able to shift into his researcher, information sifter, and categorizing self, he soon settled into my files and began to compile his own more detailed, extensive, and better structured information database. Several months later, he had readied a detailed table of contents. I was astounded—at first abashed, but soon delighted—to recognize that Jordan now knew much more than I ever had about multiplicity throughout popular culture, philosophy, religions, and science.

As we worked, we swapped stories (some included) of moments when we were aware of moving into and being in the right self, or of finding ourselves in the wrong self, or seeing people close to us in these and many other similar self-shift situations. I became more sensitized to when I had been triggered—in other words, about to snap into a different (and almost never better) self. More and more often, as we worked along, I could step back and unhook myself from a trigger in time, getting to appreciate how potentially difficult situations would resolve themselves without the intermediate steps of rancor, anger, and hurtful behavior, followed by regrets and apologies.

Like the scientists who give themselves the illness for which they think they have the cure before letting anyone else try it, we have been beta testing the ideas in this book over the past two years on ourselves and a small circle of family and friends. This personal moment is a chance for me to acknowledge that even with decades of looking at this material—and making it conscious within my family—actually settling down and writing it has made yet another level of difference.

One final confession: my family—my wife and two daughters— have been urging me to write this book for many years. When Jordan first went through my files, he asked, "Do you know that you've written eight different outlines for this book?" With that and other revelations, it became clear to me that while healthy, normal multiplicity mattered tremendously to me and that my family and some close friends all benefited from our understanding of selves, I did not seem able to take the time and focus to actually "do my book." That self did not seem to exist. However, once Jordan became a full partner, this book seemed to unfold itself, far beyond what I'd ever envisioned.

NO SERIOUS FUSS AS TO THEORIES FOR US

The general idea of selves as being natural, ordinary, healthy, and desirable is only rarely part of ordinary day-to-day conversation. Yet, many people already regularly make use of an awareness of selves. They understand the idea when they hear it, they often speak of "a part of me" or use similar language or concepts, and some even consciously practice playing their personal symphonies less as solos and more as tuneful, well-orchestrated expressions of all of who they are.

For example, in the Northern California area where we both live, quite a few therapists, bodyworkers, and other health and wellness facilitators are aware of—and make good use of—the existence of their clients' selves. Similarly, many friends, colleagues, and even strangers whom we have spoken to about healthy selves get it right away, reciting back to us examples from their own lives, confirming their understanding and adding to our own. The concept is, no doubt, also percolating up in other parts of the world.

Whether or not "a complete theory reconciling all that is known about sub-personalities"* is ever developed, *there is a whole lot of basic groundwork to be done*—people putting these ideas into practice, with low-hanging functionality and wellness fruit abundantly available. We are, in other words, so very far from a complete and full theory that overconcern about theory is neither necessary nor especially useful.

However, we believe the initial core notions presented here are valid. These include that selves really are real, that they are inherently valuable and inherently matter, that you really can not and certainly should not attempt to forcefully integrate them away against their will, and so on.

These aren't theoretical observations but *factual* observations of our actual experience, of ourselves as our selves, and of other people as their selves. Apply the ideas and practices described here and note the results. Yes, you might have to soften your disbelief, but fortunately, nearly all of what we have presented is experiential, not theoretical. If you are open and aware, you can experience the benefits of healthy selves.

A LEVEL PROPOSITION: PRIORITIZING PRAGMATIC FOCUS OVER CEASELESS DOUBTING

The name [Pragmatism] was inspired by the belief that philosophical ideas or theories should be viewed as instruments, not absolute truths, and their validity judged by their practical consequences in our lives.

LEONARD MLODINOW, *SUBLIMINAL*

---

*In the preface to his own book, John Rowan writes, "This book tries to put subpersonalities on the map. At the moment this concept is not there, and it ought to be. Because this book is a pioneering effort it . . . does not profess to put forward a complete theory reconciling all that is known about subpersonalities . . . [which] is a task for later, when the field is better developed."[1] We are not there yet, but thanks to the efforts of many thinkers and writers, including Rowan, we are now on the way.

From the beginning, we have been clear that this is a pragmatic book. We hope you will make use of the basic ideas presented here to help you experience and test things for yourself.

However, notions of "levels" and "levels of reality" can get in one's way. For example, during the process of writing this book, we have often heard statements like this: "Regardless of everything else, wouldn't you agree that, on one level, we are all just a single human being?" Or, "Wouldn't you still say, though, that on one level, different selves are really just different moods, or maybe aspects, of who we are?"

On one level, these statements seem reasonable: we only have one physical body, so you *could* say that we are indeed a single human being, and you *could* say that selves are *just* moods, despite our detailed explanations of why such an assertion is misguided. Regardless of their potential reasonableness, such objections not only miss the point but also misdirect us away from a functional and pragmatic focus.

Similarly, notwithstanding the evidence we put forth as to the reality of selves—along behavioral, subjective, physiological, and pragmatic lines—some people may still wonder about whether selves are *actually* real or only exist at some internal psychological level. This wondering costs time and energy that could be better spent simply experiencing the real-world benefits that flow from acknowledging, appreciating, and working with selves.

Our general suggestion, then, is to not get stuck on whether selves are only real on some levels but not others. Leave those sorts of nebulous inquiries for the back burner, coffee shop, and social media thread. Instead, experience and experiment with these ideas. If you become happier, healthier, and more functional, you will likely lose interest in arguments and discussions as to the reality or non-reality of selves.

Experiencing and working with your own selves and the selves of others is not an intellectual or theoretical activity; it is a level-headed approach that will assert a powerful positive impact on your ordinary, everyday, embodied life and actions.

Some Personal Reflections: Jordan

When I suggested that we should both write personal reflections, I assumed that this would be easy for me. After all, I'd already drafted tens of thousands of words on this subject, including many personal stories. But, when my first draft was finished, it was obvious to me that my reflections essay had come mainly from an editorial headspace. I'd covered the major high points, but it was rushed and flat. Apparently, my best writer self had been elsewhere.

So I rewrote it . . . but it still wasn't very good. The part of me that might have had something valuable, useful, or interesting to say just wasn't available. Not even coffee and chocolate helped; despite all of my practice, shifting into the right mind at the right time was easier said than done.

But since perseverance is the middle name of at least one of my selves, I started out today in a café with paper and pen. Experience has shown me that actual handwriting slows me down, brings me fully present, and enables me to start drafting the kind of words you are now reading. Sometimes, the subtlest of environmental or instrumental cues is all that is needed to more easily and elegantly access a desired self.

At the end of the day, there are three important things to communicate here.

First, there is no doubt that as a full human being body/mind process—as a skin-encapsulated symphony of selves—practicing what we are preaching in this book has left the whole of me better off and more effective. More patience with my own and others' selves is not just an idea; it has become my living reality. And my/our ability to know when we can get something done—professionally or personally—based on which selves are available or already present, has made me/us better at nearly everything we do. Knowing that I have selves—being aware of which self is "up" and which ones might be available or desirable (and which ones should be avoided or shied away from)—is truly a lifelong game changer.

Second, there is also no doubt that many other people have already benefited from these ideas as we wrote the book. Several close friends have expressed their gratitude for the changes they have been able to make by just sticking with the idea of healthy normal multiplicity in their work and personal lives. Even my daughter—who has for a few years now ignored most of my advice—gained an invaluable insight. A focused musician throughout high school, a few months before this book was finished she came face-to-face with her final college decision: a dual-degree program at a rural Midwest school with a great conservatory and a well-regarded liberal arts college, or a high-ranking women's college in upper Manhattan. After many agonizing back-and-forths, she finally made a decision. Soon after, she texted me: "Dad, I get it. You're a genius! Part of me really does want to go to Manhattan, but more of me definitely wants to go for the dual-degree. It makes total sense now, why I felt so conflicted, just like your book says it does. There's more than one part of me, and that's totally normal."

Finally, I want to be very clear that all of me truly marvels at the parts of Jim Fadiman that have been working on this subject since about 1985, and thinking about them for longer than that. I heard Jim give a public talk on this exact subject the first time I ever laid eyes on him in 1989, and that same part of him has persevered for more than three decades in collecting articles and graduate papers, giving workshops, and thinking long and hard on what was missing. The one thing that was missing, as it turned out, was me.

Different parts of Jim and Jordan, you see, needed each other. Jim needed someone who could help him articulate, flesh out, and expand his original insights . . . and make it through his files and outlines. And Jordan needed someone like Jim, who had had a powerful set of insights (the existence and desirability of healthy, normal multiplicity as well as the recognition of the Single Self Assumption and the role it plays) and who needed a book written.

Mediated by physical proximity (we live two miles apart), intersecting social and professional circles, and deepening personal relationships in both our households, the magic of fate and destiny was able to bring us together after twenty-five years of friendship to write this book. For my part—for all of my parts—I remain extraordinarily delighted and excited, and unceasingly thankful and grateful.

One Last Anecdote:
A Wistful Wish Fulfilled

I (Jordan) was walking on a central path in our home garden and there, right at eye level, ready to smack me in the face, was an overhanging branch of blooming wisteria. Normally I would have pushed it aside, with a brief, irritated grumble that it "violated the corridor rule" and needed pruning.

But instead—wonder of wonders—I was able to shift into being someone who would just naturally relax, enjoy, and appreciate this eye-level bundle of beauty. I stopped still in my tracks; took several deep, fragrant whiffs; and reveled in the redolent, sun-glinting purple-lilac flowers for a long, lovely while.

Then I simply let it be, as I moved on to other needful things. Becoming that other me was easy and rewarding—a simple, natural flowering of the right self in the right time. It's not a big deal to proactively shift selves—for any of us, it requires just a moment of attention.

GETTING STARTED WITH LANGUAGE

Using "healthy selves language" in everyday life is both interesting and beneficial. Earlier we looked at research on how people talk to themselves (both in their heads and aloud). Those studies suggested that talking in other than the first person—other than in the "I" voice—brings greater emotional control in difficult situations. A recent study states, "The simple act of silently talking to yourself in the third person during stressful times may help you control emotions without any additional mental effort than what you would use for first-person self-talk."[2] To shift your own language, merely substitute in non-I words for references to yourself (your selves). Thus, you can try substituting in "this self" for "me," or "selves" for "self," and so on. Here are some examples of things you might say:

- "That makes part of me really happy."
- "That's pretty selves evident, isn't it?"
- "How is that self doing today?"
- "What's really bothering that part of me?"
- "The part of me that did that . . . that's not all of me. I need to work things out with that part of myself."
- "Not all of me is really behind that" or "All of me feels pretty good about that right now."

Similarly, with regard to others, you can try out phrases like "Which of you am I talking to?" or "Are all of you okay?" (For those hailing from the U.S. South, this is a good time to call on your "y'all" and "all of y'all" heritage, as described earlier.)

When you are alone, the use of some of these phrases may feel silly or contrived, or make you uncomfortable. Don't force things. Instead, see when and where such phrases not only fit without too much trouble but also make sense and feel right. Eventually, you might feel comfortable and even happy communicating about one or several of your selves in spoken or written communications, a common tactic in comedy, movies, television series, and other cultural expressions. As we become more aware of and move into the healthy new normal, our language and communication patterns—which are already always evolving anyway—will likely come to fully embrace healthy multiplicity. In this way we move beyond the Single Self Assumption not just cognitively, or even experientially, but self-reflectively, descriptively, and functionally as well.

FINAL WORDS AND MANY BLESSINGS TO ALL OF YOU

Robert Anton Wilson had a remarkable talent for leading readers to question assumptions that they didn't even know that they had, and redefine their unconsciously constructed notions of reality. He had an uncanny ability to lead his readers, unsuspectingly, into a mutable state of mind where

they are playfully tricked into "aha" experiences that caused
them to question their most basic assumptions about what is
real and what isn't.

DAVID JAY BROWN, NEW INTRODUCTION TO
ROBERT ANTON WILSON'S *QUANTUM PSYCHOLOGY*

We are neither as subtle nor as clever as Robert Anton Wilson was. Nonetheless, we hope we have led you to recognize your own "mutable state of mind"—your own changeable self-states—as well as the self-states of others. We hope we have occasioned you to question an inaccurate basic psychological assumption—the Single Self Assumption—that posits that only a single self is real.

Aware of both your own selves and the selves of others, you can get better and better at consciously shifting and harmonizing your selves to be in the right mind at the right time. You can also become increasingly aware of how the people in your life are *also shifting their selves,* which will lead you to be more understanding, patient, and compassionate. Generally speaking, when you see things more fully and accurately, your interactions with others will tend to go better.

As you become more cohesive and learn to consistently take advantage of the many capabilities found within your current constellation of selves, you will experience new types of growth and more success overall. Expanding the Delphic Oracle's maxim from "Know Thyself" to "Know Thy Many Selves" is inherently rewarding and self-validating—personally, interpersonally, and functionally. Knowledge, rewards, and greater camaraderie are immediately available, as simply and freely as breathing, and just as close.

Let us know how it goes. Email us at info@symphonyofselves.com.

Thank you for coming along with us on this journey, and many blessings to all of you and all of yours.

—JAMES FADIMAN
—JORDAN GRUBER

APPENDIX

Dissociation

Origins and Usage; Problems and Suggestions

Dissociation has been used by many people, in many contexts, to mean many things. For this and other reasons addressed here, it is an inherently problematic term. Moreover, despite its having been "the object of intense scholarly and scientific interest in recent years,"[1] it does not appear to be necessary—or even all that useful—in understanding and exploring healthy normal selves. As chapter 12 noted, we made very little use of the term throughout, and even then, it was mostly in historical references.

Nonetheless, since it is so ubiquitous and pervasive—a terminological elephant in the middle of a crowded room—it may be useful to look at dissociation's origins, meanings, and some of the problems with its use.

ORIGINS:
FROM DISSOCIATION TO
DÉSAGRÉGATION AND BACK AGAIN

Like the idea of the unconscious, the notion of dissociation did not suddenly spring forth from a single person's mind. Ernest Hilgard tells us that in the late-nineteenth century there was "nothing especially new about the concept of 'dissociation,' defined as the splitting off* of certain mental processes from the main body of consciousness with various degrees of autonomy."[2] Indeed, what was later identified as dissociation had been the focus of several nineteenth-century thinkers including Benjamin Rush, Frederick Myers, Charles Richet, Maine de Biran, Moreau de Tours, Gilles de la Tourette, and of course, Jean-Martin Charcot, among others.[†]

The phrase "dissociation of ideas" was apparently first used by Jacques-Joseph Moreau de Tours in 1845.[‡] And by 1880, Josef Breuer—who would share ideas, methods, money, and publishing credit with Sigmund Freud—had begun working with the patient Anna O., trying to explain her hysterical symptoms in terms of the trauma she suffered and the "double consciousness" she seemed to exhibit.[§]

It was, however, Pierre Janet who brought the term into focus. Janet, in an article in the *Revue Philosophique*,[3] "first used the term 'dissociation' in May 1887 to describe the phenomenon of 'double consciousness' in hypnotism, hysteria, spirit possession, and mediumship."[4] Then, in his 1889 book, *L'automatisme psychologique,* Janet switched over to the term *désagrégation* (in English, "disaggregation"). Janet uses the term dozens of times throughout the book. Chapter 3, for example, is

---

*Right from the start we find references to splitting off from an implied original, single, whole, real thing—the assumed, original, special Single Self. Even if the supposedly split-off thing, part, or self is healthy, independent, and autonomous, it is somehow seen as being less than, broken, or simply *not* the real thing. Our assumption in this book is radically different: there just *are* independent selves—a brute fact of nature—and these selves are not split off from a single original real self, nor are they otherwise less than or defective in any way.

†"There can be little doubt that Janet's thinking . . . was deeply influenced by his reading of then-contemporary authorities on automatism—Prosper Despite, Edmund Gurney, Frederick Myers, and Charles Richet."[5]

‡In 1845, Jacques-Joseph Moreau de Tours "in a paper about the altered state of consciousness 'of inebriation provoked by hashish,' coins, for the first time, the expression 'dissociation of ideas.'"[6]

§"By the mid 1890s Janet in France and Freud, with his collaborator Joseph Breuer, in Vienna had arrived independently at strikingly similar formulations: hysteria was a condition caused by psychological trauma. Unbearable emotional reactions to traumatic events produced an altered state of consciousness, which in turn induced the hysterical symptoms. Janet called this alteration in consciousness 'dissociation.' Breuer and Freud called it 'double consciousness.'"[7]

titled "Diverses Formes De La Désagrégation Psychologique" ("Various Forms of Psychological Disaggregation").[8]

In a section titled "Spiritism and Psychological Désagrégation," Janet refers to the previous efforts of his colleagues, Richet and Myers, work, "which I had tried to complete myself," and refers to it being "perfectly expressed" in an anonymous 1855 "short brochure of 93 pages."[9]

After Janet coined the term *désagrégation,* William James (in his 1890 book, *Principles of Psychology*) then used "the term dissociation to translate to English . . . Janet's concept of disaggregation."[10] Ernest Hilgard's etymological review suggests that James might have better translated *désagrégation* as "disaggregation":

> When "association" was the favorite process to describe the binding between two ideas, it is not surprising that a word was selected to represent their separation, or "dis-association." Janet (1889) used the French word désagrégation, which might have been better translated as "disaggregation" in English. However, the term dissociation became accepted in English, as used by William James in his *Principles of Psychology* (1890), and by Janet himself in his Harvard lectures, *The Major Symptoms of Hysteria* (1907).[11]

However, the notion that "dissociation" was simply a poor translation choice for *désagrégation* has been challenged. A 2006 letter to the editor of the *American Journal of Psychiatry* highlights "a common misunderstanding among North American students of dissociation":

> It is true that in *L'automatisme psychologique* Janet spoke of *désagrégation.* . . . However, both before and after this monumental publication, he regularly used the term dissociation, thereby following a tradition that may have started with Moreau de Tours. Consequently, Janet's use of the term dissociation in his Harvard lectures (published in 1907), for example, was not the simple result of translation. Rather, his use of the word dissociation reflected prior usage of the term by himself and others in French publications. Thus the term dissociation as evidenced in the literature today was

present in the French literature prior to Janet and does not owe its psychiatric existence to being the closest English translation for the French term *désagrégation*.[12]

We doubt that the history of psychology would have been different if instead of dissociation James had translated Janet's "désagrégation" as "disaggregation" and it had stuck. In any case, the idea of dissociation has a long and complicated history. It should not be surprising, then, that there have been inconsistencies and complications with later definitions and actual usage. "Although the construct of dissociation was introduced into psychiatry at the end of the 19th century by Pierre Janet, the term still lacks a coherent conceptualization. . . . Despite its clinical importance, dissociation represents a semantically open term leading to conceptual confusions."[13] Or as clinical psychologist Paul F. Dell noted in 2006, "Despite more than a century of research, there is still no generally accepted definition of disassociation."[14]

DEFINITIONS AND USAGES

Dissociation is defined in a wide variety of ways, depending on context and who is using it for what purpose. We will briefly look at its definitions and usage in a variety of contexts:

- as defined in general and medical dictionaries
- as defined in the DSM-V and the ICD-10
- as a scored output on modern psychological test instruments
- as used in ordinary conversation

Dictionary Definitions
Consider three general all-purpose dictionary definitions, starting with the Free Dictionary:

Psychiatry. A disintegration or fragmentation of the mind in which memories, thoughts, or aspects of the personality become disconnected, as in multiple personality disorder or some kinds of amnesia.[15]

This definition assumes that selves are real—as did the older "official" term, *multiple personality disorder* (MPD)—and then frames the mechanism of dissociation as being some kind of disintegration, fragmentation, or disconnection.

Dictionary.com, in turn, defines dissociation like this:

> The splitting off of a group of mental processes from the main body of consciousness, as in amnesia or certain forms of hysteria.[16]

In this simple definition, the connection between "splitting off" and the production and existence of selves is not clear.

Finally, *Merriam-Webster's* provides this definition:

> The separation of whole segments of the personality (as in multiple personality disorder) or of discrete mental processes (as in the schizophrenias) from the mainstream of consciousness or of behavior.[17]

This definition implies that something about the kind of "separation" that goes on between (a) whole segments of the personality and (b) discrete mental processes is similar enough to justify the use of dissociation both with regard to MPD and schizophrenia. However, as discussed earlier, the existence of selves—certainly healthy, and even pathological—is a completely distinct phenomena from the deep systems meltdown that schizophrenia encompasses.

The definitions found in medical dictionaries are more detailed. Here are three.

1. **The Free Dictionary: Medical Dictionary**
    —An unconscious separation of a group of mental processes from the rest, resulting in an independent functioning of these processes and a loss of the usual associations; for example, a separation of affect from cognition.
    —A state used as an essential part of a technique for healing in psychology and psychotherapy; for instance, in hypnotherapy or the neurolinguistic programming technique of Time-Line therapy.[18]

2. **MedTerms Dictionary (MedicineNet.com)**

   In psychology and psychiatry, a perceived detachment of the mind from the emotional state or even from the body. Dissociation is characterized by a sense of the world as a dreamlike or unreal place and may be accompanied by poor memory of specific events.[19]

3. **MedicalDictionary.Com (from the Dictionary of Cell and Molecular Biology)**

   A defense mechanism in which a group of mental processes are segregated from the rest of a person's mental activity in order to avoid emotional distress, as in the dissociative disorders or in which an idea or object is segregated from its emotional significance. . . . A defect of mental integration in which one or more groups of mental processes become separated off from normal consciousness and, thus separated, function as a unitary whole.[20]

The Free Dictionary's Medical Dictionary refers to "independent functioning" of a group of mental processes, and MedicalDictionary.com refers to selves that "function as a unitary whole." MedicineNet .com, however, does not mention selves or sub-personalities and instead focuses on depersonalization (where you feel detached from who you are, as if you were a fake or not a real person) and derealization (where feelings of detachment and unreality are experienced with regard to your environment and other people). While the Free Dictionary's Medical Dictionary allows the possibility that in some cases a dissociative state can be "an essential part of a technique for healing," MedicalDictionary.com states flatly that dissociation is "a defect of mental integration."

Overall, both the regular and medical dictionaries seem to mainly define dissociation in terms of a process or function—some kind of splitting or separating—that produces independent selves (mental processes, unitary wholes). However, they are inconsistent in their definitions and sporadic in their inclusion of schizophrenia and other dysfunctional conditions or symptoms such as amnesia, depersonalization, and derealization.

DSM-V (and ICD-10)

The Diagnostic and Statistical Manual V (the DSM-V), the bible of American psychiatry, and the ICD-10, the World Health Organization's International Classification of Diseases, tenth revision, both address dissociative disorders from a clinical medical perspective. We need focus only on the DSM-V here because DSM codes and ICD codes are the same codes.

The DSM-V, released in 2013, lists five dissociative disorders,* with the most important of these being Dissociative Identity Disorder (DID), DSM-V code 300.14 (ICD-10 F44.81). TraumaDissociation.com provides us a bit of quick history:

> Dissociative disorders were included in the DSM-I as "dissociative reaction," and became a separate category in the 1980[s], with the publication of the DSM-III. In that edition, Multiple Personality Disorder became a separate diagnosis rather than a subtype of a more general condition. MPD was renamed Dissociative Identity Disorder in the 1994 DSM-IV.[21]

Further, according to TraumaDissociation.com, these "dissociative disorders are mutually exclusive and appear in a hierarchy, with Dissociative Identity Disorder taking precedence over Dissociative Amnesia and Depersonalization/Derealization Disorder";[22] that is, the first of these is the "worst" diagnosis you can receive, and subsumes the others. Depersonalization and derealization, then, are lower down in the hierarchy than DID.

The DSM-V states five criteria for DID (300.14). Economically restated, they are:

---

*Here are the five diagnoses: • Dissociative Identity Disorder (DID), DSM-V code 300.14 (ICD-10 F44.81) • Dissociative Amnesia including Dissociative Fugue, DSM-V code 300.12 (ICD-10 F44.0) • Depersonalization/Derealization Disorder, DSM-V code 300.6 (ICD-10 F48.1) • Other Specific Dissociative Disorder, DSM-V code 300.16 (ICD-10 F44.89) • Unspecified Dissociative Disorder, DSM-V code 300.15 (ICD-10 F44.9)[23]

1. disruption of identity characterized by two or more distinct personality states;
2. recurrent gaps in memory inconsistent with ordinary forgetting;
3. the symptoms cause clinically significant distress or impairment in social, occupational, or other important areas of functioning;
4. the disturbance is not a normal part of a broadly accepted cultural or religious practice; and
5. the symptoms are not attributable to the physiological effects of a substance.

Consider the first two sentences of the full first criterion: "Disruption of identity characterized by two or more distinct personality states, which may be described in some cultures as an experience of possession. The disruption in identity involves marked discontinuity in sense of self and sense of agency, accompanied by related alterations in affect, behavior, consciousness, memory, perception, cognition, and/or sensory-motor functioning." The DSM-V thus recognizes that people can experience "two or more distinct personality states." It also can be read as equating to having two or more distinct personality states as inherently being a "disruption."

Alternatively, the DSM-V here can also be read as saying that having two or more personality states is *not* a problem in and of itself. First, having those states must produce a disruption not just of "sense of self" but also of "sense of agency." On top of that, this dual disruption must also be "accompanied by related alterations in affect, behavior, consciousness, memory, perception, cognition, and/or sensory-motor functioning."

Thus, suppose someone does have two distinct recurring personality states and arguably therefore experiences a disruption of their "sense of self." But if they do not also have a disruption in their "sense of agency"—think about all the ways consciously shifting selves can actually increase one's effectiveness and agency in the world—then it seems that this diagnosis would not fit. And even if their sense of agency is disrupted, for the diagnosis to fit, it must be accompanied by problems with feeling, acting, remembering, thinking, or moving their bodies. The upshot is that even under the DSM-V, while having "distinct personality states" is necessary for DID, it is nowhere near sufficient.

Significantly, *the DSM itself never simply and precisely defines dissociation or the underlying mechanisms behind it.* It sets out the five different types of dissociative disorders, it uses the term *dissociative* in its titles and headings, and in the preamble to the section on dissociative disorders it tells us that the "dissociative disorders are frequently found in the aftermath of trauma." In a section titled "Development and Course," we are told that "dissociation in children may generate problems with memory, concentration, attachment, and traumatic play," but no mechanism or process for dissociation itself is precisely defined here.

Instead, we are left to backfill for ourselves if we want to construct a consistent and delimited definition of dissociation. It apparently has something to do with experiencing distinct personality states and is somehow related to amnesia and clinical dysfunction. Or, if we are looking at some of the lesser diagnoses, it also seems to have something to do with losing track of time (fugues), feelings of detachment and unreality (depersonalization or derealization), or memory loss (amnesia*). Ultimately, we have an edifice of interlocking definitions and symptoms used to regulate the medical industry, not a consistent and direct definition.

Psychological Test Instruments

Mental health professionals use a variety of different tests—interviews, surveys, or other scored instruments—to determine an individual's level of dissociation. These tests include structured interviews with patients or persons of interest, clinical/parent rating scales,

---

*Perhaps most amnesia is a memory of events not easily—or not at all—shared between selves. "Lost" memories, then, can often be recovered when hypnosis or other means are used to shift one back into a self or constellation of selves that had the memory and can communicate about it.

and self-report rating scales. Older tools are replaced or upgraded, and even newer ones are frequently revised.*

For example, there is the Dissociative Experiences Scale (DES-II), which comes from the original DES-I developed by Eve Carlson and Frank Putnam.[24] Following are the first two questions from the twenty-eight-item questionnaire.

> 1. Some people have the experience of driving or riding in a car or bus or subway and suddenly realizing that they don't remember what has happened during all or part of the trip. Select the number to show what percentage of the time this happens to you.
>
> 0% (Never) 10 20 30 40 50 60 70 80 90 100% (Always)
>
> 2. Some people find that sometimes they are listening to someone talk and they suddenly realize that they did not hear part or all of what was said. Select the number to show what percentage of the time this happens to you.
>
> 0% (Never) 10 20 30 40 50 60 70 80 90 100% (Always)[25]

These first two questions—and others focused on sometimes hearing voices or talking aloud while alone—concern behaviors that, as discussed throughout this book, are arguably not abnormal at all. Other questions center on dysfunctional hyper-focus, memory loss, or feelings of unreality. Only question 22 directly addresses the experience of having independent selves.

> 22. Some people find that in one situation they may act so differently compared with another situation that they feel almost as if

---

*Available test instruments include: • The Dissociative Disorders Interview Schedule (DDIS) • The Structured Clinical Interview for DSM-V Dissociative Disorders (SCID-5-PD) • Clinician Administered Dissociative States Scale (CADSS) • The Dissociative Experience Scale (DES, DES-II) • Questionnaire of Experiences of Dissociation (QED) • Dissociation Questionnaire (DIS-Q) • Somatoform Dissociation Questionnaire (SDQ-5) • Multidimensional Inventory of Dissociation (MID) • Multiscale Dissociation Inventory (MDI0) • Child/Adolescent Dissociative Checklist • Child Dissociative Checklist • Adolescent Dissociative Experiences Scale (ADES)[26] they were two different people. Select the number to show what percentage of the time this happens to you.[27]

0% (Never) 10 20 30 40 50 60 70 80 90 100% (Always)

As with the DSM and ICD, the primary purpose of all of these instruments is to enable mental health professionals to assess troubled individuals and diagnose them for specific treatment and insurance billing purposes. These tests are based on a commonly agreed sense as to what is and is not normal, problematic, and treatable.

However, few of these test instruments specifically and clearly define dissociation, and no two of them define it in exactly the same way. Additionally, when we compare them, we find that they vary significantly in their focus on (a) experiencing separate identities or selves; (b) spacing out or in (lack of focus *or* over absorption); (c) memory loss; (d) detachment from self, others, and the world; or (e) inappropriate behavior and social dysfunction. In short, these instruments fail to provide standardized grading for symptoms in pathological cases of substantial dysfunction. Moreover, they do not move us very far along in understanding the relationship between dissociation—whatever exactly it is—and the existence of both pathological and, more importantly for our purposes, normal, healthy selves.

Conversational Usage—Asserting Someone Else's "Where" or "How" Is Wrong

When average laypeople with no professional mental health background say that someone else—or perhaps you—are dissociating, they tend to mean one of three things:

- The person is *not fully present* through either lack of focus (spacing out) or hyper-focus (spacing in).
- The person is *detached from reality*, either depersonalized or derealized.
- The person has, in a noticeable and perhaps distressing manner, moved from one self to another.

In the first of these, the "where" of someone else's focus is assessed as being wrong or inappropriate. Thus, someone who demonstrates a lack of real-time presence and has an inability to focus is considered to be "spaced out," "a million miles away," or "not really here." Alternatively, someone can be overfocused or hyper-focused, perhaps lost in a screen or a book. Here, once again (according to another person), someone is so deeply involved in what they are doing or experiencing that they are not *where* they are supposed to be and are sometimes then said to be dissociated.

The second and third lay usages of dissociation come from the assessment that *how someone else is behaving* is inappropriate, wrong, or off-base. Thus, in the second lay usage, someone might be said to be dissociated if they experience—or are noticed as experiencing—either depersonalization or derealization.*

In the third main common usage, to say to someone else that they have dissociated is essentially to notify them that *how* they are acting in the moment is wrong or inappropriate. They have either shifted or switched selves in a manner that the other person has noticed—and usually does not approve of. Suppose one of John's front-and-center selves is talking to Mary when a difficult subject comes up. If (from Mary's perspective) John abruptly and obviously moves into a different self, then Mary might say, "You are dissociating again."† But from John's perspective, it might have been a perfectly sensible shift into a more useful self. It all depends upon whose perspective you take.

---

*Notice how this definition from the *Merck Manual* is fairly typical in how it presents dissociation, derealization, and depersonalization in one bundle: "Depersonalization/derealization disorder is a type of dissociative disorder that consists of persistent or recurrent feelings of being detached (dissociated) from one's body or mental processes, usually with a feeling of being an outside observer of one's life (depersonalization), or of being detached from one's surroundings (derealization)."[28]

†Interestingly, the DSM-V's Code 300.14, which defines DID, ends its first paragraph by stating, "These signs and symptoms may be observed by others or reported by the individual." In conversational usage, however, more often than not instead of self-reporting it is one person telling another that the other person has a problem and is dissociating.

PROBLEMS WITH ITS USE

The term *dissociation* is burdened with five significant problems:

1. Variable and inconsistent definitions*
2. Emotionally charged usage
3. Reification according to cultural norms
4. Conversational deconstruction
5. Pervasive but unconscious reassertion of the Single Self Assumption

The first problem is the variability and incoherence of the definitions given to dissociation, as just demonstrated. As a quick review, we have:

- general and medical dictionaries, no two of which give the same definition, that rely on a wide range of meanings;
- official diagnoses, like the DSM-V, that never clearly and specifically define the term;
- test instruments with scored outputs, which mix and match a wide variety of definitions and are mainly designed for the medical and insurance industries; and
- commonplace lay usage that can refer to a lack or presence or focus (the wrong "where"), or someone being too detached or having too much movement from one self-state or constellation of selves to another (the wrong "how").

This lack of precision, and the non-existence of a simple, consistent definition, enables people to use the term *dissociation* in a wide variety of contexts to mean just what they want or need it to mean according to their current purposes.

The second problem is the use of the term in such an emotionally

---

*"Since there is no consistent agreement about precisely what dissociation 'is' . . ." begins one section in a 2006 *World Psychiatry* article on recent developments in dissociation.[29]

charged manner that no further discussion or constructive conversation is possible. Early on, Jordan was telling a friend about the main themes of this book. She unhesitatingly and emphatically stated that she was close to someone "who dissociated, who had absolutely ruined his life" and that therefore "advocating dissociation in any way, shape, or form is just wrong."

Dissociation, then, is often so loaded with negative associations and judgments that anything that can be taken as dissociation—or that even resembles what dissociation is supposed to be—can bring forth dismissive, angry, or negative reactions. Ironically, in this case, the mere mention of the word *dissociation* triggered or switched someone into a very judgmental self with regard to both dissociation and healthy multiplicity.

The third problem is the desire to button-down dissociation with a simple, culturally familiar definition. Stanley Krippner has written:

> Westerners are prone to take terms with which they are familiar and superpose them on phenomena in other cultures with which they are unfamiliar. Like other hypothetical constructs in the social sciences, the term "dissociation" is an attempt by social groups to describe, explain, or otherwise account for the world in which they live. . . . So called "dissociative" phenomena have been given varied labels and interpretations in different eras and locations, as well as in diverse historically and geographically situated interchanges among people. An understanding of this situation should prevent the reification of such expressions as "dissociation" and "dissociative disorders," and the uncritical acceptance of the Western construction of these phenomena.[30]

When Krippner talks about preventing the reification of the term *dissociation,* he means to not oversimplify it by making it into a thing and giving it definite concrete form.

The fourth problem relates to the third conversational usage described earlier, where one person has moved—in a noticeable manner, according to the other person—from one self to another. Continuing with our example, after a difficult subject has come up, Mary feels that John has clearly moved into a self that is not his normal and approved of self, so she tells him that he has dissociated.

But from *John's perspective,* there are a number of different possibilities. First, he might not have changed selves at all, but instead, Mary might have moved into another self—and from the perspective of Mary's different self, it might have looked to her that it was John who changed selves. Second, again from John's perspective, he may have consciously shifted—as opposed to having abruptly switched—into an appropriate self, and thus Mary's disapproval with his asserted dissociation would make no sense to him.

Following postmodern techniques of deconstruction, then, depending on whose perspective we take, the assertion that someone else has dissociated can be seen as a manipulation. If I move from one self to another in a way that you dislike, disapprove of, or feel uncomfortable with, then you can claim I dissociated—but perhaps it is really more about how you feel or what you have done than what I have done.

Finally, the term *dissociation* can be seen as doing a lot of the ongoing legwork needed to maintain the Single Self Assumption. If only a single self is possible, then any movement or shifting away from that single self—whether through gentle and intentional shifting or through abrupt and unconscious switching or triggering—is necessarily characterized as being undesirable and pathological. Almost all standard uses of the term *dissociation* thus reinforce the Single Self Assumption.

DEFINITIONAL SUBSTITUTION: COHESIVENESS FOR DISSOCIATION

The process, function, or state that dissociation has been taken to refer to plays a deeply ingrained role within the functional grammar of today's interlocking medical-psychology-insurance system. Even though we did not need or make much use of the term throughout this book, it is unlikely that dissociation as a term of art will go away completely any time soon.*

For now, as was suggested in chapter 12, we suggest substituting *cohesiveness* for *dissociation* as a means for facilitating a more fruitful discussion. Cohesiveness is defined in terms of how well integrated someone is in their function and presentation. Cohesiveness can be further evaluated in terms of:

- the congruence between someone's current words and behavior juxtaposed with their previous words, behavior, intentions, and plans;
- the coherence with which they present themselves and are experienced in human interactions and relationships; and
- the compassion they demonstrate both to their own selves and the selves of others.

The next time someone throws out some form of the term *dissociation* in conversation, consider for a moment whether whatever is being discussed might also be reframed so it can be described in terms of cohesiveness. Working from a positive map that is not derived from pathology, the use of a straightforward term like *cohesiveness*—instead of a hopelessly muddled and problematic one like *dissociation*—will set you on a better and more selves-aware course.

---

*Not surprisingly, a number of other interesting and creative attempts at redefining or expanding dissociation have also been made. These include Bennett Braun's "BASK Model of Dissociation," which "maps the process of dissociation along the lines of Behavior, Affect, Sensation and Knowledge";[31] Stanley Krippner's paper in which he contrasts Dissociation (Interrupted Flow) and Integrated Awareness (Flow) on one axis, and Control and Lack of Control on another;[32] and Judith Springer's 1994 master's thesis for the Institute of Transpersonal Psychology titled "Awareness, Access, and Choice: A Transpersonal Perspective on Dissociation, Association, Health and Illness" develops a model in which she shows that we can be too associated or too dissociated across a number of experiential dimensions.[33]

Notes

ONE. WHAT THIS IS ABOUT AND WHAT WE HOPE TO ACCOMPLISH

1. See Helen Green's website for her illustrations.
2. Jim Farber, "David Bowie Speaks on Musical Influences, 'Ziggy Stardust' Era and Getting Older in Final In-Depth Interview with the Daily News," *New York Daily News* website, updated January 11, 2016.
3. Oliver James, "Upping Your Ziggy," 47–48.
4. Oliver James, "Upping Your Ziggy," 48.
5. Jevon Dängeli, "Transpersonal Psychology: New Perspectives," at Authentic Self Empowerment website.
6. Goleman, "Probing the Enigma of Multiple Personality."

TWO. THE BENEFITS OF THE HEALTHY SELVES MODEL

1. William James, preface to *The Meaning of Truth,* ix–xxiv.
2. Kirkpatrick, "Walker: A Renaissance Man."
3. Madison Park, "Nearing 50, Renaissance Jock Herschel Walker Breaks Fitness Rules," CNN website, October 11, 2010.
4. The Athletic Build website, "Herschel Walker Bio, Workout, and Diet Plan," June 22, 2012, accessed July 1, 2017.
5. Daniel Williams, "Football Fit: A Look at Herschel Walker's Football Routine," at NFL website, updated February 1, 2017.
6. Walker, *Breaking Free,* 13.
7. Walker, prologue to *Breaking Free.*
8. Walker, *Breaking Free,* 6.
9. Walker, *Breaking Free,* xv.
10. Carter Strickland, "Herschel Walker Reveals He Suffers from Multiple Personality Disorder," *Star Tribune,* March 15, 2008.

11. Transcribed from video interview: "Herschel Walker: Man of Many Talents," YouTube, accessed June 1, 2016 (no longer available).

12. "Herschel Walker: Man of Many Talents," YouTube (no longer available).

13. "Herschel Walker: Man of Many Talents," YouTube (no longer available).

14. Strickland, "Herschel Walker Reveals He Suffers from Multiple Personality Disorder."

15. Strickland, "Herschel Walker Reveals He Suffers from Multiple Personality Disorder."

16. Walker, *Breaking Free*, 14.

17. Walker, *Breaking Free*, 18.

18. Lester, *On Multiple Selves*, 176.

19. Shah, *The Commanding Self*, 7.

20. Rowan, *Subpersonalities*, 105, quoting Genie Laborde.

21. Rowan, *Subpersonalities*, 189.

22. Fadiman, *Unlimit Your Life*.

23. Haddock, *The Dissociative Identity Disorder Sourcebook*, 50.

24. Kaufman and Gregoire, *Wired to Create*, xxvi.

25. Sliker, *Multiple Mind*, 35.

26. Kaufman and Gregoire, *Wired to Create*, xx.

27. Grierson, "What If Aging Is Nothing but a Mind-Set?"

28. Keyes, *The Minds of Billy Milligan*, xvii.

29. Walker, *Breaking Free*, 52.

30. Walker, *Breaking Free*, 54.

31. Walker, *Breaking Free*, 53–54.

32. Walker, *Breaking Free*, 130.

33. Kenyon, *Brain States*, 159.

34. "Psychotherapy and the Treatment of Alcohol Dependence," at Alcohol MD website, accessed July 1, 2017.

35. Romans 7:15–19, New International Version at Bible Gateway website, accessed January 13, 2020.

36. Rowan, *Subpersonalities*, 189.

37. Wikipedia, s.v. "Alvin Toffler," accessed July 1, 2017.

38. See Russell Goldman, "Here's a List of 58 Gender Options for Facebook Users," at ABC News website, February 13, 2014.

39. Mick Cooper, "If You Can't Be Jekyll Be Hyde: An Existential-Phenomenological Exploration on Lived-Plurality," in Rowan and Cooper, *The Plural Self*, 68–69.

40. Carter, *The People You Are*, 249.

THREE. MENTAL HEALTH IS BEING IN THE RIGHT MIND AT THE RIGHT TIME

1. Ray Grasse, personal communication to Jordan Gruber, November 18, 2015.
2. Ramos, *Dissociation*, 59.
3. "Howard Stern and Jerry Seinfeld Discuss Transcendental Meditation," YouTube, accessed January 9, 2017 (no longer available).
4. Ferriss, *The 4-Hour Body*. (For a list of his online resources, see "Becoming Uberman: Sleeping Less with Polyphasic Sleep" on his blog [Tim.blog], linked from "The 4-Hour Body Tools" page.)
5. Tom McCook, personal conversation with Jordan Gruber, October 2017.

FOUR. LANGUAGE, VOICES, AND POPULAR CULTURE

1. Ramos, *Dissociation*, 47.
2. Noricks, *Parts Psychology*, 2.
3. Baldwin, *Four and Twenty Blackbirds*, 31.
4. Carter, *The People You Are*, 81.
5. Carter, *The People You Are*, 81.
6. Lester, *On Multiple Selves*, xi.
7. Ferris, "Lent 1, Adam's Legacy, Romans 5:12–19," in Killen et al., *Sermons on the Second Readings*, 139–40.
8. *Fiddler on the Roof* movie script, Script-O-Rama website, accessed January 7, 2017.
9. Jen Nowell, "Keeble & Shucat Closing," *Palo Alto Daily Post*, September 16, 2016.
10. Arika Okrent, "Can 'Y'all' Be Used to Refer to a Single Person?," at Mental Floss website, September 10, 2014.
11. Wikipedia, s.v. "Y'all," accessed January 7, 2017.
12. Mencken, The American Language: Supplement 2, 337.
13. Okrent, "Can 'Y'all' Be Used to Refer to a Single Person?"
14. American Dialect Society, "2015 Word of the Year is singular 'they,'" American Dialect website, January 8, 2016.
15. Augustine, *Augustine of Hippo*, 94.
16. Jad Abumrad and Robert Krulwich, "The Voices Inside You," RadioLab, at WNYC studios (podcast), June 26, 2013.
17. Peter Moseley, "Talking to Ourselves," *Guardian*, August 21, 2014.
18. Mental Health Foundation, "Hearing Voices," at Mental Health website, accessed January 6, 2017.

19. Mental Health Foundation, "Hearing Voices."

20. Nancy A. Stewart, "The Devil Made Me Do It?!?!," Faith & Grace blog, July 12, 2016 (no longer available).

21. Laura Wiley, "Why Do People Talk to Themselves?"

22. Guy Winch, "Why You Should Start Talking to Yourself," at *Psychology Today,* The Squeaky Wheel blog, May 29, 2014.

23. Laura Wiley, "Why Do People Talk to Themselves?"

24. See also Michigan State University, "Talking to Yourself in the Third Person Can Help You Control Emotions," at *ScienceDaily* website, July 26, 2017.

25. Jean Houston, interview by Rebecca McClen Novick and David Jay Brown, "Jean Houston PhD Awakening Human Potential," at Awaken website, posted April 3, 2015, accessed November 13, 2019.

26. James S. Grotstein, "The Alter Ego and Déjà vu Phenomena: Notes and Reflections," in Rowan and Cooper, *The Plural Self,* 33.

27. Cardin, "Those Sorrows Which Are Sent to Wean Us from the Earth."

28. Prince, *Psychotherapy and Multiple Personality,* 201.

29. Hesse, *Steppenwolfe,* 40–59.

30. Nin, *The Diary of Anaïs Nin,* 47.

31. Nin, *The Diary of Anaïs Nin,* 241.

32. Joy, *Avalanche,* 61–62.

33. Joy, *Avalanche,* 69–70.

34. Colin Wilson, *Mysteries,* 210.

35. Colin Wilson, *Mysteries,* 223.

36. Colin Wilson, *Mysteries,* 229.

37. Kaufman and Gregoire, *Wired to Create,* xxi.

38. Gergen, "Multiple Identity," 31–35, 64–66.

39. Carroll, *Alice's Adventures in Wonderland,* 19–21.

40. Thomas, *The Medusa and the Snail,* 42–44.

41. Ellenberger, *The Discovery of the Unconscious,* 167.

42. Rowan, *Subpersonalities,* 9, quoting Mary Louise von Franz, as transcribed from a film interview.

43. Ferguson, *Aquarius Now,* 52.

44. Carter, *The People You Are,* xii–xiv.

45. Carter, *The People You Are,* 249.

46. Khakpour, "Epic: An Interview with Salman Rushdie," 54–65.

47. Maugham, *A Writer's Notebook,* 23.

48. Wikipedia, s.v. "Virginia Woolf," accessed January 7, 2017.

49. Woolf, *Orlando,* 308–9 (cited in Bromberg, *Awakening the Dreamer,* 52).

50. Braun, *Treatment of Multiple Personality Disorder*, xi.

51. Wikipedia, s.v. *The Three Faces of Eve*, accessed January 7, 2017.

52. Lynn Neary, "Real 'Sybil' Admits Multiple Personalities Were Fake," at NPR website, October 20, 2011, accessed January 7, 2017.

53. Lynn Neary, "Real 'Sybil' Admits Multiple Personalities Were Fake."

54. Eagleman, *Incognito*, 19.

55. Eagleman, *Incognito*, 104.

56. Eagleman, *Incognito*, 104.

57. "Lohan Says Fiancé Was Abusing Her," *Palo Alto Daily Post*, August 8, 2016, 22.

58. Dave McGuinness, "A Brief History of the Comic Resurgence," at GeekOutInc.wordpress blog, accessed January 7, 2017.

59. Darrick Mattsen, "Creative Superhero Art Illustrates Their Secret Identities," at Walyou website, November 15, 2011.

60. See "Comic Book Characters and Multiple Personality Disorder," at Comic Collector Live web forum, accessed January 7, 2017.

61. Carter, *The People You Are*, 73.

62. Carter, *The People You Are*, 73.

63. Wikipedia, s.v. *I'm not There*, accessed December 16, 2019.

64. Tracy Smith, "Unraveling the Secret of 'Alters,'" CBS News website, March 8, 2009.

65. Gibran, "The Seven Selves," in *The Madman—His Parables and Poems*.

66. Jalaluddin Rumi, "The Guest House," translated by Coleman Barks, available at Scottish Poetry Library website.

67. Czeslaw Milosz, "Ars Poetica?," translated by Czeslaw Milosz and Lillian Vallee, available at Poetry Foundation website.

68. Elton John, "Multiple Personality," YouTube, posted August 10, 2016.

69. Jules Evans, "On Pop Stars' Alter-Egos," at Philosophy for Life: The Website of Jules Evans blog, September 11, 2015.

FIVE. SOULS AND SELVES
IN RELIGION AND PHILOSOPHY

1. Smith, *The Lost Teachings of the Cathars*, 59.

2. Schwartz and Falconer, *Many Minds, One Self*, 16.

3. Christine Wilson Owens, "Hmong Cultural Profile," May 1, 2007, available at EthnoMed (website of University of Washington Health Sciences Libraries and Harborview Medical Center).

4. Wikipedia, s.v. "Hmong Customs and Culture," accessed January 9, 2017.

5. "The Split Horn: Hmong Rituals," PBS website, commentary on *The Split*

Horn: Life of a Hmong Shaman in America, a film by Taggart Siegel.

6. M. Alan Kazlev, "The Ancient Egyptian Conception of the Soul," at Kheper website, July 27, 1998, modified October 10, 2005.

7. M. Alan Kazlev, "The Ancient Egyptian Conception of the Soul."

8. See the Chinese Buddhist Encyclopedia website for a basic description of polytheism.

9. See "What are some examples of polytheistic religions?" at Reference.com, accessed January 9, 2017.

10. Cited in Ferguson, *Aquarius Now,* 53.

11. V. Jayaram, "An Overview of Hindu Gods and Goddesses," at Hinduwebsite .com, accessed January 9, 2017.

12. Subhamoy Das, "Symbolism of Hindu Deities Explained," at LearnReligions .com, updated February 20, 2019.

13. Webster, "Working Polytheism," 45–46.

14. Stone and Winkelman, *Embracing our Selves,* 243.

15. See Wikipedia, s.v. "Akhenaten," accessed January 10, 2017.

16. Lynn Blanch, "Why Didn't Monotheism in Ancient Egypt Work?," at Classroom.Synonym.com, accessed January 10, 2017.

17. Hofstadter, *I Am a Strange Loop,* 222.

18. Green, *Radical Judaism,* 39.

19. See generally Patai, *The Hebrew Goddess.*

20. Dell Markey, "What Effects Did the Babylonian Exile Have on the Jewish Religion?," at Classroom.Synonym.com, updated June 25, 2018, accessed January 10, 2017.

21. For a detailed review of Jewish conceptions of "soul," see Kaufmann Kohler, Isaac Broydé, and Ludwig Blau, "Soul," at JewishEncyclopedia.com, accessed January 10, 2017.

22. Rabbi Ari Cartun of Congregation Etz Chayim, Palo Alto, California, personal communication to Jordan Gruber, July 2016.

23. From Congregation Etz Chayim newsletter with transcript of homily.

24. Sommer, *The Bodies of God and the World of Ancient Israel,* 129.

25. Augustine, *Augustine of Hippo,* 94.

26. Ellenberger, *The Discovery of the Unconscious,* 126.

27. Schwartz and Falconer, *Many Minds, One Self,* 24.

28. See "Good Angel, Bad Angel," at All the Tropes (Wiki contributor website), accessed January 10, 2017.

29. O'Connor, *Our Many Selves,* 6.

30. Robert L., "Dissociative Identity Disorder and Demons," at Great Bible Study website, accessed January 10, 2017.

31. Wikipedia, s.v. "Islam," accessed January 10, 2017.

32. Zia H. Shah, "Possessed by Jinns: Many Medieval Muslim Scholars Need Exorcism," *Muslim Times,* July 27, 2014.

33. Frager and Fadiman, *Personality and Personal Growth,* 388–90.

34. Arsen Darnay, "One Self or Many?," at Borderzone blog, April 4, 2011.

35. Ramos, *Dissociation,* 22.

36. Luke Mastin, "Essentialism," Basics of Philosophy website, accessed January 10, 2017.

37. Encyclopedia.com, s.v. "Essentialism," updated October 22, 2019, accessed December 3, 2019.

38. Powell, "The Multiple Self," 1482.

39. McKellar, *Mindsplit,* 9.

40. Hamilton and Cairns, *Plato: The Collected Dialogues,* 684–86.

41. Lee Archie and John G. Archie, "'The Socratic Paradox' by Plato," chapter 18 of *Introduction to Ethical Studies: An Open Source Reader,* available online at Philosophy.lander.edu, accessed January 10, 2017.

42. Butler, *The Works of Bishop Butler,* 158.

43. Hood, prologue to *The Self Illusion,* xi.

44. Daniel Bonevac, "Notes on Hume and Kant," University of Texas at Austin, accessed January 10, 2017 (no longer available).

45. Kluft and Fine, *Clinical Perspectives on Multiple Personality Disorder,* 374.

46. Nietzsche, *Beyond Good and Evil,* § 19.

47. William McDonald, *Stanford Encyclopedia of Philosophy* online, s.v. "Soren Kierkegaard," Winter 2017 edition.

48. Russell, Irigaray, and Kierkegaard, *On the Construction of the Self,* 8.

SIX. MANY MINDS ON MANY MINDS: PSYCHOLOGISTS AND MULTIPLICITY

1. Ross, *Multiple Personality Disorder,* 9.

2. Ross, *Multiple Personality Disorder,* 12–16.

3. Anonymous, "The History of Multiple Personality Disorder," Dissociative Identity/Multiple Personality: Case Studies and Presentations, at MultipleSelf.wordpress website, June 25, 2014, accessed December 8, 2016.

4. Richardson, Best, and Bromley, *The Satanism Scare,* 152.

5. van der Hart, Lierens, and Goodwin, "Jeanne Fery: A Sixteenth-Century Case of Dissociative Identity Disorder," 1.

6. Putnam, *Diagnosis & Treatment of Multiple Personality Disorder,* 28.

7. Russell A. Dewey, "Multiple Personality," Psych Web website, 2017–2018 revision, accessed January 27, 2020.

8. Ellenberger, *The Discovery of the Unconscious,* 128.

9. Putnam, *Diagnosis & Treatment of Multiple Personality Disorder,* 28.

10. Putnam, *Diagnosis & Treatment of Multiple Personality Disorder,* 29.

11. Ross, *Multiple Personality Disorder,* 30.

12. Ellenberger, *The Discovery of the Unconscious,* 89.

13. Ellenberger, *The Discovery of the Unconscious,* 89.

14. Paul R. McHugh, "Multiple Personality Disorder," cited in Skeptic's Dictionary website, s.v. "hystero-epilepsy," updated November 5, 2015, accessed December 4, 2019.

15. *New World Encyclopedia* online, s.v. "Pierre Janet," accessed December 8, 2016.

16. *Encyclopædia Britannica* online, s.v. "Pierre Janet," accessed December 8, 2016.

17. Van den Berg, *Divided Existence and Complex Society,* 26.

18. William James, *The Principles of Psychology,* 227–28.

19. Ross, *Multiple Personality Disorder,* 23.

20. Duncan, *The Fractured Mirror,* 6.

21. Cohen, Giller, and W., *Multiple Personality Disorder from the Inside Out,* xix.

22. O'Regan, "Multiple Personality—Mirrors of a New Model of Mind?," 9.

23. Ellenberger, *The Discovery of the Unconscious,* 143–44.

24. Ross, *Multiple Personality Disorder,* 29–30.

25. Rowan, *Subpersonalities,* 16.

26. Myers, "Human Personality," 637, cited in *The Nineteenth Century* (Vol. 29): *A Monthly Review,* ed. James Knowles (London: Kegan Paul, Trench, Trubner, 1891), 158.

27. Kelly, "F. W. H. Myers and the Empirical Study of the Mind-Body Problem," 79.

28. Wikipedia, s.v. "Morton Prince," accessed December 8, 2016.

29. Lester, *On Multiple Selves,* 163–64.

30. Prince, *Psychotherapy and Multiple Personality,* 204.

31. William James, introduction to *The Psychology of Suggestion,* by Boris Sidis.

32. Hilgard, *Divided Consciousness,* 5.

33. Bruce, "The Riddle of Personality," 242.

34. Rowan, *Subpersonalities,* 16–17.

35. Sidis and Goodhart, *Multiple Personality,* 58.

36. Sidis and Goodhart, *Multiple Personality,* 75–78.

37. Russell Goodman, *Stanford Encyclopedia of Philosophy* online, s.v. "William James," accessed December 8, 2016.

38. Robert D. Richardson, *William James*, 335.

39. Putnam, *Diagnosis & Treatment of Multiple Personality Disorder*, 3.

40. Frager and Fadiman, *Personality and Personal Growth*, 208.

41. Taylor, *William James on Exceptional Mental States*, 73–91.

42. Kluft and Fine, *Clinical Perspectives on Multiple Personality Disorder*, 357.

43. Kluft and Fine, *Clinical Perspectives on Multiple Personality Disorder*, 358.

44. Putnam, *Diagnosis & Treatment of Multiple Personality Disorder*, 28.

45. Steinberg, *Handbook for the Assessment of Dissociation—A Clinical Guide*, 184.

46. Janet, *The Major Symptoms of Hysteria*, 92.

47. Bromberg, *Awakening the Dreamer*, 1–2.

48. Hilgard, *Divided Consciousness*, 4.

49. Saul McLeod, "Id, Ego and Superego," at Simply Psychology website, updated 2019, accessed December 17, 2019.

50. Manning and Manning, "Legion Theory," 840.

51. See Pavi Sandhu, "Step Aside, Freud: Josef Breuer Is the True Father of Modern Psychotherapy," *Scientific American: Mind* (guest blog), June 30, 2015.

52. Josef Breuer and Sigmund Freud, *Preliminary Communications* (1893), cited in Paul Kiritsis, "The Concept of Dissociation: Breuer, Freud, and the Break from Janet," Down the Rabbit Hole blog, July 12, 2013, accessed July 21, 2017.

53. Wikipedia, s.v. "Pierre Janet," attributed to Sigmund Freud, *Five Lectures on Psycho-Analysis* (1995): 25–33.

54. Kiritsis, "The Concept of Dissociation: Breuer, Freud, and the Break from Janet," Down the Rabbit Hole blog.

55. Wikipedia, s.v. "Pierre Janet," accessed July 21, 2017.

56. Kiritsis, "The Concept of Dissociation: Breuer, Freud, and the Break from Janet." See also Bennet, "The Freud-Janet Controversy: An Unpublished Letter," 52–53.

57. Mark L. Manning and Rana L. Manning, "Dissociative Identity Disorder and Freud," at LegionTheory.com website, accessed December 8, 2016 (no longer available).

58. Ross, *Multiple Personality Disorder*, 103.

59. Cohen, Giller, and W., *Multiple Personality Disorder from the Inside Out*, xix–xx.

60. Mark L. Manning and Rana L. Manning, "Dissociative Identity Disorder and Freud."

61. Sliker, *Multiple Mind*, 7.

62. Colin Wilson, *Mysteries*, 205.

63. Colin Wilson, *Mysteries*, 205.

64. Colin Wilson, *Mysteries,* 206.

65. Colin Wilson, *Mysteries,* 207.

66. Kendra Cherry, "Sigmund Freud Photobiography," at VeryWellMind website, updated October 24, 2017, accessed December 5, 2019.

67. "The Well-Documented Friendship of Carl Jung and Sigmund Freud," at Historacle.org website, accessed December 8, 2016.

68. Kendra Cherry, "Sigmund Freud Photobiography."

69. "When Freud Met Jung," All Psychology Schools website, accessed December 8, 2016.

70. Carl Golden, "The 12 Common Archetypes," SoulCraft website, accessed December 8, 2016.

71. Wikipedia, s.v. "Jungian Archetypes," accessed December 8, 2016.

72. Paul Levy, "Glossary of Terms," at Awaken in the Dream website, s.v. "Archetypes," accessed December 5, 2019.

73. Lester, *On Multiple Selves,* 3.

74. Sliker, *Multiple Mind,* 22–23, quoting Carl Jung, *Collected Works,* vol. 8, *The Structure and Dynamics of the Psyche* (Princeton, N.J.: Princeton University Press, 1960), 96.

75. Sliker, *Multiple Mind,* 22–23.

76. Jung, *Collected Works of C. G. Jung,* vol. 13, *Alchemical Studies,* 42.

77. Wilhelm and Jung, *The Secret of the Golden Flower,* 116.

78. Rosselli and Vanni, "Roberto Assagioli and Carl Gustav Jung," 7.

79. Sliker, *Multiple Mind,* 7.

80. Wikipedia, s.v. "Psychosynthesis," accessed December 8, 2016.

81. McGuire, *The Freud/Jung Letters,* 138.

82. Lester, *On Multiple Selves,* 73.

83. Dattilo, Ferrucci, and Ferrucci, *Roberto Assagioli in his own words,* 32–33.

84. Ferrucci, *What We May Be,* 42.

85. Sliker, *Multiple Mind,* 13–14.

86. Ferrucci, *What We May Be,* 3.

87. Ferrucci, *What We May Be,* 53–54.

88. Ferrucci, *What We May Be,* 55–56.

89. Sliker, *Multiple Mind,* 9, 26.

90. London, "From Little Acorns."

91. Sanford L. Drob, "The Depth of the Soul: James Hillman's Vision of Psychology," The New Kabbalah website, accessed December 8, 2016.

92. Hillman, *Re-Visioning Psychology,* 25.

93. Hillman, *Re-Visioning Psychology,* 24.

94. Rowan, *Subpersonalities,* 35.

95. Hillman, "Psychology: Monotheistic or Polytheistic?," 193–94.

96. Hillman, "Psychology: Monotheistic or Polytheistic?," 196.

97. Hillman, "Psychology: Monotheistic or Polytheistic?," 206.

98. Taves, "Religious Experience and the Divisible Self," 310–11.

99. "Karl Menninger, 96, Dies; Leader in U.S. Psychiatry," *The New York Times,* July 19, 1990.

100. McKellar, *Mindsplit,* 13.

101. "Karl Menninger, 96, Dies; Leader in U.S. Psychiatry."

102. Wikipedia, s.v. "Karl Menninger," accessed December 8, 2016.

103. Baldwin, *Four and Twenty Blackbirds,* 8.

104. Rowan, *Subpersonalities,* 78.

105. O'Connor, *Our Many Selves,* 13.

106. Richeport, "The Interface between Multiple Personality, Spirit Mediumship, and Hypnosis."

107. Ramos, *Dissociation,* 50.

108. Watkins and Watkins, foreword to *Unity and Multiplicity,* by John O. Beahrs, xiv.

109. Alistair Horscroft, "Understanding the 5 Human Stress Responses Can Help Us Create Powerful Relationships," at Soul Sessions website, September 1, 2013.

110. Satir, *Your Many Faces,* 63.

111. Rowan, *Subpersonalities,* 103–4.

112. Cited in Kaufman and Gregoire, *Wired to Create,* xx.

113. McKellar, *Mindsplit,* 17.

114. Ramos, *Dissociation,* 30.

115. Frager and Fadiman, *Personality and Personal Growth,* 207.

116. Frager and Fadiman, *Personality and Personal Growth,* 207.

117. John G. Watkins and Helen H. Watkins, foreword to *Unity and Multiplicity,* by John O. Beahrs, xiv.

118. Watkins and Watkins, "Ego-State Therapy in the Treatment of Dissociative Disorders," 277–79.

119. Siegel, *Mindsight,* 198, 200, 203–4, 208.

SEVEN. AT THE CONVERGENCE OF BUDDHISM, SCIENCE, AND POSTMODERN THINKING

1. Frager and Fadiman, *Personality and Personal Growth,* 237.

2. Frager and Fadiman, *Personality and Personal Growth,* 283, 285.

3. McHugh and Stewart, *The Self and Perspective Taking,* 38.

4. Eagleman, *Incognito,* 106–7.

5. Minsky, *The Society of Mind,* 290.

6. Ferguson, *Aquarius Now,* 53.

7. Gazzaniga, "The Split Brain in Man."

8. "Why Do the Borg Refer to Themselves as 'We' and Not 'I,'" SciFi Stack Exchange web forum, October 29, 2014.

9. Panikkath, Panikkath, Mojumder, and Nugent, "The Alien Hand Syndrome," 219–20.

10. Rowan, *Subpersonalities,* 166.

11. Gazzaniga, *The Social Brain,* 4.

12. Ornstein, *Multimind,* 81.

13. Robert Ornstein, "Current Lectures: Multimind," at Robert Ornstein website, accessed November 21, 2016.

14. Ornstein, *Multimind,* 25.

15. Ornstein, *Multimind,* 143–44.

16. Ornstein, *Multimind,* 185.

17. Ornstein, *Multimind,* 103.

18. Ornstein, *Multimind,* 189–90.

19. Hofstadter, *Metamagical Themas,* §§ 781–82.

20. Hofstadter, *Metamagical Themas,* §§ 789–90.

21. Hofstadter, *Metamagical Themas,* §§ 788–89.

22. Kahneman, *Thinking, Fast and Slow,* 13.

23. Kahneman, *Thinking, Fast and Slow,* 28–29.

24. *The Economist,* Free Exchange, "A Cooler Head: Thomas Schelling," December 24, 2016, 94.

25. "Nagasena and the Chariot," at Practically Zen blog, October 23, 2009.

26. Lester, *On Multiple Selves,* xii.

27. Ingrid Fischer-Schreiber, Franz-Karl Ehrhard, Kurt Friedrichs, and Michael S. Diener, *The Encyclopedia of Eastern Philosophy and Religion: Buddhism, Taoism, Zen, Hinduism,* s.v. "Anātman" (Boulder, Colo.: Shambhala, 1989), 12.

28. Fischer-Schreiber, Ehrhard, Friedrichs, and Diener, *The Encyclopedia of Eastern Philosophy and Religion: Buddhism, Taoism, Zen, Hinduism,* s.v. "Anātman," 12.

29. Tashi Phuntsok, "Dalai Lama and Oracle," posted on Facebook, September 27, 2012.

30. Gopnik, "American Nirvana," 71.

31. Olivia Goldhill, "You're Not the Same: Neuroscience Backs up the Buddhist Belief That 'the Self' Isn't Constant, but Ever-Changing," at Quartz website, September 20, 2015.

32. Christopher Keep, Tim McLaughlin, and Robin Parmar, "Defining Postmodernism," at Electronic Labyrinth website, accessed November 22, 2016.

33. Powell, "The Multiple Self," 1494.

34. Hoffman, Stewart, Warren, and Meek, "Multiple Selves in Postmodern Theory."

35. "Identity and the Self," at Shifting to 21st Century Thinking website, accessed November 22, 2016.

36. "Postmodern Psychology and Socially Constructed Selves," at All About Worldview website, accessed November 22, 2016.

37. J. R. Hustwit, *Internet Encyclopedia of Philosophy* website, s.v. "Process Philosophy," accessed November 23, 2016.

38. Hustwit, *Internet Encyclopedia of Philosophy* website, s.v. "Process Philosophy."

39. Russell and Suchocki, "The Multiple Self," 191–92.

40. Lucas, *The Rehabilitation of Whitehead,* 146.

41. Russell and Suchocki, "The Multiple Self," 191.

EIGHT. SELVES EXPLANATIONS: ORIGINS, ATTRIBUTES, AND ROLES

1. Watkins and Watkins, "Ego-State Therapy in the Treatment of Dissociative Disorders," 278.

2. Watkins and Watkins, "Ego-State Therapy in the Treatment of Dissociative Disorders," 279.

3. Ludwig, "Altered States of Consciousness," 225–34.

4. Tart, *Waking Up,* 4–5.

5. James Kingsland, "Could Meditation Really Help Slow the Ageing Process?," at The Guardian website, March 3, 2016.

6. Thomas B. Roberts, "Multistate Theory," at Academia website, derived from "New Horizons: Potential Benefits of Psychedelics for Humanity" (lecture, World Psychedelic Forum, Basel, Switzerland, March 23, 2008), accessed March 27, 2017.

7. Elster, *The Multiple Self,* 1.

8. Bromberg, *Awakening the Dreamer,* 3.

9. See Jim Rutt, "In Search of the Fifth Attractor," at Medium website, February 3, 2017. Although this presentation is focused on past, current, and future political scenarios, it would be easy to apply it to an analysis of selves.

10. Gregg Henriques, "One Self or Many Selves?," at *Psychology Today* website, April 25, 2014.

11. Baldwin, *Four and Twenty Blackbirds,* 246.

12. Kramer and Bressan, "Humans as Superorganisms," 464–81.

13. Robin Andrews, "19 Pieces of Non-Human DNA Found in Human Genome," at IFL Science website, March 23, 2016, accessed July 11, 2019.

14. Raymond MacDougall, "NIH Human Microbiome Project Defines Normal Bacterial Makeup of the Body," at News Releases of National Institutes of Health website, June 13, 2012.

15. David Robson, "Is Another Human Living Inside You?," at BBC Future website, September 18, 2015.

16. See, Dietart, *The Human Superorganism.*

17. Kohn, "When Gut Bacteria Change Brain Function."

18. Ohio State University, "Autism Symptoms Improve after Fecal Transplant, Small Study Finds," at Science Daily website, January 23, 2017.

19. Spafford C. Ackerly, "Inner Smile and Six Healing Sounds Practices," at Universal Healing Tao website, accessed January 27, 2017.

20. Liam Galleran, personal communication to Jordan Gruber, January 23, 2018.

21. Coryn, "The Bodily Seats of Consciousness," 209.

22. Rajvanshi, "Brain, Heart and Gut Minds."

23. Darin Stevenson, Facebook Timeline post, June 14, 2016, used with permission.

24. Rajvanshi, "Brain, Heart and Gut Minds."

25. MacLean, *The Triune Brain in Evolution.*

26. Wikipedia, s.v. "Triune Brain," accessed January 27, 2017.

27. Ferguson, *Aquarius Now,* 48.

28. Wikipedia, s.v. "Default Mode Network," accessed March 20, 2017.

29. Mehl-Madrona, *Remapping Your Mind,* 6.

30. Mehl-Madrona, *Remapping Your Mind,* 66.

31. Mlodinow, *Subliminal,* 35.

32. Mehl-Madrona, *Remapping Your Mind,* 71–72.

33. Grasse, "The Crowd Within," 43.

34. Crabtree, "The Phenomenology of Multiple Personality and Possession-Type Experiences," 5.

35. Crabtree, "The Phenomenology of Multiple Personality and Possession-Type Experiences," 6.

36. Crabtree, "The Phenomenology of Multiple Personality and Possession-Type Experiences," 7–9.

37. Crabtree, "The Phenomenology of Multiple Personality and Possession-Type Experiences," 9.

38. Crabtree, "The Phenomenology of Multiple Personality and Possession-Type Experiences," 13.

39. Rowan, *Subpersonalities,* 197.

40. Alice Robb, "Multilinguals Have Multiple Personalities," at *New Republic* website, April 23, 2014.

41. Colin Wilson, *Mysteries,* 223.

42. Colin Wilson, *Mysteries,* 232.

43. Colin Wilson, *Mysteries,* 227–29.

44. Colin Wilson, *Mysteries,* 231–32.

45. Carter, *The People You Are,* 23–26.

46. Carter, *The People You Are,* 160.

47. Carter, *The People You Are,* 160–61.

48. Rowan, *Subpersonalities,* 86–87.

49. "Alters in Dissociative Identity Disorder (MPD) and DDNOS," at Trauma Dissociation website, accessed December 8, 2019.

50. Grasse, "The Crowd Within," 42.

51. "Alters in Dissociative Identity Disorder (MPD) and DDNOS," at Trauma Dissociation website, accessed December 8, 2019.

52. Robert Anton Wilson, "Robert Anton Wilson—Interview—An Incorrigible Optimist," at YouTube, from the Enlightenment.Com interview (Capitola, California, March 1, 2006), accessed March 29, 2017.

53. Perel, "Why Happy People Cheat."

54. Lilienfeld and Arkowitz, "Facts & Fictions in Mental Health," 64–65.

55. Crabtree, "The Phenomenology of Multiple Personality and Possession-Type Experiences," 88.

56. "Alters in Dissociative Identity Disorder (MPD) and DDNOS," at Trauma Dissociation website, accessed December 8, 2019.

57. Herbert, "The Three Brains of Eve," 356.

58. Heidegger, "Possession's Many Faces," in *The Principle of Reason,* 18–19.

59. Millman, *Everyday Enlightenment.*

60. Bromberg, *Awakening the Dreamer,* 3.

61. Noricks, *Parts Psychology,* 3.

NINE. HOW SELVES COOPERATE

1. Bromberg, "Standing in the Spaces," 4.

2. Noricks, *Parts Psychology,* 1–2.

3. Thomas, *The Medusa and the Snail,* 42–44.

4. Quigley, *Alchemical Hypnotherapy,* 51.

5. Bloom, "First Person Plural."

6. Capps, *Still Growing,* 164.

7. Baldwin, *Four and Twenty Blackbirds,* 16, quoting Peg Boyles who is quoting Verlaine Crawford.

8. Crawford, *Ending the Battle Within,* 2.

9. Baldwin, *Four and Twenty Blackbirds,* 63.

10. Keyes, *The Minds of Billy Milligan,* xviii.

11. Rowan, *Subpersonalities,* 205–6.

12. Rowan, *Subpersonalities,* 207.

13. Baldwin, *Four and Twenty Blackbirds,* 250.

14. Steven Johnson, "Mind Wide Open," *The New York Times,* May 9, 2004.

15. Beahrs, *Unity and Multiplicity,* 6–7.

16. Ramos, *Dissociation,* 51.

17. Grasse, "The Crowd Within," 43.

18. Fadiman, "Who's Minding the Store?," 133.

19. Dictionary.com, s.v. "Band," accessed March 13, 2017.

20. James Woodall, "Ringo's No Joke. He Was a Genius and the Beatles Were Lucky to Have Him," *The Spectator* website, July 4, 2015.

21. John O'Leary. "Who's the Leader of the Band?," at Business Lessons from Rock blog, October 24, 2012.

22. Regine P. Azurin and Yvette Pantilla, review of *The 17 Indisputable Laws of Teamwork,* by John C. Maxwell, at Refresher website, December 1, 2001.

23. Kotler and Wheal, *Stealing Fire,* 11–12.

24. Baldwin, *Four and Twenty Blackbirds,* 139.

25. Sliker, *Multiple Mind,* 69.

26. Ramos, *Dissociation,* 53.

27. Crabtree, "The Phenomenology of Multiple Personality and Possession-Type Experiences," 5.

28. Ferguson, *Aquarius Now,* 47.

29. Cooper-White, *Braided Selves,* 214–15.

30. Crabtree, "The Phenomenology of Multiple Personality and Possession-Type Experiences," 2.

31. Baldwin, *Four and Twenty Blackbirds,* 71.

32. Rowan, *Subpersonalities,* 150.

33. Ellenberger, *The Discovery of the Unconscious,* 270.

34. Shapiro, *The Selves Inside You,* 35.

35. Baldwin, *Four and Twenty Blackbirds,* 38.

36. Shapiro, *The Selves Inside You,* 35.

37. Shapiro, *The Selves Inside You,* 35.

38. Business Dictionary website, s.v. "Workgroup," accessed April 2, 2017.

39. Weiss, "A Flight of Fancy Mathematics," 172.
40. Berardelli, "When Pigeons Flock, Who's in Command?"
41. Murphy, *Jacob Atabet*, 108.

TEN. TOOLS, TECHNIQUES, AND STRATEGIES FOR SELVES WORK

1. Carter, *The People You Are*, 90.
2. Ferrucci, *What We May Be*, 52.
3. Winter and Reed, *Towards a Radical Redefinition of Psychology*, 106.
4. Ferrucci, *What We May Be*, 53–54.
5. Rowan and Cooper, *The Plural Self*, 8.
6. Keyes, *The Minds of Billy Milligan*, 61.
7. Rowan, *Subpersonalities*, 68–69.
8. Rowan, *Subpersonalities*, 70, citing Robert Johnson.
9. Rowan, *Subpersonalities*, 70, citing Robert Johnson.
10. Rowan, *Subpersonalities*, 198. The list has been reordered.
11. Rowan, *Subpersonalities*, 198–99.
12. Rowan, *Subpersonalities*, 199.
13. Ross, *Multiple Personality Disorder*, 103.
14. Metzner, *Ecology of Consciousness*, 254.
15. Ferrucci, *What We May Be*, 48.
16. Rowan, *Subpersonalities*, 200.
17. Rowan, *Subpersonalities*, 200.
18. Ed Yong, "What Bird Flocks and Fish Schools Can Teach Us about the Future," Talking with Neal Conan, June 13, 2013, transcript available at NPR website, 24.
19. Rolling, *Swarm Intelligence*, 89–90.
20. Rolling, *Swarm Intelligence*, 89–90.
21. Miller, "The Genius of Swarms."
22. Sliker, *Multiple Mind*, 81.
23. Fox, *Winning from Within*, xxiv.
24. Rowan, *Subpersonalities*, 202.
25. Sliker, *Multiple Mind*, 32.
26. Sliker, *Multiple Mind*, 79.
27. Ferrucci, *What We May Be*, 51.
28. *Merriam-Webster Dictionary* online, s.v. "Presence," accessed April 7, 2017.
29. Luther Kitahata, Certified Integral Coach, personal communication to Jordan Gruber.
30. Wikipedia, s.v. "Active Imagination," accessed December 19, 2017.

31. Rowan and Cooper, *The Plural Self,* 259.

32. Baldwin, *Four and Twenty Blackbirds,* 176.

33. Personal communication from friend to James Fadiman; names have been changed.

34. Sasportas, "Subpersonalities and Psychological Conflicts," in Greene and Sasportas, *The Development of the Personality,* 191–92.

35. O'Connor, *Our Many Selves,* 23.

36. Jamie Wheal and Steven Kotler, "Opinion: What Navy SEAL Team 6 Can Teach Us about How to Succeed at Work," at Market Watch website, May 20, 2017.

37. Wheal and Kotler, "Opinion: What Navy SEAL Team 6 Can Teach Us about How to Succeed at Work."

38. Personal communication between Kintla Striker and Jordan Gruber, June 27, 2017.

39. Willow, "How We Work *with* Our Dissociation, instead of Struggling against It," 2.

40. Rowan, *Subpersonalities,* 201.

ELEVEN. SPIRITUAL, THERAPEUTIC, AND SOCIOCULTURAL RESPONSES

1. Aurobindo, *Letters on Yoga* 1:79.

2. Aurobindo, *Letters on Yoga* 1:80.

3. Aurobindo and the Mother, *Our Many Selves,* xvii.

4. Aurobindo and the Mother, *Our Many Selves,* 3–4.

5. Wikipedia, s.v. "George Gurdjieff," accessed May 24, 2017.

6. Ouspensky, *In Search of the Miraculous,* 53–54.

7. Ouspensky, *In Search of the Miraculous,* 59–60.

8. Nicoll, *Psychological Commentaries on the Teaching of Gurdjieff and Ouspensky* 1:20.

9. Lester, *On Multiple Selves,* 7.

10. Jean Houston, "Awakening to Your Life's Purpose," at Evolving Wisdom website, accessed May 24, 2017.

11. Jean Houston, "Awakening to Your Life's Purpose," at Evolving Wisdom website, accessed May 24, 2017.

12. "Polyphrenia," at Blogspot, April 30, 2007.

13. Jean Houston, interview by Douglas Eby, "Interviews," at TalentDevelop .com, accessed May 24, 2017. See also Jean Houston, interview by Jordan Gruber, at Enlightenment.Com (audio file), January 28, 2003.

14. Pamela Bloom, "The Moon, Jean Houston, and You," at Science of Mind website.
15. Wikipedia, s.v. "Psychosynthesis," accessed May 30, 2017.
16. Ferrucci, *What May Be,* 42.
17. Wikipedia, s.v. "Psychosynthesis," accessed July 14, 2019.
18. Jung quoted in Kerr, *A Most Dangerous Method,* 214–15.
19. Rowan, *Subpersonalities,* 74.
20. "Jacob Moreno," at GoodTherapy website, last updated July 3, 2015, accessed May 30, 2017.
21. Wikipedia, s.v. "Psychodrama," accessed May 30, 2017.
22. Rowan, *Subpersonalities,* 76.
23. Rowan, *Subpersonalities,* 76.
24. Rowan, *Subpersonalities,* 77.
25. Rowan, *Subpersonalities,* 77.
26. Hal Stone and Sidra Stone, Voice Dialogue International website, accessed June 7, 2017.
27. Stone and Winkelman, *Embracing Our Selves,* 12–13.
28. Stone and Winkelman, *Embracing Our Selves,* 25.
29. Stone and Winkelman, *Embracing Our Selves,* 23.
30. Stone and Winkelman, *Embracing Our Selves,* 62.
31. Stone and Winkelman, *Embracing Our Selves,* 61.
32. Stone and Stone, at Voice Dialogue International website.
33. Stone and Stone, at Voice Dialogue International website.
34. Wikipedia, s.v. "Internal Family Systems Model," accessed June 7, 2017.
35. Center for Self Leadership, "The Internal Family Systems Model Outline," at Self Leadership website, accessed June 7, 2017.
36. Richard Bolstad, "Parts Integration and Psychotherapy," at Transformations International website, accessed June 7, 2017.
37. Bolstad, "Parts Integration and Psychotherapy."
38. Bob Hoffman, "The Hoffman Process: A Path to Personal Freedom and Love," Hoffman Institute website, last revised December 2015.
39. Amy Mindell and Arnold Mindell, "Deep Democracy's Relationship To 'Regular' Democracy," at Amy and Arnold Mindell website, accessed June 17, 2017.
40. "The Inside Team," at CRR Global website, accessed July 15, 2019.
41. Fox, *Winning from Within.*
42. "The Hakomi Principles," at Hakomi Institute Southwest website, accessed December 13, 2019.

43. "R-CS: Re-Creation of the Self Model of Human Systems," at Mindful Experiential Therapy Approaches (M.E.T.A.) website, accessed June 7, 2017.

44. Ross, *Multiple Personality Disorder,* 28.

45. Roberts, "Multiple Realities: How MPD Is Shaping Up Our Notions of the Self, the Body and Even the Origins of Evil," 26.

46. Duncan, *The Fractured Mirror,* 7.

47. "Schizophrenia," at National Institute of Mental Health website, accessed June 29, 2017.

48. Lexico website, s.v. "Schizophrenia," accessed December 13, 2019.

49. Braun, *Treatment of Multiple Personality Disorder,* 4.

50. Ross, *Multiple Personality Disorder,* 39.

51. Ross, *Multiple Personality Disorder,* 38.

52. Wilber, *The Religion of Tomorrow,* 275–76.

53. Baldwin, *Four and Twenty Blackbirds,* 37.

54. Carter, *The People You Are,* 84.

55. Beahrs, *Unity and Multiplicity,* xiii.

56. The Free Dictionary website, s.v. "Mens Rea," accessed June 7, 2017.

57. Hood, *The Self Illusion,* 243.

58. Hood, *The Self Illusion,* 243.

59. Eagleman, "The Brain on Trial."

60. Wikipedia, s.v. "Twinkie Defense," accessed June 7, 2017.

61. Halleck, "Dissociative Phenomena and the Question of Responsibility," 298–314.

62. Rowan, *Subpersonalities,* 19–20.

63. Rowan, *Subpersonalities,* 34, quoting James Vargiu.

64. Noricks, *Parts Psychology,* 8.

65. Baldwin, *Four and Twenty Blackbirds,* 108–9.

66. Mooallem, "One Man's Quest to Change the Way We Die," *The New York Times Magazine,* January 3, 2017.

67. Betsy Carroll, "Demarginalizing Multiple Identities," at Leading Virtually website, March 5, 2009.

68. Benjamin Grosser, "How the Technological Design of Facebook Homogenizes Identity and Limits Personal Representation," at Ben Grosser blog, September 24, 2011.

TWELVE. FROM THE TRADITIONAL CONTINUUM TO THE EXPANDED FULL SPECTRUM

1. *Cambridge Dictionary* website, s.v. "Continuum," accessed June 7, 2017.

2. Lexico website, s.v. "Continuum," accessed December 14, 2019.

3. Ramos, *Dissociation,* 59. We have redrawn Ramos's continuum, which she credits to "Adapted Terms from Ross, *Multiple Personality Disorder: Diagnosis, Clinical Features and Treatment* and Beahrs, *Unity and Multiplicity.*"
4. Bergmann, "Hidden Selves," 238.
5. Rowan, *Subpersonalities,* 9.
6. Carter, *The People You Are,* 67.
7. Ross, *Multiple Personality Disorder.*
8. Ross, *Multiple Personality Disorder,* 1194–95.
9. Baldwin, *Four and Twenty Blackbirds,* 68.

THIRTEEN. CONCLUSION:
RECAPS, REFLECTIONS, REMINDERS

1. Rowan, *Subpersonalities,* 1.
2. Michigan State University, "Talking to Yourself in the Third Person Can Help You Control Emotions," at *ScienceDaily* website, July 26, 2017.

APPENDIX. DISSOCIATION: ORIGINS
AND USAGE; PROBLEMS AND SUGGESTIONS

1. LeBlanc, "The Origins of the Concept of Dissociation," 57.
2. Hilgard, "Dissociation and Theories of Hypnosis," 69.
3. Janet, "L'anesthésie systématisée et la dissociation des phénomènes psychologiques," 449–72.
4. *New World Encyclopedia* online, s.v. "Pierre Janet," accessed July 5, 2017.
5. Dell and O'Neil, *Dissociation and the Dissociative Disorders,* 719. See also van der Hart and Horst, "The Dissociation Theory of Pierre Janet."
6. Di Fiorino and Figueira, "An Introduction to Dissociation," citing Jacques-Joseph Moreau de Tours, "Du Haschisch et de l'Aleliénation Mentale, 1845," Pyster website, *Bridging Eastern and Western Psychiatry* 1 no. 1 (2003).
7. Herman, *Trauma and Recovery,* 7.
8. Janet, *L'Automatisme Psychologique,* 366, translated by Google Translate.
9. Janet, *L'Automatisme Psychologique,* 397, translated by Google Translate.
10. Di Fiorino and Figueira, "An Introduction to Dissociation."
11. Hilgard, "Dissociation and Theories of Hypnosis," 69.
12. Van der Hart and Dorahy, letter to the editor, 1646.
13. Spitzer, Barnow, Freyberger, and Grabe, "Recent Developments in the Theory of Dissociation," 82.
14. Dell, "The Multidimensional Inventory of Dissociation (MID)," 98.
15. The Free Dictionary website, s.v. "Dissociation," accessed July 5, 2017.

16. Dictionary.com, s.v. "Dissociation," accessed July 5, 2017.

17. *Merriam-Webster Dictionary* online, s.v. "Dissociation," accessed July 5, 2017.

18. Medical Dictionary website, s.v. "Dissociation," accessed July 5, 2017.

19. MedTerms Dictionary, at MedicineNet.com, s.v. "Dissociation," accessed July 5, 2017.

20. Medical Dictionary website, s.v. "Dissociation," accessed July 5, 2017 (no longer available).

21. "DSM-5 Dissociative Disorders," at Trauma Dissociation website.

22. "DSM-5 Dissociative Disorders," at Trauma Dissociation website.

23. "DSM-5 Dissociative Disorders," at Trauma Dissociation website.

24. See "Dissociative Experiences Scale II," at Trauma Dissociation website, accessed July 27, 2017.

25. See "Dissociative Experiences Scale II," at Trauma Dissociation website.

26. Peterson, "Assessment and Treatment Tools for Dissociative Disorders."

27. See "Dissociative Experiences Scale II," at Trauma Dissociation website.

28. David Spiegel, "Depersonalization/Derealization Disorder," at *Merck Manual* online, last revised March 2019.

29. Spitzer, Barnow, Freyberger, and Grabe, "Recent Developments in the Theory of Dissociation," 82.

30. Krippner, "The Varieties of Dissociative Experience," 82–83.

31. Braun, "The BASK Model of Dissociation."

32. Krippner, "The Varieties of Dissociative Experience," 82–83.

33. Springer, "Awareness, Access, and Choice."

Bibliography

Augustine. *Augustine of Hippo: Selected Writings*. Translated by Mary T. Clark. Mahwah, N.J.: Paulist Press, 1984.

Aurobindo, Sri. *Letters On Yoga*. Vol. 1. Pondicherry, India: Sri Aurobindo Ashram Trust, 2012.

Aurobindo, Sri, and The Mother. *Our Many Selves: Practical Yogic Psychology*. Twin Lakes, Wis.: Lotus Press, 2002.

Baldwin, Peter. *Four and Twenty Blackbirds: Personae Theory and the Understanding of Our Multiple Selves*. Las Vegas, Nev.: Bramble Books, 1997.

Beahrs, John O. *Unity and Multiplicity: Multilevel Consciousness of Self in Hypnosis, Psychiatric Disorder and Mental Health*. New York: Brunner/ Mazel, 1982.

Bennet, Edward A. "The Freud-Janet Controversy: An Unpublished Letter." *British Medical Journal* 1, no. 5426 (January 2, 1965): 52–53.

Berardelli, Phil. "When Pigeons Flock, Who's in Command?" *Science* (April 8, 2010).

Bergmann, Uri. "Hidden Selves: Treating Dissociation in the Spectrum of Personality Disorders." In *Healing the Heart of Trauma and Dissociation with EMDR and Ego State Therapy,* edited by Carol Forgash and Margaret Copeley. New York: Springer, 2008.

Bloom, Paul. "First Person Plural." *The Atlantic,* November 2008.

Braun, Bennett G. "The BASK Model of Dissociation." *Dissociation* 1, no. 1 (March 1988): 4–23.

———, ed. *Treatment of Multiple Personality Disorder*. Washington, D.C.: American Psychiatric Press, 1986.

Bromberg, Philip M. *Awakening the Dreamer: Clinical Journeys*. New York: Routledge, 2011.

———. "Standing in the Spaces: The Multiplicity of Self and the Psychoanalytic Relationship," *Contemporary Psychoanalysis*, 32. no. 4 (1996): 509–35.

Bruce, H. Addington. "The Riddle of Personality." *Appleton's Magazine* 9 (February 1907): 241–46.

Butler, Joseph. *The Works of Bishop Butler.* Vol 1. Edited by J. H. Bernard. Glasgow: Glasgow University Press, 1900.

Capps, Donald. *Still Growing: The Creative Self in Older Adulthood.* Cambridge, UK: Lutterworth Press, 2015.

Cardin, Matt. "Those Sorrows Which Are Sent to Wean Us from the Earth: The Failed Quest for Enlightenment in Mary Shelley's *Frankenstein.*" Term paper, Missouri State University, Summer 2001.

Carroll, Lewis. *Alice's Adventures in Wonderland.* London: Macmillan, 1865.

Carter, Rita. *The People You Are.* London: Little, Brown, 2008.

Cohen, Barry M., Esther Giller, and Lynn W., eds. *Multiple Personality Disorder from the Inside Out.* Derwood, Md.: Sidran Press, 1991.

Cooper-White, Pamela. *Braided Selves: Collected Essays on Multiplicity, God, and Persons.* Eugene, Ore.: Cascade Books, 2011.

Coryn, Herbert. "The Bodily Seats of Consciousness: 1." *The Path* 10, no. 7 (October 1895): 209–13. Available at The Theosophical Society International Headquarters website, accessed January 27, 2017.

Crabtree, Adam. "The Phenomenology of Multiple Personality and Possession-Type Experiences: Starting Point for a Reassessment of Human Personality." Address to the Transpersonal Psychology Interest Group at the American Psychological Association Meeting, Toronto, Ontario, August 25, 1984.

Crawford, Verlaine. *Ending the Battle Within: How to Create a Harmonious Life Working with your Sub-Personalities.* Laguna Woods, Calif.: High Castle, 1992.

Dattilo, Yoav, Piero Ferrucci, and Vivien Reid Ferrucci. *Roberto Assagioli in his own words: Fragments of an autobiography.* Firenze: Edizioni Instituto de Psicosintesi, 2019.

Dell, Paul F., and John A. O'Neil, eds. *Dissociation and the Dissociative Disorders: DSM-V and Beyond.* New York: Routledge, 2009.

———. "The Multidimensional Inventory of Dissociation (MID): A Comprehensive Measure of Pathological Dissociation." *Journal of Trauma & Dissociation* 7 no. 2 (2006): 98.

Dennett, Daniel. *Consciousness Explained.* New York: Little, Brown, 1991.

Dietart, Rodney. *The Human Superorganism: How the Microbiome Is Revolutionizing the Pursuit of a Healthy Life.* New York: Dutton, 2016.

Di Fiorino, Mario, and Maria Luisa Figueira, eds. "Dissociation: Dissociative Phenomena; Questions and Answers." Special Issue *Bridging Eastern and Western Psychiatry* 1, no. 1 (2003).

Duncan, C. W. *The Fractured Mirror: Healing Multiple Personality Disorder.* Deerfield Beach Fla.: Health Communications, 1994.

Eagleman, David. "The Brain on Trial." *The Atlantic,* July/August 2011.

———. *Incognito: The Secret Lives of the Brain.* New York: Vintage Books, 2012.

Economist. "A Cooler Head: Thomas Schelling." December 24, 2016.

Ellenberger, Henri F. *The Discovery of the Unconscious: The History and Evolution of Dynamic Psychiatry.* New York: Basic Books, 1970.

Elster, Jon, ed. *The Multiple Self.* Cambridge, UK: Cambridge University Press, 1987.

Fadiman, James. *Unlimit Your Life: Setting and Getting Goals.* Berkeley, Calif.: Celestial Arts, 1989.

———. "Who's Minding the Store? A Comment on Frick's Defense of Unitary Personality." *Journal of Humanistic Psychology* 33, no. 2 (April 1993): 129–33.

Ferguson, Marilyn. *Aquarius Now: Radical Common Sense and Reclaiming Our Personal Sovereignty.* York Beach, Maine: Weiser Books, 2005.

Ferris, Timothy. *The 4-Hour Body: An Uncommon Guide to Rapid Fat-Loss, Incredible Sex and Becoming Superhuman.* New York: Harmony, 2010.

Ferrucci, Piero. *What We May Be: Techniques for Psychological and Spiritual Growth through Psychosynthesis.* New York: Tarcher/Penguin, 2002.

Fox, Erica Ariel. *Winning from Within: A Breakthrough Method for Leading, Living, and Lasting Change.* New York: HarperCollins, 2013.

Frager, Robert, and James Fadiman. *Personality and Personal Growth.* 7th ed. Upper Saddle River, N.J.: Pearson, 2013.

Gazzaniga, Michael S. *The Social Brain: Discovering the Networks of the Mind.* New York: Basic Books, 1985.

———. "The Split Brain in Man." *Scientific American* 217, no. 2 (1967): 24–29.

Gergen, Kenneth J. "Multiple Identity: The Healthy, Happy Human Being Wears Many Masks." *Psychology Today* 5, no. 12 (May 1972): 31–35, 64–66.

Gibran, Kahlil. *The Madman—His Parables and Poems.* New York: Alfred A. Knopf, 1918. Available at The Project Gutenberg website.

Goleman, Daniel. "Probing the Enigma of Multiple Personality." *The New York Times,* June 28, 1988, section C page 1.

Gopnik, Adam. "American Nirvana: Is There a Science of Buddhism?" *The New Yorker,* August 7/14, 2017, 69–74.

Grasse, Ray. "The Crowd Within: Multiple Personality Disorder and Traditional Esoteric Psychologies." *Quest* 5, no. 3 (Autumn 1992): 38–43.

Green, Arthur. *Radical Judaism: Rethinking God & Tradition.* New Haven, Conn.: Yale University Press, 2010.

Greene, L., and Howard Sasportas. *The Development of the Personality: Seminars in Psychological Astrology*. London: Routledge (1987).

Grierson, Bruce. "What If Aging Is Nothing but a Mind-Set?" *The New York Times Magazine,* October 22, 2014.

Haddock, Deborah Bray. *The Dissociative Identity Disorder Sourcebook*. New York: McGraw Hill Education, 2001.

Halleck, Seymour L. "Dissociative Phenomena and the Question of Responsibility." *International Journal of Clinical and Experimental Hypnosis* 38, no. 4 (1990): 298–314.

Heidegger, Martin. *The Principle of Reason*. Bloomington: Indiana University Press, 1991.

Herbert, W. "The Three Brains of Eve: EEG Data." *Science News* 121, no. 22 (May 29, 1982): 356.

Herman, Judith. *Trauma and Recovery: The Aftermath of Violence—from Domestic Abuse to Political Terror*. New York: Basic Books, 1992.

Hesse, Herman. *Steppenwolfe*. New York: Picador, Henry Holt, 1963.

Hilgard, Ernest R. "Dissociation and Theories of Hypnosis." In *Contemporary Hypnosis Research,* edited by Erika Fromm and Michael R. Nash, 69–101. New York: Guilford Press, 1992.

———. *Divided Consciousness: Multiple Controls in Human Thought and Action*. New York: John Wiley, 1977.

Hillman, James. "Psychology: Monotheistic or Polytheistic?" Postscript in *The New Polytheism,* by David L. Miller. New York: Spring Publications, 1981. Previously published in *Spring,* 1971, 193–208.

———. *Re-Visioning Psychology*. New York: Harper & Row, 1975.

Hoffman, Louis, Sharon Stewart, Denise Warren, and Lisa Meek. "Multiple Selves in Postmodern Theory: An Existential Integrative Critique 1." Paper presented at the American Psychological Association's Annual Convention, New Orleans, La., August 2006.

Hofstadter, Douglas R. *I Am a Strange Loop*. New York: Basic Books, 2007.

———. *Metamagical Themas: Questing for the Essence of Mind and Pattern*. New York: Basic Books, 1985.

Hood, Bruce. *The Self Illusion: How the Social Brain Creates Identity*. New York: Oxford University Press, 2013.

Humphrey, Nicholas, and Daniel Dennett. "Speaking for Ourselves: An Assessment of Multiple Personality Disorder." *Raritan* 9, no. 1 (January 1989): 68–98.

James, Oliver. "Upping Your Ziggy." *Watkins Mind Body Spirit* 49 (Spring 2017): 47–48.

James, William. *The Meaning of Truth*. Great Books in Philosophy Series. Amherst, New York: Prometheus Books, 1997. First published 1911 by Longmans, Green, and Co.

———. *The Principles of Psychology*. Vol. 1. New York: Dover, 1950. First published 1890 by Henry Holt.

Janet, Pierre. "L'anesthésie systématisée et la dissociation des phénomènes psychologiques." *Revue Philosophique* 23 (1887): 449–72.

———. *L'Automatisme Psychologique*. Paris: Felix Alcan, 1889.

———. *The Major Symptoms of Hysteria: Fifteen Lectures Given in the Medical School of Harvard University*. New York: Macmillan, 1920. Available at Archive.org.

Johnson, Steven. "Mind Wide Open." *The New York Times* (May 9, 2004).

Joy, W. Brugh. *Avalanche: Heretical Reflections on the Dark and the Light*. New York: Random House, 1990.

Jung, Carl. *Collected Works of C. G. Jung*. Vol. 13, *Alchemical Studies*. Bollingen Series. Princeton, N.J.: Princeton University Press, 1967.

Kahneman, Daniel. *Thinking, Fast and Slow*. New York: Farrar, Straus and Giroux, 2011.

Kaufman, Scott Barry, and Carolyn Gregoire. *Wired to Create: Unraveling the Mysteries of the Creative Mind*. New York: TarcherPerigee, 2015.

Kelly, Emily Williams. "F. W. H. Myers and the Empirical Study of the Mind-Body Problem." Chap. 2 in *Irreducible Mind: Toward a Psychology for the 21st Century*, by Edward F. Kelly, Emily Williams Kelly, Adam Crabtree, Alan Gauld, and Michael Grosso. Lanham, Md.: Rowman & Littlefield, 2009.

Kenyon, Tom. *Brain States*. Lithia Springs, Ga.: World Tree Press/New Leaf, 2001.

Kerr, John. *A Most Dangerous Method: The Story of Jung, Freud, and Sabina Spielrein*. New York, Vintage Books, 1994.

Keyes, Daniel. *The Minds of Billy Milligan*. New York: Random House, 1981.

Khakpour, Porochista. "Epic: An Interview with Salman Rushdie." *Poets & Writers*, September/October 2017, 54–65.

Killen, James L., Richard W. Ferris, William G. Carter, Jeff Wedge, and Rick Brand. *Sermons on the Second Readings: Series I, Cycle A*. Lima, Ohio: CSS, 2004.

Kirkpatrick, Curry. "Walker: A Renaissance Man." *Sports Illustrated*, October 3, 2007.

Kluft, Richard, and Catherine Fine, eds. *Clinical Perspectives on Multiple Personality Disorder*. Washington, D.C.: American Psychiatric Press, 1993.

Kohn, David. "When Gut Bacteria Change Brain Function." *The Atlantic,* June 24, 2015.

Kotler, Steven, and Jamie Wheal. *Stealing Fire: How Silicon Valley, the Navy SEALs, and Maverick Scientists Are Revolutionizing the Way We Live and Work.* New York: HarperCollins, 2017.

Kramer, Peter, and Paola Bressan. "Humans as Superorganisms: How Microbes, Viruses, Imprinted Genes, and Other Selfish Entities Shape Our Behavior." *Perspectives on Psychological Science* 10, no. 4 (2015): 464–81.

Krippner, Stanley. "The Varieties of Dissociative Experience: A Transpersonal, Postmodern Model." *International Journal of Transpersonal Studies* 18, no. 2 (1999): 82–83.

Langer, Ellen J. *Counterclockwise: Mindful Health and the Power of Possibility.* New York: Ballantine Books, 2009.

LeBlanc, André. "The Origins of the Concept of Dissociation: Paul Janet, His Nephew Pierre, and the Problem of Post-hypnotic Suggestion." *History of Science* 39, no. 1 (2001): 57–69.

Lester, David. *On Multiple Selves.* New Brunswick, N.J.: Transaction, 2015.

Lilienfeld, Scott O., and Hal Arkowitz. "Facts & Fictions in Mental Health: Can People Have Multiple Personalities?" *Scientific American Mind* 22, no. 4 (September 2011): 64–65.

London, Scott. "From Little Acorns: A Radical New Psychology." *The Sun,* March 1998. Also available at Scott London website as "On Soul, Character and Calling: A Conversation with James Hillman."

Lucas, George R., Jr. *The Rehabilitation of Whitehead: An Analytic and Historical Assessment of Process Philosophy.* New York: State University of New York Press, 1989.

Ludwig, Arnold. "Altered States of Consciousness." *Archives of General Psychiatry* 15, no. 3 (1966): 225–34.

MacLean, Paul D. *The Triune Brain in Evolution: Role in Paleocerebral Functions.* New York: Springer, 1990.

Manning, Mark L., and Rana Manning. "Legion Theory: A Meta-psychology." *Sage Publications* 17, no. 6 (December 1, 2007): 840.

Margulis, Lynn, and Dorion Sagan. *What Is Life?* New York: Simon & Schuster, 1995.

Maugham, W. Somerset. *A Writer's Notebook.* London: Heinemann, 1949.

McGonigal, Kelly. *The Willpower Instinct.* New York: Penguin, 2012.

McGuire, William. *The Freud/Jung Letters.* Princeton, N.J.: Princeton University Press, 1974.

McHugh, Louise, and Ian Stewart. *The Self and Perspective Taking: Contributions and Applications from Modern Behavioral Science.* Vancouver: Raincoast Books, 2012.

McKellar, Peter. *Mindsplit: The Psychology of Multiple Personality and the Dissociated Self.* London: J. M. Dent & Sons, 1979.

Mehl-Madrona, Lewis. *Remapping Your Mind: The Neuroscience of Self-Transformation through Story.* Rochester, Vt.: Bear & Company, 2015.

Mencken, H. L. *The American Language; An Inquiry into the Development of English in the United States:* Supplement 2. New York: Alfred A. Knopf, 1948.

Metzner, Ralph. *Ecology of Consciousness: The Alchemy of Personal, Collective, and Planetary Transformation.* Oakland, Calif.: New Harbinger, 2017.

Miller, Peter. "The Genius of Swarms." *National Geographic,* July 2007.

Millman, Dan. *Everyday Enlightenment.* New York: Grand Central Publishing, 1998.

Minsky, Marvin. *The Society of Mind.* New York: Simon and Schuster, 1986.

Mlodinow, Leonard. *Subliminal: How Your Unconscious Mind Rules Your Behavior.* New York: Random House, 2012.

Mooallem, Jon. "One Man's Quest to Change the Way We Die," *New York Times Magazine* (January 3, 2017).

Murphy, Michael. *Jacob Atabet: A Speculative Fiction.* Millbrae, Calif.: Celestial Arts, 1977.

Myers, Frederick. "Human Personality," *Fortnightly Review* 38, no. 227 (1885): 637–55.

Nathan, Debbie. *Sybil Exposed: The Extraordinary Story Behind the Famous Multiple Personality Case.* New York: Free Press, 2011.

Nicoll, Maurice. *Psychological Commentaries on the Teaching of Gurdjieff and Ouspensky.* Vol. 1. York Beach, Maine: Weiser Books, 1996.

Nietzsche, Friedrich. *Beyond Good and Evil: Prelude to a Philosophy of the Future,* New York: Vintage Books, 1989, §19.

Nin, Anaïs. *The Diary of Anaïs Nin 1931–1934.* San Diego: Mariner Books, 1969.

Noricks, Jay. *Parts Psychology: A Trauma-Based Self-State Therapy for Emotional Healing.* Los Angeles: New University Press, 2011.

O'Connor, Elizabeth. *Our Many Selves: A Handbook for Self-Discovery.* New York: Harper & Row, 1971.

O'Regan, Brendan, ed. "Multiple Personality—Mirrors of a New Model of Mind?" *Investigations: A Research Bulletin of the Institute of Noetic Sciences* 1, no. 3/4 (1985).

Ornstein, Robert. *Multimind: A New Way of Looking at Human Behavior.* New York: Macmillan, 1986.

Ouspensky, P. D. *In Search of the Miraculous: The Teachings of G.I. Gurdjieff.* San Diego: Harvest, 2001.

Panikkath, Ragesh, Deepa Panikkath, Deb Mojumder, and Kenneth Nugent. "The Alien Hand Syndrome." *Baylor University Medical Center Proceedings* 27, no. 3 (2014): 219–20.

Patai, Raphael. *The Hebrew Goddess.* Detroit: Wayne State University Press, 1990.

Perel, Esther. "Why Happy People Cheat," *The Atlantic* (October 2017).

Peterson, Gary. "Assessment and Treatment Tools for Dissociative Disorders." Slideshow presentation at the Clinical Lecture Series for University of North Carolina–Chapel Hill, School of Social Work, November 15, 2010.

Plato. *Plato: The Collected Dialogues.* Edited by Edith Hamilton and Huntington Cairns. Bollingen Series. Princeton, N.J.: Princeton University Press, 1973.

Powell, John A. "The Multiple Self: Exploring Between and Beyond Modernity and Postmodernity." *Minnesota Law Review* 81 (1996): 1481.

Prince, Morton. *Psychotherapy and Multiple Personality: Selected Essays.* Cambridge, Mass.: Harvard University Press, 1975.

Putnam, Frank W. *Diagnosis & Treatment of Multiple Personality Disorder.* New York: Guilford, 1989.

Quigley, David. *Alchemical Hypnotherapy: A Manual of Practical Techniques.* Fort Bragg, Calif.: Lost Coast Press, 1984.

Rajvanshi, Anil K. "Brain, Heart and Gut Minds," *The Times of India,* October 7, 2011.

Ramos, Celia. *Dissociation: Potential Key to Optimal Mental Function.* Master's Thesis, University of Houston–Clear Lake, Texas, 1993.

Richardson, James T., Joel Best, and David G. Bromley, eds. *The Satanism Scare.* Oxfordshire, UK: Routledge, 1991.

Richardson, Robert D. *William James: In the Maelstrom of American Modernism, A Biography.* New York: Houghton Mifflin Books, 2006.

Richeport, M. M. "The Interface between Multiple Personality, Spirit Mediumship, and Hypnosis." *American Journal of Clinical Hypnosis* 34, no. 3 (1992): 168–77.

Roberts, Susan C. "Multiple Realities: How MPD Is Shaping Up Our Notions of the Self, the Body and Even the Origins of Evil." *Common Boundary,* May 1992, 26.

Rolling, James Haywood, Jr. *Swarm Intelligence: What Nature Teaches Us About Shaping Creative Leadership.* New York: St. Martin's Press, 2013.

Ross, Colin A. *Multiple Personality Disorder.* New York: John Wiley & Sons, 1989.

Rosselli, Massimo, and Duccio Vanni. "Roberto Assagioli and Carl Gustav Jung." *Journal of Transpersonal Psychology* 46, no. 1 (2014): 7–34.

Rowan, John. *Subpersonalities: The People Inside Us*. London: Routledge, 1990.

Rowan, John, and Mick Cooper, eds. *The Plural Self: Multiplicity in Everyday Life*. London: Sage Publications, 1999.

Russell, Helene Tallon. *Irigaray and Kierkegaard: On the Construction of the Self*. Macon, Georgia, Mercer University Press, 2010.

Russell, Helene Tallon, and Marjorie Hewitt Suchocki. "The Multiple Self." In *In Search of Self: Interdisciplinary Perspectives on Personhood,* edited by J. Wentzel van Huyssteen and Erik. P. Wiebe. Grand Rapids, Mich.: Wm. B. Eerdmans, 2011.

Satir, Virginia. *Your Many Faces*. Berkeley, Calif.: Celestial Arts, 1978.

Schwartz, Richard C., and Robert R. Falconer. *Many Minds, One Self: Evidence for a Radical Shift in Paradigm*. Oak Park, Ill.: Trailhead Publications, 2017.

Shah, Idries. *The Commanding Self*. London: Octagon Press, 1994.

Shapiro, Stewart B. *The Selves Inside You*. Berkeley, Calif.: Explorations Institute, 1976.

Sidis, Boris. *The Psychology of Suggestion: A Research into the Subconscious Nature of Man and Society*. With introduction by William James. New York: D. Appleton, 1898.

Sidis, Boris, and Simon P. Goodhart. *Multiple Personality: An Experimental Investigation into the Nature of Human Individuality*. New York: D. Appleton, 1904.

Siegel, Daniel J. *Mindsight*. New York: Bantam Books, 2011.

Sliker, Gretchen. *Multiple Mind: Healing the Split in Psyche and World*. Boulder, Colo.: Shambhala, 1992.

Sommer, Benjamin. *The Bodies of God and the World of Ancient Israel*. Cambridge: Cambridge University Press, 2009.

Smith, Andrew Phillip. *The Lost Teachings of the Cathars: Their Beliefs & Practices*. London: Watkins Media, 2015.

Spitzer, Carsten, Sven Barnow, Harald J. Freyberger, and Hans Joergen Grabe, "Recent Developments in the Theory of Dissociation." *World Psychiatry* 5, no. 2 (June 2006): 82.

Springer, Judith. "Awareness, Access, and Choice: A Transpersonal Perspective on Dissociation, Association, Health, and Illness." M.A. Thesis, Institute of Transpersonal Psychology, Palo Alto, Calif., April 1994.

Steinberg, Marylene. *Handbook for the Assessment of Dissociation—A Clinical Guide*. Washington, D.C.: American Psychiatric Press, 1990.

Stone, Hal, and Sidra Winkelman. *Embracing Our Selves: The Voice Dialogue Manual.* Los Angeles: DeVorss, 1985.

Tart, Charles T. *Waking Up: Overcoming the Obstacles to Human Potential.* Boulder, Colo.: New Science Library, 1986.

Taves, Ann. "Religious Experience and the Divisible Self: William James (and Frederic Myers) as Theorist(s) of Religion." *Journal of the American Academy of Religion* 71, no. 2 (June 2003): 303–26.

Taylor, Eugene. *William James on Exceptional Mental States: The 1896 Lowell Lectures.* Portsmouth, NH: Jetty House, 1982.

Thomas, Lewis. *The Medusa and the Snail: More Notes of a Biology Watcher.* New York: Penguin Books, 1975.

Van den Berg, J. H. *Divided Existence and Complex Society.* New York: Humanities Press, 1974.

Van der Hart, Onno, and Martin Dorahy. Letter to the editor, *American Journal of Psychiatry* 163, no. 9 (September, 2006): 1646.

Van der Hart, Onno, and Rutger Horst. "The Dissociation Theory of Pierre Janet." *Journal of Traumatic Stress* 2, no. 4 (1989): 397–412.

Van der Hart, Onno, Ruth Lierens, and Jean Goodwin. "Jeanne Fery: A Sixteenth-Century Case of Dissociative Identity Disorder." *Journal of Psychohistory* 24, no. 1 (Summer 1996): 1–12.

Walker, Herschel. *Breaking Free: My Life with Dissociative Identity Disorder.* New York: Touchstone, 2008.

Watkins, Helen H., and John G. Watkins. "Ego-State Therapy in the Treatment of Dissociative Disorders." In *Clinical Perspectives on Multiple Personality Disorder,* edited by Richard Kluft, and Catherine Fine, 277–300. Washington, D.C.: American Psychiatric Press, 1993.

Webster, Sam. "Working Polytheism." *Gnosis Magazine,* no. 28 (Summer 1993): 45–46.

Weiss, Rick. "A Flight of Fancy Mathematics: Chaos Brings Harmony to a Birder's Puzzle." *Science News* 137, no. 11 (March 17, 1990): 172.

Wilber, Ken. *The Marriage of Sense and Soul: Integrating Science and Religion.* Vol. 8 of *The Collected Works of Ken Wilber.* Boulder, Colo.: Shambhala, 2000.

———. *The Religion of Tomorrow: A Vision for the Future of the Great Traditions—More Inclusive, More Comprehensive, More Complete.* Boulder, Colo.: Shambhala, 2017.

Wilhelm, Richard, and Carl Jung. *The Secret of the Golden Flower: A Chinese Book of Life.* Oxfordshire, UK: Routledge, 2001.

Willow, "How We Work *with* Our Dissociation, instead of Struggling Against It." *Many Voices: Words of Hope for People Recovering from Trauma & Dissociation* 7, no. 2 (April 1995): 2.

Wilson, Colin. *Mysteries: An Investigation into the Occult, the Paranormal and the Supernatural.* New York: Perigee Books, 1978.

Wilson, Robert Anton. *Quantum Psychology: How Brain Software Programs You and Your World.* Grand Junction, Colo.: Hilaritas Press, 2016.

Winter, David, and Nick Reed, eds. *Towards a Radical Redefinition of Psychology: The Selected Works of Miller Mair.* Oxfordshire: Routledge, 2014.

Woolf, Virginia. *Orlando: A Biography.* New York: Harcourt Brace, 1928.

Index